Mediterranean Dish

Cookbook for Beginners

Easy & Flavorful Mediterranean Diet Recipes and
4-Week Meal Plan for Anyone to Cook Gourmet

Marcie Janes

Contents

Introduction

The Mediterranean is not a new diet. It is one of the most famous and healthiest diets you can adopt. This diet is based on the regular eating patterns of those living in the Mediterranean regions such as France, Turkey, Greece, Spain, Italy, etc.

The Mediterranean diet consists of fresh food and health benefits. It is about enjoying fresh ingredients and meals prepared from starch as much as possible. The Mediterranean diet is endowed with fresh, healthy, natural, and wholesome foods from all food groups, such as fruits, vegetables, legumes, seafood, etc.

Following the Mediterranean diet, you will not only enjoy delicious foods, but you'll also take pleasure in a healthy diet. It is simple to adopt a diet. You didn't need to skip your favorite food. A healthy relationship with food is essential for good health. It means that we should put the same effort into nurturing our bond with food as we nurture other relationships. Healthy food makes us feel good. Moreover, by taking a good diet, you may feel calm, improved health, have high energy, and have a positive body image. It is important to understand what diet we should take.

The Mediterranean diet is one of the best choices ever. The Mediterranean diet is the right diet to start. It is a plant-based diet rich in green vegetables, healthy fats, carbohydrates, and protein. This diet comprises beans, green leafy vegetables, nuts, grains, legumes, etc. Olive oil is the main ingredient in this diet. You should use olive oil for making all foods. It is healthy oil. You should eat less red meat and sweet dairy foods on this diet. Doctors recommend this diet because it is good for heart health. You can consume red wine in small amounts and drink a lot of water on this diet.

This cookbook will get healthy and delicious Mediterranean diet recipes for you and your family. All recipes are simple to follow and healthy for your diet. Choose a good diet and stay healthy! Keep ready!

Fundamentals of Mediterranean Diet

▶▶▶ What Is Mediterranean Diet?

The Mediterranean diet is rich in fruits, vegetables, whole grains, healthy fats, carbohydrates, proteins, seafood, grains, nuts, seeds, and olive oil. Olive oil is healthy oil, and you should cook all meals with olive oil. This diet pattern also includes smaller portions of eggs, poultry, fermented dairy products, and the occasional glass of wine with your meals. There are more than 20 countries are the part of Mediterranean region. It includes Croatia, Turkey, Greece, Italy, France, Morocco, Spain, Tunisia, Egypt, and Syria. One of the attractive things about this diet is its flexible and versatile diet. Consume fresh vegetables, fruits, legumes, whole grain, nuts, seeds, olive oil, seafood and limiting to eat poultry, red meat, processed food, processed meat, and dairy products. Avoid alcohol, sugar, high fat foods, and unhealthy foods.

▶▶▶ Principles of the Mediterranean Diet

The Mediterranean diet is always focused on healthy foods. This diet is based on the following straightforward principles:

Eat vegetables and fruits: On this diet, you should eat many seasonal green vegetables and fresh fruits. Your plate should be full of colorful vegetables and fruits in each meal. When you eat food according to season, you will always enjoy the freshness and varieties of foods.

Choose fresh herbs and spices: On this diet, you should buy or choose fresh herbs such as coriander, chives, parsley, and many more. These are important for any meal. The spices should be fresh because it makes your health good or bad. Spices add flavor, color, and health benefits to your meals.

Focus on healthy fats: The Mediterranean diet focuses on always healthy fats. It features healthy

and healthy quality sources of fat. Olive oil is the main ingredient in this diet, and it is a staple ingredient in every kitchen. Olive oil, olives, nuts, and seeds are good sources of healthy fats.

Consume less meat: You should change your mind about meat. The Mediterranean diet calls for a small amount of red meat, focusing on seafood and legumes. You can eat the meat in moderation and on special occasions.

Enjoy quality dairy foods: Unsweetened plain or Greek yogurt and cheese are traditional in the Mediterranean diet. You can eat it in moderation. It would be best if you focused on green vegetables and fruits only.

Enjoy grains: The Mediterranean diet features whole and cracked grains like bulgur, oats, barley,

farro, etc. Whole grain bread is a staple ingredient.

Avoid processed foods: You should not eat processed food on this diet because these are unhealthy for you.

Eat fruit desserts: Fruits are full of natural sugar. When they are combined with nuts, seeds, small portion of cheese and baked into dessert, they are good nutrients and satisfy your tooth.

Drink plenty of water: You should drink plenty of water on this diet. If you don't want to drink water, you can drink different juices and smoothies.

If you want to change your life-style, you should follow this advanced diet. Choose healthy fats, consume fresh vegetables, fruits, legumes, grains, and drink plenty of water.

• Keep yourself hydrated

The Mediterranean diet revolves around fresh produce, whole grains, and the inclusion of fish. While it may be a great way to lose weight, it is essential to stay well hydrated while you are on it (as diets can be dehydrating). Some dieters complain that they feel weak, cold, and emotionally unstable when dieting. This is due to the considerable reduction in sodium as many healthy foods contain naturally high amounts of salt — so eating healthily does mean cutting down on salty snacks. As a result of the low sodium levels, your immune system may run low on some minerals that can only be replenished by eating more foods high in those minerals —potassium, and magnesium. Rest assured, though, that these symptoms usually subside after about ten days as your body adjusts to the new eating pattern.

• Have your vitamins and supplements properly

Vitamins and minerals can be found in both plants and animals. However, more fruit and vegetables are generally more vital sources of them. When we consume other animals, we are destroying the total of all the energy and health benefits they also consumed throughout their lives. This might sound like a great deal on paper, but remember that the pig you're eating has squandered away its daily nutrition allotment, so it's only going to have a little left in store for you to benefit from it. But when you eat fruits and vegetables, your body is given first-hand access to calcium, vitamin K, and vitamin C. Each day your body requires a fresh intake of each one

• Prepare your meal and portion control planning

Meal prepping can seem like a tricky habit to get into, but there are a lot of benefits to doing it, and others are typically surprised by how easy it is. All you have to do is plan out your meals for the week the night or two before or the weekend before so that when it's time to head off to work, you grab one with you and heat it throughout the day. If you plan enough, this can even mean that on days when you don't need any snacks and eat out at lunch venues instead of bringing in food from home, you might be able to take extra portions along as extras in case anyone else stays hungry after... Try not to freeze solid the food as much as possible - let them sit on the countertop for a little while so they'll be easier to thaw later during your preparation time!

• Track macronutrients

Tracking your macronutrients to calculate the nutritional value of your meals and portions is as easy as stepping on a kitchen scale. And you should have one as soon as possible. If you're new to keeping track of what you eat, don't worry, it becomes second nature after a while. You won't need to spend time calculating or strategizing anymore because we've covered that in the rewrote portion below!

• Counting calories and forming a deficit

If you wish to lose weight, one can only do it - and that is by reducing your calorie intake by cutting back on unhealthy eating in your diet while increasing physical activity levels as well. It is not that you have to count calories every day until you see the pounds drop off - but I am saying that if you are serious about weight management, then what you eat will always matter above all else. A healthy rate of weight loss for most adults should come to about 1-2 lbs. per week. A daily caloric intake of 1500 throughout the week doesn't give any weight changes but increases each Friday over the weekend. It's possible to shed 2lbs over three days with extra workouts or make more intelligent choices when eating (like fewer carbs!).

You'll lose around a pound if you cut out calories every day for just one week. But remember that this depends on several factors, including how much physical activity you get per day, fitness level, and overall calorie needs, so your body burns more or less than the average person. If you need to adjust the definition of one Mediterranean meal to match your weight loss program and your genetic makeup and metabolism, that's fine - don't go over on meat! It doesn't matter if you put extra wasabi on it or drink a glass of seaweed juice after; trust us, we've tried it!

• Set your goal to meet your achievements

One of the most important things to stay in control is to set clear and bright goals. Stepping through all the aspects that you should work on before setting off requires some discipline as it will ensure that you're aware of what you need to do during your journey, and this is one way to ensure that you will be okay throughout your diet. It has been found that even if a diet is healthy, it can still be very demanding compared to the usual meals we eat daily. However, one can still get used to having natural fruits and vegetables instead of junk food. One may lose up to two pounds per week while following a Mediterranean diet; any faster than this would not be recommended since your body needs time to get healthier properly. Thus, it is okay for you to allow yourself a certain period wherein you would like - for instance, six months or so - to accomplish this goal.

▌▌▶ Health Benefits of the Mediterranean Diet

The Mediterranean diet is satisfying and tasty, and easy-to-follow for life. This diet has a lot of health benefits.

Lower the risk of heart diseases:

The Mediterranean diet boosts the energy level and reduces the risk of heart diseases. It promotes heart health. Studies say that by following the Mediterranean diet, you will stay healthy. The Mediterranean diet can help lower diastolic and systolic blood pressure, good for health. Cardiovascular was reduced by following the Mediterranean diet supplemented with olive oil or nuts.

Another study shows that men who consumed fish twice a week reduced the risk by 23% of death from heart diseases! The doctor recommended the Mediterranean diet to heart patients because this diet is good for heart health. This diet encourages the consumption of many vegetables and fruits while limiting the consumption of red meat and dairy products. It focuses on fresh and natural ingredients rich in vitamins and minerals than processed foods. These factors result in a high in heart-healthy nutrients and low in saturated fats and added sugars.

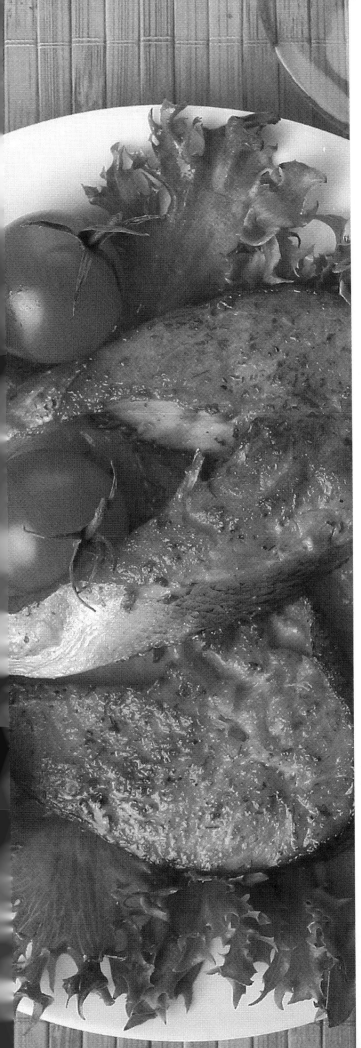

Improve digestion:

The Mediterranean diet also improves digestion. It consists of healthy digestive foods that easily digest and keep you healthy. It improves bowel function. It focuses on a healthy diet only. It does not recommend any unhealthy and un-digestive food. That's why; the Mediterranean diet is the perfect choice for your good health.

Maintain body weight:

The Mediterranean diet encourages high-quality meals only. Taking a walk to a nearby grocery shop instead of driving, reducing portions, and eating healthy foods keep you active, and you will maintain and manage your body weight. Taking healthy nutrients and consuming less saturated fats can help you reach a healthy body weight.

Reduce the risk of cancer:

The health care professionals show that following the Mediterranean diet is linked to reduced overall cancer rates. The positive relationship between cancer and the Mediterranean diet is due to high anti-inflammatory nutrients that consist of vegetables, fresh fruits, nuts, and olive oil, which protect the human from cancer disease. Epidemiological studies show that the Mediterranean diet is a model of a good eating diet that promotes better health quality of life and reduces the risk of stroke, cancer, and other diseases.

Maintain a healthy blood sugar level:

The Mediterranean diet focuses on sugar-free foods. It does not recommend you to eat added-sugar foods. The fruits have natural sugar, so it does not affect their health. Multiple studies have shown that the Mediterranean diet could lower fasting blood sugar levels and enhance hemoglobin levels.

Keep the brain healthy:

The Mediterranean diet is good for the brain. It improves cognition, brain volume, and memory. It offers a good effect on brain health and lowers the risk of brain diseases.

Asthma:

In both Mediterranean and non-Mediterranean countries, researchers have found that the Mediterranean diet seems to have a protective effect against Asthma and wheeze the kids. The Mediterranean diet is based on a high intake of vegetables, legumes, seafood, fruits, olive oil, and cereals, which is involved in the reduction of Asthma in children.

Increase longevity:

The Mediterranean diet lowers the risk of both cancer and heart diseases. It also reduces the risk of death by 20% at all ages.

Protect against type-2 diabetes:

The Mediterranean diet recommends sugar-free foods. This diet is high in fiber, easily digested, prevents high blood pressure sugar levels, and helps maintain body weight.

High cholesterol:

The Mediterranean diet lowers the risk of heart diseases because people eating this way have a lower level of LDL blood cholesterol. LDLs are bad cholesterol, which is more apt to build up deposits in arteries. The researcher reviewed 40 diets in 2018 in the US. Health care professionals have proven that the Mediterranean diet is one of the best diets.

Enhance gut health:

The Mediterranean diet is rich in fiber, minerals, vitamins, and antioxidants due to the high intake of fresh fruits, green vegetables, and whole grains. It may lead to an increase the gut health. Gut health is connected to mental health.

Improve sleep:

The Mediterranean diet can help older people to improve better sleep.

Lower blood pressure:

The Mediterranean diet has healthy fats, which is the main key to lowering blood pressure.

Keeps you active and strong:

The Mediterranean diet can reduce the risk of developing muscle weakness and other diseases up to 70% in adults. It means that if you are healthy, you can enjoy your life like a young, healthy person.

Improve mood and reduce stress:

The Mediterranean diet can reduce the risk of stress and improve mood. This diet encourages good and healthy food. It focuses on daily exercise, physical activities, and an active lifestyle. These factors improve mood and mental health. This diet keeps your mood always good and you feel always fresh and healthy.

▷ What Foods Are Allowed to Be Eaten?

The Mediterranean diet allows you to eat fresh fruits, vegetables, legumes, whole grains, seafood, nuts, seeds, and olive oil. If you want to stay healthy and active, you should follow this diet strictly. It does not keep you from your favorite food. You can enjoy your favorite food in a small portion, such as poultry, red wine, dairy products, etc.

Fresh fruits and vegetables:

The Mediterranean diet allowed you to eat fresh fruits such as Oranges, bananas, apples, pears, Clementine, lemons, grapefruit, dates, limes, cantaloupe, figs, grapes, melon, peach, apricot, plums, pomegranate, strawberries, blueberries, raspberries, blackberries, cherries, and avocados, etc. You will eat fresh vegetables on this diet such as spinach, kale, tomatoes, Swiss chard, collard green, arugula, broccoli, cauliflower, celery, Brussels sprout, carrots, cucumbers, green beans, eggplant, zucchini, squash, onions, scallions, shallots, garlic, bell pepper, mushrooms, artichokes, cabbage, fennel, leeks, asparagus, potatoes, sweet potatoes, turnips, and yams, etc. Fiber, vitamins, nutrients, and complex carbohydrates are present in fruit and vegetables, reducing the risk of many diseases and keeping to always healthy and active. It lowers the risk of heart and cancer diseases.

Nuts and seeds:

Nuts are seeds allowed in the Mediterranean diet; almonds, walnuts, macadamia nuts, hazelnuts, cashews, pistachios, pine nuts, sesame seeds, sunflower seeds, pumpkin seeds, etc. Nuts and seeds have polyunsaturated, monounsaturated fats, healthy fats, and proteins which may lower the risk of diseases. You can add them to the different meals, especially in the desserts. It is also used for topping different desserts.

Legumes:

Beans, lentils, and peas are good sources of plant-based protein and iron, potassium, and other important nutrients, which are good for health. You should eat 3 cups serving a week on the Mediterranean diet. It consists of essential nutrients, and you can add them to make the soup, burgers, salad, dips, hummus, etc.

• Beans: Kidney beans, cannellini, white kidney beans, Fava are different varieties and good for your health. You can make soups and salad to increase the flavor of the meal. You can make dips and hummus also.

- Peas: You can make peas blend for kids and add to the pasta and salads to add the flavors.
- Lentils: Make the lentil soups and salad for extra protein.
- Chickpeas: You can make tahini, dips, or hummus.

Whole grains:

- Whole oats: You can make overnight oats baked oatmeal dishes using whole oats.
- Brown rice: It is used in many dishes, and you can serve it with your favorite vegetable dish.
- Barley: You can add barley into soups and salad. It is good to pair with mushrooms.
- Bulgur: Toss into a salad with roasted veggies and olive oil.
- Buckwheat: It is used to make muffins or pancakes, and you can add it to the soups and salad.
- Corn: Corn is family-favorite grain. You can sauté the corn in olive oil.
- Whole-grain bread: Use whole-grain bread. Mash the avocado and spread it over the whole-grain bread.
- Pita bread: Spread mashed avocado or hummus over the pita bread.
- Pasta: Pasta is a kid-friendly dish. You can make shrimp pasta or veggie pasta for your family.
- Couscous: Add it to the vegetable dish.
- Farro: Make a salad with olives and lemon juice.
- Quinoa: Add it to the salad or veggie dish.

Fish and seafood:

Seafood is rich in omega-3 fatty acids, and it is a main source of protein in the Mediterranean diet. You should use 3 to 4 oz of seafood per week.

- Tuna: You can add tuna into the salad and serve it as a side dish with your main vegetable dish.
- Anchovies: Only purchase canned in olive oil. It is a good source of healthy fat.
- Sardines: You can toss the sardine with pasta or salad dressing with olive oil.

- Mackerel: Serve it with a vegetable dish.
- Herring: You can pickle or smoke the herring and serve it on sandwiches or in the salad.
- Salmon: Salmon is a healthy fish. You can roast, bake, and grill the salmon. Serve it as a main dish.
- Trout: You can grill it, and it is a good source of vitamin D and protein.
- Cod: You can steam, grill, or bake the cod and serve it as a main dish.
- Barramundi: It is good to pair with citrus and olives
- Sea bass: You can roast, grill, or steam the sea bass.
- Shrimp: Sauté the shrimp in olive oil and serve a salad or toss with pasta.
- Crab: You can make crab stew and serve it at dinner.
- Oysters: Use fresh oysters and rub them with lemon juice.
- Mussels: You can steam it with herbs.
- Clams: Toss the steamed clams with pasta and olive oil.
- Octopus: Grill it and serve with a drizzle of olive oil and lemon juice.

Meat:

The Mediterranean diet focuses on plant-based foods such as vegetables, fresh fruits, legumes, and seafood, but poultry can also be included. You should select skinless white meat and consume it in a small portion. Limit eating pork, beef, and lamb.

- Chicken
- Duck
- Cornish game hens
- Turkey

Cheese and dairy products:

Low-fat dairy products are allowed in the Mediterranean diet. Choose fat-free milk.

- Cheese: Haloumi, ricotta, parmesan, manchengo, feta, chevre, and labneh are allowed in the

Mediterranean diet.

- Greek yogurt
- Eggs
- Fat-free milk

Herb and Spices:

- Rosemary
- Sage
- Nutmeg
- Pepper

- Mint
- Basil
- Garlic
- Cinnamon

Healthy fats:

Extra-virgin olive oil: Olive oil is the main ingredient in this diet. It is rich in monounsaturated fat and good for your heart. Olive oil is better than other oils. It reduces the risk of many diseases such

as cancer, heart disease, and inflammatory diseases like asthma. It assists with weight loss.

Avocado oil: You can use avocado oil for making different meals. It is also healthy oil. Avocado is allowed in this diet. That's why; avocado oil can be used for making Different Dishes.

Which Foods Are Not Allowed to Be Eaten?

Added sugar foods: Ice creams, cookies, baked goods, cakes, candies, soda, and syrup, fried and processed foods, canola oil, cottonseed oil, grapeseed oil, vegetable oil, corn oil, safflower oil, soybean oil, Processed sausage, deli meats, hot dogs, and beef jerky, popcorn, granola bars, fast food, bacon, sugary beverages, sugary desserts, sodas, cheeses, white bread, white pasta, alcohol, and butter, etc. Avoid these unhealthy and processed foods while following the Mediterranean diet.

The Mediterranean Food Pyramid

The Mediterranean Diet Pyramid is one of the oldest known still-used models of health; it is believed to have been the first diet in human

history. It is thought that this was because the Grecian doctors and India discovered that foods could be ordered in a sequence according to their medicinal properties.

How Is the Pyramid Laid Out?

Tier 1: Olive oil, fruits, vegetables, whole grains, legumes, beans, nuts & seeds, spices & herbs:

If you're trying to keep things healthy in the kitchen and learn a new way of cooking, then there are a few things you should always ensure are at the root of your meals. These foods go well with most dishes and help bring out their flavors. It shouldn't be hard to find foods that fall into these categories daily. Olive oil is fundamental - this should be your primary fat source in most recipes. Herbs and spices are excellent replacements for salt, which you typically use when cooking dishes, so feel free to add them generously! If you can't get hold of fresh herbs or if they are too expensive for your budget, dried varieties will still do the job

nicely. You can even freeze them for longer storage life. Finally, garlic and ginger roots provide great flavor enhancers for almost any dish. They will also help boost the immune system over time by adding beautiful nutrients to your body that it needs daily.

Tier 2: Fish & seafood:

These are essential staples of the Mediterranean diet that should be consumed often as a protein source. Products such as salmon, trout, tuna, mussels, and crab are excellent sources of- protein that you should try and include in your diet at least twice per week. Additionally, seafood like prawns or shrimp can be formed into salads or sandwiches for a delicious meal. Canned goods are also available when cooking meals or tossing into a salad with fresh vegetables or roasted nuts/seeds for a tasty flavor burst!

Tier 3: Cheese, yogurt, eggs & poultry:

When eating according to the Mediterranean diet, there are several ingredients you should use sparingly throughout the week. Keeping in mind that eggs are usually used as a main course for lunch or dinner when on this diet, you want to try not to overindulge in them - instead of saving them for special occasions. Another tip is to use healthier varieties of cheese like Parmesan, ricotta, and feta as toppings or garnishes on your dishes.

Tier 4: Red meat & sweets:

These items will be consumed less frequently on the Mediterranean diet. If you are eating them,

you want to be sure it is only in small quantities and prefer lean meat versions with less fat. Most studies recommend a maximum of 12 to 16 ounces per month. You can still have red meat occasionally to add some variety to your diet, but you want to reduce how often you have it. That's because of all the health concerns with sugar and red meat. The Mediterranean diet is working to improve cardiovascular health and reduce blood pressure. At the same time, red meat tends to be dangerous in terms of cardiac health due to fat levels associated with heart disease or strokes, which can jeopardize your life long-term. The residents of Greece ate very little red meat and instead had fish or seafood as their primary source of protein, which was

healthier for their heart

Water:

The Mediterranean diet encourages you to be hydrated, so drinking more than your daily water intake. Doctors recommend 9 glasses each day for women and 13 for men. If a woman is pregnant or breastfeeding, she should drink more to keep hydrated because water is essential to the development and function of cells.

Wine:

Drinking wine in moderation is encouraged in the Mediterranean diet. Studies have shown that drinking alcohol in moderation can reduce the risk of heart disease. That can mean one glass per day for women. Men tend to have a higher body mass to consume 1-2 drinks each. Remember what your doctor would recommend regarding wine consumption based on your health and family history. Remember that overconsumption of alcohol may increase the risk of various health problems, including obesity, gout, arthritis, and heart issues!

▶▶ Common Mistakes During Diet

When you start a new diet, it always helps to remember that you're likely to make some mistakes when you first begin. Dieters always find themselves in situations where they're uncertain about what to do next. Avoid future pitfalls and get on the Mediterranean diet plan more quickly by considering the following common mistakes!

• All or nothing

The diet you choose will determine how your body reacts to the food you consume. The most common reason people give up on dieting is that they struggle with the monotony of the foods they are required to eat. You should be mentally prepared for the cultural shift that accompanies a new diet before giving it a try, and there is no more significant source of information than from

others who have adopted this way of life! First-hand accounts are crucial here - so look for friends who can help you decide what kind of diet best suits you by talking about their experiences instead of relying on quick factoids found online! It's also important not to start a new diet with an all-or-nothing approach - make gradual changes that your body can get used to over time and work your way up.

• Repeating same things

Don't eat the same things over and over again, every day. One of the most common mistakes people make is that they think that eating the same kind of cuisine will satisfy their hunger and keep them satisfied for hours on end - but this is incorrect. The Mediterranean diet doesn't have you eating only one ingredient throughout the week. Instead, it allows you to have multiple dishes throughout the week as long as you control your portions and maintain a healthy weight.

• Deprivation

Some dieters will try to convince you that starvation is the only way to manage weight loss. While slightly cutting calories can help, it's important to note that focused exercises can maintain energy levels and appetite regulation as part of a healthy diet. Starvation won't provide you with enough energy and will weaken you in the long run, so if we're talking about having your cake and eating it too - this shouldn't be taken literally!

• Giving up

Don't give up in the middle of following a diet. The Mediterranean diet is meant to help, not hinder you. If you see your efforts paying off and think, "Okay, I can have sweet things now..." then it means you haven't been committed enough. Get rid of that mindset and realize that a diet should not be indulged

in as much as it should be followed: no matter what, no matter how tempting it may be! Try alternative healthy treats and reject foods that are bad if they'll mess up your progress! In any case, our bodies need time to adjust and stabilize our food, so switching back and forth simply won't do.

• Not setting goals

Many people either skip meals or end up not eating correctly daily, which makes this strategy ineffective. Your body undergoes specific changes when you follow a regime, which can take some time to adjust. While most people in the field of dieting believe that it takes four weeks for one's body to adapt to the new regime, others believe that it may take longer or shorter depending on individual cases. If you have a goal regarding how much weight you would like to lose over time, try a gradual and slow change to accommodate your body's current needs. If you happen to be so determined and decide that specific steps need to be taken faster, give yourself enough breaks so as not to cause your body too many problems in the process of making swift changes.

• Following the wrong plan

Many people do not know what the best plan for them is. For example, if you decide to follow the Mediterranean diet, consult a professional nutritional counselor to help you select an appropriate, safe, and effective protocol for your specific lifestyle. While many choose to combine elements of the Mediterranean diet with their personal lifestyle choices, other factors will make or break your experience with this relatively simple diet. It is important to note that this style of eating alone will not guarantee success as one can modify recipes in many ways that may cause one or two nutrients to be lacking. So it's crucially important to consult a registered dietician who can help you select the right foods and such to get all the necessary vitamins and minerals needed to achieve your goals successfully!

4-Week Diet Plan

Week-1

	Breakfast	Lunch	Snack	Dinner	Dessert
Day-1	Breakfast: Granola Parfait with Greek Yogurt	Lunch: Cauliflower Steaks with Tahini Sauce	Snack: Roasted Spiced Cashews	Dinner: Fried Steak with Salsa Verde	Dessert: Mixed Berry Frozen Yogurt Bar
Day-2	Breakfast: Fig and Ricotta Toast	Lunch: Vegetarian Pockets	Snack: Tasty Spicy-Sweet Roasted Walnuts	Dinner: Pesto-Glazed Stuffed Chicken Breasts	Dessert: Red Grapefruit Granita
Day-3	Breakfast: Berry-Honey Pancakes	Lunch: Gnocchi with Chickpeas	Snack: Easy Sweet-and-Savory Popcorn	Dinner: Sirloin Steak with Vegetable Mix	Dessert: Pistachio Cookies
Day-4	Breakfast: Avocado Trout Toast	Lunch: Grilled Eggplant Sandwich	Snack: Easy Sweet Potato Sticks	Dinner: Homemade Chicken Cacciatore	Dessert: Roasted Honey-Cinnamon Apples
Day-5	Breakfast: Baked Yogurt Peach Oatmeal	Lunch: Pasta with Lentil-Beet Balls	Snack: Terrific Marinated Olives	Dinner: Beef Stuffed Cabbage Rolls	Dessert: Fruit Salad with Yogurt
Day-6	Breakfast: Potato Shakshuka	Lunch: Broccoli and Chickpea Couscous	Snack: Healthy Sauerkraut Avocado Mash	Dinner: Beef Stew with Mushrooms	Dessert: Wine Poached Pears
Day-7	Breakfast: Harissa Shakshuka	Lunch: Grilled Veggie Pita	Snack: Pesto Cucumber Boats with Walnuts	Dinner: Chicken Thighs with Red Wine Sauce	Dessert: Cretan Cheese Pancakes

Week-2

	Breakfast	Lunch	Snack	Dinner	Dessert
Day-1	Breakfast: Cherry Smoothie Bowl	Lunch: Vegetarian Skillet Lasagna	Snack: Tasty Avocado Pudding	Dinner: Prosciutto and Fresh Mozzarella Burgers	Dessert: Vanilla Pudding with Strawberries
Day-2	Breakfast: Egg Stuffed in Pepper Ring with Avocado	Lunch: Chickpea Salad Sandwich	Snack: Refreshing Citrus-Kissed Melon	Dinner: Healthy Chicken Almond Phyllo Pie	Dessert: Toasted Almonds with Honey
Day-3	Breakfast: Morning Muffins	Lunch: Vegetable Tagine	Snack: Rosemary Olives	Dinner: Pomegranate-Glazed Lamb Shanks with Vegetables	Dessert: Red Grapefruit Granita
Day-4	Breakfast: Sweet Potato Toast	Lunch: Falafel-Stuffed Pita	Snack: Easy Stuffed Grape Leaves	Dinner: Beef Meatballs	Dessert: Wine Poached Pears
Day-5	Breakfast: Fried Eggs and Polenta with Sautéed Chard	Lunch: Vegan Paella	Snack: Savory Walnut and Red Pepper Spread	Dinner: Poached Chicken with Tarragon	Dessert: Grilled Peaches with Yogurt
Day-6	Breakfast: Breakfast Bruschetta	Lunch: Quinoa-Stuffed Peppers	Snack: Beet Chips	Dinner: Roasted Herb Whole Chicken	Dessert: Fruit with Crème Fraiche
Day-7	Breakfast: Scrambled Eggs with Smoked Salmon	Lunch: Asparagus with Lemon Zest	Snack: Yogurt Deviled Eggs	Dinner: Moroccan Chicken with Cinnamon and Olives	Dessert: Strawberry Parfaits

Week-3

	Breakfast	Lunch	Snack	Dinner	Dessert
Day-1	Breakfast: Breakfast Parfaits with Grapes	Lunch: Pumpkin Mac 'N' Cheese	Snack: Filo-Wrapped Brie	Dinner: Cheesy Beef Stuffed Peppers	Dessert: Baked Apples with Walnuts
Day-2	Breakfast: Honey Nut Granola	Lunch: Mediterranean Buddha bowl	Snack: Refreshing Café Cooler	Dinner: Hearty Veggie and Chicken Stew	Dessert: Honey-Cinnamon Doughnuts
Day-3	Breakfast: Baked Berry Oatmeal	Lunch: Tofu Pesto Panini	Snack: Easy Sweet Potato Sticks	Dinner: Honey Pork Chops	Dessert: Churro Bites with Chocolate Sauce
Day-4	Breakfast: Mini Frittatas	Lunch: Rosemary-Roasted Tofu	Snack: Garlicky Tomato Bruschetta	Dinner: Herb-Roasted Turkey Breast	Dessert: Yogurt with Honey and Pomegranates
Day-5	Breakfast: Chickpea Avocado Toast	Lunch: Zucchini Alfredo	Snack: Diary-free and Easy Hummus	Dinner: Mediterranean Lamb Bowl with Feta Cheese	Dessert: Churro Bites with Chocolate Sauce
Day-6	Breakfast: Quinoa Almond Bowl	Lunch: Stuffed Artichoke Hearts	Snack: Spinach-Walnut Fatayers	Dinner: Roasted Rib Eye Steak with Onions	Dessert: Vanilla Pudding with Strawberries
Day-7	Breakfast: Breakfast Polenta	Lunch: Garlic and Cauliflower Mash	Snack: Diary-Free Baba Ganoush	Dinner: Spanish Chicken in Almond Sauce	Dessert: Pistachio Cookies

Week-4

	Breakfast	Lunch	Snack	Dinner	Dessert
Day-1	Breakfast: Overnight Almond Oats	Lunch: Garlic-Roasted Veggies	Snack: Fruit Cheese Board	Dinner: Beef Stew with Orange Slice	Dessert: Strawberry Parfaits
Day-2	Breakfast: Scrambled Eggs with Cheese	Lunch: Avocado-Chickpea Sandwich	Snack: Terrific Spiced Almonds	Dinner: Stuffed Chicken and Ricotta	Dessert: Date Energy Balls
Day-3	Breakfast: Marinara Eggs	Lunch: Mediterranean Fettuccine	Snack: Honey Crostini with Goat Cheese	Dinner: Beef Feta Pitas	Dessert: Greek Yogurt with Chocolate
Day-4	Breakfast: Overnight Raspberries Oats	Lunch: Shawarma Lettuce Wrap	Snack: Mediterranean Crostini	Dinner: Roasted Chicken with Garlic	Dessert: Pineapple and Melon
Day-5	Breakfast: Pumpkin Parfait	Lunch: Green Veggie Sandwich	Snack: Honey-Rosemary Almonds	Dinner: Mediterranean Chimichurri Skirt Steak	Dessert: Baked Apples with Walnuts
Day-6	Breakfast: Spinach Pie with Parmesan Cheese	Lunch: Marinated Zucchini	Snack: Savory Popcorn	Dinner: Homemade Yogurt-Marinated Chicken Kebabs	Dessert: Mixed Berry Frozen Yogurt Bar
Day-7	Breakfast: Quinoa Porridge	Lunch: Roasted Root Vegetables	Snack: Fig- Energy Bites	Dinner: Cheesy Lamb Pita Breads with Nuts	Dessert: Honey-Cinnamon Doughnuts

Chapter 1 Breakfast Recipes

Baked Yogurt Peach Oatmeal

Prep time: 5 minutes | Cook time: 30 minutes | Serves: 6

Olive oil cooking spray
2 cups certified gluten-free rolled oats
2 cups unsweetened almond milk
¼ cup raw honey, plus more for drizzling (optional)
½ cup nonfat plain Greek yogurt
1 teaspoon vanilla extract
½ teaspoon ground cinnamon
¼ teaspoon salt
1½ cups diced peaches, divided, plus more for serving (optional)

1. Preheat the air fryer to 380°F; while preheating, lightly coat a 6-inch cake pan with olive oil cooking spray. 2. In a large bowl, mix together the oats, almond milk, honey, yogurt, vanilla, cinnamon, and salt until well combined; fold in ¾ cup of peaches. 3. Pour the mixture into the prepared cake pan and then sprinkle the remaining peaches over the mixture. Bake the food in the preheated air fryer for 30 minutes. 4. When the time is up, let the food rest for 5 minutes before serving. You can enjoy with additional fresh fruit and honey.
Per Serving: Calories 235; Fats 10.71g; Sodium 146mg; Carbs 50.46g; Fiber 5.8g; Sugar 29.23g; Protein 10.71g

Harissa Shakshuka

Prep time: 10 minutes | Cook time: 20 minutes | Serves: 4

1½ tablespoons extra-virgin olive oil
2 tablespoons harissa
1 tablespoon tomato paste
½ onion, diced
1 bell pepper, seeded and diced
3 garlic cloves, minced
1 (28-ounce) can no-salt-added diced tomatoes
½ teaspoon kosher salt
4 large eggs
2 to 3 tablespoons fresh basil, chopped or cut into ribbons

1. Preheat your oven to 375°F. 2. In your skillet, heat the olive oil over medium heat; add the harissa, tomato paste, onion, bell pepper and sauté for 3 to 4 minutes; add the garlic and cook for 30 seconds or until fragrant.; add the diced tomatoes, salt and simmer for about 10 minutes. 3. Make 4 wells in the sauce and gently break 1 egg into each. Carefully transfer the food cooking tray in the oven and bake them for 10 to 12 minutes until the egg whites are cooked and the yolks are set. 4. When cooked, allow the food to cool for 3 to 5 minutes; garnish with the basil, and carefully spoon onto plates. Enjoy.
Per Serving: Calories 176; Fats 10.48g; Sodium 501mg; Carbs 13.22g; Fiber 5.1g; Sugar 8.11g; Protein 8.89g

Egg Stuffed in Pepper Ring with Avocado

Prep time: 15 minutes | Cook time: 10 minutes | Serves: 4

4 bell peppers, any color
1 tablespoon extra-virgin olive oil
8 large eggs
¾ teaspoon kosher salt, divided
¼ teaspoon freshly ground black pepper, divided
1 avocado, peeled, pitted, and diced
¼ cup red onion, diced
¼ cup fresh basil, chopped
Juice of ½ lime

1. Remove the stems and seeds from bell peppers and cut 2 rings from each pepper. Chop the remaining bell pepper into small dice and set aside. 2. In your skillet, heat the olive oil over medium heat; add 4 bell pepper rings and then crack 1 egg in each ring; season each egg with ¼ teaspoon of salt and ⅛ teaspoon of black pepper, cook them for 2 to 3 minutes until the egg whites are mostly set but the yolks are still runny. 3. Gently flip the pepper rings and cook 1 additional minute for over easy. Move the egg–bell pepper rings to a platter or onto plates, and cook the remaining 4 bell pepper rings with the same steps. 4. In a medium bowl, mix the avocado, onion, basil, lime juice, reserved diced bell pepper, the remaining salt and black pepper well. 5. Divide the mixture among the pepper rings. Enjoy.
Per Serving: Calories 276; Fats 20.39g; Sodium 585mg; Carbs 10.55g; Fiber 4.3g; Sugar 3.4g; Protein 14.63g

Fried Eggs and Polenta with Sautéed Chard

Prep time: 5 minutes | Cook time: 30 minutes | Serves: 4

For the Polenta
2½ cups water
½ teaspoon kosher salt
¾ cups whole-grain cornmeal
¼ teaspoon freshly ground black
pepper
2 tablespoons grated Parmesan cheese
For the Chard
1 tablespoon extra-virgin olive oil
1 bunch (about 6 ounces) Swiss chard, leaves and stems chopped and separated
2 garlic cloves, sliced
¼ teaspoon kosher salt
⅛ teaspoon freshly ground black pepper
Lemon juice (optional)
For the Eggs
1 tablespoon extra-virgin olive oil
4 large eggs

To Make the Polenta: 1. In your skillet, add the water and salt and boil the water over high heat; slowly add the cornmeal, whisking constantly. 2. Decrease the heat to low, cover the skillet and cook for 10 to 15 minutes, stirring often to avoid lumps. Stir in the pepper and Parmesan, then divide the polenta among 4 bowls. Clean your skillet.
To Make the Chard: 1. In your skillet, heat the oil over medium heat; add the chard stems, garlic, salt, pepper and sauté for 2 minutes; add the chard leaves and cook for 3 to 5 minutes or until wilted. 2. Add a spritz of lemon juice (optional), toss together, and divide evenly on top of the polenta.
To Make the Eggs: 1. Still in the skillet, heat the oil over medium-high heat and then crack 1 egg into it at a time, taking care not to crowd the skillet and leaving space between the eggs. Cook the eggs for 2 to 3 minutes until the whites are set and golden around the edges (you can cook the eggs for 1 minute longer for over easy). 2. Place one egg on top of the polenta and chard in each bowl.
Per Serving: Calories 222; Fats 11.3g; Sodium 684mg; Carbs 21.39g; Fiber 2.5g; Sugar 1.12g; Protein 9.79g

Scrambled Eggs with Smoked Salmon

Prep time: 5 minutes | Cook time: 5 minutes | Serves: 2

4 large eggs
1 tablespoon milk
1 tablespoon fresh chives, minced
1 tablespoon fresh dill, minced
¼ teaspoon kosher salt
⅛ teaspoon freshly ground black pepper
2 teaspoons extra-virgin olive oil
2 ounces smoked salmon, thinly sliced

1. In a large bowl, add the eggs, milk, chives, dill, salt and pepper. Mix well. 2. In the skillet, heat the olive oil over medium heat; add the egg mixture and cook for about 3 minutes, stirring occasionally; add the salmon and cook for 1 minute longer until the eggs are set but moist. 3. Serve and enjoy.
Per Serving: Calories 242; Fats 16.79g; Sodium 559mg; Carbs 3.09g; Fiber 0.8g; Sugar 0.78g; Protein 19.24g

Baked Berry Oatmeal

Prep time: 10 minutes | Cook time: 45-50 minutes | Serves: 8

2 cups gluten-free rolled oats
2 cups (10-ounce bag) frozen mixed berries (blueberries and raspberries work best)
2 cups plain, unsweetened almond milk
1 cup plain Greek yogurt
¼ cup maple syrup
2 tablespoons extra-virgin olive oil
2 teaspoons ground cinnamon
1 teaspoon baking powder
1 teaspoon vanilla extract
½ teaspoon kosher salt
¼ teaspoon ground nutmeg
⅛ teaspoon ground cloves

1. Preheat your oven to 375°F. 2. In a large bowl, mix all the ingredients together and then pour the mixture into a 9-by-13-inch baking dish. Bake the mixture in the preheated oven for 45 to 50 minutes or until golden brown. 3. Serve and enjoy.
Per Serving: Calories 176; Fats 6.42g; Sodium 218mg; Carbs 31.7g; Fiber 5g; Sugar 13.88g; Protein 7.29g

Quinoa Almond Bowl

Prep time: 10 minutes | Cook time: 15 minutes | Serves: 4

1½ cups water
1 cup quinoa
2 cinnamon sticks
inch knob of ginger, peeled
¼ teaspoon kosher salt
1 cup plain Greek yogurt
½ cup dates, pitted and chopped
½ cup almonds (raw or roasted), chopped
2 teaspoons honey (optional)

1. In the saucepan, bring the water, quinoa, cinnamon sticks, ginger, and salt to a boil over high heat. Reduce the heat and then cover the saucepan, simmer them for 10 to 12 minutes. 2. Remove the cinnamon sticks and ginger, fluffy with a fork; add the yogurt, dates, and almonds to the quinoa and mix together. Divide evenly among 4 bowls and garnish with ½ teaspoon of honey per bowl (optional). Enjoy.
Per Serving: Calories 263; Fats 3.01g; Sodium 175mg; Carbs 47.01g; Fiber 4.7g; Sugar 16.83g; Protein 13.66g

Fig and Ricotta Toast

Prep time: 5 minutes | Cook time: 0 | Serves: 2

¼ cup ricotta cheese
2 pieces' whole-wheat bread, toasted

4 figs, halved
2 tablespoons walnuts, chopped
1 teaspoon honey

1. Spread 2 tablespoons of ricotta cheese and place 4 fig halves on each piece of toast, pressing firmly to keep the figs in the ricotta. 2. Sprinkle 1 tablespoon of walnuts and drizzle ½ teaspoon of honey on each piece of toast. Enjoy.
Per Serving: Calories 235; Fats 9.93g; Sodium 174mg; Carbs 29.01g; Fiber 4.1g; Sugar 12.52g; Protein 9.92g

Avocado Trout Toast

Prep time: 10 minutes | Cook time: 0 | Serves: 2

1 avocado, peeled and pitted
2 teaspoons lemon juice, plus more for serving
¾ teaspoon ground cumin
¼ teaspoon kosher salt
¼ teaspoon red pepper flakes,

plus more for sprinkling
¼ teaspoon lemon zest
2 pieces' whole-wheat bread, toasted
1 (3.75-ounce) can smoked trout

1. In a medium bowl, add the avocado, lemon juice, cumin, salt, red pepper flakes, and lemon zest, mix them well. 2. Spread half the avocado mixture on each piece of toast and top each piece of toast with half the smoked trout. Garnish with a pinch of red pepper flakes (optional) or a sprinkle of lemon juice (optional).
Per Serving: Calories 337; Fats 19.98g; Sodium 478mg; Carbs 23.53g; Fiber 8.8g; Sugar 2.5g; Protein 18.92g

Granola Parfait with Greek Yogurt

Prep time: 10 minutes | Cook time: 35 minutes | Serves: 4

For the Granola
¼ cup honey or maple syrup
2 tablespoons vegetable oil
2 teaspoons vanilla extract
½ teaspoon kosher salt
3 cups gluten-free rolled oats
For the Parfait
2 cups plain Greek yogurt
1 cup fresh fruit, chopped

1 cup mixed raw and unsalted nuts, chopped
¼ cup sunflower seeds
1 cup unsweetened dried cherries

(optional)

To Make the Granola: 1. Preheat the oven to 325°F. Line a baking sheet with parchment paper. 2. In the saucepan, add the honey, oil, vanilla, salt and heat them over medium heat. Simmer them for 2 minutes and stir together well. 3. In a large bowl, combine the oats, nuts, and seeds. Stir in the warm oil mixture. Spread in a single layer on the prepared baking sheet. 4. Bake the food for 30 minutes, stirring halfway through. Remove from the oven and add in the dried cherries. Cool completely. This dish can be stored in an airtight container at room temperature for up to 3 months.
To Make the Parfait: For one serving: In a bowl or lowball drinking glass, spoon in ½ cup of yogurt, ½ cup of granola and ¼ cup of fruit (optional). Layer in whatever pattern you like.
Per Serving: Calories 554; Fats 33.61g; Sodium 632mg; Carbs 50.32g; Fiber 6.1g; Sugar 22.4g; Protein 26.1g

Potato Shakshuka

Prep time: 10 minutes | Cook time: 20 minutes | Serves: 4

2 tablespoons olive oil
1 cup chopped shallots
1 cup chopped red bell peppers
1 cup finely diced potato
1 teaspoon garlic powder
1 (14.5-ounce) can diced

tomatoes, drained
¼ teaspoon turmeric
¼ teaspoon paprika
¼ teaspoon ground cardamom
4 large eggs
¼ cup chopped fresh cilantro

1. At 350 degrees F, preheat your oven. 2. In an oven-safe sauté pan or skillet, heat the olive oil over medium-high heat and sauté the shallots for 3 minutes until fragrant, stirring occasionally. 3. Add the bell peppers, potato, and garlic powder, cover the pan or skillet and cook them for 10 minutes, stirring every 2 minutes. 4. Add the tomatoes, turmeric, paprika, and cardamom to this skillet and mix well. Once bubbly, crack the eggs into this skillet so the yolks are facing up. 5. Transfer this skillet in the oven and cook for an additional 5 to 10 minutes, until eggs are cooked to your preference. 6. Garnish with the

cilantro and serve.
Per Serving: Calories 185; Total Fat 11.7g; Sodium 140mg; Total Carbs 16.13g; Fiber 4.2g; Sugars 5.55g; Protein 5.19g

Morning Muffins

Prep time: 10 minutes | Cook time: 15 minutes | Serves: 12 muffins

Nonstick cooking spray
1½ cups granulated sugar
½ cup brown sugar
¾ cup all-purpose flour
2 teaspoons pumpkin pie spice
1 teaspoon baking soda
¼ teaspoon salt

Pinch nutmeg
3 mashed bananas
1 (15-ounce) can of pure pumpkin puree
½ cup yogurt
½ cup (1 stick) butter, melted
2 large egg whites

1. At 350 degrees F, preheat your oven. Grease a muffin tray with cooking spray. 2. In a suitable bowl, mix the sugars, flour, pumpkin pie spice, baking soda, salt, and nutmeg. 3. In a separate bowl, stir the pumpkin puree, bananas, yogurt, and butter. 4. Slowly mix the wet ingredients into the dry ingredients. 5. In a suitable glass bowl, using a mixer on high, whip the egg whites until stiff and fold them into the batter. 6. Pour the batter into a muffin tray, filling each cup halfway. 7. Bake the muffins for 15 minutes, or until a fork inserted in the center comes out clean. 8. When done, serve and enjoy.
Per Serving: Calories 294; Total Fat 9g; Sodium 132mg; Total Carbs 43.5g; Fiber 0.7g; Sugars 37.4g; Protein 12.4g

French Toast

Prep time: 10 minutes | Cook time: 15 minutes | Serves: 6

1 cup whole milk
3 large eggs
2 teaspoons grated orange zest
1 teaspoon vanilla extract
⅛ teaspoon ground cardamom

⅛ teaspoon ground cinnamon
1 loaf of boule bread, sliced 1 inch thick
1 banana, sliced
¼ cup berry and honey compote

1. In a suitable, shallow dish, mix the milk, eggs, orange zest, vanilla, cardamom, and cinnamon. 2. Heat a suitable nonstick sauté pan over medium-high heat. 3. Working in batches, dredge the bread slices in the egg mixture and put in the hot pan. 4. Cook the food for 5 minutes per side, or until golden brown. 5. Top the toast with banana and drizzled with honey compote, enjoy.
Per Serving: Calories 101; Total Fat 4.3g; Sodium 94mg; Total Carbs 10.4g; Fiber 0.8g; Sugars 5.5g; Protein 5.2g

Sweet Potato Toast

Prep time: 10 minutes | Cook time: 35 minutes | Serves: 4

2 plum tomatoes, halved
6 tablespoons olive oil
Salt
Black pepper
2 large sweet potatoes, sliced lengthwise
1 cup fresh spinach

8 medium asparagus, trimmed
4 large cooked eggs
1 cup arugula
4 tablespoons pesto
4 tablespoons shredded asiago cheese

1. At 450 degrees F, preheat your oven. 2. On the baking sheet, brush the plum tomato halves with 2 tablespoons of olive oil and season with black pepper and salt. 3. Roast the tomatoes in the oven for almost 15 minutes, then remove from the oven and allow to rest. 4. Put the sweet potato slices on a separate baking sheet and brush about 2 tablespoons of oil on each side and season with black pepper and salt. 5. Bake the sweet potato slices for almost 15 minutes, flipping halfway through, until just tender. Remove the sweet potato slices from the oven and set aside. 6. Heat the remaining olive oil in the sauté pan over medium heat and sauté the fresh spinach until just wilted. 7. In the same pan, stir in the asparagus and sauté, turning throughout. Transfer to a paper towel-lined dish. 8. Place the slices of grilled sweet potato on serving plates and divide the spinach and asparagus evenly among the slices. 9. Place a prepared egg on top of the spinach and asparagus. Top this with ¼ cup of arugula. 10. Finish by drizzling with 1 tablespoon of pesto and sprinkle with 1 tablespoon of cheese. 11. Serve with 1 roasted plum tomato.
Per Serving: Calories 471; Total Fat 35.9g; Sodium 527mg; Total Carbs 27.5g; Fiber 5.3g; Sugars 5g; Protein 13.7g

Mini Frittatas

Prep time: 10 minutes | Cook time: 35 minutes | Serves: 6

Nonstick cooking spray, olive oil, or butter	4 large eggs
1½ tablespoons olive oil	4 large egg whites
¼ cup chopped red potatoes	½ cup skim milk
¼ cup minced onions	Salt
¼ cup chopped red bell pepper	Black pepper
¼ cup asparagus, sliced	½ cup shredded mozzarella cheese

1. At 350 degrees F, preheat your oven. Grease a 12-count muffin pan with nonstick cooking spray. 2. In a suitable sauté pan, preheat the oil over medium heat and sauté the potatoes and onions for almost 4 minutes, until the potatoes are fork-tender. 3. Add the bell pepper and asparagus and sauté for almost 4 minutes, until just tender. Transfer the contents of a pan onto a paper-towel-lined plate to cool. 4. In a suitable bowl, Beat together the eggs, egg whites, and milk. Season with black pepper and salt. 5. Once the vegetables are cooled to room temperature, add the vegetables and ¼ cup of mozzarella cheese. 6. Using a spoon or ladle, evenly distribute the contents of the bowl into the prepared muffin pan, filling the cups about halfway. 7. Sprinkle the rest ¼ cup of cheese over the top of the cups. 8. Bake the food for 25 minutes, until eggs reach an internal temperature of 145°F or the center is solid. 9. Allow the mini frittatas to rest for 5 to 10 minutes before removing from muffin pan and serving.
Per Serving: Calories 186; Total Fat 16.2g; Sodium 80mg; Total Carbs 3.5g; Fiber 0.4g; Sugars 2g; Protein 7.6g

Overnight Almond Oats

Prep time: 10 minutes | Cook time: 0 minute | Serves: 2

½ cup vanilla, unsweetened almond milk	sweetener
½ cup rolled oats	1 teaspoon chia seeds
2 tablespoons sliced almonds	¼ teaspoon ground cardamom
2 tablespoons simple sugar liquid	¼ teaspoon ground cinnamon

1. In a mason jar, mix all the ingredients, and shake them well. 2. Store the mixture in the refrigerator for 8 to 24 hours. 3. Serve cold or heated.
Per Serving: Calories 263; Total Fat 4.4g; Sodium 6mg; Total Carbs 22.1g; Fiber 3g; Sugars 7g; Protein 4g

Overnight Raspberries Oats

Prep time: 10 minutes | Cook time: 0 minute | Serves: 2

⅔ cup almond milk	¼ teaspoon turmeric
⅓ cup rolled oats	⅛ teaspoon ground cinnamon
¼ cup raspberries	Pinch ground cloves
1 teaspoon honey	

1. In a mason jar, mix all the ingredients, and shake them well. 2. Keep the mixture in the refrigerator for at least 8 hours and up to 24 hours. 3. Serve cold or heated.
Per Serving: Calories 271; Total Fat 1.1g; Sodium 7mg; Total Carbs 22.9g; Fiber 2.5g; Sugars 12.5g; Protein 2g

Spinach Pie with Parmesan Cheese

Prep time: 10 minutes | Cook time: 25 minutes | Serves: 8

Nonstick cooking spray	¼ teaspoon ground nutmeg
2 tablespoons olive oil	4 large eggs, divided
1 onion, chopped	1 cup grated parmesan cheese, divided
1 pound frozen spinach, thawed	
¼ teaspoon garlic salt	2 puff pastry doughs, at room temperature
¼ teaspoon freshly ground black pepper	4 hard-boiled eggs, halved

1. At 350 degrees F, preheat your oven. 2. Grease a suitable baking sheet with nonstick cooking, and set aside. 3. Heat a sauté pan over medium-high heat. Put in the oil and onion, and sauté the onion for almost 5 minutes, until translucent. 4. Squeeze the excess water from the spinach, then add to pan and cook them so that any excess water from the spinach can evaporate. Add the garlic salt, pepper, and nutmeg. 5. In a suitable bowl, crack 3 eggs and mix well. Add the eggs and ½ cup parmesan cheese to the cooled spinach mix. 6. On the prepared baking sheet, roll out the pastry dough. Layer the spinach mix on top of dough, leaving 2 inches around each edge. 7. Once the

spinach is spread onto the pastry dough, place hard-boiled egg halves evenly throughout the pie, then cover with the second pastry dough. Pinch the edges closed. 8. Crack the rest egg in a suitable bowl and mix well. 9. Spread the egg wash over the pastry dough. 10. Bake the food in the preheated oven for 15 to 20 minutes, until golden brown and warmed through. 11. When the time is up, serve and enjoy.
Per Serving: Calories 195; Total Fat 13.9g; Sodium 183mg; Total Carbs 9g; Fiber 1.7g; Sugars 1.4g; Protein 10g

Berry-Honey Pancakes

Prep time: 10 minutes | Cook time: 15 minutes | Serves: 4

1 cup almond flour	¼ teaspoon salt
1 cup plus 2 tablespoons skim milk	2 tablespoons olive oil
2 large eggs, beaten	1 sliced banana or 1 cup sliced strawberries, divided
⅓ cup honey	2 tablespoons berry and honey compote
1 teaspoon baking soda	

1. In a suitable bowl, mix together the almond flour, milk, eggs, honey, baking soda, and salt. 2. In a suitable sauté pan, heat the olive oil over medium-high heat and pour ⅓ cup of pancake batter into this pan. 3. Cook the batter for 2 to 3 minutes. 4. Right before pancake is ready to flip, add half of the fresh fruit and flip to cook for 2 to 3 minutes on the other side, until cooked through. 5. Top with the rest fruit, drizzle with berry and honey compote and serve.
Per Serving: Calories 462; Total Fat 26g; Sodium 572mg; Total Carbs 47.7g; Fiber 4.3g; Sugars 34.7g; Protein 12.2g

Cherry Smoothie Bowl

Prep time: 10 minutes | Cook time: 0 minute | Serves: 4

1 (16-ounce) bag frozen dark sweet cherries	desired
	1 teaspoon vanilla extract
1½ cups 2% plain Greek yogurt, plus more if desired	¾ teaspoon ground cinnamon
	6 ice cubes
¾ cup pomegranate juice	½ cup chopped pistachios
⅓ cup 2% milk, plus more if	½ cup fresh pomegranate seeds

1. In a suitable blender, add the cherries, yoghurt, pomegranate juice, milk, vanilla, cinnamon, and ice cubes, and purée them until smooth and well mix. 2. The prepared combination should be slightly thicker than a typical smoothie, but not too thick to pour. 3. Add a few teaspoons of milk if the smoothie is too thick; if it's too thin, add a few tablespoons of yoghurt. 4. Fill four bowls with the smoothie. 5. Serve with 2 tablespoons of pistachios and 2 tablespoons of pomegranate seeds on top of each.
Per Serving: Calories 390; Total Fat 8.1g; Sodium 189mg; Total Carbs 44.2g; Fiber 3.6g; Sugars 33.7g; Protein 34.7g

Breakfast Bruschetta

Prep time: 10 minutes | Cook time: 20 minutes | Serves: 4

¼ teaspoon salt	3 large eggs
6 cups broccoli rabe, chopped	1 tablespoon milk
1 tablespoon olive oil	¼ teaspoon black pepper
2 garlic cloves, minced	4 teaspoons grated parmesan cheese
1-ounce prosciutto, cut or torn into ½-inch pieces	
	1 garlic clove, halved
¼ teaspoon crushed red pepper	8 (¾-inch-thick) slices baguette-style whole-grain bread
Nonstick cooking spray	

1. Bring a suitable stockpot of water to a boil. Add the salt and broccoli rabe, and boil for 2 minutes. Drain in a colander. 2. Heat the oil in the suitable skillet over medium heat. 3. Add the garlic, prosciutto, and crushed red pepper, and cook for 2 minutes, stirring often. 4. Add the broccoli rabe and cook for an additional 3 minutes, stirring a few times. 5. Transfer to a suitable bowl and set aside. 6. Place this skillet back on the stove over low heat and coat with nonstick cooking spray. 7. In a suitable bowl, beat together the eggs, milk, and pepper. 8. Pour the egg mixture into this skillet. Stir and cook until the eggs are soft scrambled, 3 to 5 minutes. 9. Add the broccoli rabe mixture back to this skillet along with the cheese. 10. Stir and cook for almost 1 minute, until heated through. Now remove it from the heat. 11. Toast the bread, then apply the cut sides of the garlic clove halves onto one side of each slice of the toast. 12. Spoon the egg mixture onto each piece of toast and serve.
Per Serving: Calories 210; Total Fat 13.5g; Sodium 462mg; Total Carbs 6.6g; Fiber 0.1g; Sugars 0.5g; Protein 17g

Breakfast Parfaits with Grapes

Prep time: 10 minutes | Cook time: 25 minutes | Serves: 4

1½ pounds seedless grapes (about 4 cups)	2 cups plain Greek yogurt
1 tablespoon olive oil	½ cup chopped walnuts
	4 teaspoons honey

1. Place a suitable, rimmed baking sheet in the oven. At 450 degrees F, preheat the oven with this pan inside. 2. Dry on a clean kitchen towel, and put in a suitable bowl. Drizzle with the oil, and toss to coat. 3. Remove the hot pan from the oven, and pour the grapes onto this pan. Bake the food for 20 to 23 minutes, until slightly shriveled, stirring once halfway through. 4. Remove this baking sheet from the oven and cool on a wire rack for 5 minutes. 5. While the grapes are cooling, assemble the parfaits by spooning the yogurt into four bowls or tall glasses. Top each bowl or glass with 2 tablespoons of walnuts and 1 teaspoon of honey. 6. When the grapes are slightly cooled, top each parfait with a quarter of the grapes. 7. Scrape any accumulated sweet grape juice onto the parfaits and serve.
Per Serving: Calories 323; Total Fat 8.2g; Sodium 32mg; Total Carbs 59.4g; Fiber 3.4g; Sugars 55.4g; Protein 9.6g

Chickpea Avocado Toast

Prep time: 10 minutes | Cook time: 0 minute | Serves: 4

1 (15-ounce) can chickpeas, drained and rinsed	lemon juice or 1 tablespoon orange juice
1 avocado, pitted	½ teaspoon freshly ground black pepper
½ cup (2 ounces) diced feta cheese	4 pieces' multigrain toast
2 teaspoons freshly squeezed	2 teaspoons honey

1. Put the chickpeas in a suitable bowl. 2. Scoop the avocado flesh into the bowl. 3. Mash the chickpea mixture together until smooth. 4. Stir in lemon juice, feta, and pepper, and mix well. 5. Divide the prepared mash onto the four pieces of toast and spread with a knife. 6. Drizzle the food with honey and serve.
Per Serving: Calories 366; Total Fat 13.5g; Sodium 159mg; Total Carbs 48.3g; Fiber 14.6g; Sugars 10.2g; Protein 16.1g

Honey Nut Granola

Prep time: 10 minutes | Cook time: 20 minutes | Serves: 6

2½ cups regular rolled oats	2 tablespoons ground flaxseed
⅓ cup coarsely chopped almonds	¼ cup honey
⅛ teaspoon kosher or sea salt	¼ cup olive oil
½ teaspoon ground cinnamon	2 teaspoons vanilla extract
½ cup chopped dried apricots	

1. At 325 degrees F, preheat your oven. Line a suitable, rimmed baking sheet with parchment paper. 2. In the skillet, mix the oats, almonds, salt, and cinnamon. Turn the heat to medium-high and cook the oat mixture for almost 6 minutes. 3. While the oat mixture is toasting, in a microwave-safe bowl, mix the apricots, flaxseed, honey, and oil. Heat the mixture in the microwave for high for almost 1 minute, or until very hot and just beginning to bubble. 4. Stir the vanilla into the honey mixture, then pour it over the oat mixture in this skillet. Stir well. 5. Spread out the prepared granola on the prepared baking sheet. 6. Bake the granola for 15 minutes, until lightly browned. 7. Allow the granola cool for a few mixture before serving.
Per Serving: Calories 313; Total Fat 15.4g; Sodium 4mg; Total Carbs 38.8g; Fiber 5.4g; Sugars 13.7g; Protein 6.8g

Breakfast Polenta

Prep time: 10 minutes | Cook time: 10 minutes | Serves: 6

2 (18-ounce) tubes plain polenta	½ cup chopped pecans
2¼ to 2½ cups milk	¼ cup plain Greek yogurt
2 oranges, peeled and chopped	8 teaspoons honey

1. Slice the plain polenta into rounds and place in a microwave-safe bowl. 2. Heat in the microwave for high for 45 seconds. 3. Transfer the polenta to a suitable pot, and mash it with a potato masher or fork until mashed. Place the pot on the stove over medium heat. 4. In a suitable, microwave-safe bowl, preheat the milk in the Heat in the microwave for high for 1 minute. 5. Add 2 cups of the warmed milk into the pot with the polenta, and stir with a whisk. Continue to stir and mash with the whisk, adding the rest milk a few tablespoons at a time, until the polenta is fairly smooth and heated through, about 5 minutes. 6. Divide the polenta among four serving bowls. 7. Top each bowl with one-quarter of the oranges, 2 tablespoons of pecans, 1 tablespoon of yogurt, and 2 teaspoons of honey before serving.
Per Serving: Calories 286; Total Fat 6.4g; Sodium 135mg; Total Carbs 42g; Fiber 2.1g; Sugars 25.6g; Protein 16.7g

Ricotta with Pears

Prep time: 10 minutes | Cook time: 35 minutes | Serves: 4

Nonstick cooking spray	1 tablespoon sugar
1 (16-ounce) container whole-milk ricotta cheese	1 teaspoon vanilla extract
2 large eggs	¼ teaspoon ground nutmeg
¼ cup white whole-wheat flour or whole-wheat pastry flour	1 pear, cored and diced
	2 tablespoons water
	1 tablespoon honey

1. At 400 degrees F, preheat your oven. 2. Grease four 6-ounce ramekins with nonstick cooking spray. 3. In a suitable bowl, beat together the ricotta, eggs, flour, sugar, vanilla, and nutmeg. Spoon into the ramekins. 4. Bake the ricotta for 22 to 25 minutes, or until the ricotta is just about set. Remove from the oven and cool slightly on racks. 5. While the ricotta is baking, in a suitable saucepan over medium heat, simmer the pear in the water for 10 minutes, until softened then add honey. 6. Serve the ricotta ramekins topped with the warmed pear.
Per Serving: Calories 162; Total Fat 6.2g; Sodium 86mg; Total Carbs 20.5g; Fiber 1.3g; Sugars 12.6g; Protein 7.1g

Chicken Vegetable Risotto

Prep time: 10 minutes | Cook time: 30 minutes | Serves: 4

For the Dressing:

Juice and zest of 1 lemon	¼ cup grated parmesan cheese
½ teaspoon minced garlic	Sea salt
¼ cup olive oil	Black pepper

For the Risotto:

1 cup brown rice, soaked overnight and drained	1 yellow bell pepper, finely chopped
1½ cups water	1 carrot, finely chopped
2 cups chopped store-bought rotisserie chicken or leftover cooked chicken	2 tomatoes, seeded and diced
	1 scallion, sliced
1 cup finely chopped cauliflower	2 tablespoons chopped fresh oregano

To make the dressing: 1. In a suitable bowl, beat together the lemon juice, lemon zest, garlic, olive oil, and parmesan cheese. 2. Add salt and black pepper and set aside.
To make the risotto: 1. In a suitable pot, mix the soaked rice and water. Bring to a boil, then reduce its heat to low, cover the pot, and simmer for 20 to 30 minutes, until tender. 2. Transfer the cooked rice to a dish and refrigerate until cool. 3. In a suitable bowl, mix together the cooled rice, chicken, cauliflower, bell pepper, carrot, tomatoes, scallion, and oregano. 4. Stir in the dressing and toss to mix. Serve.
Per Serving: Calories 433; Total Fat 16.8g; Sodium 95mg; Total Carbs 45.6g; Fiber 4.8g; Sugars 4.7g; Protein 26.2g

Mediterranean Bulgur Bowl

Prep time: 10 minutes | Cook time: 15 minutes | Serves: 6

1½ cups uncooked bulgur	8 dried (or fresh) figs, chopped
2 cups milk	½ cup chopped almonds
1 cup water	¼ cup loosely packed fresh mint, chopped
½ teaspoon ground cinnamon	Warm milk (optional)
2 cups frozen (or fresh, pitted) dark sweet cherries	

1. In a suitable saucepan, mix the bulgur, milk, water, and cinnamon. Stir once, then bring just to a boil. 2. Cover the saucepan, reduce its heat to medium-low, and simmer the mixture for 10 minutes or until the liquid is absorbed. 3. Turn off the heat, but keep this pan on the stove, and stir in the frozen cherries (no need to thaw), figs, and almonds. 4. Stir well, cover the saucepan, and wait for 1 minute, then let the hot bulgur thaw the cherries and partially hydrate the figs. 5. Stir in the mint, and scoop into serving bowls. 6. Serve with warm milk.
Per Serving: Calories 310; Total Fat 3.8g; Sodium 31mg; Total Carbs 63.5g; Fiber 14g; Sugars 12.2g; Protein 10.5g

Scrambled Eggs with Cheese

Prep time: 10 minutes | Cook time: 10 minutes | Serves: 4

1½ teaspoons extra-virgin olive oil	¼ teaspoon kosher or sea salt
1 cup chopped bell peppers	2 tablespoons water
2 garlic cloves, minced (about 1 teaspoon)	½ cup crumbled goat cheese
6 large eggs	2 tablespoons loosely packed chopped fresh mint

1. Heat the oil in the suitable skillet over medium-high heat. 2. Add the chopped peppers and sauté for 5 minutes with occasional stirring. 3. Toss in the garlic and cook for 1 minute. 4. While the peppers are cooking, in a suitable bowl, beat together the eggs, salt, and water. 5. Lower the heat to medium-low, and pour the prepared egg mixture over the peppers. 6. Let the eggs cook undisturbed for 1 to 2 minutes, until they begin to set on the bottom. 7. Sprinkle with the goat cheese. 8. Cook the eggs for almost 1 to 2 more minutes, stirring slowly, until the eggs are soft-set and custardy. 9. Top with the fresh mint and serve.
Per Serving: Calories 238; Total Fat 19g; Sodium 272mg; Total Carbs 3.6g; Fiber 0.4g; Sugars 2.4g; Protein 14.2g

Pumpkin Parfait

Prep time: 10 minutes | Cook time: 0 | Serves: 4

1 (15-ounce) can of pure pumpkin puree	¼ teaspoon ground cinnamon
4 teaspoons honey	2 cups Greek yogurt
1 teaspoon pumpkin pie spice	1 cup honey granola

1. In a suitable bowl, mix the pumpkin puree, honey, pumpkin pie spice, and cinnamon. 2. Cover this bowl and refrigerate for at least 2 hours. 3. To make the parfaits, in each cup, pour ¼ cup of pumpkin mix, ¼ cup of yogurt and ¼ cup of granola. 4. Repeat Greek yogurt and pumpkin layers, and top with honey granola. 5. Enjoy.
Per Serving: Calories 153; Total Fat 1.6g; Sodium 74mg; Total Carbs 29.2g; Fiber 1.7g; Sugars 16.5g; Protein 4.6g

Marinara Eggs

Prep time: 10 minutes | Cook time: 15 minutes | Serves: 6

1 tablespoon olive oil	added
1 cup chopped onion (about ½ medium onion)	6 large eggs
2 garlic cloves, minced (about 1 teaspoon)	½ cup chopped fresh flat-leaf (Italian) parsley
2 (14.5-ounce) cans Italian diced tomatoes, undrained, no salt	Crusty Italian bread and grated parmesan or Romano cheese (optional)

1. Heat the oil in a skillet over medium-high heat. 2. Toss in the onion and cook for 5 minutes with occasional stirring. 3. Stir in the garlic and cook for 1 minute. 4. Pour the tomatoes with their juices over the onion mixture and cook until bubbling, 2 to 3 minutes. 5. While waiting for the tomato mixture to bubble, crack one egg into a suitable custard cup. 6. When the tomato mixture bubbles, lower the heat to medium. 7. Then use a suitable spoon to make six indentations in the tomato mixture. 8. Gently pour the first cracked egg into one indentation and repeat, cracking the rest eggs, one at a time, into the custard cup and pouring one into each indentation. 9. Cover the hot skillet and let it cook for 6 to 7 minutes. 10. Top with the parsley, and serve with the bread and grated cheese.
Per Serving: Calories 107; Total Fat 7.3g; Sodium 76mg; Total Carbs 3.8g; Fiber 1.1g; Sugars 1.2g; Protein 6.9g

Quinoa Porridge

Prep time: 10 minutes | Cook time: 20 minutes | Serves: 4

½ cup quinoa	almond milk
1 cup water	¼ cup pumpkin seeds
1 cup gluten-free rolled oats	¼ cup chopped pecans
½ cup unsweetened vanilla	1 tablespoon honey

1. In a suitable saucepan, mix the quinoa and water and cook to a boil over medium heat. 2. Reduce its heat to low and cook until the liquid is absorbed, 10 to 15 minutes. 3. In a suitable bowl, stir the cooled quinoa, oats, almond milk, pumpkin seeds, pecans, and honey until well mixed. 4. Transfer the mixture to a storage container and store in the refrigerator, sealed, overnight. 5. Stir in more almond milk in the morning if needed to adjust the texture. Serve.

Per Serving: Calories 242; Total Fat 8g; Sodium 27mg; Total Carbs 35.9g; Fiber 4.6g; Sugars 4.6g; Protein 8.9g

Chia-Pomegranate Smoothie

Prep time: 10 minutes | Cook time: 0 minute | Serves: 2

1 cup pure pomegranate juice	3 Medjool dates, pitted and chopped
1 cup frozen berries	Pinch ground cinnamon
1 cup chopped kale	
2 tablespoons chia seeds	

1. In a suitable blender, add all the ingredients to a blender, and then pulse them until smooth. 2. Pour the smoothie into glasses and serve.
Per Serving: Calories 384; Total Fat 9g; Sodium 27mg; Total Carbs 74.9g; Fiber 15.7g; Sugars 50.5g; Protein 7.7g

Oatmeal Pancakes

Prep time: 10 minutes | Cook time: 20 minutes | Serves: 4

4 large egg whites	1 teaspoon vanilla extract
1 large egg	½ teaspoon ground cinnamon
1 cup low-fat cottage cheese	1 cup gluten-free rolled oats
2 tablespoons honey	Coconut oil, for cooking

1. In a suitable bowl, beat together the egg whites, egg, cottage cheese, honey, vanilla, and cinnamon until well blended and most of the lumps are gone. Beat in the rolled oats until blended. 2. Place a suitable skillet over medium heat and lightly coat it with coconut oil. 3. Add about ¼ cup of batter to this skillet, and cook for 3 minutes per side. 4. Repeat with the rest of the batter. 5. Serve warm or cold.
Per Serving: Calories 212; Total Fat 4.1g; Sodium 281mg; Total Carbs 27.4g; Fiber 2.7g; Sugars 9.3g; Protein 16.5g

Olive and Sweet Pepper Frittata

Prep time: 10 minutes | Cook time: 15 minutes | Serves: 4

1 tablespoon olive oil	½ cup pitted, sliced kalamata olives
1 sweet onion, chopped	¼ cup chopped fresh oregano
1 red bell pepper, chopped	½ cup crumbled goat cheese
1 teaspoon minced garlic	Sea salt
8 large eggs	Freshly ground black pepper
½ cup low-fat milk	

1. Preheat the oven to broil. 2. In a suitable bowl, beat together the olives, milk, eggs, and oregano until blended. 3. Heat the olive oil in the skillet over medium heat; sauté the bell pepper, onion, and garlic for 4 minutes. 4. Pour the prepared egg mixture into this skillet and as the prepared mixture starts to set, lift the edges with a spatula, and let the egg flow under the cooked portions. 5. Continue cooking and lifting for 5 to 7 minutes until the egg mixture is almost set. 6. Sprinkle the top of the frittata with goat cheese and place the entire skillet in the oven. 7. Broil the food for 2 minutes until the eggs are set and the top is golden brown. 8. Season with black pepper and salt, and serve.
Per Serving: Calories 240; Total Fat 15.9g; Sodium 186mg; Total Carbs 10.5g; Fiber 2.9g; Sugars 5.3g; Protein 15.8g

Quinoa and Spinach Salad with Figs

Prep time: 10 minutes | Cook time: 15 minutes | Serves: 4

½ cup quinoa	¼ cup sunflower seeds
1 cup water	½ cup store-bought balsamic dressing
6 cups chopped spinach	½ cup crumbled goat cheese
8 ripe figs, quartered	

1. In a suitable saucepan, mix the quinoa and water and cook to a boil over medium heat. 2. Reduce its heat to low and cook, uncovered, until the liquid is absorbed, 10 to 15 minutes. 3. Transfer the food to a dish and refrigerate until cool. 4. In a suitable bowl, toss the spinach, cooled quinoa, figs, and sunflower seeds until well mixed. 5. Add the dressing, toss to coat, and transfer the salad to serving plates. 6. Top with goat cheese and serve.
Per Serving: Calories 216; Total Fat 4.6g; Sodium 55mg; Total Carbs 40.2g; Fiber 6.5g; Sugars 18.6g; Protein 7.2g

Cucumber Quinoa

Prep time: 10 minutes | Cook time: 20 minutes | Serves: 4

1 cup quinoa
2 cups water
2 English cucumbers
2 plum tomatoes, cut into eighths
1 cup chopped broccoli
½ cup pitted, sliced green olives
1 scallion, chopped
1 tablespoon chopped fresh oregano
¼ cup olive oil
2 tablespoons white wine vinegar
Sea salt
Freshly ground black pepper

1. In a suitable saucepan, mix the quinoa and water and cook to a boil over medium heat. 2. Reduce its heat to low and cook the quinoa for 10 to 15 minutes until the liquid is absorbed. 3. Transfer the cooked quinoa to a dish and refrigerate until cool. 4. While the quinoa is cooking, use a vegetable peeler to shave the cucumbers into long strips. 5. Arrange the cucumbers on a suitable platter. 6. In a suitable bowl, stir together the cooled quinoa, tomatoes, broccoli, olives, scallion, and oregano. 7. Spoon the prepared quinoa mixture into the center of the cucumber noodles. 8. In a suitable bowl, beat together the olive oil and vinegar, and season with black pepper and salt. 9. Drizzle the prepared dressing over the entire dish, and serve.
Per Serving: Calories 318; Total Fat 16g; Sodium 57mg; Total Carbs 38.6g; Fiber 5.6g; Sugars 5.5g; Protein 8.6g

Kale Smoothie

Prep time: 10 minutes | Cook time: 0 minute | Serves: 2

1 cup low-fat plain Greek yogurt
½ cup apple juice
1 apple, cored and quartered
4 Medjool dates
3 cups packed chopped kale
Juice of ½ lemon
4 ice cubes

1. In a suitable blender blend the yogurt, apple juice, apple, and dates and pulse until smooth. 2. Add the kale and lemon juice and pulse until blended. 3. Add the ice cubes and blend until smooth and thick. 4. Pour the smoothie into glasses and serve.
Per Serving: Calories 366; Total Fat 0.5g; Sodium 105mg; Total Carbs 79.9g; Fiber 8.3g; Sugars 58.1g; Protein 17.4g

Hummus Toasts

Prep time: 10 minutes | Cook time: 3 minutes | Serves: 4

4 multigrain bread slices
½ cup hummus
½ cup sliced English cucumber
½ cup shredded carrot
¼ cup chopped oil-packed sun-
dried tomatoes
1 scallion, julienned
¼ cup crumbled feta cheese
2 tablespoons sliced kalamata olives

1. Toast the bread and spread 2 tablespoons of hummus on each slice. 2. Divide the cucumber, carrot, sun-dried tomatoes, scallion, feta cheese, and olives between the toasts. Serve.
Per Serving: Calories 174; Total Fat 7.7g; Sodium 472mg; Total Carbs 19.5g; Fiber 4.4g; Sugars 3.5g; Protein 8.1g

Apple Cheese Omelet

Prep time: 10 minutes | Cook time: 20 minutes | Serves: 4

2 tablespoons olive oil
8 asparagus spears, chopped
1 garlic clove, minced
1 cup chopped spinach
¼ cup peeled chopped apple
1 tablespoon chopped fresh oregano
1 tablespoon chopped fresh basil
Sea salt
¼ cup chopped roasted red peppers
6 large eggs
¼ cup low-fat milk
⅓ cup crumbled feta cheese

1. In a suitable skillet, heat 1 tablespoon of olive oil over medium heat. Sauté the asparagus for 4 to 5 minutes, or until softened. 2. Add garlic and sauté for 1 minute. 3. Add the spinach, apple, oregano, and basil. Season lightly with salt and continue cooking for 5 minutes until the apples are softened and spinach has cooked down. 4. Stir in the roasted red peppers and transfer the vegetables to a plate. 5. In a suitable bowl, beat the eggs with the milk. 6. Wipe out this skillet, then preheat the rest 1 tablespoon of olive oil over medium heat and pour the eggs into this pan. As the eggs firm up, lift the edges and let the uncooked egg flow underneath, cooking them for 7 to 8 minutes until the eggs are almost set but still moist. 7. Season with salt. 8. Spoon the prepared vegetable mixture onto one side of the omelet and sprinkle with the feta cheese. 9. Fold the other half of the omelet over the cheese mixture and cook for 1 to 2 minutes more. 10. Cut into slices and serve.
Per Serving: Calories 194; Total Fat 14.7g; Sodium 140mg; Total Carbs 6.3g; Fiber 2.2g; Sugars 3.5g; Protein 11.1g

Goat Cheese Egg Frittata

Prep time: 10 minutes | Cook time: 15 minutes | Serves: 4

1 tablespoon olive oil
2 cups spinach
1 sweet onion, chopped
1 teaspoon minced garlic
5 large eggs
5 large egg whites
Sea salt
Black pepper
½ cup chopped roasted red peppers
½ cup crumbled goat cheese
1 tablespoon chopped fresh parsley

1. Preheat the oven to broil. 2. In the ovenproof skillet, heat the olive oil over medium-low heat and sauté the spinach, onion, and garlic for 5 minutes until softened. 3. Beat the eggs and egg whites and stir in salt and pepper. Pour the eggs into this skillet. 4. As they firm up, lift the edges with a spatula and let the uncooked egg flow underneath. Cook the eggs for 7 to 8 minutes until they are almost set. 5. Scatter the roasted red peppers and goat cheese over the top of the frittata and broil for 1 to 2 minutes until the top is completely set and the cheese is melted. 6. Serve topped with parsley.
Per Serving: Calories 178; Total Fat 11.2g; Sodium 209mg; Total Carbs 5.6g; Fiber 1.2g; Sugars 3.1g; Protein 14.4g

Chard Scramble

Prep time: 10 minutes | Cook time: 15 minutes | Serves: 4

12 large egg whites
½ cup unsweetened almond milk
¼ teaspoon ground nutmeg
Sea salt
Black pepper
1 tablespoon olive oil
1 red bell pepper, chopped
½ sweet onion, chopped
1 teaspoon minced garlic
2 cups shredded Swiss chard
1 tablespoon chopped fresh parsley

1. In a suitable bowl, beat the egg whites, almond milk, and nutmeg until mix. Season lightly with black pepper and salt and set aside. 2. In a suitable skillet, preheat the olive oil over medium-high heat and sauté the bell pepper, onion, and garlic until softened, about 4 minutes. Stir in the chard and sauté until wilted, about 3 minutes more. 3. Lower the heat to medium and pour the egg white mixture into this skillet. Scramble the egg whites with the vegetables for 4 minutes, creating fluffy thick curds, until the egg whites are moist but cooked through. 4. Serve topped with parsley.
Per Serving: Calories 107; Total Fat 4.3g; Sodium 162mg; Total Carbs 5.5g; Fiber 1.2g; Sugars 3g; Protein 11.8g

Salmon Breakfast Casserole

Prep time: 10 minutes | Cook time: 45 minutes | Serves: 6

2 tablespoons olive oil
2 cups chopped fresh broccoli
1 sweet onion, chopped
1 red bell pepper, chopped
2 teaspoons minced garlic
10 large eggs, beaten
1 cup unsweetened almond milk
1 tablespoon chopped fresh dill
Sea salt
Black pepper
6 ounces smoked salmon, chopped

1. Preheat the oven to 350 degrees F. 2. Heat the olive oil in the skillet over medium-high heat. Sauté the broccoli, onion, bell pepper, and garlic for 5 minutes until softened. 3. In a suitable bowl, beat together the eggs, almond milk, and dill until well blended and season with black pepper and salt. 4. Transfer the vegetable mixture to a 9-by-13-inch baking dish and top with the smoked salmon. 5. Pour the prepared egg mixture over the salmon and vegetables. 6. Bake the food for 35 to 40 minutes, until a knife inserted in the center comes out clean and the casserole is golden. 7. Serve.
Per Serving: Calories 226; Total Fat 14.9g; Sodium 726mg; Total Carbs 6.8g; Fiber 1.7g; Sugars 3g; Protein 17.2g

Overnight Porridge with Cherries

Prep time: 10 minutes | Cook time: 0 minute | Serves: 4

2 cups unsweetened vanilla almond milk
1 cup steel-cut oats
2 tablespoons chia seeds
2 tablespoons honey

¼ teaspoon ground cinnamon
2 cups frozen or fresh pitted black cherries
½ cup sliced almonds
¼ cup sunflower seeds

1. In a suitable bowl, stir together the almond milk, oats, chia seeds, honey, and cinnamon until well mixed. Cover the bowl and refrigerate overnight, stirring a few times. 2. Spoon the oats into bowls and top with cherries, almonds, and sunflower seeds. Serve.
Per Serving: Calories 363; Total Fat 14.3g; Sodium 595mg; Total Carbs 53.9g; Fiber 8.8g; Sugars 37.9g; Protein 7.8g

Avocado-Blueberry Smoothie

Prep time: 10 minutes | Cook time: 0 minutes | Serves: 2

½ cup unsweetened vanilla almond milk
½ cup low-fat plain Greek yogurt
1 ripe avocado, peeled, pitted, and chopped

1 cup blueberries
¼ cup gluten-free rolled oats
½ teaspoon vanilla extract
4 ice cubes

1. Add the almond milk, yogurt, avocado, blueberries, oats, and vanilla to the blender, and pulse until well blended. 2. Add the ice cubes and blend until thick and smooth. 3. Serve.
Per Serving: Calories 170; Total Fat 10.8g; Sodium 40mg; Total Carbs 15.1g; Fiber 5g; Sugars 5.2g; Protein 5.2g

California Egg Scramble

Prep time: 10 minutes | Cook time: 10 minutes | Serves: 4

10 large egg whites
1 tablespoon chopped fresh parsley
1 teaspoon chopped fresh basil
½ teaspoon chopped fresh thyme
Sea salt
Pinch black pepper
1 tablespoon olive oil

1 ripe avocado, pitted, peeled, and chopped
1 cup halved cherry tomatoes
1 scallion, diced
2 tablespoons chopped fresh cilantro
1 tablespoon minced jalapeño

1. In a suitable bowl, beat together the egg whites, parsley, basil, and thyme and season with black pepper and salt. 2. In a suitable skillet, preheat the olive oil over medium heat. 3. Pour the prepared egg mixture into this skillet and swirl this pan lightly. Scramble the eggs for 5 minutes or until cooked through but still moist. 4. Spoon the prepared eggs onto a platter and top with avocado, tomatoes, scallion, cilantro, and jalapeño. 5. Serve.
Per Serving: Calories 189; Total Fat 7.5g; Sodium 186mg; Total Carbs 10.8g; Fiber 2.6g; Sugars 6.8g; Protein 20.1g

Oatmeal Bowls with Blackberries

Prep time: 10 minutes | Cook time: 12 minutes | Serves: 4

2 cups water
¾ cup gluten-free rolled oats
¼ cup quinoa
2 tablespoons flaxseed
Pinch sea salt
½ cup unsweetened almond milk

½ teaspoon ground cinnamon
Pinch ground cloves
1 cup blackberries
¼ cup pumpkin seeds
2 tablespoons honey

1. In a suitable saucepan, stir together the water, oats, quinoa, flaxseed, and salt and cook to a boil over medium-high heat. Cook them for 5 minutes, stirring constantly. 2. Lower the heat to low and cook for 5 to 7 minutes until thick and creamy. 3. Stir in the almond milk, cinnamon, and cloves. 4. Divide into bowls and top with the blackberries, pumpkin seeds, and honey. 5. Serve.
Per Serving: Calories 189; Total Fat 7.5g; Sodium 186mg; Total Carbs 10.8g; Fiber 2.6g; Sugars 6.8g; Protein 20.1g

Pumpkin Smoothie

Prep time: 10 minutes | Cook time: 0 minute | Serves: 2

2 cups unsweetened almond milk
1 cup pure pumpkin purée
¼ cup gluten-free rolled oats

¼ cup pure cranberry juice
1 tablespoon honey
¼ teaspoon ground cinnamon

Pinch ground nutmeg

1. Add all the ingredients to the blender, and blend them until smooth.
2. Pour into glasses and serve immediately.
Per Serving: Calories 166; Total Fat 4.8g; Sodium 187mg; Total Carbs 32.7g; Fiber 6g; Sugars 16.6g; Protein 4.2g

Walnut Pancakes

Prep time: 10 minutes | Cook time: 15 minutes | Serves: 4

¾ cup whole-wheat flour
¼ cup ground walnuts
2 teaspoons baking powder
¼ teaspoon ground cinnamon
1 cup cooked quinoa

½ cup unsweetened almond milk
2 tablespoons honey
2 large eggs
2 teaspoons pure vanilla extract
Nonstick olive oil cooking spray

1. In a suitable bowl, stir together the flour, ground walnuts, baking powder, and cinnamon. 2. In a suitable bowl, beat together the quinoa, almond milk, honey, eggs, and vanilla until well blended. Add the quinoa mixture to the flour mixture and stir until mixed. 3. Heat a suitable skillet over medium heat and grease with cooking spray. 4. Scoop about ¼ cup of batter per pancake into this skillet, making about 4 pancakes per batch, and cook for 3 minutes until puffed up and browned on the bottom. 5. Flip and cook for almost 2 minutes more, until browned. 6. Transfer to a plate and repeat with remaining batter. 7. Serve with your favorite toppings.
Per Serving: Calories 372; Total Fat 10.4g; Sodium 63mg; Total Carbs 56.6g; Fiber 4.4g; Sugars 9.2g; Protein 13.6g

Strawberry Brown Rice

Prep time: 10 minutes | Cook time: 45 minutes | Serves: 4

1 cup brown rice
1 cup water
1 cup light coconut milk
1 teaspoon pure vanilla extract
¼ teaspoon ground cinnamon

2 cups sliced strawberries
¼ cup sunflower seeds
¼ cup shredded unsweetened coconut
2 tablespoons honey

1. In a suitable saucepan, stir together the rice, water, coconut milk, vanilla, and cinnamon over medium-high heat. 2. Bring to a boil, and then lower the heat to low; cover the saucepan, and cook for 35 to 40 minutes, until the liquid is absorbed and the rice is tender. 3. Divide the rice between bowls. 4. Top each bowl with strawberries, arranging them to cover half the rice. 5. Add the sunflower seeds and coconut to the bowls so they each cover one-quarter of the rice. 6. Drizzle with honey and serve.
Per Serving: Calories 403; Total Fat 18.9g; Sodium 15mg; Total Carbs 55.3g; Fiber 5.2g; Sugars 14.7g; Protein 6.2g

Fruit Overnight Bulgur

Prep time: 10 minutes | Cook time: 0 minute | Serves: 4

2 cups low-fat plain Greek yogurt
1 cup instant bulgur
½ cup light coconut milk
¼ cup chopped pecans
¼ cup maple syrup

½ teaspoon ground ginger
3 plums, pitted and chopped
1 peach, pitted and chopped
1 cup pitted frozen or fresh black cherries

1. In a suitable bowl, stir together the yogurt, bulgur, coconut milk, pecans, maple syrup, and ginger until well mixed. 2. Evenly divide the prepared mixture between bowls and top with the plums, peaches, and cherries. Cover the bowls and refrigerate overnight. 3. Serve.
Per Serving: Calories 275; Total Fat 8.4g; Sodium 77mg; Total Carbs 38.1g; Fiber 4.1g; Sugars 26.1g; Protein 15.2g

Chapter 2 Chicken and Poultry Recipes

Homemade Chicken Cacciatore

Prep time: 10 minutes | Cook time: 4 hours | Serves: 4 to 6

8 chicken thighs with skin and bones
1 teaspoon salt
¼ teaspoon freshly ground black pepper
2 tablespoons extra-virgin olive oil
1 onion, chopped
1 red bell pepper, seeded and chopped
3 garlic cloves, sliced
½ cup red wine
1 (28-ounce) can crushed tomatoes
1 cup chicken broth or water
1 tablespoon capers
2 teaspoons dried oregano

1. Season the chicken with pepper and salt, and put in the bottom of a slow cooker. Together with the onion, bell pepper, red wine, olive oil, water or chicken broth, oregano, capers, garlic, tomatoes, and then pour over the chicken. Then, close and cook on high for 4 hours. 2. This is a hearty recipe that can last 1 week in the refrigerator or for several months in the freezer. Since it makes a big pot, it's good to freeze in single servings for a fast lunch or supper.
Prep tip: You can substitute beef short ribs for the chicken in this recipe. Once cooked, remove the bones and you have a hearty sauce for pasta.
Per Serving: Calories 851; Fat 60.54g; Sodium 1150mg; Carbs 11.12g; Fiber 4g; Sugar 5.99g; Protein 63.45g

Chicken Thighs with Red Wine Sauce

Prep time: 15 minutes | Cook time: 4 hours | Serves: 4 to 6

2 tablespoons extra-virgin olive oil
8 chicken thighs with skin and bones
1 teaspoon salt
¼ teaspoon freshly ground black pepper
3 shallots, thinly sliced
1 pound mushrooms, thinly sliced
1 cup red wine
1 cup chicken broth
1 sprig fresh thyme

1. Place a large skillet over high heat. Add the olive oil and cook the chicken until browned on all sides, about 3 to 4 minutes per side. Transfer the chicken and all the pan juices to a slow cooker. Sprinkle with the salt and pepper. 2. Add the mushrooms, chicken broth, red wine, shallots, and thyme to the slow cooker. Close and cook on high for 4 hours.(For a Dutch oven or a heavy pot with a lid, remove the chicken and set it aside. Add the shallots and mushrooms to the same pot and sauté for 5 minutes. Then add the wine, broth, salt, pepper, and thyme, and turn the chicken to the pot. Bring to a boil, cover, and reduce to a simmer. Simmer for 1 hour.) Get the thyme sprig away and serve. 3. Because this recipe can make a big quantity, we do suggest that freeze it in double potions or single for easy meals. Besides, this kind of recipe can be kept in the refrigerator for 1 week, or even frozen for several months.
Per Serving: Calories 848; Fat 60.35g; Sodium 924mg; Carbs 9.01g; Fiber 1.8g; Sugar 4.32g; Protein 65.08g

Healthy Chicken Almond Phyllo Pie

Prep time: 30 minutes | Cook time: 35 minutes | Serves: 6 to 8

2 tablespoons butter
2 tablespoons extra-virgin olive oil
1 large onion, chopped
2 garlic cloves, chopped
1¾ teaspoons ground cinnamon, divided
1 teaspoon cayenne pepper
1 teaspoon powdered ginger
½ teaspoon ground turmeric
¼ cup chicken broth or water
1 pound boneless chicken thigh meat, chopped into ¼-inch pieces
1 teaspoon salt
¼ teaspoon freshly ground black pepper
¼ cup finely chopped Preserved Lemons or 2 tablespoons lemon juice
¼ cup chopped fresh flatleaf parsley
4 eggs, beaten
1 cup ground unsalted almonds
2 tablespoons sugar
6 ounces butter, melted
12 sheets phyllo (filo)
⅓ cup powdered sugar

1. Place a Dutch oven or a heavy pot with a lid over high heat and add the butter and olive oil. 2. Add the garlic and onion and sauté several minutes. Then add the cayenne, turmeric, 1 teaspoon cinnamon and fry 5 minutes. 3. To the pot, add the broth, chicken, salt, and pepper, and simmer 10 minutes or until the chicken is cooked through and the liquid has evaporated. Remove the chicken from the pot and place in a large bowl. Let cool at least 15 minutes. 4. Add the lemon juice, preserved lemons, eggs as well as parsley. Then set them aside. 5. Combine sugar, ½ teaspoon cinnamon, ground almonds in a small bowl and set them aside. Heat the oven to 375°F ahead of cooking. 6. Brush a 9-by-13-inch baking pan with a little melted butter. 7. Place 1 sheet of phyllo in the buttered pan and brush with more butter. Top with another layer of phyllo and brush with butter, then add a third layer and brush with butter. 8. First, spread one-half of the almond mixture over the phyllo. Then, put three more sheets of phyllo on top of them, brushing each sheet with butter. 9. Next, over the phyllo, please spoon one-half of the chicken. Top with three sheets of phyllo, brushing in between each sheet with butter. Add the remaining almond mixture. Finish the dish with the remaining chicken followed by the last three sheets of phyllo, brushing with butter in between each sheet. 10. Brush the top layer with butter. Using a sharp knife, score the top layers of phyllo into 12 pieces. This will prevent the phyllo from cracking as it rises in the oven. 11. Bake for 25 to 35 minutes or until golden brown. Remove from the oven and let cool for 10 minutes. After garnish with the remaining ¼ teaspoon cinnamon and powdered sugar, then keep the warm.
Prep tip: The number of ingredients is daunting, but it's really not complicated. There are three elements: the chicken filling, the almond filling, and the phyllo. The fillings can be made ahead for last-minute assembly, or the whole dish can be made ahead and frozen uncooked for several months. It can go from freezer to oven; this will extend the baking time, since the filling will be frozen. Garnish with the powdered sugar and cinnamon after baking.
Per Serving: Calories 666; Fat 49.49g; Sodium 823mg; Carbs 32.39g; Fiber 3.9g; Sugar 9.41g; Protein 25.68g

Poached Chicken with Tarragon

Prep time: 10 minutes | Cook time: 25 to 35 minutes | Serves: 4

6 boneless, skinless chicken breasts
½ cup white wine
1 cup chicken broth or water
1 shallot, sliced
3 sprigs fresh tarragon, plus 1 teaspoon chopped for garnish
1 teaspoon salt
¼ teaspoon freshly ground black pepper

1. Heat the oven to 375°F ahead of time. In a single layer in a 9-by-13-inch pan, please set the chicken breasts. 2. Add the broth or water, shallot, salt, pepper as well as the wine. Slightly stir to combine ingredients. 3. Cover with foil and place in the oven for 25 to 35 minutes, or until the chicken is firm to the touch. 4. Carefully remove the foil, since it will release hot steam. Let the chicken rest 10 minutes in the poaching liquid before serving. 5. Remove the chicken from the pan with a slotted spoon and garnish with the chopped tarragon. Cooked chicken can be kept for 1 week in the refrigerator.
Serving Suggestion: Save the poaching liquid, since it's loaded with flavor and can be used to make sauces and soups. The liquid can be kept in a jar and frozen until you're ready to use it.
Per Serving: Calories 255; Fat 7.53g; Sodium 889mg; Carbs 1.92g; Fiber 0.2g; Sugar 0.71g; Protein 42.04g

Moroccan Chicken with Cinnamon and Olives

Prep time: 10 minutes | Cook time: 20 minutes | Serves: 4

½ cup rice flour
1 teaspoon ground cumin
1 teaspoon ground ginger
1 teaspoon ground cinnamon
½ teaspoon salt
¼ teaspoon freshly ground black pepper
4 boneless, skinless chicken breasts
3 tablespoons extra-virgin olive oil
1 garlic clove, thinly sliced
½ cup wine
½ cup chicken broth or water
Several saffron threads
½ cup salt-cured olives
1 orange, sliced
¼ cup chopped fresh cilantro

1. Together with cumin, rice flour, cinnamon, ginger, pepper as well as salt in a small shallow bowl. Then, in the spice mixture, dredge each piece of chicken. 2. Place a large skillet over high heat and add the olive oil. Add the chicken and brown on all sides, about 3 to 4 minutes per side. 3. Add the garlic, wine, broth or water, and saffron to the pan and bring to a boil. Reduce to a simmer and cook for 15 minutes. 4. Add the olives and orange slices, cover, and turn off the heat. Let it sit for 5 minutes to combine the flavors. Open the lid, then add the cilantro, and serve. Besides, this recipe can be kept in the refrigerator for 5 days.
Prep tip: If you don't like the sweet-salty combination of oranges and olives, you can omit the olives and add ½ cup chopped dried apricots instead.
Per Serving: Calories 314; Fat 15.02g; Sodium 559mg; Carbs 23.34g; Fiber 2.8g; Sugar 3.52g; Protein 21.68g

Spanish Chicken in Almond Sauce

Prep time: 15 minutes | Cook time: 30 minutes | Serves: 4

1 tablespoon extra-virgin olive oil	½ teaspoon ground nutmeg
1 tablespoon butter	¼ teaspoon ground turmeric
4 boneless, skinless chicken breasts	½ cup chicken broth
½ medium onion, sliced	¼ cup dry sherry
1 garlic clove, sliced	1 teaspoon salt
¼ cup blanched (skinless) unsalted almonds	¼ teaspoon freshly ground black pepper
½ teaspoon ground cinnamon	1 tablespoon chopped fresh flatleaf parsley

1. First of all, set a large skillet over high heat. Then, on all sides until firm, add the butter, olive oil and cook the chicken breasts which can spend 5 to 7 minutes per side or so. Besides, Remove the chicken and set them aside. 2. Add the garlic, onion, cinnamon, almonds, nutmeg, and sauté and turmeric to the same pan until the almonds are lightly brown which will spend 1 to 2 minutes. 3. Set chicken broth, salt, sherry, pepper, the almond mixture in food processor, a blender, and process until the mixture is smooth. If the sauce is too thick, add additional chicken broth to get the consistency of heavy cream. 4. Return the chicken to the pan and add the almond sauce. Reduce the heat to low and let the sauce warm through. Be careful not to simmer the sauce, because it will separate. 5. Arrange the chicken and sauce on a serving platter, top with parsley, and serve. This kind of recipe can be kept in the refrigerator for 4 days.

Serving Suggestion: The sauce can be made several days ahead, and is best reheated very gently over a very low flame or on the top of a double boiler.

Per Serving: Calories 236; Fat 13.47g; Sodium 776mg; Carbs 7.61g; Fiber 2g; Sugar 4.25g; Protein 21.65g

Stuffed Chicken and Ricotta

Prep time: 30 minutes | Cook time: 45 minutes | Serves: 4

4 ounces ricotta cheese	breasts
2 tablespoons chopped sun-dried tomatoes	2 tablespoons extra-virgin olive oil
1 garlic clove, chopped	¼ teaspoon freshly ground black pepper
½ teaspoon chopped fresh thyme	1 cup white wine
1½ teaspoons salt, divided	½ lemon
4 boneless, skin-on chicken	

1. Heat the oven to 375°F ahead of time. Combine the sun-dried tomatoes, thyme, ½ teaspoon salt, as well as the ricotta. 2. Place the chicken skin side up on a work surface. Under the skin slide your fingers and slightly pull the skin partially away from the chicken breast, being carefully not to tear it. 3. Place about 2 tablespoons of filling under the skin of each breast. In a 9-inch-square baking dish, place the skin side up, stuffed breasts, tucking the ends of the breasts under so that breasts are round and plump. 4. Brush the breasts with olive oil and sprinkle with the remaining 1 teaspoon salt and the pepper. 5. Pour the wine into the pan, and bake 35 to 45 minutes or until the skin is golden brown. Squeeze the lemon juice and get away from the oven over the stuffed breasts. 6. Let take a break for 10 minutes before serving. The breasts can be kept in the refrigerator for 5 days.

Prep tip: You can stuff the breasts several hours ahead and roast them later. For best results, let them sit 30 minutes at room temperature before cooking them. It's important to let the chicken breasts rest after they've been baked as well, because if you cut them while they are very hot, the ricotta will ooze out.

Per Serving: Calories 1038; Fat 63.93g; Sodium 2101mg; Carbs 6.49g; Fiber 0.6; Sugar 3.03g; Protein 104.37g

Roasted Chicken with Garlic

Prep time: 15 minutes | Cook time: 75 minutes | Serves: 4

1 whole chicken	oil
1 teaspoon salt	40 garlic cloves (about 3 to 4 heads), peeled
¼ teaspoon freshly ground black pepper	1 cup white wine
2 tablespoons butter	1 sprig fresh thyme
2 tablespoons extra-virgin olive	

1. Heat the oven to 375°F ahead of time. Keep the chicken dry with a pepper towel and scatter with the pepper and salt. 2. Place a large Dutch oven or a heavy pot with a lid over high heat. Add the butter and olive oil. Brown the chicken on all sides, about 5 to 7 minutes per side, using tongs to carefully turn it without breaking the skin. Get the chicken away and set them aside. 3. Add the garlic to the same pot and sauté for 5 minutes to soften. Return the chicken to the pot and add the wine and thyme. Close the pot and set it in the oven for 1 hour. Then, carefully get the chicken away from the pot and keep it rest for 15 minutes. 4. Carve the chicken and arrange it on a platter. Remove the thyme sprig. Spoon the garlic and pan drippings over the chicken and serve.

Prep tip: Some markets sell peeled garlic. If yours doesn't, there are several ways to easily remove the skin. One is to blanch the garlic in boiling water for a minute, drain it, and slip off the skins. Another technique is to use a garlic roller—a rubber tube you place the garlic inside and roll, pressing down, to release the skins from the cloves. Garlic rollers are available in some grocery stores, online, and in cookware stores.

Per Serving: Calories 424; Fat 19.12g; Sodium 815mg; Carbs 10.8g; Fiber 0.7g; Sugar 0.95g; Protein 50.78g

Pesto-Glazed Stuffed Chicken Breasts

Prep time:20 minutes | Cook time: 15 minutes | Serves: 4

¼ cup plus 1 tablespoon extra-virgin olive oil, divided	pepper
4 boneless, skinless chicken breasts	1 packed cup fresh basil leaves
	1 garlic clove, minced
½ teaspoon salt	¼ cup grated Parmesan cheese
¼ teaspoon freshly ground black	¼ cup pine nuts

1. Heat 1 tablespoon of the olive oil over medium-high heat in a heavy, large skillet. 2. Season the chicken breasts with salt and pepper and place in the skillet. Cook for 10 minutes on the first side, then turn and cook for 5 minutes. 3. In the meanwhile, combine the garlic, parmesan cheese, basil as well as pine nuts, and blend on high in a blender or food processor. Gradually pour in the remaining ¼ cup olive oil and blend until smooth. 4. Spread 1 tablespoon pesto on each chicken breast, cover the skillet, and cook for 5 minutes. Serve the chicken pesto side up.

Per Serving: Calories 306; Fat 23.26g; Sodium 442mg; Carbs 2.34g; Fiber 0.4g; Sugar 0.32g; Protein 22.14g

Hearty Veggie and Chicken Stew

Prep time: 20 minutes | Cook time: 40 minutes | Serves: 4

1½ pounds boneless, skinless chicken thighs	1¼ cups no-salt-added chicken stock
1 teaspoon kosher salt, divided	¼ cup white wine vinegar
¼ teaspoon freshly ground black pepper	2 tablespoons lemon juice
2 tablespoons olive oil	1 tablespoon lemon zest
1 onion, julienned	1 (14-ounce) can artichoke hearts, drained
4 garlic cloves, sliced	¼ cup olives, pitted and chopped
1 teaspoon ground turmeric	1 teaspoon capers, rinsed and chopped
1 teaspoon ground cumin	
½ teaspoon ground coriander	1 tablespoon fresh mint, chopped
½ teaspoon ground cinnamon	1 tablespoon fresh parsley, chopped
¼ teaspoon red pepper flakes	
1 dried bay leaf	

1. Season the chicken with ½ teaspoon of salt and pepper. 2. In your skillet, heat the olive oil over medium heat; cook the chicken for 2 to 3 minutes on each side. Transfer to a plate and set aside. 3. Still in the skillet, add the onion and sauté for 5 minutes until translucent; add the garlic and sauté for 30 seconds; then add the remaining salt, the turmeric, cumin, coriander, cinnamon, red pepper flakes, bay leaf and sauté them for 30 seconds; add ¼ cup of the chicken stock and adjust the heat to medium-high to deglaze the pan, and scraping off any brown bits from the bottom, then add the remaining stock, the lemon zest and lemon juice, cover the skillet and reduce the heat to low, simmer the liquid for 10 minutes. 4. When the time is up, add the artichokes, olives, and capers and mix well; add the reserved chicken and nestle it into the mixture. Remove the lid and simmer for 10 to 15 minutes until the chicken fully cooks through. Garnish with the mint and parsley. Serve.

Per Serving: Calories 424; Fats 17.85g; Sodium 1156mg; Carbs 48.43g; Fiber 7.2g; Sugar 11.6g; Protein 18.55g

Roasted Herb Whole Chicken

Prep time:25 minutes | Cook time: 70 minutes | Serves: 6

1 (3 to 3½-pound) roasting chicken
1 tablespoon extra-virgin olive oil
4 sprigs rosemary
6 sprigs thyme
4 fresh sage leaves
1 bay leaf
1 teaspoon freshly squeezed lemon juice
1 teaspoon salt
½ teaspoon freshly ground black pepper

1. Heat the oven to 400°F. Place a rack inside a large baking pan ahead of time. 2. Rub the olive oil all over the chicken. As you do, gently loosen the skin over the breast to form a pocket. 3. Slide half of the rosemary and thyme sprigs underneath the skin over the breast, and put the sage leaves, bay leaf, and remaining sprigs inside the cavity. Then season with pepper and salt as well as rub with the lemon juice. 4. Roast the chicken until an instant-read thermometer inserted into registers 165°F, 50 to 60 minutes. Get away from the oven and make them rest for 10 minutes before carving.
Per Serving: Calories 247; Fat 15.4g; Sodium 485mg; Carbs 0.86g; Fiber 0.4g; Sugar 0.04g; Protein 25.3g

One Skillet Chicken with Lemon-Garlic

Prep time: 10 minutes | Cook time: 15 minutes | Serves: 4

¼ cup freshly squeezed lemon juice
4 tablespoons olive oil, divided
6 garlic cloves, minced
1 tablespoon chopped fresh oregano
1 teaspoon ground cumin
1 teaspoon ground coriander
1 pound boneless, skinless chicken breast tenders
Sea salt
Freshly ground black pepper
1 onion, sliced
2 lemons, cut into wedges
Chopped fresh parsley, for garnish

1. Combine 2 tablespoons of olive oil, oregano, garlic, cumin, the lemon juice, coriander and then mix well in a medium bowl. 2. Season the chicken with salt and pepper and then place the chicken and the onion in the marinade. Toss to coat. Cover and let stand for at least 20 minutes or refrigerate it for up to 8 hours. 3. In a large cast iron skillet, heat remaining 2 tablespoons olive oil over medium heat. In a single layer, add the chicken tenders to the skillet, and remove any marinade left behind. 4. Cook on each side for 6 to 7 minutes, flipping once, until browned and the juices run clear. After putting the onions and chicken into a serving platter, you can garnish with parsley and use the lemon wedges.
Substitution Tip: Replace the chicken breast tenders with boneless, skinless chicken thighs if desired. Or if you have chicken breasts on hand, simply prepare them for this recipe by cutting each breast into four or five lengthwise strips.
Per Serving: Calories 341; Fat 20.3g; Sodium 459mg; Carbs 29.55g; Fiber 2.6g; Sugar 7.3g; Protein 11.5g

Chicken with Greek Yogurt-Mint Sauce

Prep time: 10 minutes | Cook time: 25 minutes | Serves: 4

1 cup low-fat plain Greek yogurt
¼ sweet onion, finely chopped
1 tablespoon chopped fresh mint
1 teaspoon chopped fresh dill
1 teaspoon minced garlic
1 teaspoon ground cumin
Pinch red pepper flakes
4 (3-ounce) boneless, skinless chicken breasts

1. Whisk together the onion, mint, dill, garlic, cumin, red pepper flakes as well as yogurt until blended in a medium bowl. Transfer ½ cup of the yogurt to a small bowl. Set aside, covered, in the refrigerator. 2. Add the chicken to the remaining yogurt mixture, turning to coat. Cover and place the chicken in the refrigerator to marinate for 3 hours. Heat the oven to 400°F ahead of time. 3. Transfer the chicken breasts to a baking sheet and roast until the chicken is cooked through, 20 to 25 minutes. Serve with the reserved yogurt-mint sauce.
Per Serving: Calories 203; Fat 6.03g; Sodium 274mg; Carbs 25.5g; Fiber 1.8g; Sugar 10.52g; Protein 11.72g

Mango Salsa Turkey Burgers

Prep time: 15 minutes | Cook time: 10 minutes | Serves: 6

1½ pounds ground turkey breast
1 teaspoon sea salt, divided
¼ teaspoon freshly ground black pepper
2 tablespoons extra-virgin olive oil
2 mangos, peeled, pitted, and cubed
½ red onion, finely chopped
Juice of 1 lime
1 garlic clove, minced
½ jalapeño pepper, seeded and finely minced
2 tablespoons chopped fresh cilantro leaves

1. Form the turkey breast into 4 patties and season the patties with ½ teaspoon of sea salt and the pepper. 2. In the skillet, heat the olive oil over medium-high heat until it shimmers; add the seasoned turkey patties and cook them for 5 minutes on each side until browned. 3. Mix up the mango, red onion, lime juice, garlic, jalapeño, cilantro, and remaining sea salt in a small bowl. Spoon the salsa over the turkey patties and serve.
Per Serving: Calories 260; Fats 4.81g; Sodium 542mg; Carbs 18.86g; Fiber 2.1g; Sugar 16.01g; Protein 35.36g

Tasty Moussaka

Prep time: 10 minutes | Cook time: 45 minutes | Serves: 8

5 tablespoons extra-virgin olive oil, divided
1 eggplant, sliced (unpeeled)
1 onion, chopped
1 green bell pepper, seeded and chopped
1 pound ground turkey
3 garlic cloves, minced
2 tablespoons tomato paste
1 (14-ounce) can chopped tomatoes, drained
1 tablespoon Italian seasoning
2 teaspoons Worcestershire sauce
1 teaspoon dried oregano
½ teaspoon ground cinnamon
1 cup unsweetened nonfat plain Greek yogurt
1 egg, beaten
¼ teaspoon freshly ground black pepper
¼ teaspoon ground nutmeg
¼ cup grated Parmesan cheese
2 tablespoons chopped fresh parsley leaves

1. Preheat the oven to 400°F. 2. In your skillet, heat 3 tablespoons of olive oil over medium-high heat; cook the eggplant slices for 3 to 4 minutes per side. When cooked, transfer them to paper towels to drain. 3. In the same skillet, heat the remaining olive oil; then add the onion, green bell pepper and cook for about 5 minutes, stirring, until the vegetables are soft. Transfer them from the pan and set aside. 4. Still in the skillet, add and heat the turkey for about 5 minutes, crumbling with a spoon, until browned; add garlic and sauté for 30 seconds; add the tomatoes, Italian seasoning, Worcestershire sauce, oregano, tomato paste, cinnamon and place the eggplant slices and bell pepper back to it, sauté them for 5 minutes. 5. In a small bowl, whisk the egg, yogurt, pepper, nutmeg and cheese. 6. Spread half the meat mixture in the baking dish. Layer with half the eggplant. Add the remaining meat mixture and the remaining eggplant. Spread with the yogurt mixture. Bake the food for about 20 minutes until golden brown. 7. Garnish with the parsley and serve.
Per Serving: Calories 254; Fats 15.4g; Sodium 272mg; Carbs 11.89g; Fiber 3.9g; Sugar 6.62g; Protein 18.42g

Tuscan Chicken

Prep time: 10 minutes | Cook time: 25 minutes | Serves: 6

¼ cup extra-virgin olive oil, divided
1 pound boneless, skinless chicken breasts, cut into ¾-inch pieces
1 onion, chopped
1 red bell pepper, chopped
3 garlic cloves, minced
½ cup dry white wine
1 (14-ounce) can crushed tomatoes, undrained
1 (14-ounce) can chopped tomatoes, drained
1 (14-ounce) can white beans, drained
1 tablespoon dried Italian seasoning
½ teaspoon sea salt
⅛ teaspoon freshly ground black pepper
⅛ teaspoon red pepper flakes
¼ cup chopped fresh basil leaves

1. In a large skillet, heat 2 tablespoons of olive oil over medium-high heat until it shimmers; add the chicken breast pieces and cook for 6 minutes, stirring constantly, until browned. Transfer them to the plate and cover them with aluminum foil to keep warm. 2. Still in the skillet, heat the remaining olive oil until it shimmers; add onion, red bell pepper and sauté for 6 minutes or until the vegetables are soft; add the garlic and sauté for 30 seconds. 3. Stir in the wine, and use the side of the spoon to scrape and fold in any browned bits from the bottom of the pan; cook for 1 minute longer; add white beans, tomatoes, red pepper flakes, Italian seasoning, sea salt and pepper, bring them to a simmer and then reduce the heat to medium, sauté them for 5 minutes. 4. Return the chicken pieces and any juices that have collected to the skillet, cook them for 1 to 2 minutes until the chicken pieces heat through. 5. Stir in the basil before serving.
Per Serving: Calories 288; Fats 15.97g; Sodium 809mg; Carbs 26.58g; Fiber 5.3g; Sugar 9.41g; Protein 11.12g

Herb-Roasted Turkey Breast

Prep time: 15 minutes | Cook time: 1 hour 30 minutes | Serves: 6

2 tablespoons extra-virgin olive oil
4 garlic cloves, minced
Zest of 1 lemon
1 tablespoon chopped fresh thyme leaves
1 tablespoon chopped fresh rosemary leaves
2 tablespoons chopped fresh

Italian parsley leaves
1 teaspoon ground mustard
1 teaspoon sea salt
¼ teaspoon freshly ground black pepper
1 (6-pound) bone-in, skin-on turkey breast
1 cup dry white wine

1. Preheat the oven to 325°F. 2. In a small bowl, mix up the olive oil, garlic, lemon zest, thyme, rosemary, parsley, mustard, sea salt, and pepper. Evenly rub the surface of the turkey breast with the herb mixture, and loosen the skin and rub underneath as well. 3. Place the turkey breast in a roasting pan on a rack, skin-side up; pour the wine in the pan. Roast the turkey breast for 1 to 1½ hours until the turkey reaches an internal temperature of 165°F. 4. Remove the turkey from the oven and let rest for 20 minutes, tented with aluminum foil to keep it warm, before carving.
Per Serving: Calories 441; Fats 16.09g; Sodium 1865mg; Carbs 1.95g; Fiber 0.3g; Sugar 0.34g; Protein 68.13g

Braised Chicken with Tomatoes

Prep time: 30 minutes | Cook time: 1 hour 15 minutes | Serves: 8

2 tablespoons extra-virgin olive oil
4 pounds' bone-in chicken, breast and thighs, skin removed
1½ teaspoon kosher salt, divided
¼ teaspoon freshly ground black pepper
1 onion, julienned

6 garlic cloves, sliced
1 cup white wine
2 pounds' tomatoes, chopped
¼ teaspoon red pepper flakes
2 jars roasted red peppers, drained
⅓ cup fresh parsley, chopped
1 tablespoon lemon juice

1. Season the chicken with ¾ teaspoon of the salt and the pepper. 2. In a large pot, heat the olive oil over medium-high heat; add half of the chicken and brown for 2 minutes on each side. Transfer to a plate, and cook another half of the chicken with the same steps. 3. Still in the pot, sauté the onion for about 5 minutes over medium heat; add the garlic and sauté for 30 seconds; add the wine and adjust the heat to medium-high, and then bring to a boil to deglaze the pot, scraping off any brown bits from the bottom. Reduce liquid by half for about 5 to 7 minutes. 4. Add the tomatoes, red pepper flakes, the remaining salt and mix well; place the chicken back to the pot, cover, reduce the heat to low and then simmer for 40 minutes, turning the chicken halfway through the cooking time. 5. While simmering, chop the bell peppers into 1-inch pieces and set aside. 6. Once the chicken is cooked through, transfer it to a plate. Adjust the heat to high and then bring the mixture to a boil. Reduce by half, about 10 minutes. 7. When the chicken is cool enough to handle, remove the meat from the bone and return it to the pot with the bell peppers, then simmer them for 5 minutes to heat through. Stir in the parsley and lemon juice. 8. Serve and enjoy.
Per Serving: Calories 299; Fats 8.56g; Sodium 2858mg; Carbs 15.76g; Fiber 2.1g; Sugar 6.99g; Protein 41.28g

Homemade Yogurt-Marinated Chicken Kebabs

Prep time: 10 minutes | Cook time: 20 minutes | Serves: 4

½ cup plain Greek yogurt
1 tablespoon lemon juice
½ teaspoon ground cumin
½ teaspoon ground coriander
½ teaspoon kosher salt

¼ teaspoon cayenne pepper
1½ pound skinless and boneless chicken breast, cut into 1-inch cubes

1. In a large bowl, combine the yogurt, lemon juice, cumin, coriander, salt, and cayenne pepper, then add the chicken breast. Marinate chicken breast for at least 30 minutes and up to overnight in the refrigerator. 2. Transfer the chicken from marinade and thread it on 4 metal skewers. 3. Preheat the oven to 425°F. Line a baking sheet with parchment paper. Bake the skewers in the preheated oven for 20 minutes, turning the chicken over once halfway through the cooking time. 4. When the time is up, serve and enjoy.
Per Serving: Calories 227; Fats 4.69g; Sodium 380mg; Carbs 1.72g; Fiber 0.1g; Sugar 1.25g; Protein 41.92g

Skillet-Cooked Sausage with Vegetables

Prep time: 10 minutes | Cook time: 20 minutes | Serves: 6

2 tablespoons extra-virgin olive oil
6 Italian chicken sausage links
1 onion, thinly sliced
1 red bell pepper, seeded and sliced thinly
3 garlic cloves, minced

1 green bell pepper, seeded and sliced thinly
½ cup dry white wine
½ teaspoon sea salt
¼ teaspoon freshly ground black pepper
Pinch red pepper flakes

1. In a large skillet, heat the olive oil over medium-high heat until it shimmers; cook the sausages for 5 to 7 minutes, turning occasionally, until they turn brown and reach an internal temperature of 165°F. When cooked, transfer the sausages to a plate and cover them with aluminum foil to keep warm. 2. Still in the skillet, add the onion, red bell pepper, green bell pepper and cook them for 5 to 7 minutes, stirring them often, until all the vegetables become to brown; then add the garlic and cook for 30 seconds, stirring constantly. 3. Stir in the wine, sea salt, pepper, and red pepper flakes. Use the side of a spoon to scrape and fold in any browned bits from the bottom of the pan. Simmer for about 4 minutes more, stirring, until the liquid reduces by half. 4. Spoon the peppers over the sausages and serve.
Per Serving: Calories 182; Fats 11.12g; Sodium 861mg; Carbs 4.72g; Fiber 0.4g; Sugar 1.29g; Protein 16.11g

Chicken Piccata with Parsley

Prep time: 10 minutes | Cook time: 15 minutes | Serves: 6

½ cup whole-wheat flour
½ teaspoon sea salt
⅛ teaspoon freshly ground black pepper
1½ pounds boneless, skinless chicken breasts, cut into 6 pieces
3 tablespoons extra-virgin olive oil

1 cup unsalted chicken broth
½ cup dry white wine
Juice of 1 lemon
Zest of 1 lemon
¼ cup capers, drained and rinsed
¼ cup chopped fresh parsley leaves

1. In a shallow dish, whisk the flour, sea salt and pepper. Dredge the chicken breasts in the flour and tap off any excess. 2. In a large skillet, heat the olive oil over medium-high heat until it shimmers; cook the chicken breasts for 4 minutes on each side until browned. Transfer them to a plate and cover them with aluminum foil to keep warm. 3. Still in the skillet, add the broth, wine, lemon juice, lemon zest, and capers; use the side of a spoon to scrape and fold in any browned bits from the bottom of the pan. Simmer the liquid for 3 to 4 minutes, stirring, until the liquid thickens. Remove the skillet from the heat and return the chicken to the skillet. Turn to coat. 4. Stir in the parsley and serve.
Per Serving: Calories 313; Fats 13.1g; Sodium 1148mg; Carbs 8.87g; Fiber 1.2g; Sugar 0.69g; Protein 39.46g

Easy Chicken Kapama

Prep time: 10 minutes | Cook time: 1 hour 20 minutes | Serves: 4

1 (32-ounce) can chopped tomatoes, drained
¼ cup dry white wine
2 tablespoons tomato paste
3 tablespoons extra-virgin olive oil
¼ teaspoon red pepper flakes
1 teaspoon ground allspice

½ teaspoon dried oregano
2 whole cloves
1 cinnamon stick
½ teaspoon sea salt
⅛ teaspoon freshly ground black pepper
4 boneless, skinless chicken breast halves

1. In a large pot over medium-high heat, add the tomatoes, wine, tomato paste, olive oil, red pepper flakes, allspice, oregano, cloves, cinnamon stick, sea salt, and pepper. Bring them to a simmer, stirring occasionally. 2. Reduce the heat to medium-low and simmer the mixture for 30 minutes, stirring occasionally. Remove and discard the whole cloves and cinnamon stick from the sauce and let the sauce cool. 3. Preheat the oven to 350°F. 4. Transfer the chicken breasts in the baking dish; pour the sauce over the chicken breasts and cover the pan with aluminum foil. Bake the chicken breasts for 40 to 45 minutes, or until the they reach an internal temperature of 165°F. 5. Serve the chicken breasts with the tomato mixture.
Per Serving: Calories 393; Fats 12.84g; Sodium 863mg; Carbs 11.29g; Fiber 5.2g; Sugar 6.97g; Protein 57g

Spinach Stuffed Chicken Breasts

Prep time: 10 minutes | Cook time: 45 minutes | Serves: 4

2 tablespoons extra-virgin olive oil
pound fresh baby spinach
3 garlic cloves, minced
Zest of 1 lemon
½ teaspoon sea salt
⅛ teaspoon freshly ground black pepper
½ cup crumbled feta cheese
4 boneless, skinless chicken breast halves, pounded to ½-inch thickness

1. Preheat the oven to 350°F. 2. In a large skillet, heat the olive oil over medium-high heat until it shimmers; add the spinach and sauté for 3 to 4 minutes until wilted; add the lemon zest, garlic, sea salt, pepper and sauté for 30 seconds; cool the spinach slightly and then mix in the cheese. 3. Spread the spinach and cheese mixture in an even layer over the chicken pieces and roll the breast around the filling. Hold closed with toothpicks or butcher's twine. 4. Place the breasts in a 9-by-13-inch baking dish and bake them for 30 to 40 minutes, or until the chicken reaches an internal temperature of 165°F. 5. Remove the chicken breasts from the oven and let rest for 5 minutes before slicing and serving.
Per Serving: Calories 176; Fats 12.07g; Sodium 656mg; Carbs 6.52g; Fiber 2.6g; Sugar 1.57g; Protein 12.43g

Rosemary Chicken Drumsticks

Prep time: 5 minutes | Cook time: 1 hour | Serves: 6

2 tablespoons chopped fresh rosemary leaves
1 teaspoon garlic powder
½ teaspoon sea salt
⅛ teaspoon freshly ground black pepper
Zest of 1 lemon
12 chicken drumsticks

1. Preheat the oven to 350°F. 2. In a small bowl, mix up the rosemary, garlic powder, sea salt, pepper, and lemon zest. Arrange the chicken drumsticks in the baking dish and then sprinkle with the rosemary mixture. 3. Bake the chicken drumsticks for about 1 hour, or until the chicken reaches an internal temperature of 165°F. 4. When done, serve and enjoy.
Per Serving: Calories 423; Fats 23.98g; Sodium 470mg; Carbs 1.37g; Fiber 0.2g; Sugar 0.21g; Protein 47.15g

Baked Veggie and Chicken Leg-Thigh

Prep time: 5 minutes | Cook time: 45 minutes | Serves: 4

2 cups fingerling potatoes, halved
4 fresh figs, quartered
2 carrots, julienned
2 tablespoons extra-virgin olive oil
1 teaspoon sea salt, divided
¼ teaspoon freshly ground black pepper
4 chicken leg-thigh quarters
2 tablespoons chopped fresh parsley leaves

1. Preheat the oven to 425°F. 2. In a small bowl, mix up the potatoes, figs, and carrots with the olive oil, ½ teaspoon of sea salt, pepper and then spread them in the baking dish. 3. Season the chicken leg-thigh quarters with the remaining sea salt; place them on top of the vegetables. 4. Bake them for 35 to 45 minutes, or until the vegetables are soft and the chicken reaches an internal temperature of 165°F. 5. Sprinkle with the parsley and serve.
Per Serving: Calories 342; Fats 14.84g; Sodium 1146mg; Carbs 21.62g; Fiber 3.4g; Sugar 6.07g; Protein 30.68g

Chicken Gyros

Prep time: 10 minutes | Cook time: 1 hour | Serves: 6

1 pound ground chicken breast
1 onion, grated with excess water wrung out
2 tablespoons dried rosemary
1 tablespoon dried marjoram
6 garlic cloves, minced
½ teaspoon sea salt
¼ teaspoon freshly ground black pepper
Tzatziki Sauce

1. Preheat the oven to 350°F. 2. In your food processor, add the chicken, onion, rosemary, marjoram, garlic, sea salt, pepper and then blend them for about 2 minutes until the mixture forms a paste. 3. Press the mixture into a loaf pan. Bake them for about 1 hour until it reaches an internal temperature of 165°F. Remove from the oven and let rest for 20 minutes before slicing. 4. Slice the gyro and spoon the Tzatziki sauce over the top.
Per Serving: Calories 164; Fats 5.98g; Sodium 291mg; Carbs 3.47g; Fiber 0.7g; Sugar 1.06g; Protein 23.08g

Onion Chicken Meatballs

Prep time: 20 minutes | Cook time: 25 minutes | Serves: 4

2 whole-wheat bread slices
1¼ pounds ground turkey
1 egg
¼ cup seasoned whole-wheat bread crumbs
3 garlic cloves, minced
¼ red onion, grated
¼ cup chopped fresh Italian
parsley leaves
2 tablespoons chopped fresh mint leaves
2 tablespoons chopped fresh oregano leaves
½ teaspoon sea salt
¼ teaspoon freshly ground black pepper

1. Preheat the oven to 350°F. Line a baking sheet with parchment paper. 2. Wet the bread slices under water and squeeze out any excess. Tear the wet bread into small pieces and place it in a clean bowl; add the garlic, egg, turkey, red onion, oregano, sea salt, pepper, mint and parsley, mix them well and then form them into ¼-cup-size balls. 3. Arrange the meatballs to the baking sheet and bake them in the preheated oven for 25 minutes or until they reach an internal temperature of 165°F. 4. Serve and enjoy.
Per Serving: Calories 302; Fats 12.91g; Sodium 514mg; Carbs 13.93g; Fiber 1.9g; Sugar 1.55g; Protein 32.56g

Bomba Chicken

Prep time: 10 minutes | Cook time: 35 minutes | Serves: 4

2 pounds boneless, skinless chicken thighs
Sea salt
Freshly ground black pepper
2 tablespoons olive oil, divided
1 onion, chopped
3 garlic cloves, minced
1 cup chicken broth
1 tablespoon bomba sauce or harissa
2 (15-ounce) cans chickpeas, drained and rinsed
¼ cup chopped fresh Italian parsley

1. Season the chicken thighs with salt and pepper. 2. In the skillet, heat 1 tablespoon of olive oil over medium-high heat; add the chicken thighs and cook for 2 to 3 minutes on each side, or until browned. Transfer the chicken thighs to a plate and set aside for later use. 3. Still in the skillet, heat the remaining olive oil; add the onion, garlic and sauté for 4 to 5 minutes, until softened. Return the chicken to the skillet, then add the broth and bomba sauce. 4. Bring them to a boil and then reduce the heat to low, cover the skillet and simmer the food for 15 minutes, or until the chicken is cooked through; when the time is up, add the chickpeas and simmer for 5 minutes longer. 5. Garnish with the parsley, serve and enjoy.
Per Serving: Calories 621; Fats 27.5g; Sodium 2092mg; Carbs 28.81g; Fiber 7.6g; Sugar 5.92g; Protein 63.91g

Chicken Spinach Pasta

Prep time: 15 minutes | Cook time: 45 minutes | Serves: 4

1 pound boneless, skinless chicken thighs or breasts
1½ cups dried farfalle (bow-tie) pasta
½ (15-ounce) can chickpeas, drained and rinsed
2 cups fresh baby spinach
½ English cucumber, chopped
¼ cup sun-dried tomatoes,
chopped
¼ cup shredded Parmesan cheese
¼ cup shredded carrot
Juice of ½ lemon
2 tablespoons olive oil
½ teaspoon dried thyme
¼ teaspoon dried marjoram
Sea salt
Freshly ground black pepper

1. In the stockpot, add the chicken in a large stockpot and pour in enough water to cover the chicken by 1 inch. Bring the water to a boil over high heat, then reduce the heat to low, and simmer the chicken for 30 minutes, or until the chicken is cooked through. Transfer the chicken to a plate and set aside. 2. Still in the stockpot, bring the water to a boil over high heat; add the pasta and cook for 10 to 12 minutes (or according to the package directions) until al dente; drain the pasta and rinse with cold water to stop the cooking process. Transfer the pasta to a large bowl. 3. Chop the chicken into 2-inch pieces and add them to the bowl with the pasta; add the chickpeas, spinach, cucumber, sun-dried tomatoes, Parmesan, carrot, lemon juice, olive oil, thyme, and marjoram, mix them well. 4. Season with salt, pepper and then you can enjoy.
Per Serving: Calories 546; Fats 26.88g; Sodium 1273mg; Carbs 43.87g; Fiber 7.6g; Sugar 3.44g; Protein 33.45g

Delectable Chicken Skewers

Prep time: 10 minutes | Cook time: 15 minutes | Serves: 4

¼ cup olive oil
Zest of 1 lemon
Juice of 2 lemons
2 tablespoons dried oregano
1 tablespoon dried thyme
2 garlic cloves, minced
Sea salt
Freshly ground black pepper
3 pounds boneless, skinless chicken breasts, cut into 2-inch cubes

1. In a suitable bowl, mix up the olive oil, lemon zest, lemon juice, oregano, thyme, garlic, salt and pepper; thoroughly coat the chicken with the herb mixture. Cover the bowl and refrigerate them for at least 20 to 30 minutes. 2. Thread the chicken pieces onto skewers, 4 or 5 pieces per skewer. 3. In your skillet, place the skewers in the skillet, about 3 skewers per batch, and cook for 5 to 7 minutes, turning frequently, until the chicken pieces are cooked through and reach an internal temperature of 165°F. 4. Cook the remaining skewers with the same steps. Serve and enjoy.
Per Serving: Calories 646; Fats 25.66g; Sodium 2114mg; Carbs 4.53g; Fiber 1g; Sugar 0.99g; Protein 96.25g

Chicken Thighs Tagine

Prep time: 15 minutes | Cook time: 35 minutes | Serves: 4

3 tablespoons olive oil
1 onion, sliced
2 carrots, cut into long ribbons
2 red bell peppers, coarsely chopped
3 garlic cloves, minced
3 pounds boneless, skinless chicken thighs
1 cup chicken broth
1 tablespoon tomato paste
1 teaspoon ground coriander
½ teaspoon ground turmeric
1 to 2 tablespoons harissa
¼ cup chopped dried apricots
Sea salt
Freshly ground black pepper

1. In a small bowl, stir together the broth, tomato paste, coriander, turmeric, and harissa until well combined. 2. In your skillet, heat the olive oil over medium-high heat; add the onion, carrots, bell peppers, garlic and sauté them for 5 to 7 minutes, until softened; add the chicken thighs and cook for 7 minutes, turning to brown the chicken thighs evenly on all sides; add the broth mixture and stir well; add the apricots and then season with salt and pepper. 3. Bring the food to a boil and then reduce the heat to low, cover the skillet and simmer for 20 minutes, or until the chicken thighs are cooked through and each of them has an internal temperature of 165°F. 4. Serve and enjoy.
Per Serving: Calories 741; Fats 37.49g; Sodium 2362mg; Carbs 13.64g; Fiber 3g; Sugar 8.96g; Protein 85g

Scrambled Chicken Thighs with Vegetables

Prep time: 10 minutes | Cook time: 30 minutes | Serves: 4

2 tablespoons olive oil
1 onion, diced
2 carrots, chopped
2 celery stalks, chopped
4 garlic cloves, minced
1 shallot, diced
1 pound boneless, skinless chicken thighs
pound pork sausages, casings removed, cut into 2-inch pieces
2 tomatoes, diced, or 1 (15-ounce)
can diced tomatoes with their juices
1 tablespoon tomato paste
½ teaspoon dried thyme
2 bay leaves
Sea salt
Freshly ground black pepper
½ cup chicken broth, as needed
2 (15-ounce) cans cannellini beans, drained and rinsed

1. In the skillet, heat the olive oil over medium-high heat; add the onion, carrots, celery, garlic, shallot and sauté for 5 minutes, or until the vegetables are softened; add the chicken thighs, sausage and sauté for 5 minutes, turning to brown the chicken on all sides. 2. Add the diced tomatoes, tomato paste, thyme, bay leaves, salt, pepper and half the broth. Bring to a boil and then reduce the heat to medium-low, and simmer for 15 minutes, or until the chicken is cooked through; add the beans and cook for 5 minutes, adding more broth as needed so that the mixture is just slightly soupy. 3. Serve and enjoy.
Per Serving: Calories 473; Fats 20.37g; Sodium 2420mg; Carbs 42.14g; Fiber 7.6g; Sugar 14.52g; Protein 33.19g

Herbed Chicken Gyro

Prep time: 20 minutes | Cook time: 10 minutes | Serves: 4

3 tablespoons olive oil
Zest and juice of ½ lemon
1 tablespoon dried oregano
1½ teaspoons dried thyme
1 garlic clove, minced
¼ teaspoon sea salt
¼ teaspoon freshly ground black pepper
2 pounds boneless, skinless chicken thighs, cut into ½-inch-
thick strips
4 pita breads
3 Roma (plum) tomatoes, diced
½ red onion, thinly sliced
½ cup Tzatziki
¼ cup crumbled feta cheese

1. In a large bowl, stir together the olive oil, lemon zest, lemon juice, oregano, thyme, garlic, salt, and pepper. Evenly coat the chicken strips with the herb mixture. Cover the bowl and marinate the chicken strips in the refrigerator for 30 minutes. 2. In the skillet, heat the marinated chicken strips (discard the marinade) for 7 to 10 minutes, until cooked through. Transfer the chicken to a plate. 3. Place the pitas on a clean work surface and top each with 3 or 4 strips of chicken. Evenly divide the tomatoes, onion, tzatziki, and feta among the pitas. 4. Fold the pitas over to enclose the toppings and then you can enjoy.
Per Serving: Calories 664; Fats 33.65g; Sodium 1387mg; Carbs 25.32g; Fiber 2.5g; Sugar 6.58g; Protein 63.65g

Lemony Chicken Avgolemono

Prep time: 10 minutes | Cook time: 60 minutes | Serves: 4

1½ pounds boneless, skinless chicken breasts
6 cups chicken broth, as needed
¾ cup dried Greek orzo
3 large eggs
Juice of 2 lemons
Sea salt
Freshly ground black pepper

1. Place the chicken breasts in a stockpot and add enough broth to cover the chicken breasts by 1 inch. Bring to a boil over high heat and then reduce the heat to low; cover the stockpot and simmer for 30 to 45 minutes, until the chicken breasts are cooked through. Transfer the chicken breasts to a bowl and set aside. 2. Still in the stockpot, increase the heat to medium-high and bring the broth back to a boil, then add the orzo and cook for 7 to 10 minutes, until tender. 3. While cooking the orzo, shred the chicken breasts with two forks and then return them to the pot when orzo is done. 4. Crack the eggs into a small bowl and whisk until frothy, then stir in the lemon juice. While stirring continuously, slowly pour in 1 cup of the hot broth to temper the eggs. Pour the egg mixture back into the pot and stir. Simmer for 1 minute more, season with salt and pepper. 5. Serve and enjoy.
Per Serving: Calories 245; Fats 4.96g; Sodium 3757mg; Carbs 18.58g; Fiber 1.6g; Sugar 11.85g; Protein 33.28g

Veggie Chicken Moussaka

Prep time: 10 minutes | Cook time: 45 minutes | Serves: 4

For the Moussaka
1 eggplant, cubed
¼ cup extra-virgin olive oil, divided
pound lean ground chicken
⅔ yellow onion, diced
3 garlic cloves, minced
⅛ teaspoon sea salt
1 (16-ounce) can diced tomatoes
1 tablespoon tomato paste
1 teaspoon paprika
¾ cup water, as needed
For the Béchamel Sauce (Optional)
⅓ cup extra-virgin olive oil
⅓ cup all-purpose flour
2 cups unsweetened nondairy
milk
Sea salt
Freshly ground black pepper

1. Preheat the oven to 400°F. 2. Place the eggplant cubes on a rimmed baking sheet and then toss them with ⅛ cup of olive oil; roast them in the oven for 20 minutes or until tender. 3. In the skillet, brown the ground chicken over high heat until cooked through, then transfer to the plate and set aside for later use. 4. In the same skillet, heat the remaining olive oil; add the onion, garlic and sauté them for 5 to 6 minutes, until the onion is translucent and soft. 5. Add the cooked chicken, roasted eggplant cubes, salt, diced tomatoes, tomato paste, paprika, stir well and then lower the heat, bring to a simmer and simmer for about 15 minutes, adding water as needed. 6. To make the béchamel sauce (optional): In a small saucepan, heat the olive oil over medium heat; add the flour, milk and whisk the mixture well so no clumps form. Continue whisking to prevent the sauce from burning. The sauce is finished when it has thickened; season them with salt and pepper. 7. Divide the chicken moussaka among 4 plates, top each dish with the béchamel sauce, and allow to cool for 5 minutes before eating.
Per Serving: Calories 453; Fats 24.64g; Sodium 1193mg; Carbs 32.6g; Fiber 7.7g; Sugar 17.62g; Protein 28.27g

Rosemary Chicken in White Wine

Prep time: 5 minutes | Cook time: 50 minutes | Serves: 4

1 tablespoon olive oil	3 garlic cloves, minced
2 pounds boneless, skinless	¼ cup white wine
chicken breasts	¼ teaspoon chopped fresh
8 ounces cremini (baby bella)	rosemary
mushrooms, quartered	Sea salt
½ onion, diced	Freshly ground black pepper

1. In a large skillet, heat olive oil over medium-high heat; cook the chicken for 5 to 7 minutes, turning halfway through. Place the chicken in a plate and set aside. 2. Still in the skillet, add the mushrooms, onion, garlic and cook them for 7 to 10 minutes, until the vegetables are tender; then add the cooked chicken, rosemary, white wine, salt, pepper and bring them to a boil, reduced the heat to low; then cover the skillet and simmer for 20 to 30 minutes until the chicken is cooked through. 3. Serve and enjoy.
Per Serving: Calories 391; Fats 4.89g; Sodium 2950mg; Carbs 50.4g; Fiber 7g; Sugar 2.48g; Protein 43.96g

Skillet-Fried Chicken Breasts in Cream Sauce

Prep time: 10 minutes | Cook time: 40 minutes | Serves: 6

3 tablespoons olive oil	3 garlic cloves, minced
6 (4-ounce) boneless, skinless	½ teaspoon dried thyme
chicken breasts	½ teaspoon dried marjoram
½ zucchini, chopped into 2-inch	½ teaspoon dried basil
pieces	½ cup baby spinach
1 celery stalk, chopped	1 cup heavy (whipping) cream
1 red bell pepper, thinly sliced	¼ cup chopped fresh Italian
2 tomatoes on the vine, chopped	parsley (optional)

1. In a large skillet, heat olive oil over medium-high heat; cook the chicken breasts for 8 to 10 minutes per side, until cooked through. Place the chicken breasts in a plate and set aside. 2. Still in the skillet, add the garlic, zucchini, celery, bell pepper, tomatoes and sauté for 8 to 10 minutes, until the vegetables are softened; add the thyme, marjoram, basil and cook for 1 minute; add the spinach and cook for 3 minutes until wilted; add the cream and mix well. 3. Return the chicken breasts to the skillet and cook them for 4 minutes until warmed through. 4. Garnish with the parsley (optional) and serve.
Per Serving: Calories 161; Fats 14.66g; Sodium 225mg; Carbs 3.88g; Fiber 0.7g; Sugar 1.19g; Protein 4.58g

Garlicky Roasted Whole Chicken

Prep time: 10 minutes | Cook time: 1 hour 40 minutes | Serves: 4-6

1 (3½- to 4-pound) whole chicken	3 tablespoons olive oil
Zest and juice of 1 lemon	2 tablespoons unsalted butter, at
4 tablespoons dried oregano,	room temperature
divided	Sea salt
3 garlic cloves, crushed	Freshly ground black pepper

1. Preheat the oven to 375°F. 2. In a small bowl, mix up the garlic, lemon zest, half the lemon juice and 3 tablespoons of oregano. 3. Place the chicken in the roasting pan and then add the garlic mixture in the chicken's cavity; place the two juiced lemon halves in the cavity as well; rub the chicken with the olive oil, butter and the remaining lemon juice, and then sprinkle it with the salt, pepper and the remaining oregano. 4. Roast the chicken, basting it occasionally with the pan juices, for 20 minutes per pound, plus an additional 20 minutes, until the skin is golden brown and the juices run clear when the thigh is pierced. 5. When there are 15 minutes left in the cooking time, cover the chicken loosely with aluminum foil to prevent the skin from burning. 6. Carve the chicken and spoon the juices from the bottom of the pan onto each plate. Serve.
Per Serving: Calories 433; Fats 17.68g; Sodium 811mg; Carbs 3.77g; Fiber 1.7g; Sugar 0.37g; Protein 62.12g

Lemony Chicken Thighs with Olives

Prep time: 15 minutes | Cook time: 45 minutes | Serves: 4-5

2 tablespoons olive oil	Sea salt
⅓ cup all-purpose flour	Freshly ground black pepper
¼ teaspoon paprika	3 pounds' chicken thighs
½ teaspoon dried basil	1 cup halved pitted kalamata
⅛ teaspoon red pepper flakes	olives

2 carrots, diced	½ cup water
1 onion, diced	Juice of ½ lemon
3 garlic cloves, minced	1 cup fresh baby spinach

1. In a small bowl, mix up the flour, paprika, basil, red pepper flakes salt and black pepper. Dip the chicken thighs into the flour mixture., shake off any excess. 2. In a large skillet, heat the olive oil over medium heat; cook the chicken thighs for 6 to 8 minutes, turning occasionally, until browned. Transfer the chicken thighs to a plate and set aside. 3. Still in the skillet, add the carrots, onion, olives, garlic and sauté them for 3 to 5 minutes; add the water and bring to a boil; add the cooked chicken thighs and then reduce the heat to low; cover the skillet and simmer for 25 to 30 minutes until the chicken thighs are cooked through; when there are 5 minutes left in the cooking time, add the lemon juice. 4. Add the spinach and turn off the heat, cover the skillet and wait a few minutes until the spinach wilted. 5. Serve and enjoy.
Per Serving: Calories 434; Fats 18.55g; Sodium 1266mg; Carbs 14.03g; Fiber 2.5g; Sugar 2.35g; Protein 53.97g

Chicken Thighs with Mushroom

Prep time: 10 minutes | Cook time: 40 minutes | Serves: 4

2 tablespoons olive oil, divided	8 ounces cremini (baby bella)
2 pounds boneless, skinless	mushrooms, chopped
chicken thighs	½ cup pinot grigio
1 small onion, diced	½ cup chicken broth
2 garlic cloves, minced	1 cup heavy (whipping) cream
3 tablespoons unsalted butter	

1. In the skillet, heat 1 tablespoon of olive oil over medium-high heat; cook the chicken thighs for 12 to 15 minutes, turning often, until cooked through. Transfer the chicken thighs to a plate and set aside. 2. In the same skillet, heat the remaining olive oil over medium-high heat; then add the onion and garlic, sauté them for 5 to 7 minutes until translucent; add the butter, mushrooms and cook for 5 to 7 minutes, until the mushrooms have released their liquid. 3. Add the wine and scrape up any browned bits from the bottom of the pan with a spoon, simmer for 3 to 4 minutes; add the broth and simmer for 5 minutes until it has reduced by about three-quarters; add the cream and simmer for 3 to 5 minutes; add the cooked the chicken thighs and cook them for 4 minutes until heated through. 4. Serve and enjoy.
Per Serving: Calories 656; Fats 41.81g; Sodium 1153mg; Carbs 5.56g; Fiber 0.9g; Sugar 2.85g; Protein 58.56g

Chicken Spaghetti with Cauliflower Sauce

Prep time: 10 minutes | Cook time: 30 minutes | Serves: 4

4 boneless, skinless chicken	2 teaspoons extra-virgin olive oil
breasts	1 white onion, diced
1 teaspoon sea salt, divided	3 garlic cloves, minced
1 teaspoon freshly ground black	Juice of 1 lemon
pepper, divided	¾ cup unsweetened nondairy
4 cups frozen cauliflower florets	milk, divided
8 ounces dried whole-grain	⅓ cup Parmesan "Cheese"
spaghetti	

1. Preheat the oven to 375°F. 2. Cut the chicken breasts into 1-inch strips and season them with ½ teaspoon of salt and ½ teaspoon of pepper; arrange the chicken strips to the baking sheet and cook in the oven for 20 minutes, turning halfway through. 3. Boil a large pot of water to a boil over high heat and then add the frozen cauliflower florets; cook the cauliflower florets for 6 to 7 minutes or until fork-tender; drain them and transfer them to your food blender. 4. Cook the spaghetti according to the package directions. 5. While cooking the spaghetti, in your skillet, heat the olive oil over medium heat and sauté the onion and garlic for about 5 minutes, or until the onion is translucent and fragrant. 6. transfer the cooked onion and garlic to the food blender as well; add the lemon juice, ¼ cup of milk, and the remaining salt and pepper to the food blender and then blend them until smooth and creamy (you can add more of the milk if the mixture is too thick). 7. After the spaghetti is cooked and drained, put it back into the pot, add the cooked chicken strips, and pour in the cauliflower sauce. Mix well. 8. Plate and top with the Parmesan "Cheese."
Per Serving: Calories 470; Fats 11.11g; Sodium 912mg; Carbs 29.17g; Fiber 6.3g; Sugar 7.2g; Protein 63.2g

Chapter 3 Fish and Seafood Recipes

Herbed Pollock Veggie Pitas

Prep time: 5 minutes | Cook time: 15 minutes | Serves: 4

1 pound pollock, cut into 1-inch pieces	¼ teaspoon cayenne
¼ cup olive oil	4 whole wheat pitas
1 teaspoon salt	1 cup shredded lettuce
½ teaspoon dried oregano	2 Roma tomatoes, diced
½ teaspoon dried thyme	Nonfat plain Greek yogurt
½ teaspoon garlic powder	Lemon, quartered

1. Preheat the air fryer to 380°F. 2. In a bowl, coat the pollock pieces with olive oil, salt, oregano, thyme, garlic powder, and cayenne. 3. Transfer the pollock pieces to the air fryer basket and cook them in the preheated air fryer for 15 minutes. 4. Serve the pollock pieces inside pitas with lettuce, tomato, and Greek yogurt with a lemon wedge on the side.
Per Serving: Calories 316; Fats 15.18g; Sodium 1113mg; Carbs 21.92g; Fiber 3.1g; Sugar 4.57g; Protein 24.57g

Roasted Whole Red Snapper with Lemon Wedges

Prep time: 5 minutes | Cook time: 35 minutes | Serves: 4

1 teaspoon salt	snapper, cleaned and patted dry
½ teaspoon black pepper	2 tablespoons olive oil
½ teaspoon ground cumin	2 garlic cloves, minced
¼ teaspoon cayenne	¼ cup fresh dill
1 (1- to 1½-pound) whole red	Lemon wedges, for serving

1. Preheat the air fryer to 360°F 2. In a small bowl, mix together the salt, pepper, cumin, and cayenne. 3. Coat the outside of the red snapper with olive oil and sprinkle it with the seasoning blend; stuff the minced garlic and dill inside the cavity of the fish, then transfer the stuffed red snapper to the air fryer basket of the air fryer. 4. Roast the food for 20 minutes at first; when the time is up, flip the snapper over, and roast for 15 minutes more, or until the snapper reaches an internal temperature of 145°F.
Per Serving: Calories 181; Fats 8.41g; Sodium 655mg; Carbs 1.79g; Fiber 0.2g; Sugar 0.34g; Protein 23.52g

Herb-Cooked Shrimps with Tomatoes and Olives

Prep time: 5 minutes | Cook time: 8 minutes | Serves: 4

½ cup olive oil	1 Roma tomato, diced
4 garlic cloves, minced	¼ cup Kalamata olives
1 tablespoon balsamic vinegar	1 pound medium shrimp, cleaned
¼ teaspoon cayenne pepper	and deveined
¼ teaspoon salt	

1. Preheat the air fryer to 380°F. 2. Mix up the olive oil, garlic, balsamic, cayenne and salt in a small bowl. 3. Divide the tomatoes, olives and shrimps among four small ramekins in order, then pour a quarter of the oil mixture over the shrimps. 4. Cook the food in the preheated air fryer for 6 to 8 minutes, or until the shrimps are cooked through.
Per Serving: Calories 357; Fats 28.47g; Sodium 356mg; Carbs 3.14g; Fiber 0.6g; Sugar 0.64g; Protein 23.42g

Salmon Burgers with Broccoli Slaw

Prep time: 15 minutes | Cook time: 10 minutes | Serves: 4

For the Salmon Burgers

1 pound salmon fillets, bones and skin removed	1 teaspoon salt
1 egg	½ teaspoon cayenne pepper
¼ cup fresh dill, chopped	2 garlic cloves, minced
1 cup whole wheat bread crumbs	4 whole wheat buns

For the Broccoli Slaw

3 cups chopped or shredded broccoli	2 garlic cloves, minced
½ cup shredded carrots	½ teaspoon salt
¼ cup sunflower seeds	2 tablespoons apple cider vinegar
	1 cup nonfat plain Greek yogurt

To make the Salmon Burgers: 1. Preheat the air fryer to 360°F. 2. In a food processor, add the salmon fillets and pulse them until they are finely chopped. 3. In a bowl, mix up the chopped salmon, egg, dill, bread crumbs, salt, cayenne, and garlic until it comes together. 4. Form the salmon into 4 patties and then transfer them to the air fryer basket, making sure that they don't touch each other. 5. Bake the salmon patties for 10 minutes, flipping halfway through.
To Make the Broccoli Slaw: 1. In a large bowl, mix up all of the ingredients for the broccoli slaw. 2. Serve the salmon burgers on toasted whole wheat buns, and top with a generous portion of broccoli slaw.
Per Serving: Calories 499; Fats 17.72g; Sodium 1757mg; Carbs 42.76g; Fiber 5.4g; Sugar 5.41g; Protein 42.25g

Garlicky Grouper with Tomatoes

Prep time: 5 minutes | Cook time: 12 minutes | Serves: 4

4 grouper fillets	¼ cup sliced Kalamata olives
½ teaspoon salt	¼ cup fresh dill, roughly chopped
3 garlic cloves, minced	Juice of 1 lemon
1 tomato, sliced	¼ cup olive oil

1. Preheat the air fryer to 380°F. 2. Arrange the grouper fillets to the air fryer basket, season them with salt on all sides, then top them with the minced garlic, tomato slices, olives and fresh dill; drizzle the olive oil and lemon juice on the top. 3. Bake the food in the preheated air fryer for 10 to 12 minutes, or until the internal temperature reaches 145°F.
Per Serving: Calories 374; Fats 17.09g; Sodium 491mg; Carbs 2.28g; Fiber 0.4g; Sugar 0.42g; Protein 50.5g

Herb-Seasoned Tuna Steaks

Prep time: 5 minutes | Cook time: 10 minutes | Serves: 4

1 teaspoon garlic powder	4 tuna steaks
½ teaspoon salt	2 tablespoons olive oil
¼ teaspoon dried thyme	1 lemon, quartered
¼ teaspoon dried oregano	

1. Preheat the air fryer to 380°F. 2. In a small bowl, mix up the garlic powder, salt, thyme, and oregano. 3. Oil the tuna steaks and season both sides of each steak with the seasoning blend. Arrange the tums steaks to the air fryer basket in a single layer. 4. Cook the tuna steaks for 5 minutes, then flip and cook for 3 to 4 minutes longer.
Per Serving: Calories 198; Fats 8.27g; Sodium 672mg; Carbs 1.46g; Fiber 0.1g; Sugar 0.32g; Protein 30.12g

Honey-Glazed Salmon Fillets

Prep time: 5 minutes | Cook time: 12 minutes | Serves: 4

¼ cup raw honey	½ teaspoon salt
4 garlic cloves, minced	Olive oil cooking spray
1 tablespoon olive oil	4 (1½-inch-thick) salmon fillets

1. Preheat the air fryer to 380°F. 2. In a small bowl, add the honey, garlic, olive oil, and salt. Mix them well. 3. Oil the bottom of the air fryer basket with olive oil cooking spray, and place the salmon fillets in a single layer in it 4. Brush the top of each fillet with the honey-garlic mixture, and roast the food 5. for 10 to 12 minutes, or until the internal temperature reaches 145°F.
Per Serving: Calories 354; Fats 15.64g; Sodium 367mg; Carbs 18.48g; Fiber 0.1g; Sugar 17.44g; Protein 34.07g

Tuna Salad

Prep time: 10 minutes | Cook time: 0 | Serves: 4

2 tablespoons olive oil	½ cup red onion, diced
2 tablespoons lemon juice	½ cup red bell pepper, diced
2 teaspoons Dijon mustard	½ cup fresh parsley, chopped
½ teaspoon kosher salt	2 (6-ounces) cans of tuna packed
¼ teaspoon black pepper	in water, drained
12 olives, pitted and chopped	6 cups of baby spinach
½ cup celery, diced	

1. Mix the olive oil, lemon juice, mustard, salt, and black pepper in a bowl, then add the olives, celery, onion, bell pepper, and parsley. 2. Add the tuna and gently incorporate. 3. Divide the spinach evenly among four plates or bowls. 4. Spoon the tuna salad evenly on top of the spinach.
Per Serving: Calories 342; Total Fat 30g; Sodium 40mg; Total Carbs 13g; Sugar 4g; Fiber 3g; Protein 7g

Browned Salmon and Zucchini Noodles

Prep time: 10 minutes | Cook time: 25 minutes | Serves: 4

4 (5- to 6-ounce) pieces salmon
½ teaspoon kosher salt
¼ teaspoon freshly ground black pepper
1 tablespoon extra-virgin olive oil
1 cup freshly squeezed orange juice

1 teaspoon low-sodium soy sauce
2 zucchinis (about 16 ounces), spiralized
1 tablespoon fresh chives, chopped
1 tablespoon fresh parsley, chopped

1. Preheat the oven to 350°F. Season the salmon pieces with salt and black pepper. 2. In the skillet, heat the olive oil; add the salmon pieces, skin-side down, and sear for 5 minutes, or until the skin is golden brown and crispy. 3. Turn the salmon pieces over and transfer to the baking sheet, cook them in the preheated oven until your desired doneness is reached—about 5 minutes for medium-rare, 7 minutes for medium, and 9 minutes for medium-well. When done, transfer the salmon pieces to a cutting board to rest. 4. In the same skillet over medium-high heat, add the orange juice and soy sauce to deglaze it. Bring to a simmer, scraping up any brown bits, and continue to simmer 5 to 7 minutes, until the liquid is reduced by half to a syrup-like consistency. 5. Divide the zucchini noodles among 4 plates and place 1 piece of salmon on each plate; pour the orange glaze over the salmon and zucchini noodles, garnish with the chives and parsley.
Per Serving: Calories 105; Fats 4.05g; Sodium 410mg; Carbs 6.89g; Fiber 0.3g; Sugar 5.24g; Protein 9.83g

Breadcrumb-Crusted Salmon with Bell Pepper

Prep time: 15 minutes | Cook time: 15 minutes | Serves: 4

¼ cup whole-wheat bread crumbs
¼ cup mayonnaise
1 large egg, beaten
1 tablespoon chives, chopped
1 tablespoon fresh parsley, chopped
Zest of 1 lemon
¾ teaspoon kosher salt, divided
¼ teaspoon freshly ground black

pepper
2 (5- to 6-ounce) cans no-salt boneless/skinless salmon, drained and finely flaked
½ bell pepper, diced small
2 tablespoons extra-virgin olive oil, divided
1 cup plain Greek yogurt
Juice of 1 lemon

1. In a large bowl, mix up the bread crumbs, mayonnaise, egg, chives, parsley, lemon zest, ½ teaspoon of the salt, and black pepper; add the salmon and the bell pepper, coat them with the mayonnaise mixture and then form 8 patties from the mixture. 2. In the skillet, heat 1 tablespoon of the olive oil over medium-high heat. Cook half the cakes for 4 to 5 minutes until the bottoms are golden brown, flip the cakes and cook for 4 to 5 minutes longer or until golden brown. Repeat with the remaining 1 tablespoon of olive oil and the rest of the cakes. 3. In a small bowl, mix up the yogurt, lemon juice, and the remaining salt and mix well. Serve the salmon cakes with the yogurt mixture.
Per Serving: Calories 282; Fats 17.7g; Sodium 841mg; Carbs 9.94g; Fiber 0.6g; Sugar 3.73g; Protein 21.23g

Halibut in Parchment

Prep time: 15 minutes | Cook time: 15 minutes | Serves: 4

½ cup zucchini, diced small
1 shallot, minced
4 (5-ounce) halibut fillets (about 1 inch thick)
4 teaspoons extra-virgin olive oil
¼ teaspoon kosher salt

⅛ teaspoon freshly ground black pepper
1 lemon, sliced into ⅛-inch-thick rounds
8 sprigs of thyme

1. Preheat the oven to 450°F. Combine the zucchini and shallots in a medium bowl. 2. Cut 4 sheets (15x24 inches) of parchment paper. Fold each sheet in half horizontally. Draw a large half heart on one side of each folded sheet and fold along the center of the heart. Cut out the heart, open the parchment and lay flat. 3. Place a fillet near the center of each parchment heart; drizzle 1 teaspoon olive oil, sprinkle with salt and pepper over each fillet. Top each fillet with lemon slices and 2 sprigs of thyme. Sprinkle each fillet with one-quarter of the zucchini and shallot mixture. Fold the parchment over. 4. Starting at the top, fold the edges of the parchment over, and continue all the way around to make a packet. Twist the end tightly to secure. 5. Arrange the 4 packets on a baking sheet. Bake them in the preheated oven for about 15 minutes. 6. When the time is up, transfer them to a plate; cut open and you can enjoy.

Per Serving: Calories 130; Fats 9.77g; Sodium 176mg; Carbs 6.05g; Fiber 2.8g; Sugar 0.5g; Protein 6.31g

Tomato Flounder with Basil

Prep time: 10 minutes | Cook time: 20 minutes | Serves: 4

1 pound cherry tomatoes
4 garlic cloves, sliced
2 tablespoons extra-virgin olive oil
2 tablespoons lemon juice
2 tablespoons basil, cut into

ribbons
½ teaspoon kosher salt
¼ teaspoon freshly ground black pepper
4 (5- to 6-ounce) flounder fillets

1. Preheat the oven to 425°F. 2. In a baking dish, add the tomatoes, garlic, olive oil, lemon juice, basil, salt, and black pepper; mix them well; bake them in the preheated oven for 5 minutes. 3. When the time is up, arrange the flounder on top of the tomato mixture. Bake the food for 10 to 15 minutes until the fish is opaque and begins to flake. 4. When done, serve and enjoy.
Per Serving: Calories 229; Fats 10.93g; Sodium 560mg; Carbs 23.65g; Fiber 5.1g; Sugar 15.11g; Protein 11.29g

Skillet-Grilled Mahi-Mahi with Artichoke Caponata

Prep time: 25 minutes | Cook time: 30 minutes | Serves: 4

2 tablespoons extra-virgin olive oil
2 celery stalks, diced
1 onion, diced
2 garlic cloves, minced
½ cup cherry tomatoes, chopped
¼ cup white wine
2 tablespoons white wine vinegar
1 (14-ounce) can artichoke hearts, drained and chopped
¼ cup green olives, pitted and

chopped
1 tablespoon capers, chopped
¼ teaspoon red pepper flakes
2 tablespoons fresh basil, chopped
4 (5- to 6-ounces each) skinless mahi-mahi fillets
½ teaspoon kosher salt
¼ teaspoon freshly ground black pepper
Olive oil cooking spray

1. In the skillet, heat the olive oil over medium heat; add the celery, onion and sauté them for 4 to 5 minutes; add the garlic and sauté for 30 seconds; add the tomatoes and cook them for 2 to 3 minutes; add the wine and vinegar to deglaze the pan, increasing the heat to medium-high and scraping up any brown bits on the bottom of the pan. 2. Add the artichokes, olives, capers, and red pepper flakes and simmer for 10 minutes, reducing the liquid by half; mix in the basil. 3. Season the mahi-mahi with the salt and pepper. 4. Coat a grill skillet over medium-high heat with olive oil cooking spray; add the fillets and cook them for 4 to 5 minutes on each side. 5. Top with the artichoke caponata, enjoy.
Per Serving: Calories 310; Fats 18.58g; Sodium 848mg; Carbs 15.44g; Fiber 8.6g; Sugar 2.72g; Protein 21.16g

Cod Cauliflower Chowder with Cherry Tomatoes

Prep time: 15 minutes | Cook time: 40 minutes | Serves: 4

2 tablespoons extra-virgin olive oil
1 leek, white and light green parts only, cut in half lengthwise and sliced thinly
4 garlic cloves, sliced
1 medium head cauliflower, coarsely chopped
1 teaspoon kosher salt

¼ teaspoon freshly ground black pepper
2 pints' cherry tomatoes
2 cups no-salt-added vegetable stock
¼ cup green olives, pitted and chopped
1 to 1½ pounds cod
¼ cup fresh parsley, minced

1. In a pot, heat the olive oil over medium heat; add the leek and sauté for 5 minutes until lightly golden brown; add the garlic and sauté for 30 seconds; add the cauliflower, salt, black pepper and sauté them for 2 to 3 minutes. 2. Add the tomatoes and vegetable stock, increase the heat to high and bring to a boil, then turn the heat to low and simmer for 10 minutes; mix in the olives and add the cod, cover the pot and then simmer them for 20 minutes until the fish is opaque and flakes easily. 3. Gently mix in the parsley. Serve and enjoy.
Per Serving: Calories 308; Fats 10.93g; Sodium 1500mg; Carbs 12.06g; Fiber 4.5g; Sugar 4.09g; Protein 39.14g

Sardine Bruschetta with Fennel

Prep time: 10 minutes | Cook time: 0 | Serves: 4

⅓ cup plain Greek yogurt
2 tablespoons mayonnaise
2 tablespoons lemon juice
2 teaspoons lemon zest
¾ teaspoon kosher salt
One fennel bulb, cored and sliced
¼ cup fresh parsley, chopped
¼ cup fresh mint, chopped
2 teaspoons olive oil
⅛ teaspoon black pepper
Eight slices of multigrain bread, toasted
2 (4.4-ounce) cans of smoked sardines

1. Mix the yogurt, mayonnaise, 1 tablespoon of the lemon juice, the lemon zest, and ¼ teaspoon of the salt in a bowl. 2. Mix the rest ½ teaspoon of salt, 1 tablespoon of lemon juice, the fennel, parsley, mint, olive oil, and black pepper in another bowl. 3. Spoon 1 tablespoon of the yogurt mixture on each piece of toast. Evenly divide the fennel mixture on top of the yogurt mixture. 4. Divide the sardines among the toasts, placing them on the fennel mixture. Garnish with more herbs, if desired.
Per Serving: Calories 460; Total Fat 29.7g; Sodium 536mg; Total Carbs 13.1g; Fiber 6.9g; Sugars 4g; Protein 37.7g

Monkfish with Sautéed Leeks

Prep time: 10 minutes | Cook time: 35 minutes | Serves: 4

1 to 1½ pounds monkfish
3 tablespoons lemon juice
1 teaspoon kosher salt
⅛ teaspoon black pepper
2 tablespoons olive oil
1 leek, sliced
½ onion, julienned
3 garlic cloves, minced
2 bulbs fennel, cored and sliced
1 (14.5-ounce) can of no-salt-added diced tomatoes
2 tablespoons fresh parsley, chopped
2 tablespoons fresh oregano, chopped
¼ teaspoon red pepper flakes

1. Place the monkfish in the baking dish, add black pepper, 2 tablespoons of lemon juice, and ¼ teaspoon of salt, and then place the dish in the refrigerator. 2. Add the olive oil to the skillet and heat over medium heat. Add the leek and onion, and sauté for 3 minutes until translucent. 3. Stir in the garlic and sauté for 30 seconds. Add the fennel and sauté for 4 to 5 minutes. Add the tomatoes and simmer for 2 to 3 minutes. 4. Stir in the parsley, oregano, red pepper flakes, the rest salt, and the rest lemon juice. 5. Place the fish on top of the leek mixture, cover the skillet, and simmer the fish for 20 to 25 minutes, turning halfway through; when cooked, the fish should pull apart easily. 6. Garnish this dish with the fennel fronds, and serve.
Per Serving: Calories 379; Total Fat 14g; Sodium 308mg; Total Carbs 17g; Sugar 9g; Fiber 5g; Protein 43g

Sardines with Penne

Prep time: 10 minutes | Cook time: 30 minutes | Serves: 4

8 ounces' whole-wheat penne
2 tablespoons olive oil
1 bulb fennel, cored and sliced, plus ¼ cup fronds
2 celery stalks, sliced, plus ½ cup of leaves
4 garlic cloves, sliced
¾ teaspoon kosher salt
¼ teaspoon black pepper
Zest of 1 lemon
Juice of 1 lemon
2 (4.4-ounce) cans of boneless/skinless sardines

1. Cook the penne pasta according to the instructions on the package. 2. Drain the penne pasta, and reserve 1 cup of pasta water. 3. Heat the olive oil in the skillet over medium heat; add the fennel and celery, and cook for 10 to 12 minutes until tender and golden. Add garlic, and cook for 1 minute. 4. Add the penne, reserved pasta water, salt, and black pepper. 5. Remove this pan from the heat and stir in the lemon zest, lemon juice, fennel fronds, and celery leaves. 6. Break the sardines into bite-size pieces and gently mix them in, along with the oil they were packed in.
Per Serving: Calories 418; Total Fat 20g; Sodium 1121mg; Total Carbs 15g; Sugar 5g; Fiber 4g; Protein 45g

Cioppino

Prep time: 15 minutes | Cook time: 35 minutes | Serves: 4

2 tablespoons extra-virgin olive oil
1 onion, diced
1 bulb fennel, diced
16 ounces' vegetable stock
4 garlic cloves, smashed
8 thyme sprigs
1 teaspoon kosher salt
¼ teaspoon red pepper flakes
1 dried bay leaf
1 bunch kale, stemmed and chopped
1 dozen littleneck clams tightly
closed, scrubbed
1-pound fish
¼ cup fresh parsley, chopped

1. Preheat the olive oil in a stockpot over medium heat. Add the onion and fennel and sauté for about 5 minutes. 2. Add the vegetable stock, garlic, thyme, salt, red pepper flakes, and bay leaf. Adjust the heat to medium-high, and bring to a simmer. 3. Add the kale, cover, and simmer for 5 minutes. 4. Carefully add the clams, cover, and simmer for about 15 minutes until they open. Remove the clams and set them aside. Discard any clams that do not open. 5. Add the fish, cover the pot and cook on simmer for 10 minutes until opaque and easily separated. Gently mix in the parsley. 6. Divide the cioppino among four bowls. Place 3 clams in each bowl and garnish with the fennel fronds.
Per Serving: Calories 305; Total Fat 14g; Sodium 812mg; Total Carbs 8g; Sugar 2g; Fiber 2g; Protein 35g

Crab Salad with Endive

Prep time: 10 minutes | Cook time: 10 minutes | Serves: 4

1-pound lump crabmeat
⅔ cup plain Greek yogurt
3 tablespoons mayonnaise
3 tablespoons fresh chives, chopped
3 tablespoons fresh parsley, chopped
3 tablespoons fresh basil, chopped
Zest of 1 lemon
Juice of 1 lemon
½ teaspoon kosher salt
¼ teaspoon black pepper
4 endives, ends cut off, and leaves separated

1. Mix the crab, yogurt, mayonnaise, chives, parsley, basil, lemon zest, lemon juice, salt, and black pepper in a suitable bowl. 2. Place the endive leaves on four salad plates. 3. Divide the prepared crab mixture evenly on top of the endive. Garnish with additional herbs, if desired.
Per Serving: Calories 166; Total Fat 4g; Sodium 295mg; Total Carbs 13g; Fiber 2g; Sugars 4.2g; Protein 18.7g

Seared Scallops with Orange Glaze

Prep time: 10 minutes | Cook time: 20 minutes | Serves: 4

3 tablespoons olive oil
3 garlic cloves, minced
½ teaspoon kosher salt
4 blood oranges, juiced
1 teaspoon blood orange zest
½ teaspoon red pepper flakes
1-pound scallops, small side muscle removed
¼ teaspoon black pepper
¼ cup fresh chives, chopped

1. Preheat 1 tablespoon of the olive oil in a suitable saucepan over medium-high heat. Add the garlic and ¼ teaspoon of the salt and sauté for 30 seconds. 2. Add the orange juice and zest, cook to a boil; reduce its heat to medium-low, and cook for almost 20 minutes, or until the liquid reduces by half and becomes a thicker syrup consistency. 3. Mix in the red pepper flakes. 4. Season the scallops with the rest ¼ teaspoon of salt and the black pepper. 5. Heat the rest 2 tablespoons of olive oil in a suitable skillet on medium-high heat. Add the scallops gently and sear. Cook on each side for about 2 minutes. If cooking in 2 batches, use 1 tablespoon of oil per batch. 6. Serve the scallops with the blood orange glaze and garnish with the chives.
Per Serving: Calories 486; Total Fat 11.1g; Sodium 28mg; Total Carbs 76.1g; Fiber 1.9g; Sugars 0.8g; Protein 18.3g

Lemon Garlic Shrimp

Prep time: 15 minutes | Cook time: 10 minutes | Serves: 4

2 tablespoons olive oil
3 garlic cloves, sliced
½ teaspoon kosher salt
¼ teaspoon red pepper flakes
1-pound large shrimp, peeled and deveined
½ cup white wine
3 tablespoons fresh parsley, minced
Zest of ½ lemon
Juice of ½ lemon

1. Preheat the olive oil in a wok or large skillet over medium-high heat. Add the garlic, salt, and red pepper flakes and sauté for 30 seconds to 1 minute until the garlic starts to brown. 2. Add the shrimp, and wait for 4 to 6 minutes, until pink, turning halfway through. 3. Stir in the wine and deglaze the wok, scraping up any flavorful brown bits. This step will take 1 to 2 minutes. 4. Put off the heat; mix in the parsley, lemon zest, and lemon juice.
Per Serving: Calories 485; Total Fat 8.3g; Sodium 84mg; Total Carbs 82.6g; Fiber 3.7g; Sugars 3.1g; Protein 19.1g

Shrimp Fra Diavolo

Prep time: 10 minutes | Cook time: 10 minutes | Serves: 4

2 tablespoons olive oil
1 onion, diced small
1 fennel bulb, cored and diced small, plus ¼ cup fronds for garnish
1 bell pepper, diced small
½ teaspoon dried oregano
½ teaspoon dried thyme
½ teaspoon kosher salt
¼ teaspoon red pepper flakes
1 (14.5-ounce) can of no-salt-added diced tomatoes
1-pound shrimp, peeled and deveined
Juice of 1 lemon
Zest of 1 lemon
2 tablespoons fresh parsley, chopped, for garnish

1. Preheat the olive oil in a sauté pan. Add the onion, fennel, bell pepper, oregano, thyme, salt, and red pepper flakes, and sauté them for 5 minutes over medium heat until translucent. 2. Deglaze this pan with the juice from the canned tomatoes, scraping up any brown bits, and cook to a boil. 3. Add the diced tomatoes and the shrimp; reduce its heat to a simmer, cover the pan, and cook for 3 minutes until the shrimp are cooked through. 4. Put off the heat. Toss in the lemon juice and lemon zest. 5. Garnish with the parsley and the fennel fronds.
Per Serving: Calories 221; Total Fat 12.2g; Sodium 708mg; Total Carbs 5.4g; Fiber 0.1g; Sugars 0.1g; Protein 21.3g

Shrimp with White Beans

Prep time: 15 minutes | Cook time: 15 minutes | Serves: 4

3 tablespoons lemon juice
2 tablespoons olive oil
½ teaspoon kosher salt
1-pound shrimp, peeled and deveined
1 large shallot, diced
¼ cup no-salt-added vegetable stock
1 (15-ounce) can of no-salt-added
or cannellini beans, rinsed and drained
¼ cup fresh mint, chopped
1 teaspoon lemon zest
1 tablespoon white wine vinegar
¼ teaspoon black pepper
¼ cup crumbled feta cheese for garnish

1. In a suitable bowl, beat together 1 tablespoon of the lemon juice, 1 tablespoon of the olive oil, and ¼ teaspoon of the salt. Add the shrimp and set it aside. 2. Preheat the rest olive oil in a sauté pan over medium heat. 3. Stir in the shallot and sauté until translucent, about 2 to 3 minutes. 4. Add the vegetable stock and deglaze this pan, scraping up any brown bits, and cook to a boil. Add the beans and shrimp. 5. Reduce its heat to low, cover the pan, and simmer for 3 to 4 minutes until cooked through. 6. Put off the heat and add the mint, lemon zest, vinegar, and black pepper. Stir gently to mix. 7. Garnish with the feta, serve and enjoy.
Per Serving: Calories 386; Total Fat 14.8g; Sodium 113mg; Total Carbs 14.9g; Fiber 3.1g; Sugars 9.3g; Protein 46.3g

Garlicky Sardines

Prep time: 10 minutes | Cook time: 5 minutes | Serves: 4

4 (3.25-ounce) cans of sardines (about 16 sardines), packed in water or olive oil
2 tablespoons olive oil (if sardines are in water)
4 garlic cloves, minced
½ teaspoon red pepper flakes
½ teaspoon salt
¼ teaspoon black pepper

1. Preheat the broiler. 2. Line the baking dish with a huge piece of aluminum foil, then arrange the sardines in a single layer. 3. Mix the olive oil (optional), garlic, and red pepper flakes in a suitable bowl, and spoon over each sardine—season with black pepper and salt. 4. Broil them for 2 to 3 minutes just until sizzling. 5. To serve, place four sardines on each plate and top with any remaining garlic mixture collected in the baking dish.
Per Serving: Calories 227; Total Fat 14.6g; Sodium 413mg; Total Carbs 2.1g; Fiber 1g; Sugars 1.1g; Protein 22.4g

Baked Salmon

Prep time: 10 minutes | Cook time: 15 minutes | Serves: 4

4 (6-ounce) salmon fillets
2 tablespoons olive oil
½ teaspoon salt
¼ teaspoon black pepper
Juice of large Valencia orange or
tangerine
4 teaspoons orange or tangerine zest
4 tablespoons chopped fresh dill

1. At 375 degrees F, preheat your oven. 2. Apply oil to each salmon filet on both sides, and season them with salt and black pepper. 3. Place one filet in the center of one piece of foil. 4. Drizzle the orange juice over each fillet, and top with 1 teaspoon of orange zest and 1 tablespoon of dill. 5. Fold the two long sides in, and then fold the short ends to make a packet. 6. Make sure to leave about 2 inches of air space within the foil so the fish can steam. 7. Place the packets on a suitable baking sheet. 8. Bake the food for 15 minutes. Open the packets carefully, transfer the fish to 4 serving plates, and pour the sauce over the top of each.
Per Serving: Calories 469; Total Fat 22.1g; Sodium 847mg; Total Carbs 3.8g; Fiber 0.1g; Sugars 2.8g; Protein 60.8g

Poached Cod

Prep time: 10 minutes | Cook time: 30 minutes | Serves: 4

4 (6-ounce) cod fillets
½ teaspoon salt
½ teaspoon black pepper
½ cup dry white wine
½ cup seafood or vegetable stock
2 garlic cloves, minced
1 bay leaf
1 teaspoon chopped fresh sage
4 rosemary sprigs for garnish

1. At 375 degrees F, preheat your oven. 2. Season each filet with black pepper and salt and place in a suitable ovenproof skillet. Add the wine, stock, garlic, bay leaf, sage, and cover. 3. Bake them for 20 minutes or until the fish flakes easily with a fork. 4. Use a spatula to remove the filet from this skillet. 5. Place the poaching liquid over high heat and cook for 10 minutes, frequently stirring, until reduced by half. 6. Place a filet on each plate and drizzle with the reduced poaching liquid to serve. Garnish each with a fresh rosemary sprig.
Per Serving: Calories 442; Total Fat 11.5g; Sodium 950mg; Total Carbs 4.6g; Fiber 1g; Sugars 1.6g; Protein 74.3g

Mussels with White Wine

Prep time: 10 minutes | Cook time: 7 minutes | Serves: 4

4 pounds fresh, live mussels
2 cups dry white wine
½ teaspoon sea salt
6 garlic cloves, minced
4 teaspoons diced shallot
½ cup chopped fresh parsley
4 tablespoons olive oil
Juice of ½ lemon

1. In a suitable colander, scrub and rinse the mussels under cold water. 2. Discard any mussels that do not close when tapped. Use a paring knife to remove the beard from each mussel. 3. In a suitable stockpot over medium-high heat, bring the parsley's wine, salt, garlic, shallots, and ¼ cup of the parsley to a steady simmer. 4. Add the mussels, cover, and simmer for 5 to 7 minutes just until all mussels open. Do not overcook. 5. Divide the mussels among four large and shallow bowls. 6. Add the olive oil and lemon juice to the pot, stir, and pour the broth over the mussels. 7. Garnish with parsley and serve with bread.
Per Serving: Calories 251; Total Fat 7.2g; Sodium 456mg; Total Carbs 2.7g; Fiber 0.8g; Sugars 1.7g; Protein 42g

Crab Cakes with Fennel Salad

Prep time: 20 minutes | Cook time: 10 minutes | Serves: 6

¾ cup cooked baby shrimp
3 tablespoons heavy (whipping) cream
1 teaspoon sea salt
¼ teaspoon black pepper
1½ pounds lump crabmeat
6 scallions, sliced
¼ cup extra-virgin olive oil,
divided
3 fennel bulbs, cored and very sliced
2 tablespoons chopped fennel fronds
¼ cup lemon juice
½ teaspoon Dijon mustard
1 garlic clove, minced

1. In a blender, blend the shrimp, heavy cream, ½ teaspoon of sea salt, and ⅛ teaspoon of pepper until smooth. 2. In a suitable bowl, stir together the crabmeat and scallions. 3. Fold in the shrimp mousse until well mixed. Form the prepared mixture into eight patties. Refrigerate for 10 minutes. 4. In a suitable, nonstick skillet over medium-high heat, heat 2 tablespoons of olive oil until it shimmers. 5. Add the crab cakes, and cook for almost 4 minutes per side until browned on both sides. 6. In a suitable bowl, mix the fennel and fennel fronds. 7. In another bowl, beat the rest olive oil with the lemon juice, mustard, garlic, and remaining ½ teaspoon of sea salt, and ⅛ teaspoon of pepper. Toss the dressing with the fennel and serve with the crab cakes.
Per Serving: Calories 317; Total Fat 23.3g; Sodium 572mg; Total Carbs 1.1g; Fiber 0.2g; Sugars 0g; Protein 26.3g

Shrimp Scampi

Prep time: 10 minutes | Cook time: 20 minutes | Serves: 4

2 tablespoons olive oil
1 shallot, minced
1-pound shrimp, peeled, deveined
6 garlic cloves, minced
Juice of 1 lemon
Zest of 1 lemon
½ cup dry white wine
½ teaspoon sea salt
¼ teaspoon black pepper
Pinch red pepper flakes
¼ cup chopped fresh Italian parsley leaves
6 ounces' whole-wheat pasta, cooked according to package directions

1. In a suitable skillet over medium-high heat, preheat the olive oil until it shimmers. 2. Add the shallot, and cook for almost 5 minutes until soft. 3. Toss in the shrimp, and occasionally stir for 3 to 4 minutes until the shrimp is pink. 4. Stir in garlic and sauté for almost 30 seconds, stirring constantly. 5. Stir in the lemon juice and zest, wine, sea salt, pepper, and red pepper flakes. 6. Cook to a simmer, and then reduce its heat to medium-low; cook them for 2 minutes until the liquid reduces by half. 7. Turn off the heat and stir in the parsley. 8. Toss with the hot pasta and serve.
Per Serving: Calories 236; Total Fat 12.6g; Sodium 216mg; Total Carbs 4.7g; Fiber 0.8g; Sugars 0.2g; Protein 27.1g

Shrimp Mojo De Ajo

Prep time: 10 minutes | Cook time: 40 minutes | Serves: 4

¼ cup olive oil
10 garlic cloves, minced
⅛ teaspoon cayenne pepper, plus more as needed
8 ounces' mushrooms, quartered
1-pound medium shrimp,
deveined and peeled
Juice of 1 lime
½ teaspoon sea salt
¼ cup chopped fresh cilantro leaves
2 cups cooked brown rice

1. In a suitable saucepan over the lowest heat setting, bring the olive oil, garlic, and cayenne to a low simmer, so bubbles just barely break the surface of the oil. 2. Simmer the food for 30 minutes with occasional stirring. 3. Pick the garlic out, and set it aside. 4. Add the olive oil to a suitable skillet over medium-high heat and heat it until it shimmers. 5. Add the mushrooms, and cook for almost 5 minutes, stirring once or twice until browned. 6.Add the shrimp, lime juice, and sea salt. Cook for almost 4 minutes with occasional stirring until the shrimp are pink. 7. Stir in the cilantro and reserved garlic. Serve over the hot brown rice.
Per Serving: Calories 366; Total Fat 9.3g; Sodium 710mg; Total Carbs 35g; Fiber 12.4g; Sugars 15g; Protein 38.2g

Scallops with Sautéed Spinach

Prep time: 10 minutes | Cook time: 15 minutes | Serves: 4

1-pound sea scallops
1 teaspoon sea salt
½ teaspoon black pepper, divided
2 tablespoons extra-virgin olive
oil
6 cups fresh baby spinach
Juice of 1 orange
Pinch red pepper flakes

1. Season the scallops on both sides with ½ teaspoon of sea salt and ¼ teaspoon of pepper. 2. Preheat the olive oil in a skillet over medium-high heat until it shimmers. 3. Put in the scallops, and cook them for 3 to 4 minutes per side without moving until browned. Remove the scallops from this skillet and set them aside, tented with aluminum foil to keep warm. 4. Return this skillet to the heat and add the spinach, orange juice, red pepper flakes, and the remaining salt and pepper, and then stir them for 4 to 5 minutes until the spinach wilts. 5. Divide the spinach among four plates and top with the scallops. Serve immediately.
Per Serving: Calories 187; Total Fat 2.3g; Sodium 1213mg; Total Carbs 21.3g; Fiber 8.8g; Sugars 4.4g; Protein 20.6g

Roasted Salmon with Gremolata

Prep time: 10 minutes | Cook time: 10 minutes | Serves: 6

1½ pounds skin-on salmon fillet, cut into four pieces
1 teaspoon sea salt
¼ teaspoon black pepper
3 tablespoons extra-virgin olive
oil
1 bunch of fresh Italian parsley leaves, finely chopped
1 garlic clove, minced
Zest of 1 lemon, finely grated

1. At 350 degrees F, preheat your oven. 2. Season the salmon with pepper and ½ teaspoon of salt. 3. In a suitable, ovenproof skillet over medium-high heat, preheat the olive oil until it shimmers. 4. Add the salmon to this skillet, skin-side down. Cook for almost 5 minutes, gently pressing on the salmon with a spatula until the skin crisps. 5. Transfer this pan to the oven and cook the salmon for 3 to 4 minutes more until it is opaque. 6. Stir together the parsley, garlic, lemon zest, and remaining ½ teaspoon of sea salt in a suitable bowl. Sprinkle the prepared mixture over the salmon and serve.
Per Serving: Calories 241; Total Fat 8.5g; Sodium 422mg; Total Carbs 9.1g; Fiber 1.1g; Sugars 3.8g; Protein 31.4g

Salmon Burgers

Prep time: 10 minutes | Cook time: 10 minutes | Serves: 6

16 ounces canned salmon, drained
6 scallions, finely chopped
¼ cup whole-wheat bread crumbs
2 eggs, beaten
2 tablespoons fresh Italian parsley leaves, chopped
1 tablespoon dried Italian seasoning
Zest of 1 lemon
2 tablespoons extra-virgin olive oil
¼ cup unsweetened nonfat plain Greek yogurt
1 tablespoon chopped fresh dill
1 tablespoon capers, rinsed and chopped
¼ teaspoon sea salt
6 whole-wheat hamburger buns

1. Mix the salmon, scallions, bread crumbs, eggs, parsley, Italian seasoning, and lemon zest in a suitable bowl. Form the prepared mixture into six patties about ½-inch thick. 2. In a suitable nonstick skillet over medium-high heat, preheat the olive oil until it shimmers. 3. Add the salmon patties. Cook for almost 4 minutes per side until browned. 4. Beat the yogurt, dill, capers, and sea salt in a suitable bowl, spread the sauce on the buns. Top with the patties and serve.
Per Serving: Calories 303; Total Fat 12.2g; Sodium 652mg; Total Carbs 18.1g; Fiber 2.7g; Sugars 10.6g; Protein 33.5g

Swordfish Kebabs

Prep time: 20 minutes | Cook time: 10 minutes | Serves: 6

3 tablespoons extra-virgin olive oil, plus more for the grill
Juice of 2 oranges
1 tablespoon Dijon mustard
2 teaspoons dried tarragon
½ teaspoon sea salt
⅛ teaspoon black pepper
2-pound swordfish, cut into 1½-inch pieces
2 red bell peppers, cut into pieces

1. Beat the olive oil, orange juice, mustard, tarragon, sea salt, and pepper in a suitable bowl. 2. Add the swordfish and toss to coat. Let sit for 10 minutes. 3. Coat the grill pan with oil, and heat the grill pan over medium-high heat. 4. Thread the swordfish and red bell peppers onto six wooden skewers. 5. Cook the food for 8 minutes until the fish is opaque, turning halfway through. 6. Serve warm.
Per Serving: Calories 326; Total Fat 3.7g; Sodium 570mg; Total Carbs 8.5g; Fiber 1.2g; Sugars 5g; Protein 40.1g

Pollock with Roasted Tomatoes

Prep time: 10 minutes | Cook time: 45 minutes | Serves: 6

12 plum tomatoes, halved
2 shallots, significantly cut into rings
3 garlic cloves, minced
3 tablespoons plus 1 teaspoon extra-virgin olive oil
1 teaspoon sea salt, divided
½ teaspoon black pepper, divided
1 teaspoon butter (or extra-virgin olive oil)
¾ cup whole-wheat bread crumbs
6 (4-ounce) pollock fillets
¼ cup chopped fresh Italian parsley leaves

1. At 450 degrees F, preheat your oven. 2. In a suitable bowl, toss the tomatoes, shallots, and garlic with 1 tablespoon of olive oil, ½ teaspoon of sea salt, and ¼ teaspoon of pepper. Transfer to a rimmed baking sheet and arrange the food in a single layer. Bake the food for almost 40 minutes until the tomatoes are soft and browned. 3. In the nonstick skillet over medium-high heat, heat 1 tablespoon plus 1 teaspoon of olive oil until it bubbles. 4. Add the bread crumbs and cook for almost 5 minutes, stirring, until they are browned and crunchy. Remove from this pan and set aside, scraping this pan clean. 5. Return this skillet to medium-high heat and add the rest tablespoon of olive oil. 6. Season the fish with the rest ½ teaspoon of sea salt and ¼ teaspoon of pepper. Place the fish in this skillet. Cook for almost 5 minutes per side until opaque. 7. To assemble, spoon the tomatoes onto four plates. Top with the pollock and sprinkle with the bread crumbs. Garnish with parsley and serve.
Per Serving: Calories 248; Total Fat 17g; Sodium 207mg; Total Carbs 43.7g; Fiber 3g; Sugars 6g; Protein 11g

Homemade Cioppino

Prep time: 10 minutes | Cook time: 15 minutes | Serves: 8

2 tablespoons extra-virgin olive oil
1 onion, chopped
1 fennel bulb, chopped
6 garlic cloves, minced
½ cup dry white wine
2 (32-ounce) cans tomato sauce
2 cups unsalted chicken broth
1-pound shrimp, peeled, deveined, and tails removed

1-pound cod, cut into bite-size pieces
1-pound salmon, skin removed, cut into bite-size pieces
2 tablespoons Italian seasoning
½ teaspoon sea salt
⅛ teaspoon red pepper flakes
⅛ teaspoon freshly ground black pepper
¼ cup chopped fresh basil leaves

1. Heat the olive oil in a large pot over medium-high heat, until the oil shimmers. 2. Add the onion, and fennel, and sauté them for 5 minutes until they are soft. 3. Add the garlic, and sauté for 30 seconds. 4. Stir in the wine, and cook for 1 minute, constantly stirring. 5. Add the tomato sauce, broth, shrimp, cod, salmon, Italian seasoning, red pepper flakes, sea salt, and pepper, bring to a simmer; reduce the heat to medium-low, and cook the food for 5 minutes more until the fish and shrimp are opaque, occasionally stirring.
Per Serving: Calories 260; Total Fat 6.81g; Sodium 1244mg; Total Carbs 14.23g; Fiber 6.1g; Sugars 8.45g; Protein 36.25g

Halibut en Papillote with Capers

Prep time: 10 minutes | Cook time: 15 minutes | Serves: 4

4 (6-ounce) halibut fillets
2 tablespoons olive oil
½ teaspoon sea salt
¼ teaspoon black pepper
⅛ teaspoon crushed red pepper flakes
2 garlic cloves, sliced
1 cup grape tomatoes, halved

¼ cup chopped onion
2 tablespoons capers, drained
8 kalamata olives, pitted and quartered
2 tablespoons plus 2 teaspoons dry white wine
8 fresh thyme sprigs

1. Cut 4 (15-inch) squares of parchment paper or aluminum foil. Set aside. 2. At 450 degrees F, preheat your oven. 3. Brush the halibut with olive oil and sprinkle with sea salt, pepper, and red pepper flakes. Place each fillet on a parchment square. 4. Layer the fillets with garlic, tomatoes, onion, capers, and olives. Fold into packets, leaving the tops open. 5. Add 2 teaspoons of white wine to each packet and a thyme sprig. 6. Seal the packets and keep them on a rimmed baking sheet. Bake for almost 8 minutes until the fish is opaque. Serve immediately.
Per Serving: Calories 318; Total Fat 7.5g; Sodium 541mg; Total Carbs 24.8g; Fiber 2.5g; Sugars 3.8g; Protein 36g

Seafood Paella

Prep time: 10 minutes | Cook time: 35 minutes | Serves: 4

1 tablespoon olive oil
8 ounces' chicken andouille sausage links, sliced
1 small onion, diced
4 garlic cloves, minced
1 (12-ounce) can of roasted red bell peppers, drained and chopped
1 (15-ounce) can of diced tomatoes
2 cups uncooked arborio rice
1 teaspoon paprika
½ teaspoon ground turmeric
Pinch saffron threads
Sea salt

Black pepper
4 cups chicken broth
½ teaspoon red pepper flakes
1½ to 2 pounds' mussels, scrubbed and debearded
1-pound littleneck clams, soaked for at least 20 minutes and scrubbed
1-pound large shrimp (31/35 count), peeled and deveined
½ cup frozen peas
¼ cup chopped fresh Italian parsley
Lemon wedges, for serving

1. In a suitable sauté pan, heat the olive oil over medium heat. 2. Add the sausage and cook for 3 to 5 minutes. 3. Add the onion, garlic, and roasted red peppers and sauté for almost 5 minutes. 4. Add the tomatoes and cook for 1 to 2 minutes to blend the ingredients. 5. Add the rice and sauté for 1 minute. 6. Add the paprika, turmeric, and saffron and season with salt and black pepper. Sauté for 1 minute. 7. Add the broth and red pepper flakes and increase the heat to medium-high to bring the prepared mixture to a boil. 8. Reduce its heat to low, cover the pan, and simmer for 20 minutes until the liquid has been almost completely absorbed. 9. Add the mussels, clams, shrimp, and peas. Cover and increase the heat to medium. Cook for almost 10 minutes until the seafood is just cooked through. 10. Discard any clams or mussels that don't open after 10 minutes of cooking. 11. Garnish with the parsley and serve with lemon wedges alongside.

Per Serving: Calories 528; Total Fat 28.2g; Sodium 152mg; Total Carbs 4.1g; Fiber 0.8g; Sugars 0.1g; Protein 66.8g

Cod with Tomatoes and Garlic

Prep time: 10 minutes | Cook time: 20 minutes | Serves: 4

1-pound cod or your favorite white-fleshed fish
Sea salt
Black pepper
2 tablespoons olive oil
2 garlic cloves, minced

1 (15-ounce) can of diced tomatoes
¼ cup white wine
¼ cup chopped fresh Italian parsley

1. Pat the codfish fillet dry with paper towels and season with black pepper and salt. 2. In the skillet, preheat the olive oil over medium heat. 3. Add the cod to the skillet, and sear for 6 to 10 minutes, flipping halfway through. 4. Transfer the cooked fish to a plate, cover loosely with aluminum foil, and set aside. 5. Add the garlic to this skillet and sauté until fragrant, about 3 minutes. 6. Add the tomatoes and wine and increase the heat to medium-high. 7. Cook the tomato mixture for almost 4 minutes. Season with black pepper and salt. 8. Return the fish to this skillet and spoon the tomato mixture over it. 9. Serve garnished with the parsley.
Per Serving: Calories 359; Total Fat 24.7g; Sodium 177mg; Total Carbs 2.2g; Fiber 0.1g; Sugars 0.2g; Protein 29.8g

Cod with Spinach-Artichoke Spread

Prep time: 10 minutes | Cook time: 15 minutes | Serves: 4

4 tablespoons olive oil
4 (5-ounce) fresh or thawed frozen cod fillets
1 jalapeño pepper, seeded and chopped
1 (15-ounce) can of artichoke hearts, drained and chopped
1 (10-ounce) bag frozen spinach, thawed and drained

2 cups plain full-fat Greek yogurt
1½ cups grated parmesan cheese
1 (8-ounce) package of cream cheese
2 tablespoons unsalted butter
3 garlic cloves, minced
7 kalamata olives, pitted and chopped

1. Heat 2 tablespoons of olive oil in a suitable skillet over medium heat. Add the cod and cook for 4 to 5 minutes on each side until white and opaque throughout. 2. Keep this seared fish on a plate, then cover with aluminum foil to keep it warm and set aside. 3. Preheat the rest 2 tablespoons of olive oil over medium-high heat in the same skillet. Add the jalapeño and sauté for 3 to 4 minutes until fragrant. Add the artichoke hearts, spinach, yogurt, parmesan, cream cheese, butter, garlic, and olives and cook, frequently stirring, until the cheese has melted, 3 to 4 minutes. Simmer for 3 minutes more, then Now remove it from the heat. 4. Place a cod fillet on each of the four plates and spoon the artichoke mixture evenly over each piece of fish. 5. Serve.
Per Serving: Calories 354; Total Fat 19.3g; Sodium 851mg; Total Carbs 2.7g; Fiber 0.7g; Sugars 0.2g; Protein 40.9g

Mediterranean Shrimp Stir-Fry

Prep time: 10 minutes | Cook time: 10 minutes | Serves: 4

¼ cup lemon juice
¼ cup olive oil
½ teaspoon onion powder
½ teaspoon garlic powder
14 ounces' medium shrimp (36/40 count), peeled and deveined
½ onion, chopped
2 zucchinis, sliced into ½-inch pieces
½ bunch asparagus, woody ends trimmed, chopped

1 tomato, chopped
1 garlic clove, minced
1½ teaspoons dried basil
½ teaspoon dried oregano
¼ teaspoon sea salt
¼ teaspoon black pepper
Dash red pepper flakes
½ cup kalamata olives pitted
¼ cup crumbled feta cheese for topping

1. Stir together the lemon juice, olive oil, onion powder, and garlic powder in a suitable bowl. Add the shrimp, mix well, and cover with plastic wrap. Marinate in the refrigerator for 10 minutes. 2. Heat a suitable skillet over medium-high heat. Add the marinated shrimp (discard the marinade) and cook for 3 to 5 minutes until pink. 3. Remove the cooked shrimp with a spoon and set it aside in a suitable bowl. 4. In the same skillet, sauté the onion over medium-high heat for 3 minutes. Add the zucchini, asparagus, tomato, garlic, basil, oregano, salt, black pepper, and red pepper flakes, and cook for 2 to 3 minutes. 5. Return the shrimp to this skillet, add the olives, and stir to mix. 6. Serve topped with the feta.
Per Serving: Calories 290; Total Fat 15.6g; Sodium 539mg; Total Carbs 2.8g; Fiber 1.3g; Sugars 1.1g; Protein 33.4g

Shrimp Saganaki

Prep time: 10 minutes | Cook time: 25 minutes | Serves: 4

1-pound medium shrimp (36/40 count), peeled and deveined	Black pepper
½ cup plus 1 tablespoon olive oil	½ cup chopped onion
½ cup white wine	1 tomato, diced
Zest of 1 lemon	½ cup crumbled feta cheese
2 garlic cloves, minced	¼ cup chopped fresh Italian parsley
Sea salt	

1. At 400 degrees F, preheat your oven. 2. Stir together the shrimp, ½ cup of olive oil, the wine, lemon zest, and garlic in a suitable bowl. 3. Season with black pepper and salt and set aside. 4. Preheat the rest 1 tablespoon of olive oil in a Dutch oven over medium heat. 5. Stir in the onion and sauté for almost 5 minutes or until softened. Add the tomato and the shrimp mixture and cook for 3 minutes. 6. Transfer the Dutch oven to the oven and bake for 7 minutes until cooked through. Remove from the oven, top with the feta, and bake for 1 to 2 minutes. 7. Garnish with the parsley and serve.
Per Serving: Calories 285; Total Fat 19.6g; Sodium 658mg; Total Carbs 1.5g; Fiber 0.4g; Sugars 0.2g; Protein 25.7g

Mediterranean Mackerel Pasta

Prep time: 10 minutes | Cook time: 15 minutes | Serves: 4

2 tablespoons extra-virgin olive oil	3 cups water
2 garlic cloves, minced	½ cup pitted green olives
4 ounces canned mackerel, skinless and boneless	Sea salt
½ teaspoon chili flakes	Black pepper
8 ounces dried whole-grain linguine noodles	2 tablespoons freshly squeezed lemon juice
	¼ cup fresh parsley, finely chopped

1. In a suitable saucepan with a lid, warm the olive oil over medium-high heat. 2. Toss in the garlic to the hot oil and cook until fragrant, 1 to 2 minutes. 3. Break the mackerel into pieces, add the mackerel and chili flakes and stir until warmed through. 4. Add the pasta and water to the saucepan. Cover and cook to a boil and cook the pasta for 8 to 10 minutes, stirring to keep the pasta from sticking. 5. Add a splash of water if the pasta seems too dry, or use a spoon to remove excess water once the pasta is cooked through. 6. Stir in the olives and season with black pepper and salt to taste. Mix well. 7. Divide between 4 plates, sprinkle with the lemon juice and garnish with the fresh parsley.
Per Serving: Calories 268; Total Fat 12.1g; Sodium 169mg; Total Carbs 4.5g; Fiber 1.8g; Sugars 2.7g; Protein 34.2g

Mediterranean Trout

Prep time: 10 minutes | Cook time: 20 minutes | Serves: 4

2 cups basil leaves	4 trout fillets (about 5 ounces each)
Juice of ½ lemon	
2 garlic cloves	2 cups canned artichoke hearts, drained, rinsed, and chopped
¼ cup hemp hearts	
¼ teaspoon sea salt	½ cup assorted olives
¼ cup olive oil	4 tomatoes, chopped

1. At 450 degrees F, preheat your oven. 2. Layer a suitable rimmed baking sheet with parchment paper. 3. Mix the basil, lemon juice, garlic, hemp hearts, salt, and olive oil in a food processor. Pulse until smooth. 4. Place the prepared fillets on the prepared baking sheet, and arrange the artichoke hearts, olives, and tomatoes on this baking sheet. 5. Top each fillet with a generous amount of the basil mixture. 6. Bake the fillets for almost 15 minutes or until the trout is thoroughly cooked. 7. Serve warm.
Per Serving: Calories 473; Total Fat 18g; Sodium 744mg; Total Carbs 4.8g; Fiber 1.1g; Sugars 0.9g; Protein 69.5g

Steamed Mussels with Chorizo

Prep time: 10 minutes | Cook time: 15 minutes | Serves: 4

1 tablespoon olive oil	1 tomato, chopped
8 ounces cured (Spanish) chorizo, sliced	2 tablespoons unsalted butter
1 onion, chopped	½ cup white wine
3 garlic cloves, diced	1 pound mussels, scrubbed and debearded
1 teaspoon ground cumin	½ cup chopped fresh cilantro for garnish
1 teaspoon sea salt	

1 lemon, cut into wedges, for serving

1. In a Dutch oven, preheat the olive oil over medium heat. 2. Stir in the chorizo and cook for almost 2 minutes. 3. Toss in the onion, garlic, cumin, and salt and sauté for 5 minutes. 4. Add the tomato and cook for 3 minutes. Add the butter and cook until it has melted about 1 minute. 5. Pour in the wine and adjust the heat to medium-high. 6. Add the mussels and cook for 5 to 8 minutes. Discard any unopened mussels. 7. Evenly divide the mussels, chorizo, and broth among four bowls. 8. Garnish with cilantro and lemon wedges.
Per Serving: Calories 419; Total Fat 9g; Sodium 425mg; Total Carbs 1.8g; Fiber 0.9g; Sugars 1g; Protein 33.3g

Fish Tacos

Prep time: 10 minutes | Cook time: 20 minutes | Serves: 4

1-pound cod, cut into 1-inch chunks	Sea salt
Zest and juice of 1 lime	Black pepper
2 tablespoons olive oil	2 cups chopped cabbage
¼ teaspoon chili powder	¼ cup chopped fresh cilantro
¼ teaspoon ground cumin	½ cup plain full-fat Greek yogurt
	8 (6-inch) corn or flour tortillas

1. In a suitable bowl, stir together the cod, half the lime juice, 1 tablespoon of olive oil, the chili powder, and the cumin. Season with black pepper and salt and set aside. 2. In a suitable bowl, mix the rest lime juice, the cabbage, and the cilantro and set aside. 3. Stir together the yogurt and lime zest in a suitable bowl, season with black pepper and salt, and set aside. 4. Heat a suitable skillet over medium-high heat. Working in batches, warm the tortillas for 2 minutes per side. Wrap in a clean kitchen cloth or place in a tortilla warmer to keep them warm; set aside. 5. Preheat the rest 1 tablespoon of olive oil in the same skillet over medium-high heat. Add the cod and cook for 4 to 6 minutes until cooked through. 6. Divide the cooked fish evenly among the tortillas and top each with the cabbage mixture and yogurt sauce. Serve.
Per Serving: Calories 313; Total Fat 22.1g; Sodium 660mg; Total Carbs 3.4g; Fiber 1.4g; Sugars 1.2g; Protein 26.1g

Fish Stew

Prep time: 10 minutes | Cook time: 35 minutes | Serves: 4

2 tablespoons olive oil	¼ teaspoon saffron threads
2 ounces' pancetta, cubed	4 cups of fish stock
2 tomatoes on the vine, diced	2 cups water
1 onion, chopped	1 russet potato, peeled and cubed
1 leek, sliced	½ teaspoon red pepper flakes
3 garlic cloves, minced	1 bay leaf
1 tablespoon tomato paste	2 pounds prepackaged mixed seafood or your favorite fish, cut into 1-inch chunks
Sea salt	
Black pepper	

1. In a Dutch oven, preheat the olive oil over medium-high heat. 2. Add this pancetta, tomatoes, onion, leek, garlic, and tomato paste and sauté for 5 minutes—season with salt and black pepper. Add the saffron and sauté for 30 seconds. 3. Add the fish stock, water, potato, red pepper flakes, and bay leaf, and bring the prepared mixture to a boil. Reduce its heat to low and cook until the potato is tender, 15 to 20 minutes. 4. Increase the heat to medium, and add the fish; simmer the fish for 5 to 10 minutes until cooked through. 5. Remove the bay leaf and serve.
Per Serving: Calories 284; Total Fat 11.7g; Sodium 415mg; Total Carbs 1.8g; Fiber 0.6g; Sugars 0.4g; Protein 40.9g

Sauerkraut-Crusted Salmon

Prep time: 10 minutes | Cook time: 15 minutes | Serves: 2

¼ cup sauerkraut	2 (6-ounce) salmon fillets
2 tablespoons whole-grain Dijon mustard	Sea salt
2 teaspoons olive oil	Black pepper

1. At 375 degrees F, preheat your oven. 2. In a suitable bowl, mix the sauerkraut and mustard. 3. In a skillet, warm 1 teaspoon of olive oil over high heat. 4. Spread the sauerkraut mixture on one side of each salmon fillet and cook the fillets, sauerkraut-side down, in this skillet for 8 minutes. 5. Flip the fillets, and transfer them to a baking dish. Bake the fillets in the oven for an additional 8 minutes. 6. Remove the salmon from the oven and cool for 5 minutes before plating and serving with your side of choice. Add salt and pepper to taste.
Per Serving: Calories 299; Total Fat 16.4g; Sodium 697mg; Total Carbs 2.2g; Fiber 1.1g; Sugars 0.7g; Protein 34.6g

Foil-Baked Fish

Prep time: 10 minutes | Cook time: 20 minutes | Serves: 4

4 (5-ounce) cod or other white-fleshed fish fillets
2 to 3 tablespoons olive oil
2 to 3 garlic cloves, minced

1 tablespoon lemon juice
Sea salt
Black pepper

1. At 400 degrees F, preheat your oven. 2. Cut 4 (12-inches) squares of aluminum foil and lay them on a clean work surface. 3. Pat the fish dry with paper towels and place one fillet on each sheet of foil. 4. Mix the olive oil, garlic, and lemon juice in a suitable bowl and season with black pepper and salt. 5. Brush the prepared oil mixture over both sides of the fish. Fold the foil over the fish to enclose it and crimp the edges of the foil to seal. 6. Place the foil packets on a suitable baking sheet and bake for 15 to 20 minutes; the fish should flake easily with a fork when cooked. 7. Remove from the oven and serve. Tell your guests to be careful of the hot steam when opening their packets.
Per Serving: Calories 251; Total Fat 12.1g; Sodium 683mg; Total Carbs 1g; Fiber 0.6g; Sugars 0g; Protein 33.1g

Whitefish and Rice

Prep time: 10 minutes | Cook time: 15 minutes | Serves: 4

1½ cups whole-grain basmati rice, rinsed
2¼ cups water
2 cups cherry tomatoes, chopped
1 tablespoon apple cider vinegar
1 cup chopped basil leaves

½ cup kalamata olives
½ teaspoon sea salt
½ teaspoon black pepper
2 haddock fillets, cut into thirds
2 cups baby spinach leaves

1. In a suitable pot with a lid, mix the rice and water over high heat. Cover and cook to a boil; lower the heat and simmer the rice. 2. Mix the tomatoes, vinegar, ½ cup of basil leaves, olives, salt, and pepper in a suitable bowl. 3. Arrange the fish pieces over the rice after simmering for a few minutes. Pour the tomato-basil mixture over the fillet pieces and cover. Simmer for 10 minutes. 4. Add the spinach leaves in an even layer over the fillets, and simmer for 5 minutes longer, adding more water if necessary. 5. Garnish with the rest basil leaves and serve.
Per Serving: Calories 229; Total Fat 9.7g; Sodium 98mg; Total Carbs 0.9g; Fiber 0.3g; Sugars 0.1g; Protein 32.9g

Shrimp Pasta

Prep time: 10 minutes | Cook time: 15 minutes | Serves: 4

8 ounces dried whole-grain fettuccine
1-pound shrimp, peeled and deveined
¼ teaspoon sea salt

⅓ cup pesto
Juice of 1 lemon
¼ teaspoon red chili flakes
2 tablespoons finely chopped fresh parsley

1. In a suitable saucepan, cook the pasta according to the package directions. Save ½ cup of the pasta water before draining the finished pasta. 2. Cook the pasta until al dente. Set aside. 3. In a suitable skillet over medium heat, warm the ½ cup of reserved pasta water. Add the shrimp to this pan and cook for almost 2 minutes per side, or until the shrimp is no longer translucent. 4. Season with salt. 5. Mix the pasta, cooked shrimp, pesto, lemon juice, chili flakes, and parsley in a suitable bowl, and stir well to mix.
Per Serving: Calories 384; Total Fat 21.4g; Sodium 165mg; Total Carbs 3.1g; Fiber 0.6g; Sugars 2g; Protein 42.2g

Tuna Salad Chard Wrap

Prep time: 10 minutes | Cook time: 0 | Serves: 2

½ cucumber, seeded and diced
2 scallions, green and white parts, diced
½ cup cherry tomatoes halved
¼ cup chopped Kalamata olives

1 can tuna (packed in water), drained
¼ cup sumac dressing
4 rainbow Swiss chard leaves

1. Mix the cucumber, scallions, cherry tomatoes, olives, and tuna in a suitable bowl. 2. Drizzle the dressing into the bowl and stir well to mix and evenly coat the tuna salad. 3. Scoop out ¼ of the salad and place it on each rainbow chard leaf. 4. Roll the leaf slowly to wrap the salad within, or keep the leaf open for a tuna salad chard boat.
Per Serving: Calories 415; Total Fat 23.1g; Sodium 691mg; Total Carbs 6.7g; Fiber 2.3g; Sugars 2.3g; Protein 44.7g

Baked Fish with Olives

Prep time: 10 minutes | Cook time: 12 minutes | Serves: 4

2 tablespoons olive oil
½ onion, chopped
2 shallots, diced
4 garlic cloves, minced
1 (28-ounce) can of diced tomatoes, drained
Sea salt
Black pepper

1-pound cod or other white-fleshed fish
½ cup chopped pitted kalamata olives
¼ cup crumbled feta cheese for topping
¼ cup chopped fresh Italian parsley (optional)

1. At 375 degrees F, preheat your oven. 2. In a suitable oven-safe skillet, preheat the olive oil over medium-high heat. Add the onion, shallots, and garlic, and sauté for 5 to 6 minutes, until softened. 3. Stir in the tomatoes and season with black pepper and salt—Cook with occasional stirring for 4 minutes. 4. Place the fish on the tomato mixture and evenly sprinkle with the olives and feta. Transfer this skillet to the oven and bake for 15 to 20 minutes until cooked through. 5. Garnish with the parsley. 6. Enjoy.
Per Serving: Calories 313; Total Fat 11.5g; Sodium 46mg; Total Carbs 27.9g; Fiber 2.2g; Sugars 0.1g; Protein 22.3g

Shrimp Skewers

Prep time: 10 minutes | Cook time: 6 minutes | Serves: 4

¼ cup olive oil
Zest and juice of 1 lemon
1 tablespoon dried oregano
¼ teaspoon red pepper flakes (optional)

Sea salt
Black pepper
1-pound medium shrimp (36/40 count), peeled and deveined

1. If desired, stir together the olive oil, lemon zest, oregano, and red pepper flakes in a suitable bowl. Add salt and black pepper, and then add the shrimp, mix well. 2. Use plastic wrap to cover the bowl, and place it in the refrigerator to refrigerate the mixture for 15 minutes. 3. Remove the bowl from the refrigerator and thread the shrimp onto skewers. Discard any remaining marinade. 4. Heat a suitable skillet over medium heat. Place the skewers in this skillet and sear the shrimp for 3 to 4 minutes per side until just cooked through. 5. Drizzle with the lemon juice and serve.
Per Serving: Calories 399; Total Fat 27.5g; Sodium 32mg; Total Carbs 45g; Fiber 3.8g; Sugars 38.8g; Protein 3.1g

Cod and Potatoes

Prep time: 10 minutes | Cook time: 30 minutes | Serves: 4

4 cups chicken broth
1 pound of baby red potatoes, quartered
¼ cup chopped onion
3 garlic cloves, minced

Sea salt
Black pepper
4 (5-ounce) cod fillets
2 large eggs
Juice of 1 lemon

1. In a suitable stockpot, bring the broth to a boil over high heat. 2. Add the potatoes, onion, garlic, black pepper, and salt. 3. Cover the pot, reduce its heat to low, and simmer for 15 minutes. Add the cod and simmer for 7 to 10 minutes more until cooked through. 4. Beat eggs with lemon juice in the bowl. 5. While whisking continuously, slowly add 1 cup of the hot broth to the bowl with the egg mixture and beat for a few sec more to temper the egg mixture. 6. Pour the prepared mixture from the bowl back into the stockpot and stir to mix. 7. Serve.
Per Serving: Calories 219; Total Fat 9.8g; Sodium 548mg; Total Carbs 12g; Fiber 6.2g; Sugars 1.1g; Protein 22.8g

White Beans with Shrimp

Prep time: 10 minutes | Cook time: 15 minutes | Serves: 4

3 tablespoons olive oil
½ onion, diced
4 garlic cloves, minced
1 (15-ounce) can of diced tomatoes
2 (15-ounce) cans of white beans,

drained
½ to ¾ cup of water
1-pound medium shrimp (36/40 count), peeled and deveined
¼ cup chopped fresh Italian parsley

1. In a skillet, preheat the olive oil over medium-high heat. 2. Stir in the onion and garlic and sauté for 4 minutes. 3. Add tomatoes and cook for almost 2 minutes. 4. Add the beans and water, and bring to a simmer. 5. Add the shrimp and simmer for 3 to 4 minutes, until the shrimp are just cooked through. 6. Serve garnished with the parsley.
Per Serving: Calories 257; Total Fat 10.7g; Sodium 402mg; Total Carbs 0.9g; Fiber 0.4g; Sugars 0.5g; Protein 37.1g

Chapter 4 Meat Recipes

Sirloin Steak with Vegetable Mix

Prep time: 20 minutes | Cook time: 8 minutes | Serves: 4

12 ounces' boneless top sirloin steak, about 1-inch thick, trimmed of visible fat
1 tablespoon olive oil, divided
Sea salt
Freshly ground black pepper

1 yellow bell pepper, thinly sliced
1 red bell pepper, thinly sliced
1 orange bell pepper, thinly sliced
1 small red onion, thinly sliced
4 garlic cloves, crushed
Juice of 1 lemon

1. Preheat your oven. 2. Lightly grease both sides of the steak with 1 teaspoon of olive oil, then season with salt and pepper; arrange the steak to the baking sheet. 3. In a suitable bowl, mix up the onion, garlic, bell peppers and the remaining olive oil, then season with the salt and pepper as well; spread the mixture around the steak. 4. Broil the steak and vegetable mixture for 8 minutes until the steak is done to your liking, turning the steak halfway through cooking. 5. When the time is up, remove the baking sheet from the oven and let the steak rest for 10 minutes. 6. Slice thinly on the bias against the steak's grain and drizzle the vegetable mixture with lemon juice, enjoy.
Per Serving: Calories 236; Total Fat 13.17g; Sodium 631mg; Carbs 10.69g; Fiber 13.17g; Sugar 1.67g; Protein 19.21g

Delicious Pork Tenderloin Marsala

Prep time: 10 minutes | Cook time: 20 minutes | Serves: 4

4 (3-ounce) boneless pork loin chops, trimmed
Sea salt
Freshly ground black pepper
¼ cup whole-wheat flour
1 tablespoon olive oil
2 cups sliced button mushrooms

½ sweet onion, chopped
1 teaspoon minced garlic
½ cup Marsala wine
½ cup low-sodium chicken stock
1 tablespoon cornstarch
1 tablespoon chopped fresh parsley

1. Lightly season the pork chops with the salt and pepper. 2. In a plate, pour in the flour and coat both sides of the pork chops, then shake off the excess. 3. In a suitable bowl, stir together the chicken stock and cornstarch until smooth. 4. In your skillet, heat the olive oil over medium-high heat; cook the pork chops for 10 minutes until cooked through and browned, turning once halfway through cooking; when cooked, transfer the pork chops to a clean plate. 5. Still in the skillet, add the garlic, onion, and mushrooms, and sauté for 5 minutes until the vegetables are tender; stir in the wine, scraping up any bits from the skillet, and bring the liquid to a simmer; add the stock mixture and bring to boil; cook the sauce for 4 minutes until slightly thickened, stirring occasionally. 6. Serve the pork chops with the sauce and garnish with the fresh parsley.
Per Serving: Calories 119; Total Fat 5.29g; Sodium 607mg; Carbs 11.78g; Fiber 1.4g; Sugar 2.54g; Protein 6.88g

Grilled Lemon Pork Tenderloin

Prep time: 10 minutes | Cook time: 20 minutes | Serves: 4

¼ cup olive oil
¼ cup chopped fresh rosemary
Juice of 1 lemon
Juice and zest of 1 lime
1 teaspoon minced garlic

1 teaspoon ground cumin
Sea salt
12 ounces' boneless pork tenderloin

1. In a suitable bowl, add the olive oil, rosemary, lemon juice, lime juice, lime zest, garlic, and cumin and salt, whisk well; add the pork tenderloin and coat with the mixture; cover the bowl and refrigerate the coated pork tenderloin for 1 hour. 2. Preheat your grill to medium-high heat. 3. Grill the tenderloin for 15 to 20 minutes until it reaches the internal temperature of 140 degrees F, turning several times and basting with the remaining marinade during cooking. 4. When cooked, take out the pork tenderloin and cover it with foil; let it rest for 10 minutes before serving.
Per Serving: Calories 261; Total Fat 17.44g; Sodium 1089mg; Carbs 2.57g; Fiber 0.4g; Sugar 0.51g; Protein 23.16g

Roasted Lamb Chops with Fresh Cilantro

Prep time: 2 minutes | Cook time: 10 minutes | Serves: 4

4 (4-ounce) loin lamb chops with bones, trimmed
Sea salt
Freshly ground black pepper

1 tablespoon olive oil
2 tablespoons Sriracha sauce
1 tablespoon chopped fresh cilantro

1. Preheat oven to 450 degrees F. 2. Lightly season lamb chops with salt and pepper. 3. In your skillet, heat the olive oil over medium-high heat; add the lamb chops and brown them on both sides, about 2 minutes per side, then spread the chops with sriracha. 4. Transfer the lamb chops to the baking sheet and then roast them in the oven for 4 to 5 minutes, until they reach the desired doneness. 5. When cooked, top with the fresh cilantro and serve.
Per Serving: Calories 269; Total Fat 21.48g; Sodium 721mg; Carbs 4.25g; Fiber 0.5g; Sugar 2.93g; Protein 5.24g

Greek Herbed Beef Meatballs

Prep time: 10 minutes | Cook time: 20 minutes | Serves: 4

pound extra-lean ground beef
½ cup panko breadcrumbs
¼ cup grated Parmesan cheese
¼ cup low-fat milk
2 large eggs
1 tablespoon chopped fresh

parsley
1 teaspoon chopped fresh oregano
1 teaspoon minced garlic
¼ teaspoon freshly ground black pepper
Sea salt

1. Preheat oven to 400 degrees F. 2. In a suitable bowl, add the ground beef, breadcrumbs, Parmesan cheese, milk, eggs, parsley, oregano, garlic, pepper and combine well, then lightly season with salt. 3. Form 1-inch meatballs from the beef mixture and then arrange them on the baking sheet. 4. Bake the meatballs for 20 minutes until they are cooked through and browned, flipping them several times during cooking. Serve with a sauce such as Speedy Marinara Sauce or stuffed into a pita.
Per Serving: Calories 343; Total Fat 21.57g; Sodium 1218mg; Carbs 1.18g; Fiber 0.2g; Sugar 0.12g; Protein 33.26g

Roasted Pork Loin with Gremolata

Prep time: 15 minutes | Cook time: 40 minutes | Serves: 4-6

1 cup water
to 4-pound boneless pork loin roast
2 tablespoons extra-virgin olive oil, plus more to oil the roasting pan

1½ teaspoons salt
½ teaspoon freshly ground black pepper
¼ teaspoon ground nutmeg
1 recipe Gremolata

1. Preheat an oven to 400 degrees F. 2. Oil a roasting pan large enough to hold the pork roast and then add 1 cup water to it. 3. Place the pork loin roast on the pan; rub the pork loin roast with the olive oil, season with the salt, pepper and then top with the nutmeg. 4. Roast the pork loin roast in your oven for 40 minutes, or until a meat thermometer reads 150°F; when the time is up, remove the pan from oven and let stand for 10 to 15 minutes. 5. Cut the pork roast into ¼-inch slices and arrange on a platter. Spoon the Gremolata over the top, or serve it on the side. 6. Roast pork can be stored in refrigerator for about 1 week. Gremolata will last 1 week in the refrigerator or a few months in the freezer.
Per Serving: Calories 443; Total Fat 17.03g; Sodium 738mg; Carbs 0.38g; Fiber 0.1g; Sugar 0.0.4g; Protein 67.81g

Marsala Pork Chops

Prep time: 10 minutes | Cook time: 20 minutes | Serves: 4

4 thick pork chops
2½ teaspoons salt, divided
½ teaspoon freshly ground black pepper
¼ teaspoon ground cinnamon
2 tablespoons extra-virgin olive oil, plus more to oil the pan

2 shallots, thinly sliced
¾ cup chicken or beef broth
⅓ cup Marsala wine
6 dried figs, stems cut off, cut in half
1 tablespoon chopped fresh flat leaf parsley

1. Sprinkle the pork chops with the pepper, cinnamon and 1½ teaspoons of salt. 2. In your skillet, heat the olive oil over high heat; add the seasoned pork chops and cook 4 minutes per side until they are golden on both sides; remove the chops and set aside. 3. Still in the skillet, add the shallots and sauté for 5 minutes until they begin to brown; add the broth, wine, figs and the remaining salt and bring to a boil; reduce the heat and simmer the liquid; return the pork chops and cover the skillet, cook the pork chops for 3 to 5 minutes more until cooked through. 4. Arrange the chops on a serving platter and top them with the Marsala sauce; garnish with the parsley. Enjoy. 5. The leftover can be kept in the refrigerator for up to 5 days.
Per Serving: Calories 410; Total Fat 20.56g; Sodium 1665mg; Carbs 13.47g; Fiber 1.7g; Sugar 6.66g; Protein 41.28g

Lamb Meatballs

Prep time: 15 minutes | Cook time: 15 minutes | Serves: 4

1 pound ground lamb	½ teaspoon ground cumin
3 scallions, thinly sliced	¼ teaspoon red pepper flakes
2 garlic cloves, minced	(optional)
3 tablespoons rice flour	¼ teaspoon freshly ground black
1 egg	pepper
1 teaspoon dried oregano	Oil to coat the baking sheet
1 teaspoon salt	

1. Preheat an oven to 400 degrees F. 2. In a suitable bowl, mix up the ground lamb, scallions, garlic, rice flour, egg, oregano, salt, cumin, pepper and red pepper flakes (optional). 3. Oil the rimmed baking sheet. Scoop the meatballs with a 1-ounce ice cream scoop and then place them on the oiled baking sheet; leave about 1 inch around each meatball on the sheet so they brown nicely. 4. Bake the meatballs for 12 to 15 minutes or until they are firm. Serve and enjoy. 5. These meatballs can be stored in refrigerator for 1 week or frozen for several months.

Per Serving: Calories 284; Total Fat 16.68g; Sodium 673mg; Carbs 7.46g; Fiber 0.5g; Sugar 0.38g; Protein 26.01g

Delectable Stuffed Peppers

Prep time: 15 minutes | Cook time: 45 minutes | Serves: 6

3 tablespoons extra-virgin olive oil	¼ teaspoon freshly ground black pepper
1 large white onion, chopped	2 cups cooked rice
½ pound ground lamb	1 (7.5-ounce) can tomato sauce
½ pound ground beef	2 tablespoons chopped fresh flat
1 tablespoon chopped sun-dried tomatoes (optional)	leaf parsley
1 garlic clove, minced	6 large green bell peppers, tops removed and reserved, seeds
1 teaspoon salt	discarded
1 teaspoon dried oregano	1 cup chicken broth or water

1. Preheat your oven to 350 degrees F. 2. In your skillet, add the olive oil, onion and sauté for 5 to 7 minutes over high heat, or until the onion begins to brown; add the lamb, beef and cook until there is no pink left; drain any liquid from the pan; add the garlic, oregano, tomato sauce, salt, black pepper, rice and parsley, cook for 1 to 2 minutes until the sauce thickened. 3. Set the filling aside and let it sit for 10 to 15 minutes before stuffing the peppers. 4. Fill the prepared peppers with the filling and then place them in a 9-by-13-inch roasting pan; cover each pepper with its half and then carefully pour the water or broth in the pan. 5. Bake the stuffed peppers for 30 minutes or until they are soft. Let them sit for 10 minutes before serving. 6. Cooked peppers can be stored in the refrigerator for 1 week or frozen for several months.

Per Serving: Calories 421; Total Fat 25.03g; Sodium 712mg; Carbs 28.55g; Fiber 10.3g; Sugar 4.91g; Protein 32.88g

Flavorful Pork with Tzatziki on Pita Bread

Prep time: 90 minutes | Cook time: 20 minutes | Serves: 4-6

For the Pita Bread

1 cup lukewarm water	divided, plus extra for kneading
1 package dry active yeast	and rolling
½ teaspoon sugar	1 teaspoon salt
1 cup whole-wheat flour, divided	2 tablespoons extra-virgin olive
1¾ cups all-purpose flour,	oil

For the Souvlaki

1½ pounds pork shoulder, cut into	1 garlic clove, minced
1-inch pieces	1 teaspoon salt
¼ cup extra-virgin olive oil	1 teaspoon dried oregano
2 tablespoons red wine vinegar	6 to 8 skewers

To Assemble the Sandwiches

½ red onion, thinly sliced	1 tablespoon minced fresh
1 large ripe tomato, thinly sliced	oregano
1 recipe Tzatziki	

Make the Pita Bread: 1. In a bowl, add the sugar, yeast, and water in a medium bowl and then stir to combine; add ¼ cup of whole-wheat flour and ¼ cup all-purpose flour, whisk until smooth; let the mixture rest for 15 minutes in a warm spot. 2. Add the salt, olive oil, ¾ cup of all-purpose flour and the remaining ¾ cup of whole-wheat flour, mix until the mixture begins to turn into a wet sticky dough. Gradually add more all-purpose flour and knead the dough until it becomes soft and sticky. 3. On a clean work surface, lightly sprinkle

some flour and knead the dough on it until the dough is smooth, elastic and slightly sticky. 4. Place the dough back to the bowl and cover with plastic wrap, then leave it in a warm spot for 1 hour to double in bulk. 5. When the dough has risen, flatten it and cut it into 6 equal pieces, then shape each piece into ball; cover the balls with plastic wrap and let them stand for 10 minutes. 6. Preheat your oven to 425 degrees F; place a large heavy-duty baking sheet in the hot oven. While the baking sheet is heating, roll each piece of dough into a flat round, about ⅛-inch thick. 7. Remove the hot baking sheet, quickly place 3 rolled pitas on the sheet and return the sheet to the oven. After 2 to 3 minutes, the dough should puff up; flip the pitas and resume cooking for an additional 2 to 3 minutes. Remove the cooked pitas to a towel-lined plate to keep them warm. 8. Repeat the process with the remaining pita breads.

Make the Souvlaki: 1. In a bowl, add the pork shoulder pieces and coat it with the olive oil, red wine vinegar, garlic, salt, and oregano; cover the bowl and let them marinate at least 30 minutes or longer. 2. Preheat your grill to high. 3. Thread the meat on skewers. Place the meat skews on the grill and cook for 3 to 4 minutes on each side until golden brown on all sides.

Assemble the Sandwiches: 1. Prepare a serving plate and then place a warm pita on it. 2. Remove the souvlaki from a skewer and place it on top of the pita bread. 3. Top with red onions, tomatoes, Tzatziki and garnish with oregano. Serve and enjoy.

Per Serving: Calories 575; Total Fat 26.96g; Sodium 988mg; Carbs 45.78g; Fiber 4g; Sugar 1.69g; Protein 35.73g

Mediterranean Lamb Stew with Lemon Zest

Prep time: 15 minutes | Cook time: 4 hours | Serves: 4-6

3 pounds' lamb stew meat	1 bay leaf
2 onions, chopped	1½ teaspoons dried oregano
2 garlic cloves, minced	1½ teaspoons ground cumin
3 tablespoons extra-virgin olive oil	1 teaspoon salt
1 (28-ounce) can crushed tomatoes	½ teaspoon freshly ground black pepper
1 cup red wine	1 cinnamon stick
1 (5-ounce) can tomato paste	3 tablespoons honey
½ cup chopped dried apricots	2 tablespoons orange zest
	¼ cup chopped fresh cilantro

1. In a slow cooker, add Place the lamb, onions, garlic, olive oil, tomatoes, wine, tomato paste, apricots, bay leaf, oregano, cumin, salt, pepper, cinnamon stick, and honey; stir to combine and the cover the cooker; cook the food on high heat for 4 hours. 2. When the time is up, stir in the orange zest and cilantro; serve and enjoy. 3. This meal can be stored in the refrigerator for 1 week or in freezer for several months.

Per Serving: Calories 432; Total Fat 23.19g; Sodium 886mg; Carbs 31.22g; Fiber 5.7g; Sugar 23.79g; Protein 27.18g

Beef Stuffed Cabbage Rolls

Prep time: 15 minutes | Cook time: 33 minutes | Serves: 4

1 head green cabbage	1 teaspoon ground cinnamon
pound lean ground beef	2 tablespoons chopped fresh mint
½ cup long-grain brown rice	Juice of 1 lemon
4 garlic cloves, minced	Olive oil cooking spray
1 teaspoon salt	½ cup beef broth
½ teaspoon black pepper	1 tablespoon olive oil

1. Cut the cabbage in half and remove the core. Keep 12 of the larger leaves to use for the cabbage rolls. 2. Boil a large pot of salted water; drop the cabbage leaves into the hot water and boil them for 3 minutes; remove the cabbage leaves from the water and set aside for later use. 3. In a large bowl, mix up the ground beef, rice, garlic, salt, pepper, cinnamon, mint, and lemon juice until combined; divide this mixture into 12 equal portions. 4. Preheat your air fryer to 360 degrees F. Lightly coat a small casserole dish with olive oil cooking spray. 5. On the clean work surface, arrange the cabbage neatly; add a spoonful of the beef mixture on one side of the leaf and then fold the two perpendicular sides inward and then roll forward, tucking tightly as rolled; repeat the same steps to make the other rolls. 6. Place the finished rolls into the baking dish, you can stack them on top of each other if the baking dish is not large enough; pour the beef broth over the top of the cabbage rolls so that it soaks down between them, and then brush the tops with the olive oil. 7. Bake the rolls for 30 minutes at 360 degrees F.

Per Serving: Calories 546; Total Fat 25.58g; Sodium 751mg; Carbs 23.35g; Fiber 1.5g; Sugar 0.69g; Protein 52.68g

Fried Steak with Salsa Verde

Prep time: 10 minutes | Cook time: 20 minutes | Serves: 4

2 (18-ounce) bone-in rib eye steaks, about 1½ inches thick
2 tablespoons extra-virgin olive oil
1½ teaspoons salt
½ teaspoon freshly ground black pepper
1 recipe Salsa Verde

1. Preheat your oven to 400 degrees F. 2. Rub the steaks with the olive oil and sprinkle with salt and pepper. 3. Heat your skillet over high heat; when heated, there should be no more water in the skillet; add the steaks and cook them for 3 to 4 minutes or until they are a golden brown on each side. 4. Place the steaks on a rimmed baking sheet and slide it into the oven. Cook them 10 minutes for rare or 15 minutes for medium. 5. Remove the steaks from the oven and let them rest 10 to 15 minutes; slice the steaks and serve with the Salsa Verde. 6. The steaks can be kept for 5 days in the refrigerator.
Per Serving: Calories 625; Total Fat 50.93g; Sodium 1120mg; Carbs 0.74g; Fiber 0.1g; Sugar 0.5g; Protein 40.92g

Beef Stew with Mushrooms

Prep time: 10 minutes | Cook time: 4 minutes | Serves: 4-6

3 tablespoons extra-virgin olive oil
2 pounds' beef stew meat
4 ounces' pancetta or bacon, diced
1½ teaspoons salt
½ teaspoon freshly ground black pepper
2 leeks, root and top trimmed,
thinly sliced
2 cloves garlic, thinly sliced
2 large zucchinis, cut into 1-inch slices
1 pound mushrooms, halved
1 tablespoon tomato paste
1 teaspoon herbes de Provence
2 cups red wine

1. In the slow cooker, add the olive oil, beef, pancetta or bacon, salt, pepper, leeks, garlic, zucchini, mushrooms, tomato paste, herbes de Provence, and red wine, stir gently to combine; cover the cooker and cook the food on high heat for 4 hours. 2. When the time is up, you can serve. 3. This dish can be stored in the refrigerator for 1 week or frozen for several months. It's best to freeze soups and stews in single or double servings for easier thawing.
Per Serving: Calories 428; Total Fat 16.47g; Sodium 1490mg; Carbs 9.87g; Fiber 2g; Sugar 3.84g; Protein 59.72g

Beef Stew with Orange Slice

Prep time: 15 minutes | Cook time: 4 hours 10 minutes | Serves: 4-6

2 tablespoons extra-virgin olive oil
3 pounds' beef stew meat
2 teaspoons salt, divided
¼ teaspoon freshly ground black pepper
1 large white onion, sliced
1 pound small whole mushrooms
2 large carrots, peeled and cut into 1-inch pieces
1 cup orange juice
Zest of 1 orange
2 garlic cloves, minced
1 (6-ounce) can tomato paste
¼ cup balsamic or red wine vinegar
3 tablespoons honey
2 teaspoons dried cumin
2 teaspoons dried oregano
½ teaspoon ground allspice
1 orange, sliced
¼ cup fresh chopped flat leaf parsley

1. Season the beef stew meat with 1 teaspoon of salt and pepper. 2. In your skillet, heat the olive oil over high heat and then place the seasoned meat in. Being careful not to crowd the meat (you cook the meat in batches), brown the meat for about 2 to 3 minutes on each side. 3. Transfer the browned meat in the slow cooker; add the onion, mushrooms, carrots, orange juice, orange zest, garlic, tomato paste, vinegar, honey, cumin, oregano, allspice and the remaining salt, then cover the cooker and cook on high heat for 4 hours. 4. When cooked, serve the stew to your dinnerware, garnish with the orange slices and parsley. 5. This dish can be stored for 1 week in the refrigerator or frozen for several months. Freeze it in single or double portions for easy thawing and serving.
Per Serving: Calories 349; Total Fat 21.85g; Sodium 1461mg; Carbs 36.43g; Fiber 6.1g; Sugar 23.87g; Protein 6.06g

Cheesy Lamb Pita Breads with Nuts

Prep time: 15 minutes | Cook time: 25 minutes | Serves: 4

1 tablespoon extra-virgin olive oil
1 small onion, chopped
1 garlic clove, chopped
pound ground lamb
1 teaspoon ground cumin
½ teaspoon ground cinnamon
½ cup tomato sauce
¼ cup raisins
1 teaspoon salt
¼ teaspoon red pepper flakes
(optional)
4 whole-wheat pita breads
¼ cup toasted pine nuts (pignoli)
2 ounces' feta cheese, crumbled
¼ cup chopped fresh flat leaf parsley

1. Preheat your oven to 375 degrees F. 2. In your skillet, heat the olive oil over high heat; add the garlic, onion and sauté for 5 minutes until soft; add the lamb and cook for 5 minutes or until there is no pink on the meat; add the cumin, cinnamon, raisins, tomato sauce, salt and red pepper flakes, simmer the food for 5 minutes more or until most of the liquid in the tomato sauce has evaporated. 3. Arrange the pita breads on the large baking sheet and divide the lamb mixture among the four pita breads; top each pita with pine nuts, feta, and parsley. 4. Bake the pita breads for about 10 minutes until cooked through and toast the pita. Serve immediately. 5. The lamb filling can be made several days ahead. Keep in an airtight container in the refrigerator.
Per Serving: Calories 452; Total Fat 25.4g; Sodium 1396mg; Carbs 26.91g; Fiber 5.3g; Sugar 5.7g; Protein 30.59g

Roasted Lamb Kofta with Mint-Yogurt Sauce

Prep time: 40 minutes | Cook time: 10 minutes | Serves: 6

For the Kofta
1 pound ground lamb
¼ cup fresh parsley, roughly chopped
2 garlic cloves, minced
¼ white onion, diced
1 teaspoon salt
1 teaspoon ground cumin
½ teaspoon black pepper
¼ teaspoon ground cinnamon
¼ teaspoon ground allspice
¼ teaspoon cayenne pepper
¼ teaspoon ground ginger
3 tablespoons olive oil, divided

For the Mint-Yogurt Sauce
1 cup nonfat plain Greek yogurt
½ cup fresh mint, chopped
1 garlic clove, minced
2 tablespoons lemon juice
½ teaspoon ground cumin
¼ teaspoon cayenne pepper
¼ teaspoon salt
¼ teaspoon black pepper

To Make the Kofta: 1. Preheat the air fryer to 360 degrees F. 2. In a large bowl, add the ground lamb with the parsley, garlic, onion, all the spices and 2 tablespoons of olive oil, then mix them until well combined and the spices are distributed evenly. 3. Form the mixture into 4 equal long ovals, brush them with the remaining olive oil and then place them in the baking sheet that fits your air fryer. 4. Cook the food for 10 minutes at 360 degrees F, or until the internal temperature reaches 145°F.
To Make the Mint-Yogurt Sauce: 1. While the kofta is cooking, mix together the ingredients in a bowl to make the mint-yogurt sauce. 2. Enjoy each kofta with dipping them into the mint-yogurt sauce.
Per Serving: Calories 266; Total Fat 17.94g; Sodium 552mg; Carbs 3.57g; Fiber 0.5g; Sugar 1.62g; Protein 22.98g

Herb-Roasted Pork Tenderloins

Prep time: 5 minutes | Cook time: 25 minutes | Serves: 6

Nonstick cooking spray
2 medium pork tenderloins (10 to 12 ounces each)
½ teaspoon freshly ground black pepper
½ teaspoon kosher or sea salt
¼ cup 2% plain Greek yogurt
1 tablespoon chopped fresh rosemary
Tzatziki yogurt sauce from store-bought tzatziki sauce
1 to 2 tablespoons chopped fresh mint (optional)

1. Preheat the oven to 500°F. 2. Line a large, rimmed baking sheet with aluminum foil. Place a wire cooling rack on the aluminum foil, and spray the rack with nonstick cooking spray. 3. Place the pork tenderloins on the wire rack, folding under any skinny ends of the meat to ensure even cooking; sprinkle them with the pepper and salt. 4. In a small bowl, mix up the yogurt and rosemary, then rub the pork tenderloins with the yogurt mixture over all sides. 5. Roast the seasoned pork tenderloins on the wire rack for 10 minutes; turn over both pieces of pork and roast for 10 to 12 minutes longer, or until each of them reaches an internal temperature of 145°F and the juices run clear. Remove the pork from the rack and place on a clean cutting board. Let rest for 5 minutes before slicing them. 6. While roasting the pork tenderloins, make the tzatziki yogurt sauce, you can add fresh mint to the sauce. 7. Serve the sauce with the pork.
Per Serving: Calories 211; Fats 6.06g; Sodium 307mg; Carbs 0.85g; Fiber 0.2g; Sugar 0.5g; Protein 36.03g

Prosciutto and Fresh Mozzarella Burgers

Prep time: 15 minutes | Cook time: 10 minutes | Serves: 4

8 slices country Italian bread or ciabatta rolls, cut in half	drained and sliced 2 cups arugula
½ cup Pesto	1 teaspoon salt
2 tablespoons red wine vinegar	¼ teaspoon red pepper flakes (optional)
6 ounces' prosciutto, thinly sliced	
½ pound fresh mozzarella,	

1. On a clean work surface, arrange the bread slices in a single layer; spread the pesto on all bread slices. 2. Sprinkle vinegar on 4 bread slices, apportion the prosciutto between the 4 bread slices, place the mozzarella on the top of prosciutto; top each bread slice with the arugula, sprinkle each bread slice with the salt and red pepper flakes. 3. Cover these 4 bread slices with the other 4 bread slices. 4. Transfer these burgers to your skillet and cook them until the bread slices are golden down, the arugulas are welted and the cheeses are melted. Serve immediately.
Per Serving (including the red pepper flakes): Calories 490; Total Fat 29.96g; Sodium 1559mg; Carbs 23.88g; Fiber 2.6g; Sugar 1.77g; Protein 31.85g

Lamb Mint Buns

Prep time: 15 minutes | Cook time: 15 minutes | Serves: 4

8 small round dinner rolls or mini hamburger buns	¼ teaspoon freshly ground black pepper
2 pounds ground lamb	½ cup mayonnaise
1 garlic clove, minced	2 tablespoons chopped fresh mint
1 tablespoon balsamic vinegar	8 slices Roma tomatoes
1 teaspoon salt	8 thin slices red onion

1. Cut each roll in half. 2. In a medium bowl, mix up the lamb, garlic, vinegar, salt, pepper and then shape the mixture into 8 small patties. 3. Heat a stovetop grill and then place the patties in it without crowding; cook for 3 to 4 minutes on each side until both sides are dark golden. 4. When cooked, let the patties rest and during the time, stir the mayonnaise together with the mint in a suitable bowl. 5. Spread the mint mixture on both sides of each bun; place one lamb patty on the bottom side of each bun and top with the red onion slices and tomato. Enjoy. 6. The lamb patties can be mixed and formed 1 day ahead and stored in refrigerator, or frozen longer, uncooked. Thaw before cooking the burgers. The mint mayonnaise can be made 1 day ahead and refrigerated.
Per Serving: Calories 701; Total Fat 40.4g; Sodium 1238mg; Carbs 33.42g; Fiber 5.3g; Sugar 7.15g; Protein 53.31g

Pomegranate-Glazed Lamb Shanks with Vegetables

Prep time: 15 minutes | Cook time: 6 hours | Serves: 4-6

4 lamb shanks, about 1 pound each	2 garlic cloves, minced
2 teaspoons salt	2 tablespoons extra-virgin olive oil
1 teaspoon paprika	1 cup pomegranate juice
½ teaspoon freshly ground black pepper	¼ cup honey
1 onion, chopped	1 tablespoon orange zest
2 carrots, peeled and chopped	¼ cup chopped fresh flat leaf parsley

1. In a slow cooker, add the lamb shanks and season with the paprika, salt and pepper; add the carrots, onion, garlic, olive oil, pomegranate juice and honey, mix well. 2. Cover the cooker and cook the food on low heat for 6 hours. 3. When the time is up, add the orange zest and parsley; serve and enjoy. 4. Lamb shanks can be stored in the refrigerator for 1 week or in the freezer for several months. For easier defrosting, it's best to remove the meat from the bone before freezing.
Per Serving: Calories 471; Total Fat 13.67g; Sodium 1082mg; Carbs 21.34g; Fiber 1.3g; Sugar 18.47g; Protein 67.52g

Cheesy Beef Stuffed Peppers

Prep time: 10 minutes | Cook time: 30 minutes | Serves: 4

1 pound lean ground beef	½ yellow onion, diced
½ cup cooked brown rice	2 tablespoons fresh oregano, chopped
2 Roma tomatoes, diced	1 teaspoon salt
3 garlic cloves, minced	

½ teaspoon black pepper	4 ounces' goat cheese
¼ teaspoon ground allspice	¼ cup fresh parsley, chopped
2 bell peppers, halved and seeded	

1. Preheat your air fryer to 360 degrees F. 2. In a large bowl, mix up the ground beef with the rice, tomatoes, garlic, onion, oregano, salt, pepper and allspice. 3. Apportion the beef mixture equally between the halved bell peppers and top each with about ¼ of the goat cheese. 4. Place the peppers into the air fryer basket in a single layer, making sure that they don't touch each other; bake them for 30 minutes at 360 degrees F. 5. When cooked, top the stuffed peppers with fresh parsley before serving.
Per Serving: Calories 492; Total Fat 23.66g; Sodium 780mg; Carbs 26.63g; Fiber 3g; Sugar 4.28g; Protein 42.25g

Homemade Moussaka

Prep time: 25 minutes | Cook time: 85 minutes | Serves: 8

For the Eggplant

2 pounds' eggplant, cut into ¼-inch-thick slices	2 to 3 tablespoons extra-virgin olive oil
1 teaspoon salt	

For the Filling

1 tablespoon extra-virgin olive oil	¼ cup tomato paste
2 shallots, diced	1 cup low-sodium beef broth
1 tablespoon dried, minced garlic	2 bay leaves
1 pound ground lamb	2 teaspoons dried oregano
4 ounces portobello mushrooms, diced	¾ teaspoon salt
1 (14.5-ounce) can crushed tomatoes, drained	2½ cups store-bought béchamel sauce
	⅓ cup panko bread crumbs

To Make the Eggplant: 1. Preheat the oven to 450°F. 2. Line a large baking sheet with paper towels and then arrange the eggplant slices in a single layer on the paper towels, then sprinkle them with salt. Place another layer of paper towels on the eggplant slices. Continue until all eggplant slices are covered. 3. Let the eggplant sweat for 30 minutes to remove excess moisture. 4. Pat the eggplant dry. Dry and brush a baking sheet with oil and place the eggplant slices on the baking sheet. 5. Bake the eggplant slices in the preheated oven for 15 to 20 minutes, or until lightly browned and tender. Remove from oven and cool slightly before assembling the moussaka.
To Make the Filling: 1. In the skillet, heat the olive oil over high heat, add the shallots, garlic and cook them for 2 minutes, until starting to soften; add the ground lamb and brown it, breaking it up as it cooks; add the mushrooms and cook for 5 to 7 minutes, or until they have dehydrated slightly. 2. Add the tomatoes and paste, oregano, beef broth, bay leaves, and salt and stir to combine. Once the sauce comes to a boil, reduce to medium-low and cook for 15 minutes, or until it reduces to a thick sauce. 3. Remove the sauce to a separate bowl before assembly. 4. Lower the temperature to 350°F. 5. Place half of the eggplant slices in the bottom of skillet used to make the sauce. Top the slices with all the meat filling. 6. Place the remaining eggplant on top of the meat filling and pour the jarred béchamel sauce over the eggplant. Sprinkle with the bread crumbs. 7. Bake the food for 30 to 40 minutes or until golden brown. 8. Let the dish rest for 10 minutes before serving.
Per Serving: Calories 269; Fats 10.74g; Sodium 1246mg; Carbs 31.04g; Fiber 8.2g; Sugar 10.47g; Protein 17.7g

Spicy Turkey Meatballs

Prep time: 5 minutes | Cook time: 12 minutes | Serves: 4

1 pound ground turkey	1 teaspoon salt
1 egg	½ teaspoon garlic powder
¼ teaspoon red pepper flakes	½ teaspoon onion powder
¼ cup whole wheat bread crumbs	½ teaspoon black pepper

1. Preheat the air fryer to 360 degrees F. 2. In a bowl, combine all the ingredients and mix well; divide the mixture into 12 portions and then shape each portion into a ball. 3. Arrange the balls to the air fryer basket, making sure that they don't touch each other; air fry these meatballs at 360 degrees F for 10 to 12 minutes, until the meatballs are cooked through and browned. 4. When the time is up, serve and enjoy.
Per Serving: Calories215; Total Fat 10.11g; Sodium 713mg; Carbs 5.97g; Fiber 0.5g; Sugar 0.64g; Protein 24.77g

Mediterranean Lamb Bowl with Feta Cheese

Prep time: 15 minutes | Cook time: 10 minutes | Serves: 2

2 tablespoons extra-virgin olive oil
¼ cup diced yellow onion
1 pound ground lamb
1 teaspoon dried mint
1 teaspoon dried parsley
½ teaspoon red pepper flakes
¼ teaspoon garlic powder
1 cup cooked rice
½ teaspoon za'atar seasoning
½ cup halved cherry tomatoes
1 cucumber, peeled and diced
1 cup store-bought hummus
1 cup crumbled feta cheese
2 pita breads, warmed (optional)

1. In the skillet, heat olive oil over medium heat and add the onion, cook for 2 minutes, until fragrant; then add lamb and mix well, breaking up the meat when you cook. 2. Halfway through the cooking, add mint, parsley, red pepper flakes, and garlic powder. 3. In a medium bowl, mix up the cooked rice and za'atar, then apportion them into individual bowls; add the seasoned lamb, and top the bowls with tomatoes, cucumber, hummus, feta, and pita (optional).
Per Serving: Calories 1218; Fats 74.72g; Sodium 1445mg; Carbs 81.31g; Fiber 19.3g; Sugar 8.21g; Protein 74.72g

Roasted Rib Eye Steak with Onions

Prep time: 5 minutes | Cook time: 10 minutes | Serves: 4

pound rib eye steak, cubed
2 garlic cloves, minced
2 tablespoons olive oil
1 tablespoon fresh oregano
1 teaspoon salt
½ teaspoon black pepper
1 yellow onion, thinly sliced

1. Preheat your air fryer to 380 degrees F. 2. In a medium bowl, add the steak, garlic, olive oil, oregano, salt, pepper, and onion, mix until all of the beef and onion are well coated. 3. Arrange the seasoned steak mixture to the air fryer basket. Roast them at 380 degrees F for 10 minutes, stirring halfway through. 4. Let rest for 5 minutes and then you can enjoy this meal with some favorite sides.
Per Serving: Calories 371; Total Fat 30.6g; Sodium 648mg; Carbs 3.82g; Fiber 0.9g; Sugar 1.21g; Protein 20.83g

Onion Lamb Burger

Prep time: 15 minutes | Cook time: 15 minutes | Serves: 4

1 pound ground lamb
½ small red onion, grated
1 tablespoon dried parsley
1 teaspoon dried oregano
1 teaspoon ground cumin
1 teaspoon garlic powder
½ teaspoon dried mint
¼ teaspoon paprika
¼ teaspoon kosher salt
⅛ teaspoon freshly ground black
pepper
Extra-virgin olive oil, for panfrying
4 pita breads, for serving (optional)
Tzatziki Sauce, for serving (optional)
Pickled Onions, for serving (optional)

1. In a bowl, mix up the lamb, cumin, onion, parsley, oregano, paprika, garlic powder, mint, salt, and pepper. Form 4 small balls from the meat mixture and work into smooth discs. 2. In the skillet, heat a drizzle of olive oil over medium heat and then reduce the heat to medium. Then cook the patties for 4 to 5 minutes on each side, until cooked through and the juices run clear. 3. Enjoy lamb burgers in pitas, topped with tzatziki sauce and pickled onions (optional).
Per Serving: Calories 239; Fats 15.37g; Sodium 213mg; Carbs 2.03g; Fiber 0.5g; Sugar 0.44g; Protein 23.47g

Creamy Lamb Sausage Pasta

Prep time: 15 minutes | Cook time: 25 minutes | Serves: 4

3 thick lamb sausages, casing removed and chopped
1 teaspoon garlic powder
1 medium shallot, chopped
1 pound bean-based penne pasta
1½ cups diced baby portobello mushrooms
1 (14.5-ounce) can crushed tomatoes
1 tablespoon extra-virgin olive oil
4 medium Roma tomatoes, chopped
3 tablespoons heavy cream

1. In the skillet, add the lamb sausages and cook for 5 minutes over medium-high heat, stirring and breaking up the lamb sausage, until it is half cooked. 2. Reduce the heat to medium-low and add the shallot, cook for 3 minutes, until they're soft; add the mushrooms, garlic powder, olive oil and cook them for about 5 to 7 minutes, or until the mushrooms have reduced in size by half and all the water has been cooked out. 3. Cook the chopped and canned tomatoes for 7 to 10 minutes, and until the liquid thickens slightly. Lower the heat and add the cream, mixing well. 4. Boil a large pot of water and then cook the pasta according package directions, until fully cooked. Drain and set aside. 5. Plate the pasta first and top with the sausage mixture.
Per Serving: Calories 653; Fats 41.03g; Sodium 327mg; Carbs 16.77g; Fiber 6.8g; Sugar 8.45g; Protein 54.79g

Carrot Lamb Stew

Prep time: 10 minutes | Cook time: 20 minutes | Serves: 6

1 pound bone-in or boneless lamb leg steak, center cut
1 tablespoon extra-virgin olive oil
1 cup chopped onion (about ½ onion)
½ cup diced carrot (about 1 medium carrot)
1 teaspoon ground cumin
½ teaspoon ground cinnamon
¼ teaspoon kosher or sea salt
4 garlic cloves, minced (about 2 teaspoons)
2 tablespoons tomato paste
1 tablespoon chopped canned chipotle pepper in adobo sauce
2 cups water
½ cup chopped prunes
1 (15-ounce) can chickpeas, drained and rinsed
2 tablespoons freshly squeezed lemon juice (from 1 small lemon)
¼ cup chopped unsalted pistachios
Cooked couscous or bulgur, for serving (optional)

1. Slice the meat into 1-inch cubes and then pat them dry with a few paper towels. 2. In a large stockpot, heat the oil over medium-high heat; add the lamb and any bone, cook for 4 minutes, stirring only after allowing the meat to brown on one side; when cooked, transfer the lamb to a plate. 3. Still in the stockpot, add the onion, carrot, cumin, cinnamon, salt and cook them for 6 minutes, stirring occasionally; push the vegetables to the edge of the pot, add the garlic and cook for 1 minute, stirring constantly; add the tomato paste, chipotle pepper and cook for 1 minute more, stirring constantly while blending and mashing the tomato paste into the vegetables. 4. Return the lamb to the pot along with the water and prunes; increase the heat to high, and bring to a boil; reduce the heat to medium-low and cook for 5 to 7 minutes more, until the stew thickens slightly. Stir in the chickpeas and cook for 1 minute. 5. Remove the stew from the heat, and stir in the lemon juice. Sprinkle the pistachios on top and serve over couscous (optional).
Per Serving: Calories 294; Fats 9.55g; Sodium 250mg; Carbs 32.58g; Fiber 4.8g; Sugar 4.27g; Protein 22.25g

Pork Tenderloin with Pitas

Prep time: 15 minutes | Cook time: 35 minutes | Serves: 8

For the Shawarma Spice Rub
1 teaspoon ground cumin
1 teaspoon ground coriander
1 teaspoon ground turmeric
¾ teaspoon sweet Spanish paprika
½ teaspoon ground cloves
¼ teaspoon salt
¼ teaspoon freshly ground black pepper
⅛ teaspoon ground cinnamon
For the Shawarma
1½ pounds pork tenderloin
3 tablespoons extra-virgin olive oil
1 tablespoon garlic powder
Salt
Freshly ground black pepper
1½ tablespoons Shawarma Spice Rub
4 pita pockets, halved, for serving
1 to 2 tomatoes, sliced, for serving
¼ cup pickled onions, for serving
¼ cup pickled turnips, for serving
¼ cup store-bought hummus or garlic-lemon hummus

To Make the Shawarma Seasoning: In a small bowl, mix up the cumin, coriander, turmeric, paprika, cloves, salt, pepper, and cinnamon. Set aside for later use.
To Make the Shawarma: 1. Preheat the oven to 400°F. 2. Put the pork tenderloin on a plate, rub it with the garlic powder, olive oil, salt and pepper and a generous amount of shawarma spices on both sides. 3. Arrange the pork tenderloin to the roasting pan and roast for 20 minutes per pound, or until the meat begins to bounce back as you poke it. If it feels like there's still fluid under the skin, continue cooking. Check every 5 to 7 minutes until it reaches the desired tenderness and juices run clear. 4. Remove the pork from the oven and let rest for 10 minutes. 5. Serve the pork tenderloin shawarma with pita pockets, tomatoes, Pickled Onions (if using), Pickled Turnips (if using), and hummus.
Per Serving: Calories 208; Fats 6.54g; Sodium 1122mg; Carbs 12.32g; Fiber 2.2g; Sugar 0.55g; Protein 24.66g

Roasted Dijon Pork Tenderloin

Prep time: 15 minutes | Cook time: 40 minutes | Serves: 8

1½ tablespoons extra-virgin olive oil
1 (12-ounce) pork tenderloin
¼ teaspoon kosher salt
¼ teaspoon freshly ground black pepper
¼ cup apple jelly
¼ cup apple juice
2 to 3 tablespoons Dijon mustard
½ tablespoon cornstarch
½ tablespoon cream

1. Preheat the oven to 325°F. 2. In the skillet, heat the olive oil over medium heat; add the pork tenderloin and sear it on all sides; once seared, transfer it to the baking sheet and sprinkle with salt and pepper. 3. In the same skillet, with the juices from the pork, mix the apple jelly, juice, and mustard into the pan juices. Heat them thoroughly over low heat, stirring consistently for 5 minutes. Spoon over the pork in the baking sheet. 4. Put the pork in the oven and roast it for 15 to 17 minutes, or 20 minutes per pound. Every 10 to 15 minutes, baste the pork with the apple-mustard sauce. 5. When done, let the pork tenderloin rest for 15 minutes before cutting it into 1-inch slices. 6. In a small pot, blend the cornstarch with cream, heat over low heat; add the pan juices into the pot, stirring for 2 minutes, until thickened. 7. Serve the sauce over the pork.
Per Serving: Calories 123; Fats 6.27g; Sodium 231mg; Carbs 3.58g; Fiber 0.9g; Sugar 1.66g; Protein 12.82g

Honey Pork Chops

Prep time: 15 minutes | Cook time: 20 minutes | Serves: 4

4 pork chops, boneless or bone-in
¼ teaspoon salt
⅛ teaspoon freshly ground black pepper
3 tablespoons extra-virgin olive oil
5 tablespoons low-sodium chicken broth, divided
6 garlic cloves, minced
¼ cup honey
2 tablespoons apple cider vinegar

1. Season the pork chops with salt and pepper. Set aside. 2. In the skillet, heat the oil over medium-high heat, add the seasoned pork chops, sear them for 5 minutes on each side, or until golden brown. 3. Once the searing is complete, move the pork to a dish and reduce the skillet heat from medium-high to medium; add 3 tablespoons of chicken broth to the pan; this will loosen the bits and flavors from the bottom of the skillet. 4. Once the broth has evaporated, add the garlic and cook for 15 to 20 seconds, until fragrant; add the honey, vinegar, and the remaining broth, then increase the heat to medium-high and continue to cook the liquid for 3 to 4 minutes. 5. Stir periodically; the sauce is ready once it's thickened slightly. Add pork chops back into the pan, cover them with the sauce, and cook for 2 minutes. 6. Serve and enjoy.
Per Serving: Calories 343; Fats 11.24g; Sodium 346mg; Carbs 19.31g; Fiber 0.2g; Sugar 17.51g; Protein 39.92g

Flank Steak with Artichokes and Onion

Prep time: 15 minutes | Cook time: 65 minutes | Serves: 4-6

4 tablespoons grapeseed oil, divided
2 pounds' flank steak
1 (14-ounce) can artichoke hearts, drained and chopped
1 onion, diced
8 garlic cloves, chopped
1 (32-ounce) container low-sodium beef broth
1 (14.5-ounce) can diced
tomatoes, drained
1 cup tomato sauce
2 tablespoons tomato paste
1 teaspoon dried oregano
1 teaspoon dried parsley
1 teaspoon dried basil
½ teaspoon ground cumin
3 bay leaves
2 to 3 cups cooked couscous (optional)

1. Preheat the oven to 450°F. 2. In the skillet, heat 3 tablespoons of oil over medium heat; add the steak and sear it for 2 minutes per side, then transfer the steak to the baking pan and cook in oven for 30 minutes, or until desired tenderness. 3. While cooking the steak, in a large pot, mix up the remaining 1 tablespoon of oil, artichoke hearts, onion, and garlic; pour in the beef broth, tomatoes, tomato sauce, and tomato paste; stir in oregano, parsley, basil, cumin, and bay leaves. 4. Cover the pot and cook the vegetables for 30 minutes. Remove bay leaf and serve with flank steak and ½ cup of couscous per plate, if using.
Per Serving: Calories 551; Fats 21.09g; Sodium 834mg; Carbs 46.63g; Fiber 7.7g; Sugar 9.78g; Protein 44.66g

Beef Meatballs

Prep time: 10 minutes | Cook time: 20 minutes | Serves: 4

¼ cup finely chopped onion (about ⅛ onion)
¼ cup raisins, coarsely chopped
1 teaspoon ground cumin
½ teaspoon ground cinnamon
¼ teaspoon smoked paprika
1 large egg
pound ground beef (93% lean)
⅓ cup panko bread crumbs
1 teaspoon extra-virgin olive oil
1 (28-ounce) can low-sodium or no-salt-added crushed tomatoes
Chopped fresh mint, feta cheese, and/or fresh orange or lemon wedges, for serving (optional)

1. In a large bowl, mix up the onion, raisins, cumin, cinnamon, smoked paprika, and egg; add the ground beef and bread crumbs and mix gently with your hands. Apportion the mixture into 20 even portions, then wet your hands and roll each portion into a ball. 2. In the skillet, heat the oil over medium-high heat; add the meatballs and cook them for 8 minutes, rolling around every minute or so with tongs or a fork to brown them on most sides. 3. Transfer the meatballs to a paper towel–lined plate. Drain the fat out of the pan, and carefully wipe out the hot pan with a paper towel. 4. Return the meatballs to the skillet, and pour the tomatoes over the meatballs. Cover and cook on medium-high heat until the sauce begins to bubble. Lower the heat to medium, cover partially, and cook the food for 7 to 8 more minutes, until the meatballs are cooked through. 5. Garnish with fresh mint, feta cheese, and/or a squeeze of citrus, if desired, and serve.
Per Serving: Calories 308; Fats 14.96g; Sodium 117mg; Carbs 10.14g; Fiber 4.5g; Sugar 5.9g; Protein 32.99g

Beef Feta Pitas

Prep time: 10 minutes | Cook time: 15 minutes | Serves: 4

3 teaspoons extra-virgin olive oil, divided
pound ground beef (93% lean)
2 garlic cloves, minced (about 1 teaspoon)
2 (6-ounce) bags baby spinach, chopped (about 12 cups)
½ cup crumbled feta cheese (about
2 ounces)
⅓ cup ricotta cheese
½ teaspoon ground nutmeg
¼ teaspoon freshly ground black pepper
¼ cup slivered almonds
4 (6-inch) whole-wheat pita breads, cut in half

1. In the skillet, heat 1 teaspoon of oil over medium heat, add the ground beef and cook for 10 minutes, breaking it up with a wooden spoon and stirring occasionally. Remove from the heat and drain in a colander. Set aside for later use. 2. Still in the skillet, heat the remaining oil; add the garlic and cook for 1 minute, stirring constantly; add the spinach and cook for 2 to 3 minutes, or until the spinach has cooked down, stirring often. 3. Turn off the heat and mix in the feta cheese, ricotta, nutmeg, and pepper. Stir until all the ingredients are well incorporated. Mix in the almonds. 4. Divide the beef filling among the eight pita pocket halves to stuff them and serve.
Per Serving: Calories 437; Fats 21.89g; Sodium 455mg; Carbs 20.01g; Fiber 3.9g; Sugar 1.46g; Protein 40.18g

Mediterranean Chimichurri Skirt Steak

Prep time: 10 minutes | Cook time: 15 minutes | Servings: 4

¾ cup fresh mint
¾ cup fresh parsley
⅔ cup olive oil
⅓ cup lemon juice
Zest of 1 lemon
2 tablespoons dried oregano
4 garlic cloves, peeled
½ teaspoon red pepper flakes
½ teaspoon kosher salt
1 to 1½ pounds skirt steak, cut in half if more extended than a grill pan

1. Add the mint, parsley, olive oil, lemon juice, lemon zest, oregano, garlic, red pepper flakes, and salt to the blender. Process until the prepared mixture reaches your desired consistency—from slightly chunky to smooth purée. Remove a half cup of the chimichurri mixture and set aside. 2. Pour the chimichurri mixture into a suitable bowl or zip-top bag, and add the steak. Mix them well, and then marinate the steak for at least 30 minutes, and spend up to 8 hours in the refrigerator. 3. Cook the steak for 4 minutes on each side (for medium-rare) in the grill pan over medium-high heat—Cook for 2 minutes per side for medium. 4. Place the steak on a cutting board, tent it with foil to keep it warm, and let it rest for 10 minutes. 5. Slice the steak crosswise against the grain and serve with the reserved sauce.
Per Serving: Calories 434; Total Fat 16.8g; Sodium 152mg; Total Carbs 1.9g; Fiber 0.4g; Sugars 0.8g; Protein 64.8g

Mini Greek Beef Muffins

Prep time: 10 minutes | Cook time: 25 minutes | Serves: 6

Nonstick cooking spray
1 tablespoon extra-virgin olive oil
½ cup minced onion (about ¼ onion)
1 garlic clove, minced (about ½ teaspoon)
1 pound ground beef (93% lean)
½ cup whole-wheat bread crumbs
½ cup crumbled feta cheese (about 2 ounces)
1 large egg
½ teaspoon dried oregano, crushed between your fingers
¼ teaspoon freshly ground black pepper
½ cup 2% plain Greek yogurt
⅓ cup chopped and pitted Kalamata olives
2 tablespoons olive brine
Romaine lettuce or pita bread, for serving (optional)

1. Preheat the oven to 400°F. Coat a 12-cup muffin pan with nonstick cooking spray and set aside. 2. In a small skillet, heat the oil over medium heat; add the onion and cook for 4 minutes, stirring frequently; add the garlic and cook for 1 minute longer, stirring frequently. Remove from the heat. 3. In a large mixing bowl, add the ground beef, onion, garlic, bread crumbs, feta, egg, oregano, and pepper, then gently mix them together with your hands. 4. Divide the meat mixture among the muffin cups. Cook them the preheated oven for 18 to 20 minutes, or until they reach an internal temperature of 160°F. 5. While cooking the beef muffins, in a small bowl, add the yogurt, olives, and olive brine, mix them well. 6. Place the beef muffins on a serving platter and spoon the olive-yogurt sauce on top. You can also serve them on a bed of lettuce or with cut-up pieces of pita bread.
Per Serving: Calories 282; Fats 14.54g; Sodium 333mg; Carbs 10.21g; Fiber 1.1g; Sugar 2.55g; Protein 26.31g

Grilled Sirloin Steak and Veggie Skewers

Prep time: 10 minutes | Cook time: 10 minutes | Serves: 4

Nonstick cooking spray
4 garlic cloves, peeled
2 fresh rosemary sprigs (about 3 inches each)
2 tablespoons extra-virgin olive oil, divided
1 pound boneless top sirloin steak, about 1 inch thick
1 (8-ounce) package white button mushrooms
1 medium red onion, cut into 12 thin wedges
¼ teaspoon coarsely ground black pepper
2 tablespoons red wine vinegar
¼ teaspoon kosher or sea salt

1. Soak 12 (10-inch) wooden or metal skewers in water. 2. Cut a piece of aluminum foil into a 10-inch square. Place the garlic and rosemary sprigs in the center, drizzle with 1 tablespoon of oil, and wrap tightly to form a foil packet. Place it on the grill, and close the grill cover. 3. Cut the steak into 1-inch cubes. Thread the beef onto the wet skewers, alternating with whole mushrooms and onion wedges. Spray the kebabs thoroughly with nonstick cooking spray, and sprinkle with pepper. 4. Spray the cold grill with nonstick cooking spray, and heat the grill to medium-high. Cook the skewers on the covered grill for 4 to 5 minutes; turn the skewers and grill for 4 to 5 minutes longer, covered, until the meat reaches an internal temperature of 145°F (medium rare) or 160°F (medium). 5. Remove the foil packet from the grill, open, place the garlic and rosemary sprigs in a small bowl. Carefully strip the rosemary sprigs of their leaves into the bowl and pour in any accumulated juices and oil from the foil packet. Add the remaining oil, the vinegar and salt. Mash the garlic with a fork, and mix all ingredients in the bowl together. 6. Pour the sauce over the finished steak skewers and serve.
Per Serving: Calories 277; Fats 16.21g; Sodium 270mg; Carbs 6.82g; Fiber 2.1g; Sugar 2.11g; Protein 25.01g

Tasty Beef Gyros with Tahini Sauce

Prep time: 15 minutes | Cook time: 10 minutes | Serves: 4

Nonstick cooking spray
2 tablespoons extra-virgin olive oil
1 tablespoon dried oregano
1¼ teaspoons garlic powder, divided
1 teaspoon ground cumin
½ teaspoon freshly ground black pepper
¼ teaspoon kosher or sea salt
1 pound beef flank steak, top round steak, or lamb leg steak,
center cut, about 1 inch thick
1 medium green bell pepper, halved and seeded
2 tablespoons tahini or peanut butter (tahini for nut-free)
1 tablespoon hot water (if needed)
½ cup 2% plain Greek yogurt
1 tablespoon freshly squeezed lemon juice (about ½ small lemon)
1 cup thinly sliced red onion (about ½ onion)

4 (6-inch) whole-wheat pita breads, warmed

1. With the rack in it, preheat the oven broiler to high. 2. Line a large, rimmed baking sheet with foil. Place a wire cooling rack on the foil, and spray the rack with nonstick cooking spray. Set aside. 3. In a small bowl, mix up the oil, oregano, cumin, salt, pepper and 1 teaspoon of garlic powder. Rub the steak with the oil mixture on all side, saving 1 teaspoon of the mixture. Transfer the steak to the prepared rack. 4. Rub the remaining oil mixture on the bell pepper, and place on the rack, cut-side down. Press the pepper with the heel of your hand to flatten. 5. Broil the food for 5 minutes; turn the meat and the pepper pieces, and broil them for 2 to 5 minutes longer, or until the pepper is charred and the internal temperature of the meat measures 145°F on a meat thermometer. Put the pepper and steak on a cutting board to rest for 5 minutes. 6. While the meat is broiling, in a small bowl, whisk the tahini until smooth (adding 1 tablespoon of hot water if your tahini is sticky), add the remaining garlic powder, the yogurt and lemon juice, mix well. 7. Slice the steak crosswise into ¼-inch-thick strips. Slice the bell pepper into strips. 8. Divide the steak, bell pepper, and onion among the warm pita breads. Drizzle with tahini sauce and serve.
Per Serving: Calories 330; Fats 11.29g; Sodium 642mg; Carbs 25.22g; Fiber 3.6g; Sugar 5.74g; Protein 32.19g

Beef Sliders with Pepper Slaw

Prep time: 10 minutes | Cook time: 15 minutes | Serves: 4

Nonstick cooking spray
1 (8-ounce) package white button mushrooms
2 tablespoons extra-virgin olive oil, divided
1 pound ground beef (93% lean)
2 garlic cloves, minced (about 1 teaspoon)
½ teaspoon kosher or sea salt, divided
¼ teaspoon freshly ground black pepper
1 tablespoon balsamic vinegar
2 bell peppers of different colors, sliced into strips
2 tablespoons torn fresh basil or flat-leaf (Italian) parsley
Mini or slider whole-grain rolls, for serving (optional)

1. With the rack in it, preheat the oven broiler to high. 2. Line a large, rimmed baking sheet with aluminum foil. Place a wire cooling rack on the aluminum foil, and spray the rack with nonstick cooking spray. Set aside. 3. In the food processor, add half the mushrooms and pulse about 15 times, until the mushrooms are finely chopped but not puréed, similar to the texture of ground meat. Pulse the remaining mushrooms with the same step. 4. In the skillet, heat 1 tablespoon of oil over medium-high heat; add the mushrooms and cook them for 2 to 3 minutes, stirring occasionally, until the mushrooms have cooked down and some of their liquid has evaporated. Remove from the heat. 5. In a large bowl, mix the ground beef with the cooked mushrooms, garlic, ¼ teaspoon of salt, and pepper. Mix gently using your hands. Form 8 small (½-inch-thick) patties from the mixture, and place on the prepared rack, making two lines of 4 patties down the center of the pan. 6. Broil the food for 4 minutes; when the time is up, flip the burgers and rearrange them so any burgers not getting brown are nearer to the heat source; broil for 3 to 4 minutes longer, or until the internal temperature of the meat is 160°F on a meat thermometer. 7. While the burgers are cooking, in a large bowl, mix up the vinegar, the remaining 1 tablespoon of oil and ¼ teaspoon of salt. Add the peppers and basil, and coat them with the mixture by stirring them gently. 8. Serve the sliders with the pepper slaw as a topping or on the side.
Per Serving: Calories 297; Fats 15.9g; Sodium 425mg; Carbs 5.63g; Fiber 1.3g; Sugar 2.7g; Protein 31.71g

Cinnamon Lamb Meatballs

Prep time: 10 minutes | Cook time: 20 minutes | Servings: 4

Olive oil cooking spray
1-pound ground lamb
¼ cup fresh mint, chopped
¼ cup shallot, chopped
1 large egg, beaten
1 garlic clove, chopped
1 teaspoon ground coriander
1 teaspoon ground cumin
½ teaspoon kosher salt
¼ teaspoon ground cinnamon
¼ teaspoon red pepper flakes

1. At 400 degrees F, preheat your oven. 2. Brush a 12-cup muffin tray with cooking spray. 3. In a suitable bowl, mix the lamb, mint, shallot, egg, garlic, coriander, cumin, salt, cinnamon, and red pepper flakes; mix well. 4. Form the prepared mixture into 12 balls and place one in each cup of the prepared muffin tray. 5. Bake the food for 20 minutes until golden brown. 6. Serve.
Per Serving: Calories 343; Total Fat 23.8g; Sodium 692mg; Total Carbs 4.8g; Fiber 2.5g; Sugars 1.4g; Protein 26.1g

Avocado and Tomato Sandwiches

Prep time: 10 minutes | Cook time: 5 minutes | Serves: 4

8 slices whole-grain or whole-wheat bread
1 ripe avocado, halved and pitted
¼ teaspoon freshly ground black pepper
¼ teaspoon kosher or sea salt
4 romaine lettuce leaves, torn into 8 pieces
1 large, ripe tomato, sliced into 8 rounds
2 ounces' prosciutto, cut into 8 thin slices

1. Toast the bread and place on a large platter. 2. Prepare a bowl, scoop the avocado flesh out and add into the bowl; add the pepper and salt, gently mash the avocado until it resembles a creamy spread. Spread the avocado mash over all 8 pieces of toast. Take one slice of avocado toast, and top it with a lettuce leaf, tomato slice, and prosciutto slice. Top with another slice each of lettuce, tomato, and prosciutto, then cover with a second piece of avocado toast (avocado-side down on the prosciutto). 4. Repeat with the remaining ingredients to make three more sandwiches and serve.
Per Serving: Calories 262; Fats 10.19g; Sodium 624mg; Carbs 32.94g; Fiber 7.9g; Sugar 3.54g; Protein 11.76g

Balsamic Beef Kebabs

Prep time: 15 minutes | Cook time: 55 minutes | Serves: 4

¼ cup olive oil, divided
2 tablespoons balsamic vinegar
2 teaspoons Dijon mustard
1 pound beef top sirloin steak, cut into 1-inch cubes
½ sweet onion, finely chopped
1 red bell pepper, chopped
2 teaspoons minced garlic
1 cup pearled barley, rinsed
3 cups low-sodium chicken stock
4 cups chopped spinach
2 tablespoons pine nuts
1 tablespoon chopped fresh thyme
Sea salt

1. Soak bamboo skewers in warm water. 2. In a large bowl, add the balsamic vinegar, mustard and 3 tablespoons of olive oil, mix them until blended; add the beef and coat the beef with the mustard mixture; cover and marinate the beef in the refrigerator for 30 minutes. 3. In a large saucepan, heat the remaining olive oil over medium-high heat; add the onion, bell pepper, garlic and sauté them for 4 minutes until softened; add the barley and chicken stock, stir and bring to a boil, then lower the heat, cover the pan and simmer the food for 40 minutes until the barley is tender and the liquid is absorbed. 4. Remove the pan from the heat, stir in the spinach, pine nuts, thyme and salt. 5. Preheat a grill to medium high. 6. Thread the beef onto the soaked wooden skewers, leaving space between each chunk. 7. Grill the skewers for 10 minutes (medium) until the beef reaches desired doneness, turning occasionally. 8. Serve the beef skewers on the barley risotto.
Per Serving: Calories 575; Fats 28.13g; Sodium 758mg; Carbs 48.35g; Fiber 9.2g; Sugar 4.67g; Protein 33.67g

Pan-Cooked Ground Beef with Tomato-Onion Pasta

Prep time: 10 minutes | Cook time: 45 minutes | Serves: 4

6 large tomatoes (about 2 pounds), cut into wedges
1 sweet onion, coarsely chopped
½ cup chopped sun-dried tomatoes
4 garlic cloves, thinly sliced
2 tablespoons olive oil, divided
8 ounces whole-grain fettucine
8 ounces' extra-lean ground beef
½ cup pitted, halved Kalamata olives
¼ cup shredded fresh basil
Pinch red pepper flakes
Sea salt
Freshly ground black pepper
2 tablespoons grated Parmesan cheese

1. Preheat the oven to 425°F. Line a baking sheet with aluminum foil. 2. In a medium bowl, add the tomatoes, onion, sun-dried tomatoes, garlic, and 1 tablespoon of olive oil and toss them well. Transfer the tomato mixture to the baking sheet and roast in the oven for 30 minutes or until very tender. 3. While roasting the vegetables, boil a large pot of water and cook the pasta according to package instructions until al dente. Drain the pasta. 4. In the saucepan, heat the remaining olive oil over medium-high heat; add and brown the ground beef for about 10 minutes, remove any oil from the pot with a spoon and discard. 5. Add the roasted vegetables to the saucepan along with the olives, basil, and red pepper flakes and stir to combine well, breaking up any larger chunks of vegetables. Stir in the pasta. 6. Season with salt and pepper, top with Parmesan cheese and serve.
Per Serving: Calories 529; Fats 20.04g; Sodium 1036mg; Carbs 68.09g; Fiber 9.9g; Sugar 14.85g; Protein 23.84g

Greek-Style Meatloaf

Prep time: 10 minutes | Cook time: 25 minutes | Servings: 6

1-pound lean ground beef
2 eggs
2 Roma tomatoes, diced
½ white onion, diced
½ cup whole wheat bread crumbs
1 teaspoon garlic powder
1 teaspoon dried oregano
1 teaspoon dried thyme
1 teaspoon salt
1 teaspoon black pepper
2 ounces' mozzarella cheese, shredded
1 tablespoon olive oil
Fresh chopped parsley for garnish

1. At 380 degrees F, preheat your air fryer. 2. Mix the ground beef, eggs, tomatoes, onion, bread crumbs, garlic powder, oregano, thyme, salt, pepper, and cheese in a suitable bowl. 3. Form the mixture into a loaf, flattening to 1-inch thick. 4. Coat the top with olive oil; place the meatloaf into the air fryer basket and cook in the preheated air fryer for 25 minutes. 5. When cooked, let the loaf sit for 5 minutes. Garnish with a sprinkle of parsley and serve.
Per Serving: Calories 271; Total Fat 11.9g; Sodium 665mg; Total Carbs 6.4g; Fiber 2.2g; Sugars 2.7g; Protein 34.1g

Steak with Mushroom Sauce

Prep time: 10 minutes | Cooking time: 20 minutes | Servings: 4

For the Marinade and Steak
1 cup dry red wine
3 garlic cloves, minced
2 tablespoons extra-virgin olive oil
1 tablespoon low-sodium soy sauce
1 tablespoon dried thyme
1 teaspoon Dijon mustard
2 tablespoons olive oil
1 to 1½ pounds skirt steak, flat iron steak, or tri-tip steak

For the Mushroom Sauce
2 tablespoons extra-virgin olive oil
1 pound cremini mushrooms, quartered
½ teaspoon sea salt
1 teaspoon dried thyme
⅛ teaspoon freshly ground black pepper
2 garlic cloves, minced
1 cup dry red wine

To make the Marinade and Steak: 1. Beat the wine, garlic, olive oil, soy sauce, thyme, and mustard 2. In a suitable bowl, pour the mixture into a resealable bag. 3. Add the steak to the bag, and refrigerate the steak to marinate for 4 to 8 hours. 4. Take the steak out and pat it dry with paper towels. 5. In a suitable skillet over medium-high heat, preheat the olive oil until it shimmers. 6. Add the steak and cook for almost 4 minutes per side until deeply browned on each side and the steak reaches an internal temperature of 140°F. Remove the steak from this skillet and put it on a plate tented with aluminum foil to keep warm. 7. Slice the steak against the grain into ½-inch-thick slices when the mushroom sauce is ready.
To make the Mushroom Sauce: 1. In the same skillet, preheat the olive oil until it shimmers. 2. Add the mushrooms, sea salt, thyme, and pepper. Cook for almost 6 minutes, infrequently stirring, until the mushrooms are browned. 3. Stir in the garlic and cook for almost 30 seconds, stirring constantly. 4. Stir in the wine, scrape and fold in any browned bits from the bottom of this skillet. Cook for almost 4 minutes with occasional stirring until the liquid reduces by half. 5. Spoon the mushroom sauce over the steak and enjoy.
Per Serving: Calories 406; Total Fat 13.1g; Sodium 717mg; Total Carbs 4.1g; Fiber 1.2g; Sugars 1.8g; Protein 25.6g

Beef Kofta

Prep time: 10 minutes | Cook time: 20 minutes | Servings: 4

Olive oil cooking spray
½ onion, roughly chopped
1-inch piece of ginger, peeled
2 garlic cloves, peeled
⅓ cup fresh parsley
⅓ cup fresh mint
1 pound of ground beef
1 tablespoon ground cumin
1 tablespoon ground coriander
1 teaspoon ground cinnamon
¾ teaspoon kosher salt
½ teaspoon ground sumac
¼ teaspoon ground cloves
¼ teaspoon freshly ground black pepper

1. At 400 degrees F, preheat your oven. Grease a 12-cup muffin tray with olive oil cooking spray. 2. Add the onion, ginger, garlic, parsley, and mint to a food processor; process them until minced. 3. Place the onion mixture in a suitable bowl; add the beef, cumin, coriander, cinnamon, salt, sumac, cloves, and black pepper, and mix thoroughly with your hands. 4. Divide the prepared beef mixture into 12 balls and place each one in a cup of the prepared muffin tray. 5. Bake the food for almost 20 minutes, then serve.
Per Serving: Calories 383; Total Fat 20.9g; Sodium 420mg; Total Carbs 0.6g; Fiber 0.3g; Sugars 0.2g; Protein 45.4g

Ground Lamb with Lentils

Prep time: 15 minutes | Cook time: 20 minutes | Servings: 4

1 tablespoon extra-virgin olive oil	2 cups cooked, drained lentils
½ pound ground lamb	1 hothouse or English cucumber, diced
1 teaspoon red pepper flakes	⅓ cup fresh mint, chopped
½ teaspoon ground cumin	⅓ cup fresh parsley, chopped
½ teaspoon kosher salt	Zest of 1 lemon
¼ teaspoon freshly ground black pepper	1 cup plain Greek yogurt
2 garlic cloves, minced	½ cup pomegranate seeds

1. Preheat the olive oil in a suitable skillet over medium-high heat. 2. Add the lamb and season with the red pepper flakes, cumin, salt, and black pepper—Cook the lamb without stirring for 5 minutes until the bottom is brown and crispy. Stir and cook for another 5 minutes. 3. Using a spatula, break up the lamb into smaller pieces. Add the garlic and cook with occasional stirring for 1 minute. Transfer the lamb mixture to a bowl. 4. Add the lentils to this skillet and cook with occasional stirring until brown and crisp, about 5 minutes. 5. Return the lamb to this skillet, mix, and warm for about 3 minutes. Transfer to the large bowl. Mix gently with the cucumber, mint, parsley, and lemon zest. 6. Spoon the yogurt into four bowls and top each with some lamb mixture. Garnish with the pomegranate seeds. 7. Enjoy.
Per Serving: Calories 365; Total Fat 15.9g; Sodium 59mg; Total Carbs 3.9g; Fiber 0.4g; Sugars 0.5g; Protein 26.3g

Dijon Pork Tenderloin

Prep time: 10 minutes | Cook time: 20 minutes | Servings: 6

½ cup fresh Italian parsley leaves, chopped	1 tablespoon extra-virgin olive oil
3 tablespoons fresh rosemary leaves, chopped	4 garlic cloves, minced
3 tablespoons fresh thyme leaves, chopped	½ teaspoon sea salt
	¼ teaspoon freshly ground black pepper
3 tablespoons Dijon mustard	1 (1½-pound) pork tenderloin

1. At 400 degrees F, preheat your oven. 2. Blend the parsley, rosemary, thyme, mustard, olive oil, garlic, sea salt, and pepper in a blender. Process for almost 30 seconds until smooth. 3. Spread the prepared mixture evenly over the pork, and then place the pork on a rimmed baking sheet. 4. Bake the food in the preheated oven for 20 minutes, or until the meat reaches an internal temperature of 140°F. 5. Slice and serve.
Per Serving: Calories 372; Total Fat 24.3g; Sodium 440mg; Total Carbs 13.4g; Fiber 0.9g; Sugars 11.9g; Protein 23.9g

Lamb with String Beans

Prep time: 10 minutes | Cook time: 60 minutes | Servings: 6

¼ cup extra-virgin olive oil, divided	2 tablespoons tomato paste
6 lamb chops, trimmed of extra fat	1½ cups of hot water
1 teaspoon sea salt, divided	1 pound green beans, trimmed and halved crosswise
½ teaspoon freshly ground black pepper	1 onion, chopped
	2 tomatoes, chopped

1. In a skillet over medium-high heat, heat 2 tablespoons of olive oil until it shimmers. 2. Season the lamb chops with ½ teaspoon of sea salt and ⅛ teaspoon of pepper. Cook the lamb in the hot oil for almost 4 minutes per side until both sides are browned. 3. Set the meat aside on a platter. 4. Return this skillet to the heat, and heat the remaining olive oil until it shimmers. 5. In a suitable bowl, dissolve the tomato paste in hot water. Add it to the hot skillet along with the green beans, onion, tomatoes, and the rest ½ teaspoon of sea salt and ¼ teaspoon of pepper, and cook to a simmer, using the side of a spoon to scrape and fold in any browned bits from the bottom of this pan. 6. Return the lamb chops to this skillet, and bring to a boil, then reduce its heat to medium-low. Simmer for 45 minutes until the beans are soft, adding additional water as needed to adjust the thickness of the sauce. 7. Serve warm.
Per Serving: Calories 399; Total Fat 11.4g; Sodium 1244mg; Total Carbs 1.5g; Fiber 0.9g; Sugars 0.2g; Protein 44.5g

Lamb and Bean Stew

Prep time: 10 minutes | Cook time: 35 minutes | Servings: 4

4 tablespoons olive oil, divided	1 cup chopped celery
1-pound lamb shoulder, cut into 2-inch cubes	1 cup chopped tomatoes
Sea salt	1 cup chopped carrots
Freshly ground black pepper	⅓ cup tomato paste
2 garlic cloves, minced (optional)	1 (28-ounce) can of white kidney beans, drained and rinsed
1 large onion, diced	2 cups water

1. Season the lamb pieces with black pepper and salt. 2. In a stockpot, heat 1 tablespoon of olive oil over medium-high heat. Add the seasoned lamb pieces to the stockpot with the garlic (optional). 3. Brown the lamb, turning it frequently, for 3 to 4 minutes. Add the remaining olive oil, the onion, celery, tomatoes, and carrots, and cook for 4 to 5 minutes. 4. Add the tomato paste, stir to mix, and add the beans and water. 5. Bring the mixture to a boil, then reduce its heat to low, cover the stockpot, and simmer for 25 minutes, or until the lamb is fully cooked. 6. Taste, adjust the seasoning and serve.
Per Serving: Calories 525; Total Fat 7.5g; Sodium 445mg; Total Carbs 14.6g; Fiber 2.4g; Sugars 0.3g; Protein 23.8g

Roasted Lamb Leg with Potatoes

Prep time: 10 minutes | Cook time: 3 hours | Serves: 6

1 (5-pound) leg of lamb	3 garlic cloves, minced
1 to 2 tablespoons olive oil for drizzling	Sea salt
Juice of 3 lemons	Freshly ground black pepper
1 teaspoon dried oregano, plus extra for sprinkling over potatoes	3½ pounds of red potatoes, cut into 1-inch chunks
½ teaspoon dried rosemary, plus extra for sprinkling over potatoes	3 tablespoons unsalted butter
	½ cup water

1. At 300 degrees F, preheat your oven. 2. Use cold water to rinse the leg of lamb and then place it in a roasting pan, fat-side up. 3. Drizzle the lamb with the olive oil, and sprinkle with the juice of 1 lemon. Sprinkle with the oregano, rosemary, and garlic, and season with black pepper and salt. 4. Bake the leg of lamb in the oven for almost 2 hours, rotating and basting it periodically. If this pan gets too dry, add a little water. 5. Remove this pan from the oven and increase the oven temperature to 350 degrees F. Spread the potatoes around the lamb and drizzle the juice of the rest two lemons over them. 6. Sprinkle the potatoes with a little oregano and rosemary, and season with black pepper and salt. Place dabs of the butter all over the potatoes and stir in the water. 7. Place the roasting pan in the oven and bake for almost 1 hour, or until the lamb reaches an internal temperature of 145°F and the potatoes are tender. 8. Remove from the oven, slice the lamb, and serve with the potatoes.
Per Serving: Calories 502; Total Fat 26.4g; Sodium 1873mg; Total Carbs 11.5g; Fiber 2g; Sugars 7.5g; Protein 54.6g

Lebanese Stuffed Cabbage Rolls

Prep time: 10 minutes | Cook time: 65 minutes | Serves: 5-6

1 teaspoon sea salt	2 teaspoons ground cinnamon
2 heads of cabbage, cored	Sea salt
2 pounds' lean ground beef or lamb	Black pepper
1¼ cups uncooked white rice	2 cups water
1 cup olive oil	3 tablespoons tomato paste
½ onion, chopped	1 chicken bouillon cube

1. In a large stockpot, mix 10 to 12 cups of water with the salt, and cook to a boil over high heat. 2. Add the cabbage; as the heads boil and the leaves loosen, remove each leaf and set it aside in a suitable bowl of ice water. 3. Mix the ground beef, rice, olive oil, onion, and cinnamon in a suitable bowl. Season with black pepper and salt, and mix again. 4. Stir together the water, tomato paste, and bouillon cube in a bowl and set aside. 5. Place one spoonful of the meat mixture in the center of a cabbage leaf, fold the sides over the filling and roll it up from one of the open sides to create a tight roll. 6. Place the cabbage roll in the now-empty stockpot, seam-side down, and repeat until you have used all the meat mixture. 7. Pour the tomato mixture into the pot; it should reach about 1 inch below the top layer of cabbage rolls. 8. Place the stockpot over medium-high heat, cook to a boil. 9. Reduce the heat to low, cover the pot and simmer for 1 hour. 10. Serve.
Per Serving: Calories 389; Total Fat 17g; Sodium 1285mg; Total Carbs 8.9g; Fiber 4.3g; Sugars 4.8g; Protein 49.8g

Chapter 5 Vegetable Mains and Sides Recipes

Stuffed Peppers with Tabbouleh

Prep time: 10 minutes | Cook time: 0 | Serves: 4

1 pound mini sweet peppers	1 batch tabbouleh

1. Chop off the tops, and then halve the sweet peppers lengthwise. 2. Remove the seeds. Spoon the tabbouleh into the peppers and serve.
Per Serving: Calories 214; Total Fat 11.8g; Sodium 80mg; Total Carbs 4.6g; Fiber 2.5g; Sugar 2.2g; Protein 24.6g

Grilled Veggie Pita

Prep time: 10 minutes | Cook time: 15 minutes | Serves: 4

4 pita pieces of bread	½ cup plain full-fat Greek yogurt or hummus
2 tablespoons olive oil	1 teaspoon harissa
2 garlic cloves, minced	1 large tomato, sliced
1 zucchini, sliced	Sea salt
1 red bell pepper, cut into strips	Black pepper
½ red onion, sliced	

1. Toast the pitas in a skillet over medium-high heat for 3 to 4 minutes per side, then set aside. 2. In the same skillet, mix the olive oil and garlic and sauté over medium-high heat for 2 minutes. 3. Add the zucchini, bell pepper, and onion, and sauté them for 5 to 6 minutes until softened. Remove the skillet from the heat. 4. Mix the yogurt and harissa in a suitable bowl. 5. Halve the pitas crosswise and open each half to form a pocket. 6. Add 1 tablespoon of the harissa mixture to each pita pocket and spread it over the inside. 7. Spoon the cooked vegetable mixture into the pockets and top with the tomatoes—season with salt and black pepper. 8. Serve the pitas with the extra sauce on the side.
Per Serving: Calories 205; Total Fat 4g; Sodium 719mg; Total Carbs 35g; Fiber 1.3g; Sugar 5g; Protein 6g

Greek Bean Soup

Prep time: 10 minutes | Cook time: 45 minutes | Serves: 4

2 tablespoons olive oil	2 carrots, cut into long ribbons
1 large onion, chopped	⅓ teaspoon chopped fresh thyme
1 (15-ounce) can of diced tomatoes	¼ cup chopped fresh Italian parsley
1 (15-ounce) can of great northern beans, drained and rinsed	1 bay leaf
	Sea salt
2 celery stalks, chopped	Black pepper

1. In a Dutch oven, preheat the olive oil over medium-high heat. 2. Add the onion and sauté for 4 minutes, or until softened. 3. Add the tomatoes, beans, celery, carrots, thyme, parsley, and bay leaf, then add water to cover by about 2 inches. 4. Bring the soup to a boil, reduce its heat to low, cover, and simmer for 30 minutes, or until the vegetables are tender. 5. Remove the bay leaf, season with black pepper and salt, and serve.
Per Serving: Calories 214; Total Fat 11.8g; Sodium 80mg; Total Carbs 24.6g; Fiber 2.5g; Sugar 2.2g; Protein 24.6g

Vegetable Tagine

Prep time: 10 minutes | Cook time: 45 minutes | Serves: 4

3 tablespoons olive oil	1 teaspoon ground coriander
1 onion, sliced	½ teaspoon ground turmeric
5 garlic cloves, minced	½ teaspoon ground cinnamon
2 carrots, cut into long ribbons	3 cups vegetable broth
2 red bell peppers, chopped	1 sweet potato, peeled and cubed
1 (15-ounce) can of diced tomatoes	1 (15-ounce) can of chickpeas, drained and rinsed
½ cup chopped dried apricots	Sea salt
1 to 2 tablespoons harissa	Black pepper

1. In a suitable stockpot, preheat the olive oil over medium-high heat. 2. Add the onion and garlic and sauté them for 5 minutes. Add the carrots and bell peppers, and sauté for 7 to 10 minutes until the vegetables are tender. 3. Add the tomatoes, apricots, harissa, coriander, turmeric, and cinnamon, and cook for 5 minutes. Add the broth and sweet potato and cook to a boil. Reduce its heat to low, cover, and simmer for 20 minutes, or until the sweet potato is tender. 4. Add the chickpeas and simmer for 3 minutes to heat through. 5. Sprinkle the chickpeas with salt and black pepper before serving.
Per Serving: Calories 327; Total Fat 29g; Sodium 888mg; Total Carbs 6g; Fiber 1g; Sugar 1g; Protein 11g

Gnocchi with Chickpeas

Prep time: 15 minutes | Cook time: 25 minutes | Serves: 4

4 tablespoons olive oil, plus extra for drizzling	½ teaspoon Italian seasoning
1 pound store-bought gnocchi	1 (15-ounce) can of chickpeas, drained and rinsed
2 yellow squash, halved lengthwise, cut into 1-inch pieces	2 cups packed arugula
1 red bell pepper, diced	Sea salt
1 (15 ounces) can of artichoke hearts	Black pepper
	½ cup parmesan cheese, plus more for serving

1. Drain and chop the artichoke hearts. 2. Heat 2 tablespoons of olive oil in a suitable skillet over medium-high heat. Add the gnocchi and sauté for 10 to 15 minutes, until golden brown. Remove the gnocchi from this skillet with a slotted spoon and set it aside in a suitable bowl. 3. Preheat the rest 2 tablespoons of olive oil over medium-high heat in the same skillet. Add the squash, bell pepper, artichoke hearts, and Italian seasoning, and sauté for 10 to 12 minutes until softening the vegetables. 4. Add the chickpeas, and stir them for 2 minutes more. Add the arugula and cook for 30 seconds, stirring to mix. 5. Return the gnocchi to this skillet and toss to mix everything. Drizzle the gnocchi with olive oil, season with salt, black pepper, and top with the parmesan. Cover with a lid and Put off the heat. Let the prepared mixture sit for 2 minutes or until the cheese has melted. 6. Taste and adjust the seasoning. Serve topped with extra parmesan.
Per Serving: Calories 355; Total Fat 40.3g; Sodium 14mg; Total Carbs 1.3g; Fiber 0.6g; Sugars0.6g; Protein 0.7g

Cauliflower Steaks with Tahini Sauce

Prep time: 10 minutes | Cook time: 40 minutes | Serves: 4

¼ cup olive oil	cut from top to bottom into thick slabs
4 garlic cloves, minced	½ cup tahini
1 teaspoon sea salt	Juice of 1 lemon
1 teaspoon black pepper	¼ cup chopped fresh Italian parsley
2 large heads of cauliflower, stem end, trimmed (core left intact) and	

1. At 400 degrees F, preheat your oven. Line a suitable baking sheet with parchment paper. 2. Mix the olive oil, garlic, salt, and pepper in a suitable bowl. Brush the cauliflower with the olive mixture on both sides, and place them in a single layer on the baking sheet. Drizzle any remaining oil mixture over the cauliflower steaks. 3. Bake them for 45 minutes or until the cauliflower is soft. 4. While the steaks are baking, stir the tahini and lemon juice in a suitable bowl—season with black pepper and salt. 5. Transfer the cauliflower steaks to four plates. Drizzle the lemon tahini sauce evenly over the cauliflower and garnish with the parsley. Serve.
Per Serving: Calories 365; Total Fat 39.9g; Sodium 248mg; Total Carbs 3.8g; Fiber 2g; Sugars0.4g; Protein 2.5g

Grilled Eggplant Sandwich

Prep time: 10 minutes | Cook time: 20 minutes | Serves: 4

1 small eggplant, cut into ¼-inch-thick slices	2 garlic cloves, minced
Portobello mushrooms, cut into ¼-inch-thick slices (1 cup)	1 tablespoon Italian seasoning (here)
1 red bell pepper, cut into ¼-inch-thick slices	2 tablespoons extra-virgin olive oil
½ red onion, cut into ¼-inch-thick slices	4 whole-grain ciabatta buns
	¾ cup tomato sauce

1. Preheat the grill to medium-high heat, or at 425 degrees F, preheat your oven. 2. In a suitable bowl, toss together the eggplant, mushrooms, bell pepper, onion, garlic, Italian seasoning, and olive oil until well mixed. 3. Grill the vegetables on medium-high heat for 7 to 8 minutes, flipping the eggplant halfway through. If using the oven, roast the vegetables for almost 20 minutes, flipping the eggplant halfway through until the eggplant is cooked. 4. Cut open the ciabatta buns and spread the tomato sauce on the inside of both halves of each bun. 5. Top the lower half of the bun with ¼ of the grilled vegetables, add any additional toppings of your choosing, and put the top half of the bun on to close the sandwich.
Per Serving: Calories 280; Total Fat 10g; Sodium 464mg; Total Carbs 41g; Fiber 9g; Sugar 10g; Protein 9g

Vegetarian Skillet Lasagna

Prep time: 20 minutes | Cook time: 50 minutes | Serves: 4

15 ounces' ricotta cheese	1 carrot, cut into long ribbons
¼ cup chopped fresh Italian parsley	6 ounces of baby spinach
¼ teaspoon Italian seasoning	1 (28-ounce) can of crushed tomatoes
3 tablespoons olive oil	1½ cups heavy (whipping) cream
1 onion, chopped	Sea salt
3 garlic cloves, minced	Black pepper
2 yellow squash, quartered lengthwise and sliced into 1-inch pieces	9 no-bake lasagna noodles, broken into 2-inch pieces
8 ounces cremini (Baby Bella) mushrooms, quartered	1 cup grated parmesan cheese
	½ cup shredded mozzarella cheese

1. At 375 degrees F, preheat your oven. 2. Stir together the ricotta, parsley, and Italian seasoning in a suitable bowl, and set aside. 3. In an oven-safe skillet over medium-high heat, preheat the olive oil; add the onion and garlic, and sauté them for 3 minutes. Add the squash and sauté for 2 minutes more. Add the mushrooms and sauté for 4 minutes. Add the carrot and spinach and sauté for 1 minute. 4. Add the crushed tomatoes and the cream and season with black pepper and salt. Add the lasagna noodles and mix well, ensuring all the noodles are entirely covered with the sauce. 5. Evenly dollop the ricotta mixture over the tomato mixture, using the back of a spoon to spread it around gently. Evenly top with the parmesan and mozzarella. Cover this skillet with a lid and transfer it to the oven. Bake for 20 minutes, remove the lid and bake for 10 to 15 minutes more until the cheese is golden brown. 6. Remove from the oven and serve.
Per Serving: Calories 353; Total Fat 37.9g; Sodium 221mg; Total Carbs 1.2g; Fiber 0.1g; Sugars0.2g; Protein 3g

Vegetarian Pockets

Prep time: 15 minutes | Cook time: 10 minutes | Serves: 4

4 pita pieces of bread	1 onion, cut into strips
2 tablespoons olive oil	1 jalapeño pepper, seeded and chopped
1 (15-ounce) can of chickpeas, drained	2 garlic cloves, minced
3 red bell peppers, sliced	1 batch tzatziki

1. Toast the pitas in a suitable skillet over medium-high heat, turning them once, for almost 6 minutes. Remove from this skillet and set aside. 2. In the same skillet, preheat the olive oil over medium-high heat. Add the chickpeas, bell peppers, onion, jalapeño, and garlic. Cook with occasional stirring for almost 7 minutes, until the vegetables are tender. Now remove it from the heat. 3. Halve the pitas crosswise and open them to form a pocket. Spoon the chickpea-vegetable mixture into the pitas and top with the tzatziki. 4. Serve.
Per Serving: Calories 288; Total Fat 30.8g; Sodium 12mg; Total Carbs 5.2g; Fiber 3.5g; Sugars1.6g; Protein 1.5g

Chickpea Salad Sandwich

Prep time: 15 minutes | Cook time: 0 | Serves: 4

1 (15-ounce) can of chickpeas, drained and rinsed	¼ cup crème fraiche or mayonnaise
8 ounces red seedless grapes (20 to 25 grapes), halved or quartered if large	Juice of ½ lemon
2 celery stalks, sliced	1 tablespoon chopped fresh dill
2 scallions, green part only, sliced	½ teaspoon honey Dijon mustard
½ red onion, chopped	Sea salt
¼ cup sliced almonds	Black pepper
	8 slices of sourdough bread

1. In a suitable bowl, mash the chickpeas with a fork or potato masher. Stir in the grapes, celery, scallions, onion, almonds, crème Fraiche, lemon juice, dill, and mustard—season with black pepper and salt. 2. Toast the bread in a toaster, then spoon the chickpea mixture onto each slice, using about ¼ cup per slice and spreading it to the edges. 3. Serve.
Per Serving: Calories 223; Total Fat 25g; Sodium 389mg; Total Carbs 0.3g; Fiber 0g; Sugars0g; Protein 0.3g

Cheesy Polenta

Prep time: 10 minutes | Cook time: 20 minutes | Serves: 4

2 tablespoons olive oil, divided	8 ounces cremini (Baby Bella) mushrooms, sliced
1 tablespoon unsalted butter	

1 onion, chopped	polenta, cut crosswise into 1-inch-thick slices
1 shallot, chopped	1 cup shredded mozzarella cheese
3 garlic cloves, minced	½ cup shredded parmesan cheese
1 (18-ounce) tube prepared	

1. At 450 degrees F, preheat your oven. 2. Heat 1 tablespoon of olive oil and the butter over medium-high heat in a suitable oven-safe skillet. Add the mushrooms, onion, shallot, and garlic and sauté for 5 to 7 minutes until softened, then transfer them to a bowl. 3. Preheat the remaining olive oil in the same skillet over medium-high heat. If necessary, working in batches, add the polenta slices in an even layer and cook for 4 to 5 minutes per side. When done, spread the mushroom mixture over the polenta slices. 4. Sprinkle with the mozzarella and parmesan, transfer this skillet to the oven, and bake for 5 minutes to melt the cheese. 5. Remove from the oven and serve.
Per Serving: Calories 297; Total Fat 13.7g; Sodium 1129mg; Total Carbs 17.2g; Fiber 4.8g; Sugars9.3g; Protein 30.2g

Hummus

Prep time: 10 minutes | Cook time: 0 | Serves: 3-5

1 (15-ounce) can of chickpeas, drained	¼ teaspoon ground cumin
½ cup tahini	¼ teaspoon black pepper, plus more as needed
Juice of 2 lemons	2 tablespoons olive oil
2 garlic cloves	1 tablespoon pine nuts for garnish
2 tablespoons water	¼ teaspoon za'atar, homemade (see here) or store-bought, for garnish
½ teaspoon sea salt, plus more as needed	
¼ teaspoon paprika	

1. Add the chickpeas, tahini, lemon juice, garlic, water, salt, paprika, cumin, and pepper to the blender, and pulse them for 30 seconds. 2. Add the olive oil and process for almost 1 minute until smooth. 3. Taste and adjust the seasoning. 4. Drizzle the hummus with extra olive oil, garnish with the pine nuts and za'atar, and enjoy.
Per Serving: Calories 399; Total Fat 27.5g; Sodium 32mg; Total Carbs 45g; Fiber 3.8g; Sugars38.8g; Protein 3.1g

Cucumber-Yogurt Dip

Prep time: 10 minutes | Cook time: 0 | Serves: 6

½ English cucumber, peeled and grated	1 garlic clove, minced
2 cups plain full-fat Greek yogurt	2 tablespoons chopped fresh dill
3 tablespoons extra-virgin olive oil	1 to 2 teaspoons of sea salt
Juice of 1 lemon	1 teaspoon black pepper
	1 to 2 teaspoons red wine vinegar

1. Prepare a clean kitchen towel, arrange the grated cucumber on it, and twist the towel to squeeze excess liquid; place the cucumber in a suitable bowl. 2. Add the yogurt, olive oil, lemon juice, garlic, dill, salt, pepper, and vinegar and stir well. 3. Serve directly or refrigerate this dish before serving to allow the flavors to mellow.
Per Serving: Calories 256; Total Fat 24.2g; Sodium 13mg; Total Carbs 10g; Fiber 0.5g; Sugars9g; Protein 2g

Vegan Paella

Prep time: 15 minutes | Cook time: 25 minutes | Serves: 4

4 cups vegetable broth	3 cups medium-grain rice
1 teaspoon paella spice	2 tablespoons lemon juice
1 tablespoon extra-virgin olive oil	1 cup frozen peas
⅔ cup diced yellow onion	1 (16-ounce) can of white cannellini beans
4 garlic cloves, minced	1 batch tofu "chorizo" (optional)
1 cup diced red bell pepper	

1. Mix the vegetable broth and paella spice in a suitable saucepan over low heat and cook to a simmer. Do not let the prepared mixture boil. 2. In a suitable deep skillet, preheat the olive oil over medium heat. Sauté the onion, garlic, and bell pepper for 2 to 3 minutes until the onion is translucent. 3. Add the rice to this pan and sauté for 2 minutes, stirring. Add the warm vegetable broth and lemon juice, stir to mix, and reduce its heat to medium-low. 4. Bring to simmer and cook for 10 minutes, or until the rice absorbs almost all the broth and is slightly tender. 5. Add in the frozen peas, cannellini beans, and tofu "chorizo" (optional), and mix well to mix. 6. Reduce its heat to low, cover this pan, and continue to cook for 5 to 10 minutes longer until the rice is tender.
Per Serving: Calories 211; Total Fat 22g; Sodium 166mg; Total Carbs 1.1g; Fiber 0g; Sugars0.1g; Protein 2.9g

Greek Garlic Dip

Prep time: 10 minutes | Cook time: 0 | Serves: 4

2 potatoes (about 1 pound), peeled and quartered	4 garlic cloves, minced
½ cup olive oil	Sea salt
¼ cup lemon juice	Black pepper

1. Place the potatoes in a suitable saucepan and fill this pan three-quarters full with water. Bring the water to a boil over medium-high heat, then reduce its heat to medium and cook the potatoes until fork-tender, 20 to 30 minutes. 2. Stir together the olive oil, lemon juice, and garlic in a suitable bowl. 3. Once the potatoes are cooked, drain excess water and then put them back in the saucepan. 4. Stir in the oil mixture and mash with a potato masher or a fork until well mixed and smooth—taste and season with black pepper and salt. 5. Serve.
Per Serving: Calories 364; Total Fat 29.6g; Sodium 489mg; Total Carbs 27g; Fiber 10.6g; Sugars9.3g; Protein 5.5g

Asparagus with Lemon Zest

Prep time: 10 minutes | Cook time: 10 minutes | Serves: 4

¼ cup olive oil	¼ to ½ teaspoon red pepper flakes
2 pounds' asparagus, woody ends trimmed	Pinch sea salt, plus more as needed
3 to 4 garlic cloves, minced	Pinch black pepper, plus more as needed
Zest of 1 medium lemon	

1. In a suitable skillet, preheat the olive oil over medium-high heat. Add the asparagus and stir to coat with the oil. Sauté for 3 minutes. 2. Add the garlic, lemon zest, red pepper flakes, salt, and black pepper, then sauté them for 5 to 7 minutes. 3. Taste and adjust the seasonings, then serve.
Per Serving: Calories 134; Total Fat 10.8g; Sodium 124mg; Total Carbs 2.3g; Fiber 0.4g; Sugars2.1g; Protein 6.3g

Mediterranean Buddha bowl

Prep time: 20 minutes | Cook time: 0 | Serves: 2

3 cups mixed greens	½ cucumber, seeded and diced
1 cup cooked quinoa	1 cup cherry tomatoes, halved
1 cup chickpeas, drained	½ cup kalamata olives halved
⅔ cup hummus	½ cup diced orange bell pepper

1. Divide the greens evenly between 2 bowls and top each with ½ the quinoa, chickpeas, hummus, cucumber, cherry tomatoes, olives, and bell pepper. 2. Toss to mix.
Per Serving: Calories 211; Total Fat 22g; Sodium 166mg; Total Carbs 1.1g; Fiber 0g; Sugars0.1g; Protein 2.9g

Zucchini Alfredo

Prep time: 10 minutes | Cook time: 10 minutes | Serves: 2

2 zucchinis, ends trimmed	parsley
1 (16-ounce) can of white cannellini beans, cooked and drained	¼ cup nutritional yeast
	¾ to 1 cup unsweetened nondairy milk
1 garlic clove	¼ cup parmesan "cheese"
2 tablespoons chopped fresh	

1. Use a spiralizer to make zucchini noodles out of the zucchini. Set aside. 2. In a blender or food processor, mix the beans, garlic, parsley, nutritional yeast, and ¾ cup of milk. 3. Blend until smooth, adding ¼ cup of milk if you want a thinner alfredo sauce. 4. Transfer the bean sauce to a suitable saucepan over low heat. 5. While the sauce warms in a suitable skillet over medium heat, gently sauté the zucchini noodles for about 5 minutes until they are softer and less crunchy. 6. Divide the zucchini noodles between 2 plates, top with the alfredo sauce, and sprinkle with 2 tablespoons of parmesan "cheese."
Per Serving: Calories 225; Total Fat 6.3g; Sodium 7mg; Total Carbs 38.1g; Fiber 5.9g; Sugars27.7g; Protein 3.1g

Pasta with Lentil-Beet Balls

Prep time: 20 minutes | Cook time: 20 minutes | Serves: 2

1 tablespoon flaxseed	1 tablespoon dried basil
3 tablespoons water	1 tablespoon dried oregano
2 garlic cloves	1 tablespoon dried parsley

1 cup cooked red lentils, drained and cooled	6 ounces dried whole-grain spaghetti
1 cup steamed beets, drained well and cooled	1 tablespoon tomato paste
	1¼ cups tomato sauce
¼ cup quick oats	Parmesan "cheese"

1. At 375 degrees F, preheat your oven. 2. Blend the flaxseed, water, garlic, basil, oregano, and parsley in a food processor. Let sit for 2 to 3 minutes to allow the flaxseed to become gelatinous, like egg whites. 3. Add the lentils and beets to the food processor and pulse until mixed but not pureed. If the prepared mixture is too thin, stir in 1 tablespoon of oats until the ready mix is thick and doughy. 4. Scoop out 1 tablespoon of the prepared mixture and roll into a ball. It should stick together enough to make a ball but feel fragile. Continue making the balls until all the beet mixture is used. You should have 12 lentil-beet balls. 5. Heat the lentil-beet balls on a rimmed baking sheet in the oven for 20 minutes. 6. Prepare the pasta in line with the package directions while the lentil-beet balls are baking. 7. In a suitable saucepan, warm the tomato paste and sauce over medium heat, stirring, so it doesn't burn. 8. Remove the lentil-beet balls from the oven and allow them to cool for 5 minutes before lifting them from the tray. 9. Divide the pasta between 2 plates. Add 6 lentil-beet balls to each plate, top with the tomato sauce, and sprinkle the parmesan "cheese" over each dish.
Per Serving: Calories 223; Total Fat 6.3g; Sodium 7mg; Total Carbs 38.1g; Fiber 5.9g; Sugars27.7g; Protein 3.1g

Falafel-Stuffed Pita

Prep time: 10 minutes | Cook time: 20 minutes | Serves: 3

2 (16-ounce) cans of chickpeas, drained, rinsed, and patted dry	grain flour
	3 whole-grain pitas
8 garlic cloves	1 cucumber, cut into ¼-inch-thick rounds
¾ cup fresh parsley	
1 tablespoon cumin	2 Roma tomatoes, cut into
½ teaspoon sea salt	¼-inch-thick slices
4 tablespoons all-purpose whole-	⅓ cup tahini dressing or tzatziki

1. At 375 degrees F, preheat your oven. Line the rimmed baking sheet with baking paper. Set aside. 2. In a food processor, blend the chickpeas, garlic, parsley, cumin, and salt until the prepared mixture is crumbly. 3. Make sure all ingredients are well incorporated by scraping the sides of the food processor a few times. 4. Add the flour to the prepared mixture, 1 tablespoon at a time, until it becomes a dough that can be shaped into small patties without sticking to your hands. 5. Scoop out roughly 2 tablespoons of the prepared mixture, roll into a ball, and press to form a patty. Continue with all of the ready dough to make approximately 12 patties. 6. Place the patties on the prepared baking sheet, and bake in the oven for almost 20 minutes until golden brown; after 12 minutes of cooking time, turn them over. Remove from the oven. 7. Split open the top of the pitas and add 3 warm falafel patties to each, including cucumber and tomato slices. 8. Drizzle the sauce you like, and close the pita.
Per Serving: Calories 563; Total Fat 16g; Sodium 1034mg; Total Carbs 90g; Fiber 19g; Sugar 11g; Protein 23g

Quinoa-Stuffed Peppers

Prep time: 15 minutes | Cook time: 30 minutes | Serves: 6

1 cup uncooked quinoa, rinsed and drained	oil
	4 garlic cloves, minced
2 cups water	1 small onion, diced
6 bell peppers (red, green, orange, and yellow), deveined, seeded, and halved lengthwise	1 teaspoon red chili flakes
	1 teaspoon dried oregano
	2 tablespoons lemon juice
2 tablespoons extra-virgin olive	¼ cup chopped fresh parsley

1. At 425 degrees F, preheat your oven. 2. In a suitable saucepan with a lid, bring the quinoa and water to a boil over high heat. Lower the heat and cover the saucepan. Simmer the quinoa for almost 15 minutes while preparing the rest of the recipe. 3. Place the bell peppers cut-side down on a rimmed baking sheet and bake for 15 minutes. 4. In a suitable skillet over medium heat, preheat the olive oil. 5. Add the red chili flakes, garlic, and onion, and sauté for 3 to 4 minutes, or until the garlic is fragrant. 6. Add the oregano, lemon juice, and parsley and sauté for 1 more minute. 7. Add the cooked quinoa to this skillet and mix. 8. Flip the pepper over. 9. Scoop the quinoa mixture into the open peppers and return them to the oven for 5 minutes. 10. Let the pepper sit for 5 minutes before serving.
Per Serving: Calories 216; Total Fat 5.2g; Sodium 37mg; Total Carbs 37.8g; Fiber 4.3g; Sugars0.4g; Protein 8.1g

Pumpkin Mac 'N' Cheese

Prep time: 15 minutes | Cook time: 15 minutes | Serves: 4

2 cups dried macaroni noodles
1½ cups unsweetened nondairy milk
2 teaspoons garlic powder
½ cup nutritional yeast
2 teaspoons Dijon mustard

1 cup canned pumpkin puree
1 (16-ounce) can of white navy beans, drained
Sea salt
Black pepper

1. Prepare the noodles in line with the package directions. 2. While the pasta cooks, warm the milk in a suitable saucepan over medium heat. 3. Add the garlic powder, nutritional yeast, mustard, and pumpkin puree to the milk and beat until mixed. 4. Heat them for 5 minutes more over low heat. 5. In a suitable blender, blend 1 cup of the pumpkin mixture with the navy beans. 6. Blend them until smooth, then pour them into the saucepan and mix well. 7. Pour the sauce over the cooked, drained macaroni noodles, stir, and season with black pepper and salt to taste.
Per Serving: Calories 267; Total Fat 28.5g; Sodium 207mg; Total Carbs 1.5g; Fiber 0.3g; Sugars0.2g; Protein 2.4g

Rosemary-Roasted Tofu

Prep time: 10 minutes | Cook time: 25 minutes | Serves: 4

14 ounces of extra-firm tofu
1 tablespoon extra-virgin olive oil
1 tablespoon low-sodium soy sauce

½ teaspoon garlic powder
1 teaspoon finely chopped dried rosemary
2 tablespoons cornstarch

1. Wrap the tofu with a paper towel. 2. Arrange the tofu on a plate and add a second plate on top. Weigh down the top plate with a few heavy cans and leave the tofu to "press" for 5 minutes. 3. At 400 degrees F, preheat your oven. 4. In a suitable mixing bowl, beat together the olive oil, soy sauce, garlic powder, rosemary, and 1 tablespoon of cornstarch until smooth. 5. Cut the tofu half lengthwise, then cut each rectangle into about 16 pieces. 6. Toss the tofu in the sauce and stir well to mix. Add the rest 1 tablespoon of cornstarch to the mix and go well. 7. Lay the tofu cubes on a suitable baking sheet in a single layer and cook in the oven for 25 minutes, flipping them at the 15-minute mark.
Per Serving: Calories 134; Total Fat 10.8g; Sodium 124mg; Total Carbs 2.3g; Fiber 0.4g; Sugars2.1g; Protein 6.3g

Garlic and Cauliflower Mash

Prep time: 10 minutes | Cook time: 20 minutes | Serves: 4

4 cups cauliflower, raw or frozen, defrosted
4 garlic cloves, peeled
2 tablespoons, plus 1 teaspoon of

extra-virgin olive oil
1 teaspoon dried thyme
¼ teaspoon sea salt
¼ cup unsweetened nondairy milk

1. At 375 degrees F, preheat your oven. 2. Chop the cauliflower into smaller florets. 3. In a suitable bowl, toss the florets and whole garlic with 2 tablespoons of olive oil, the thyme, and the salt. 4. On a suitable, rimmed baking sheet, arrange the garlic and cauliflower, and roast them in the oven for 20 minutes, stirring halfway through. 5. Put the roasted vegetables into a blender with the milk and 1 teaspoon of olive oil. 6. Blend until smooth or to your desired mashed consistency.
Per Serving: Calories 171; Total Fat 1.5g; Sodium3mg; Total Carbs 38.2g; Fiber 20.3g; Sugars14.1g; Protein 3.8g

Garlic-Roasted Veggies

Prep time: 15 minutes | Cook time: 30 minutes | Serves: 4

1 large sweet potato
2 medium beets
2 medium carrots
1 zucchini
2 tablespoons extra-virgin olive oil
2 tablespoons balsamic vinegar

4 garlic cloves, minced
2 teaspoons dried basil
2 teaspoons dried oregano
2 cups cremini mushrooms
1 red onion, chopped
Sea salt
Black pepper

1. At 425 degrees F, preheat your oven. 2. Dice the sweet potato, beets, carrots, and zucchini into ½-inch cubes. 3. Beat the olive oil, balsamic vinegar, garlic, basil, and oregano in a suitable bowl. 4. On a rimmed baking sheet, spread the diced vegetables, the mushrooms, and the onion in a single layer and drizzle the oil mixture over the vegetables. Toss to evenly coat, and season with black pepper and salt to taste. 5. Roast the food in the oven for 15 minutes. 6. Stir the vegetables after 15 minutes and continue roasting them for an additional 10 to 15

minutes, or until the vegetables are tender.
Per Serving: Calories 270; Total Fat 7.3g; Sodium 250mg; Total Carbs 44.8g; Fiber 4.1g; Sugars9.2g; Protein 8.1g

Mediterranean Fettuccine

Prep time: 10 minutes | Cook time: 20 minutes | Serves: 2

4 ounces dried fettuccine
2 cups finely chopped kale leaves
¼ cup kalamata olives
1 tablespoon lemon juice

2 tablespoons extra-virgin olive oil
1 tablespoon nutritional yeast
⅛ teaspoon sea salt

1. Prepare the pasta in line with the package directions. 2. Once the pasta is cooked, drain excess water and rinse under cold water to prevent overcooking. Set aside for later use. 3. Still, add the kale and olives to the pot, and cook them over medium heat for 3 to 4 minutes until the kale is soft and bright green. 4. Put the pasta back in the pot, and toss lemon juice, olive oil, nutritional yeast, and salt. 5. Serve and enjoy.
Per Serving: Calories 349; Total Fat 17.2g; Sodium 284mg; Total Carbs 41.9g; Fiber 5g; Sugars21.9g; Protein 8.1g

Broccoli and Chickpea Couscous

Prep time: 10 minutes | Cook time: 15 minutes | Serves: 2

3 garlic cloves, minced
4½ tablespoons extra-virgin olive oil
1½ cups vegetable broth
1 cup whole-grain couscous
3 cups broccoli, chopped into florets

1 (16-ounce) can of chickpeas, drained
3 tablespoons lemon juice
4 tablespoons fresh parsley
Sea salt
Black pepper

1. In a suitable saucepan, sauté the garlic in ½ tablespoon of olive oil on medium-low heat until fragrant, about 3 minutes. 2. Add the vegetable broth and couscous to the saucepan and cook on low for 3 to 5 minutes until the broth is absorbed and the couscous is soft and fluffy. 3. Heat 1 tablespoon of olive oil over high heat in a suitable skillet and sauté the broccoli for 5 minutes. 4. Add the chickpeas to the broccoli, stir together, and cook for 5 minutes until the chickpeas are warmed. 5. Mix the cooked couscous with the broccoli-and-chickpea mixture. 6. Add 3 tablespoons of olive oil, lemon juice, and parsley, and stir. Season this dish with black pepper and salt, and enjoy.
Per Serving: Calories 363; Total Fat 19.1g; Sodium 67mg; Total Carbs 42.8g; Fiber 1.7g; Sugars24.2g; Protein 6.9g

Tofu Pesto Panini

Prep time: 10 minutes | Cook time: 30 minutes | Serves: 4

14 ounces of extra-firm tofu
4 tablespoons extra-virgin olive oil, divided
½ teaspoon garlic powder
½ teaspoon onion powder
½ teaspoon dried oregano
4 Roma tomatoes, halved

½ teaspoon sea salt
½ teaspoon black pepper
4 whole wheat ciabatta buns
1 cup of perfect pesto
2 cups baby spinach
½ cup fresh basil leaves

1. At 375 degrees F, preheat your oven. 2. Wrap the tofu with a paper towel. 3. Arrange the tofu on a plate and add a second plate on top. Weigh down the top plate with a few heavy cans and leave the tofu to "press" for 5 minutes. 4. Mix 1 tablespoon of olive oil, the garlic powder, the onion powder, and the oregano in a bowl. 5. Unwrap the tofu from the towel and slice it into ¼-inch-thick patties. Coat each cake in the oil-and-spice mixture. 6. Add the patties to the rimmed baking sheet. 7. Bake the patties in the oven for 25 minutes, flipping them over after 15 minutes. 8. In a single layer, arrange the tomatoes on another rimmed baking sheet, cut-side up, drizzle with 2 tablespoons of olive oil, season with the salt and pepper, then toss the tomatoes to coat them evenly—Bake in the oven for 20 minutes. 9. Half the ciabatta buns and spread each side with ¼ cup of pesto. 10. Remove the trays from the oven. Lay one tofu patty on each ciabatta bun bottom and top with 1 roasted tomato, ¼ cup spinach, and ⅛ cup basil. 11. Place the top bun over the filling and brush the exterior of each bun with the rest 1 tablespoon of olive oil. 12. In a panini press, grill each sandwich for 5 minutes if you have one. Otherwise, grill each sandwich in a pan on medium-high heat for 3 to 4 minutes on each side.
Per Serving: Calories 624; Total Fat 43g; Sodium 557mg; Total Carbs 39g; Fiber 8g; Sugar 4g; Protein 23g

Stuffed Artichoke Hearts

Prep time: 15 minutes | Cook time: 35 minutes | Serves: 4

For the Artichokes
8 cups water

10 artichokes, stemmed and cored

For the Stuffing
¼ cup olive oil
1 small onion, chopped
1 cup of fresh peas
1 carrot, peeled and diced

1 cup basmati rice
½ teaspoon ground turmeric
⅛ teaspoon salt
⅛ teaspoon black pepper

For the Sauce
2 tablespoons cornstarch
2 cups water
2 garlic cloves, minced
½ teaspoon grated peeled fresh

ginger
¼ teaspoon white pepper
¼ teaspoon grated nutmeg
⅛ teaspoon salt

To Make the Artichokes: In a suitable pot over medium-high heat, bring the water to a boil. Gently drop the artichokes into the boiling water and cook for almost 5 minutes until tender. Drain and arrange the artichokes on a serving platter.
To Make the Stuffing: 1. In a suitable saucepan over medium heat, preheat the olive oil. Add the onion and cook for 2 to 3 minutes until golden. 2. Add the peas and carrot and cook for 5 minutes more with occasional stirring. 3. Stir in the rice, turmeric, salt, and pepper. Increase the heat to bring the prepared mixture to a boil. Reduce its heat to low, cover this pan, and cook for 15 minutes. Let rest, covered, for 10 minutes.
To Make the Sauce: 1. In a suitable bowl, Beat the cornstarch and water until the cornstarch dissolves. Transfer to a suitable saucepan and place it over medium-low heat. 2. Add the garlic, ginger, white pepper, nutmeg, and salt. Cook for 5 to 8 minutes, constantly stirring, until the sauce thickens. Now remove it from the heat.
To Stuff the Artichokes: Stuff each artichoke with the rice filling and drizzle each with the sauce. Serve any remaining rice alongside the stuffed artichokes.
Per Serving: Calories 211; Total Fat 22g; Sodium 166mg; Total Carbs 1.1g; Fiber 0g; Sugars0.1g; Protein 2.9g

Three-Bean Chili

Prep time: 10 minutes | Cook time: 30 minutes | Serves: 4

2 tablespoons extra-virgin olive oil
1 yellow onion, diced
4 garlic cloves, minced
¼ cup tomato paste
2 teaspoons chili powder
1 teaspoon cumin
1 teaspoon paprika

1 cup vegetable broth
1 (16 ounces) can of diced tomatoes, drained
2 (16 ounces) cans of mixed beans, or about 4 cups of cooked chickpeas, red kidney beans, and white cannellini beans

1. In a suitable stockpot over medium heat, preheat the olive oil. 2. Add the onion and garlic to the stockpot, and sauté them for almost 4 minutes, or until fragrant. 3. Add the tomato paste, chili powder, cumin, and paprika and cook for 1 minute more. 4. Deglaze the pot with the vegetable broth, scrape the bottom, and stir well. 5. Add the diced tomatoes and mixed beans, stir well, and simmer on medium-low heat for 25 minutes with occasional stirring to keep the bottom from burning.
Per Serving: Calories 328; Total Fat 11g; Sodium 791mg; Total Carbs 46g; Fiber 13g; Sugar 11g; Protein 13g

Shawarma Lettuce Wrap

Prep time: 10 minutes | Cook time: 5 minutes | Serves: 4

1 tablespoon lemon juice
1 tablespoon tomato paste or sauce
2 tablespoons soy sauce
1 (16-ounce) can of brown lentils, drained
2 teaspoons ground cumin
1 teaspoon ground coriander

1 teaspoon paprika
¼ teaspoon ground cinnamon
¼ teaspoon ground cloves
4 large romaine lettuce leaves
½ cup diced cucumber
½ cup diced tomatoes
4 tablespoons kalamata olives
½ cup tzatziki

1. Stir together the lemon juice, tomato paste, and soy sauce until well mixed in a suitable bowl. 2. Add the lentils, cumin, coriander, paprika, cinnamon, and cloves, and stir until the lentils are evenly coated. 3. Gently warm the lentil mixture over medium heat for almost 5 minutes or until thoroughly warmed through in a suitable skillet. 4. Add ¼ of the lentil mixture to each of the four large romaine lettuce leaves. 5. Top each lettuce wrap with the cucumber, tomatoes, and olives, then drizzle the tzatziki over the filling before rolling the lettuce leaf.
Per Serving: Calories 193; Total Fat 5g; Sodium 534mg; Total Carbs 28g; Fiber 10g; Sugar 4g; Protein 13g

Potato Dumplings with Pomegranate Sauce

Prep time: 20 minutes | Cook time: 90 minutes | Serves: 6

For the Sauce
¼ cup olive oil
1 teaspoon pomegranate molasses or cranberry juice

1 teaspoon harissa, or store-bought
½ teaspoon ground coriander

For the Stuffing
¼ cup olive oil
3 onions, finely chopped
2 cups chopped walnuts
1 garlic clove, minced

1 teaspoon ground cumin
1 teaspoon ground coriander
⅛ teaspoon salt

For the Prepared Dough
2 russet potatoes
4 cups fine bulgur
6 cups of cold water
1 onion, quartered
½ cup pumpkin purée

½ cup whole-wheat flour
1 teaspoon ground cumin
Olive oil for handling the prepared dough

To Make the Sauce: Beat the olive oil, molasses, harissa, and coriander in a suitable bowl until blended. Set aside.
To Make the Stuffing: 1. In a saucepan over medium heat, preheat the olive oil. Add the onions and cook for 5 minutes. 2. Add the walnuts and cook for 5 minutes more. 3. Turn off the heat, and stir in the garlic, cumin, coriander, and salt. Set aside.
To Make the Prepared Dough: 1. Place a suitable glass bowl in the refrigerator to chill. 2. In a suitable pot, mix the potatoes and enough water to cover by 1 inch. Bring to a boil over medium-high heat. Reduce its heat to maintain a rolling boil and cook the potatoes for almost 30 minutes until soft. Drain and let cool slightly. When the potatoes are cool enough to handle, peel and quarter them. 3. While the potatoes cook, mix the bulgur and cold water in a suitable bowl and let sit for almost 10 minutes until soft. Drain and squeeze out any excess water. Set aside. 4. Mix a quarter of the onion and a quarter of the soaked bulgur in a food processor—process for 30 seconds. 5. Add a couple of potato quarters and continue to process until the prepared mixture starts to pull away from the walls of the food processor. Transfer to the chilled bowl. Repeat the process with the rest onion, bulgur, and potatoes. 6. Add the pumpkin to the bulgur dough, sprinkle with the flour, and add the cumin. Knead the prepared dough until mixed well. 7. At 400 degrees F, preheat your oven. Line a suitable baking sheet with parchment paper. 8. Coat your palms with olive oil and portion the prepared dough into 12 balls. 9. Arrange 6 dough balls on the prepared baking sheet, about 5 inches apart. 10. Flatten the balls into ⅛-inch-thick rounds. 11. Spoon the walnut stuffing onto each round. 12. Flatten the rest 6 balls in your palm and gently place them over the stuffing. Gently seal the edges and try, using your palms, to create a dome shape. Bake for 45 minutes. 13. Drizzle with the pomegranate sauce and serve.
Per Serving: Calories 196; Total Fat 13.2g; Sodium 67mg; Total Carbs 16.9g; Fiber 3.1g; Sugars8.4g; Protein 4.8g

Meatless Gyros

Prep time: 10 minutes | Cook time: 15 minutes | Serves: 4

2 cups sliced portobello mushrooms
⅔ cup sliced red onion
1½ tablespoons apple cider vinegar
1½ tablespoons reduce-sodium soy sauce
2 teaspoons ground cumin
1 teaspoon ground coriander

1 teaspoon paprika
¼ teaspoon cinnamon
¼ teaspoon ground cloves
3 to 4 tablespoons of water
⅔ cup tzatziki
4 whole-grain flatbreads
2 cups chopped lettuce
⅔ cucumber, seeded and diced

1. In a suitable saucepan with a lid over medium heat, mix the mushrooms, red onion, apple cider vinegar, soy sauce, cumin, coriander, paprika, cinnamon, and cloves. 2. Cover this pan and cook for almost 5 minutes, or until the mushrooms are browned, and the onion is soft. 3. Deglaze this pan with the water, stirring to scrape up the browned bits from the bottom, then cook, covered, for another 8 minutes. 4. Assemble the sandwich by spreading tzatziki on each flatbread, crust to crust—layer half of each flatbread with the cooked mushrooms, chopped lettuce, and diced cucumber. Fold the flatbreads in half over the fillings.
Per Serving: Calories 260; Total Fat 7g; Sodium 450mg; Total Carbs 40g; Fiber 4g; Sugar 6g; Protein 10g

Avocado-Chickpea Sandwich

Prep time: 15 minutes | Cook time: 0 | Serves: 3

1 (16-ounce) can of chickpeas, drained
1 avocado
2 teaspoons apple cider vinegar
1 garlic clove, minced
2 tablespoons dried parsley

Sea salt
Black pepper
6 slices of whole-grain bread
1 cup baby spinach
½ cucumber, cut into ¼-inch-thick rounds

1. In a suitable bowl, mash the chickpeas and avocado together with the back of a fork. 2. Add the vinegar, garlic, and parsley to the chickpea mash and stir—season with black pepper and salt to taste. 3. Spread the chickpea mash on 3 slices of bread. 4. Top each with ⅓ of the spinach and cucumber. 5. Close the sandwiches with the other 3 slices of bread and enjoy.
Per Serving: Calories 436; Total Fat 13g; Sodium 412mg; Total Carbs 64g; Fiber 15g; Sugar 8g; Protein 19g

Pita Pizza with Hummus

Prep time: 10 minutes | Cook time: 10 minutes | Serves: 2

2 teaspoons extra-virgin olive oil
¼ red bell pepper, cut into thin strips
¼ zucchini, cut into thin slices
¼ cup diced mushrooms

¼ cup diced red onion
½ cup hummus
½ cup tomato sauce (optional)
2 whole-wheat pitas
¼ cup nutritional yeast (optional)

1. At 350 degrees F, preheat your oven. 2. In a suitable skillet, preheat the oil and sauté the bell pepper, zucchini, mushrooms, and onion until the vegetables are tender. 3. Spread ¼ cup hummus and ¼ cup tomato sauce (optional) over each pita and top with the sautéed vegetables. 4. Heat the oven on a rimmed baking sheet for 8 to 10 minutes. You'll want the pita to be toasted but not burnt. 5. Sprinkle the nutritional yeast (optional) on each pizza for a cheesy flavor.
Per Serving: Calories 376; Total Fat 19g; Sodium 618mg; Total Carbs 46g; Fiber 8g; Sugar 6g; Protein 11g

Green Veggie Sandwich

Prep time: 10 minutes | Cook time: 0 | Serves: 2

1 avocado
4 slices of whole-grain bread, toasted
½ cucumber, sliced
1 cup alfalfa sprouts

1 cup baby spinach
1 teaspoon lemon juice
Sea salt
Black pepper

1. Mash ¼ of the avocado onto each slice of toast. 2. Layer the cucumber slices on 2 of the pieces of bread and push down gently, so the cucumber slices sink into the avocado. 3. Add the sprouts and spinach on top of the cucumber slices. 4. Season with lemon juice and salt and pepper to taste. 5. Top with the other two slices of toast to make the complete sandwich, and enjoy.
Per Serving: Calories 346; Total Fat 14g; Sodium 411mg; Total Carbs 46g; Fiber 11g; Sugar 5g; Protein 14g

Marinated Zucchini

Prep time: 15 minutes | Cook time: 5 minutes | Serves: 6

¼ cup balsamic vinegar
2 tablespoons stone-ground mustard
1 garlic clove, minced
2 teaspoons chopped fresh thyme

¼ cup olive oil
⅛ teaspoon salt
⅛ teaspoon black pepper
3 large zucchinis, cut diagonally into ½-inch-thick slices

1. Beat the vinegar, mustard, garlic, and thyme to mix in a suitable bowl. Gradually Beat in the olive oil until blended. Season with salt and pepper and beat again to combine. 2. Place the zucchini in a suitable bowl and drizzle ¼ cup of marinade over them. Toss well to coat. 3. Heat a grill pan or sauté pan over medium heat. 4. Place the zucchini slices in this pan. Cook for almost 5 minutes, occasionally turning, until the zucchini is tender and lightly charred. 5. Transfer the cooked zucchini back to the bowl and drizzle it with the rest marinade. Toss to coat. Cover the bowl and refrigerate the zucchini to marinate for 30 minutes or until chilled. 6. Arrange the marinated slices on a serving platter and drizzle with the marinade from the bowl to serve.
Per Serving: Calories 171; Total Fat 1.5g; Sodium3mg; Total Carbs 38.2g; Fiber 20.3g; Sugars14.1g; Protein 3.8g

Stuffed Cabbage

Prep time: 40 minutes | Cooking time: 65 minutes | Serves: 6

4 tablespoons olive oil, divided
1 small onion, chopped
2 cups short-grain rice
4 cups water
4 garlic cloves, minced
½ teaspoon dried sage
½ teaspoon crumbled dried rosemary

2 tablespoons pine nuts
1 large head cabbage, cored
1 (28-ounce) can of crushed tomatoes
¼ cup chopped olives
1 tablespoon chopped fresh rosemary

1. At 375 degrees F, preheat your oven. Line a suitable plate with a clean kitchen towel and set it aside. 2. Heat 2 tablespoons of olive oil in a pot over medium heat. Add the onion and cook for 5 minutes. 3. Add the rice and water. Increase the heat and bring the liquid to a boil. Reduce its heat to low, cover the pot, and cook for 10 minutes until the water is absorbed. 4. Transfer the rice to a suitable bowl. Add the garlic, sage, dried rosemary, and pine nuts. Toss well to mix and set aside. 5. Bring a suitable pot of water to a boil over high heat. Gently drop the cabbage into the boiling water—Cook for 5 minutes. 6. Using long, sturdy tongs, gently transfer the cabbage to the prepared plate to drain excess water. Remove the outer leaves of the cabbage; you'll need about 16 leaves. 7. Place a cabbage leaf on a flat surface. Remove the thick stem in the center but keep the leaf intact—place about ¼ cup of the stuffing in the center. Fold the sides over the filling and roll up the leaf. Place the stuffed leaf, seam-side down, in a 9-by-13-inch baking dish. Repeat until you finish stuffing all the leaves. 8. In a suitable bowl, stir together the tomatoes, remaining 2 tablespoons of olive oil, the olives, and fresh rosemary. Pour the sauce over the cabbage leaves. 9. Bake the food, uncovered, for 45 minutes. 10. Serve immediately.
Per Serving: Calories 390; Total Fat 1.9g; Sodium 7mg; Total Carbs 100.3g; Fiber 17.8g; Sugars69.7g; Protein 3.2g

Chickpea Fattah

Prep time: 10 minutes | Cook time: 15 minutes | Serves: 6

3 (9-inch) day-old pita pieces of bread, cut into 1-inch squares
3 cups plain yogurt
1 cup tahini
½ cup lemon juice
4 garlic cloves, crushed or mashed into a paste
1 teaspoon ground cumin

Salt
2 (15-ounce) cans of chickpeas, undrained
2 tablespoons ghee or store-bought
¼ cup pine nuts
2 tablespoons chopped fresh parsley

1. Arrange the bread pieces in a deep serving platter in an even layer. Set aside. 2. Beat the yogurt, tahini, lemon juice, garlic, and cumin until smooth in a suitable bowl-season with salt. Set aside. 3. Pour the chickpeas and their liquid into a saucepan and cook to a boil over medium-high heat. Reduce its heat to maintain a simmer and cook for almost 10 minutes until the chickpeas are hot. 4. Spoon the hot chickpeas and liquid evenly over the bread. Pour the yogurt sauce over the chickpeas. Set aside. 5. In a suitable saucepan over medium heat, melt the ghee. Add the pine nuts. Increase the heat to medium-high and fry the nuts for almost 1 minute or until slightly golden. 6. Pour the pine nuts and ghee over the yogurt sauce. Sprinkle with the parsley and serve.
Per Serving: Calories 256; Total Fat 24.2g; Sodium 13mg; Total Carbs 10g; Fiber 0.5g; Sugars9g; Protein 2g

Pickled Turnips

Prep time: 15 minutes | Cook time: 0 | Serves: 12

4 cups water
¼ cup salt
1 cup white distilled vinegar
1 small beet, peeled and quartered

1 garlic clove, peeled
2 pounds' turnips, peeled, halved, and cut into ¼-inch half-moons

1. In a suitable bowl, beat the water and salt until the salt dissolves. Beat in the vinegar. 2. Place the beet and garlic in a clean 2-quart glass jar with a tight-sealing lid—Layer the turnips on top. 3. Pour the vinegar mixture over the turnips to cover them. Seal the lid tightly and let the jar sit at room temperature for 1 week.
Per Serving: Calories 134; Total Fat 10.8g; Sodium 124mg; Total Carbs 2.3g; Fiber 0.4g; Sugars2.1g; Protein 6.3g

Braised Sweet Peppers

Prep time: 10 minutes | Cook time: 40 minutes | Serves: 4

¼ cup olive oil
1 red onion, sliced
3 red bell peppers, seeded and cut into 1-inch strips
3 green bell peppers, seeded and cut into 1-inch strips

2 garlic cloves, chopped
¼ teaspoon cayenne pepper
⅛ teaspoon salt
⅛ teaspoon black pepper
¼ cup vegetable broth
1 tablespoon chopped fresh thyme

1. In a suitable saucepan over medium heat, preheat the olive oil. 2. Add the red onion to the saucepan and sauté for 5 minutes. 3. Add the red and green bell peppers, garlic, cayenne, salt, and black pepper. 4. Add the vegetable broth, stir and bring to a boil. 5. Cover the saucepan and reduce its heat to low—Cook for 35 minutes with occasional stirring until the vegetables are soft but still firm. 6. Sprinkle the peppers with thyme and serve.
Per Serving: Calories 297; Total Fat 13.7g; Sodium 1129mg; Total Carbs 17.2g; Fiber 4.8g; Sugars9.3g; Protein 30.2g

Rainbow Lettuce Wrap

Prep time: 10 minutes | Cook time: 0 | Serves: 2

2 large collard green leaves
¼ cup roasted red pepper and lentil dip (optional)
¼ red bell pepper, cut into thin strips

¼ yellow bell pepper, cut into thin strips
½ carrot, peeled and cut into sticks
½ cucumber, cut into sticks

1. Roll the collard leaves a couple of times to break the fibers so they're easier to roll when assembled. 2. If using the roasted red pepper and lentil dip, spread half on each collard leaf. 3. Lay the red and yellow bell pepper, carrot, and cucumber facing the same direction in the center of each collard leaf. 4. Fold the bottom of the leaf up at first, then hold it in place while folding the top of the leaf into the center of the wrap. 5. Rotate the wrap 90 degrees, so the top and bottom become the sides, and fold the bottom side of the leaf up to the center while rolling the wrap away from you to wrap the leaf tightly around itself.
Per Serving: Calories 134; Total Fat 10.8g; Sodium 124mg; Total Carbs 2.3g; Fiber 0.4g; Sugars2.1g; Protein 6.3g

Caramelized Pearl Onions

Prep time: 5 minutes | Cook time: 15 minutes | Serves: 4

¼ cup olive oil
1 pound frozen pearl onions, thawed
3 tablespoons sugar
½ cup balsamic vinegar

1 tablespoon chopped fresh rosemary
⅛ teaspoon salt
⅛ teaspoon red pepper flakes

1. Preheat the olive oil in a sauté pan or skillet over medium heat. 2. Add the onions and cook for almost 5 minutes until they begin to brown. 3. Add the sugar and cook for almost 5 minutes more until the sugar is caramelized, gently stirring, so the onions do not stick to this plan. 4. Add the vinegar and rosemary, and cook for almost 2 minutes with occasional stirring until a syrup forms. 5. Stir in the salt and red pepper flakes. Let cool before serving.
Per Serving: Calories 168; Total Fat 3.1g; Sodium 412mg; Total Carbs 28.5g; Fiber 6.9g; Sugars5g; Protein 7.5g

Roasted Root Vegetables

Prep time: 20 minutes | Cook time: 40 minutes | Serves: 6

2 red onions, quartered
2 potatoes, peeled and cut into 2-inch cubes
2 red bell peppers, seeded and cut into 1-inch strips
2 zucchinis, cut into 2-inch sticks
1 sweet potato, peeled and cut into 2-inch cubes
¼ cup olive oil

2 garlic cloves, mashed
2 teaspoons ground coriander
1 teaspoon salt
1 teaspoon sweet paprika
½ teaspoon ground cumin
1 tablespoon chopped fresh cilantro
2 tablespoons lime juice

1. At 375 degrees F, preheat your oven. 2. Mix the red onions, potatoes, bell peppers, zucchini, and sweet potato in a suitable bowl. Set aside. 3. Beat the olive oil, garlic, coriander, salt, paprika, and cumin until well mixed in a suitable bowl. 4. Pour the olive oil mixture over the vegetables and toss well to coat. 5. Arrange the vegetables on a suitable baking sheet

in a single layer. Roast for almost 40 minutes until tender. 6. Sprinkle with the cilantro, drizzle with the lime juice and enjoy.
Per Serving: Calories 256; Total Fat 24.2g; Sodium 13mg; Total Carbs 10g; Fiber 0.5g; Sugars9g; Protein 2g

Stuffed Zucchini

Prep time: 20 minutes | Cook time: 65 minutes | Serves: 4

6 zucchinis, halved lengthwise
¼ cup olive oil
1 onion, chopped
2 cups chopped white mushrooms
1 green bell pepper, seeded and diced
4 garlic cloves, crushed
2 cups cooked lentils
1 (15-ounce) can of diced tomatoes
2 tablespoons tomato paste

2 tablespoons pomegranate molasses or cranberry juice
1 tablespoon harissa
½ cup water
⅛ teaspoon salt, plus more as needed
⅛ teaspoon black pepper, plus more as needed
½ cup feta cheese (optional)
Tzatziki sauce, for serving (optional)

1. At 375 degrees F, preheat your oven. 2. Heat a suitable pot full of water over medium heat for 10 minutes. Add the zucchini and cook for 2 to 3 minutes to blanch. Using tongs, remove the zucchini from the water and let cool. 3. Using a teaspoon, scoop out the seeds from the zucchini halves to create a cavity for the stuffing. Discard the pulp. Arrange the zucchini halves in a 9-by-13-inch baking dish, cut side up, and set aside. 4. In a skillet over medium heat, preheat the olive oil. Add the onion and cook for almost 8 minutes until golden. 5. Stir in the mushrooms, green bell pepper, and garlic—Cook for 5 minutes. Stir in the cooked lentils, tomatoes, tomato paste, molasses, harissa, water, salt, and pepper. Cover this skillet and cook for 5 minutes. Taste and season with more salt and pepper, as needed. 6. Fill the cavity of each zucchini with the lentil mixture, and spoon any remaining sauce over the zucchini. Cover the baking dish with aluminum foil. 7. Bake the food for 20 minutes. Remove the foil, sprinkle the feta cheese on top (optional), and bake for 10 minutes more or until golden brown. 8. Serve topped with tzatziki (optional).
Per Serving: Calories 184; Total Fat 2.7g; Sodium 58mg; Total Carbs 33.4g; Fiber 0.2g; Sugars5.7g; Protein 6.3g

Stuffed Potatoes

Prep time: 20 minutes | Cook time: 55 minutes | Serves: 4

¼ cup olive oil
1 onion, chopped
1 pound white mushrooms, finely chopped
¼ cup pine nuts
¼ teaspoon ground cumin
¼ teaspoon ground coriander

¼ teaspoon ground allspice
⅜ teaspoon salt
8 Yukon gold potatoes, peeled
4 cups crushed tomatoes
2 cups water
2 garlic cloves, minced
⅛ teaspoon black pepper

1. At 375 degrees F, preheat your oven. 2. In a suitable saucepan over medium heat, preheat the olive oil. 3. Add the onion and sauté for 2 to 3 minutes. 4. Add the mushrooms and cook for almost 10 minutes until their water evaporates. 5. Stir in the pine nuts, cumin, coriander, allspice, and ¼ teaspoon of salt. Set aside. 6. Using a vegetable corer, carve out the middle of each potato until the potatoes look like cups. 7. Spoon the mushroom stuffing into the cavities, filling each. Place the potatoes in a single layer, stuffing-side up, on a rimmed baking sheet. Set aside. 8. In a suitable bowl, stir together the tomatoes, water, garlic, remaining ⅛ teaspoon of salt, and pepper. Pour the tomato mixture over the potatoes. Cover the baking sheet with aluminum foil. 9. Bake the food for 40 minutes until the stuffing is hot and the potatoes are fork-tender. 10. Serve and enjoy.
Per Serving: Calories 172; Total Fat 1.8g; Sodium 135mg; Total Carbs 41.1g; Fiber 6.2g; Sugars28.7g; Protein 6.2g

Hummus-Arugula Wrap

Prep time: 10 minutes | Cook time: 0 | Serves: 2

⅔ cup hummus
2 whole-grain tortilla wraps
1 medium carrot, cut into

matchsticks
2 cups arugula
½ teaspoon paprika

1. Spread half the hummus evenly on each tortilla. 2. Add half the carrot sticks to each tortilla. 3. Top each tortilla with 1 cup arugula and sprinkle ¼ teaspoon paprika on top. 4. Roll the tortilla wraps tightly and cut them in half.
Per Serving: Calories 412; Total Fat 21g; Sodium 770mg; Total Carbs 49; Fiber 9g; Sugar 6g; Protein 12g

Buttered Potatoes

Prep time: 20 minutes | Cook time: 50 minutes | Serves: 8

8 russet potatoes, peeled
8 tablespoons (1 stick) butter, melted

1 teaspoon salt
½ teaspoon black pepper

1. At 450 degrees F, preheat your oven. 2. Using a very sharp knife, carefully cut the potatoes into uniform ⅛-inch-thick slices. 3. Generously brush the bottom of a 10-inch round ovenproof sauté pan or skillet with butter. Starting in the center of this pan, arrange the potato slices, slightly overlapping them, in a circle until you cover the bottom of this pan. Brush the potatoes with butter, sprinkle with black pepper and salt, and repeat until you have used all the potatoes. Drizzle any remaining butter over the top. 4. Cover this pan with aluminum foil—Bake the food for 40 minutes. Remove the foil and bake for 10 minutes more. 5. Remove this pan from the oven. Using a thin spatula, loosen the edges and the bottom of the potatoes. Gently invert the potatoes onto a flat plate and serve.
Per Serving: Calories 216; Total Fat 5.2g; Sodium 37mg; Total Carbs 37.8g; Fiber 4.3g; Sugars0.4g; Protein 8.1g

Eggplant Kufta

Prep time: 15 minutes | Cook time: 30 minutes | Serves: 4

1 large eggplant, cut into 2-inch cubes
¼ cup olive oil, divided
1 small onion, chopped
½ cup chopped fresh parsley
¼ cup chopped fresh cilantro
2 garlic cloves, minced

1 teaspoon sweet paprika
½ teaspoon ground coriander
¼ teaspoon cayenne pepper
⅛ teaspoon salt, plus more as needed
½ cup chopped almonds
2 cups bread crumbs

1. Preheat the broiler. 2. Mix the eggplant and 2 tablespoons of olive oil in a suitable bowl. Toss well to coat. Spread the eggplant on a suitable baking sheet. Broil for almost 5 minutes until golden. Remove and let cool. 3. Reduce the oven temperature to 400°F. 4. Transfer the cooled eggplant to a food processor and purée. Transfer the eggplant purée to a suitable bowl. 5. In the food processor, mix the onion, parsley, and cilantro. Purée them well. 6. Add this herb mixture to the eggplant, garlic, paprika, coriander, cayenne, salt, almonds, and bread crumbs. Stir until good mix. Season with more salt, if desired. 7. Moisten your palms with the rest 2 tablespoons of olive oil. Form the eggplant mixture into 3-inch balls and place them on a suitable baking sheet. You should have about 20 balls. 8. Bake for 20 minutes. Flip the balls and bake for 5 minutes more until firm.
Per Serving: Calories 297; Total Fat 13.7g; Sodium 1129mg; Total Carbs 17.2g; Fiber 4.8g; Sugars9.3g; Protein 30.2g

Pepper and Onion Tart

Prep time: 15 minutes | Cook time: 40 minutes | Serves: 6

2 tablespoons olive oil
1 red onion, chopped
All-purpose flour for dusting
1 refrigerated store-bought piecrust
1 cup ricotta
½ cup heavy cream

2 large eggs
¼ cup chopped fresh basil
⅛ teaspoon salt
⅛ teaspoon black pepper
2 red bell peppers, seeded and sliced

1. At 425 degrees F, preheat your oven 2. In a skillet over medium heat, preheat the olive oil. Add the red onion and cook for 10 minutes or until softened. 3. Dust a work surface with flour and place the crust on it. Let the crust sit for 10 minutes. Transfer the crust, flour-side down, to a 9-inch tart pan. Gently push the crust against the edges. 4. Pierce the bottom of the crust in a few places with a fork and bake for 10 minutes. Remove and set aside to cool. 5. Stir together the ricotta, heavy cream, eggs, basil, salt, and pepper in a suitable bowl. Set aside. 6. Spoon the cooked onion onto the baked pie crust. Spoon the cheese mixture over the onion and arrange the red bell peppers over the cheese. 7. Bake the food for almost 20 minutes or until the filling is set.
Per Serving: Calories 399; Total Fat 27.5g; Sodium 32mg; Total Carbs 45g; Fiber 3.8g; Sugars38.8g; Protein 3.1g

Eggplant and Lentil Tagine

Prep time: 15 minutes | Cook time: 40 minutes | Serves: 6

1 eggplant, cut into 1-inch cubes
½ cup olive oil

2 onions, sliced
1 cup chopped fresh cilantro

3 tablespoons tomato paste
2 tablespoons harissa, or store-bought
2 teaspoons ground coriander
1 teaspoon ground cumin
1 pound dried brown lentils, rinsed and picked over for debris
8 cups water

⅛ teaspoon salt, plus more as needed
⅛ teaspoon black pepper, plus more as needed
2 cups fresh baby spinach
1 cup diced dried apricots
½ cup lemon juice
2 tablespoons chopped lemons

1. Preheat the broiler. 2. Toss the eggplant with 2 tablespoons of olive oil to coat in a suitable bowl. Transfer to a suitable baking sheet and broil for almost 5 minutes until golden. Remove and set aside. 3. In a suitable soup pot over medium heat, preheat the rest 6 tablespoons of olive oil. 4. Add the onions and cook for almost 8 minutes until golden. Add the cilantro and cook for 1 minute. Transfer half the onion mixture to a suitable bowl using a slotted spoon and set aside. 5. Add the tomato paste, harissa, coriander, and cumin to the pot. Stir to mix and cook for 1 minute. 6. Stir in the lentils, water, salt, and pepper. Taste and season with more salt and pepper, as needed. Increase the heat to bring the prepared mixture to a boil. Reduce its heat to medium and cook for almost 15 minutes or until the lentils are tender. 7. Stir in the eggplant, spinach, apricots, lemon juice, and preserved lemons. Cook for 10 minutes more. 8. Spoon the tagine onto a platter and top with the rest cooked onion and cilantro mixture.
Per Serving: Calories 223; Total Fat 6.3g; Sodium 7mg; Total Carbs 38.1g; Fiber 5.9g; Sugars27.7g; Protein 3.1g

Spanakopita with Sesame Seeds

Prep time: 20 minutes | Cook time: 50 minutes | Serves: 6

1 (16-ounce) package frozen chopped spinach, thawed
¼ cup olive oil
1 onion, chopped
3 cups crumbled feta cheese
⅛ teaspoon black pepper

All-purpose flour for dusting
1 sheet puff pastry
1 large egg
1 tablespoon water
1 tablespoon sesame seeds

1. At 400 degrees F, preheat your oven. 2. Using your hands, squeeze the spinach dry, or place it in a colander and press on it with a spoon to remove excess water. Set aside. 3. In a skillet over medium heat, preheat the olive oil. Add the onion and cook for 5 minutes or until soft and translucent. Add the spinach and cook for 2 to 3 minutes more. Now remove it from the heat. 4. Stir in the feta cheese and pepper until well mixed. Spoon the spinach mixture into a 9-by-13-inch baking dish, if not using an oven-safe skillet. Set aside. 5. Dust a work surface with flour and roll out the puff pastry until it is the same size as the baking vessel. Gently cover the spinach mixture with the puff pastry. 6. In a suitable bowl, Beat the egg and water until blended. Brush the puff pastry with the egg wash. Sprinkle with the sesame seeds and cut the puff pastry into 2-inch squares. 7. Bake them for almost 40 minutes until golden. 8. Serve warm.
Per Serving: Calories 270; Total Fat 7.3g; Sodium 250mg; Total Carbs 44.8g; Fiber 4.1g; Sugars9.2g; Protein 8.1g

Spinach Ricotta Dumplings

Prep time: 30 minutes | Cook time: 5 minutes | Serves: 4

½ cup all-purpose flour
1 (10-ounce) package frozen chopped spinach, thawed
1 large egg
2 cups whole-milk ricotta
⅛ teaspoon freshly grated nutmeg

⅛ teaspoon salt, plus more for the cooking water
⅛ teaspoon black pepper
Freshly grated parmesan cheese for serving

1. Dust a suitable baking sheet with flour. 2. Using your hands, squeeze the spinach dry, or place it in a colander and press on it with a spoon to remove excess water. 3. Finely chop the spinach and place it in a suitable bowl. Add the egg, ricotta, nutmeg, flour, salt, and pepper. Mix until well mixed. 4. Dust your palms with flour to prevent the prepared dough from sticking. Take about ¼ cup of the spinach mixture, roll it into a 2-inch ball, and place it on the prepared baking sheet. Repeat with the rested dough, dusting your palms as needed. This dough should make about 20 dumplings. Refrigerate the dumplings for at least 10 minutes before cooking. 5. Bring a suitable pot of salted water to a boil over high heat. Lower the heat to medium and gently drop the dumplings into the water. Cook for almost 5 minutes until the dumplings float to the top. Using a slotted spoon, transfer the dumplings to a plate. 6. Serve topped with your favorite sauce and a sprinkle of parmesan cheese.
Per Serving: Calories 353; Total Fat 37.9g; Sodium 221mg; Total Carbs 1.2g; Fiber 0.1g; Sugars0.2g; Protein 3g

Chakchouka

Prep time: 10 minutes | Cook time: 25 minutes | Serves: 4

¼ cup olive oil
1 onion, finely chopped
1 cup chopped green bell pepper
2 garlic cloves, minced
3 ripe tomatoes, diced

1 teaspoon paprika
½ teaspoon ground cumin
½ teaspoon red pepper flakes
⅛ teaspoon salt
4 medium eggs

1. Preheat the olive oil in a suitable sauté pan or skillet over medium heat. 2. Add the onion and green bell pepper—Cook for almost 8 minutes until the vegetables soften. Add garlic and continue to cook for 1 minute more. 3. Stir together the tomatoes, paprika, cumin, red pepper flakes, and salt in a suitable bowl until well mixed. Add the tomato mixture to this pan, stir, and simmer for 8 minutes. 4. Gently crack the eggs on top of the cooked vegetables, careful not to break the yolks. Cover this pan and cook for 5 minutes or until the egg yolks are firm but not dry. 5. Serve and enjoy.
Per Serving: Calories 256; Total Fat 24.2g; Sodium 13mg; Total Carbs 10g; Fiber 0.5g; Sugars9g; Protein 2g

Asparagus and Swiss Quiche

Prep time: 20 minutes | Cook time: 50 minutes | Serves: 6

6 cups water
8 ounces' asparagus, ends trimmed, cut into 1-inch pieces
2 tablespoons olive oil
4 scallions, chopped
1 (8-inch) store-bought unbaked pie shell

2 large eggs
½ cup heavy cream
2 tablespoons chopped fresh tarragon
¼ teaspoon ground nutmeg
1 cup shredded Swiss cheese

1. At 400 degrees F, preheat your oven. 2. In a suitable pot over medium-high heat, bring the water to a boil. Drop the asparagus into the boiling water and blanch for 2 minutes. Drain and set aside. 3. In a skillet over medium heat, preheat the olive oil. Add the scallions and cook for 5 minutes. Add the asparagus and cook for 1 minute. 4. Spoon the vegetables into the unbaked pie shell. Set aside. 5. In a suitable bowl, beat the eggs, heavy cream, tarragon, and nutmeg. 6. Pour the prepared egg mixture over the asparagus. Sprinkle the Swiss cheese over the top. 7. Bake for almost 40 minutes until firm. Remove from the oven, and let the food cool to room temperature before serving.
Per Serving: Calories 364; Total Fat 29.6g; Sodium 489mg; Total Carbs 27g; Fiber 10.6g; Sugars9.3g; Protein 5.5g

Herbs, Cheese, and Pine Nut Frittata

Prep time: 20 minutes | Cook time: 30 minutes | Serves: 4

¼ cup olive oil
2 tablespoons chopped scallion, white part only
1 garlic clove, chopped
1 (16-ounce) package frozen chopped spinach, thawed
¼ cup pine nuts
2 tablespoons chopped fresh

chives
1 tablespoon chopped fresh basil
1 tablespoon chopped fresh thyme
1 teaspoon dried oregano
3 large eggs
3 tablespoons heavy cream
½ cup grated gruyere cheese

1. Preheat the olive oil in a suitable skillet over medium heat; add the scallion and garlic, and cook for 5 minutes. 2. Add spinach, pine nuts, chives, basil, thyme, and oregano. Cook, stirring, for 5 minutes. Drain any liquid. Set aside. 3. Beat the eggs, heavy cream, and gruyere cheese in a suitable bowl. Pour the prepared egg mixture into the spinach mixture and stir well. 4. Return this skillet to medium heat and cook the frittata for almost 15 minutes or until set. Press the top with a spatula to compact the ingredients. 5. Now remove it from the heat, cover this skillet with a suitable plate, and carefully flip the frittata onto the plate. Slide the frittata back into this skillet and cook over medium heat for almost 5 minutes until golden.
Per Serving: Calories 172; Total Fat 1.8g; Sodium 135mg; Total Carbs 41.1g; Fiber 6.2g; Sugars28.7g; Protein 6.2g

Zucchini and Parmesan Frittata

Prep time: 15 minutes | Cook time: 30 minutes | Serves: 6

¼ cup olive oil
1 red onion, chopped
2 zucchinis, diced
6 large eggs

¼ cup milk
¼ cup chopped fresh parsley
¼ cup freshly grated parmesan cheese

1 teaspoon dried basil
⅛ teaspoon salt

⅛ teaspoon black pepper

1. At 350 degrees F, preheat your oven. 2. In a 12-inch ovenproof skillet over medium heat, preheat the olive oil. 3. Add the red onion and cook for 2 minutes. Add the zucchini and sauté for 10 minutes. Now remove it from the heat. 4. Beat the eggs, milk, parsley, parmesan cheese, basil, salt, and pepper until mixed in a suitable bowl. Pour the prepared egg mixture over the vegetables. 5. Place this skillet in the oven and bake for 15 minutes or until the center of the frittata is set. Serve hot.
Per Serving: Calories 134; Total Fat 10.8g; Sodium 124mg; Total Carbs 2.3g; Fiber 0.4g; Sugars2.1g; Protein 6.3g

Spinach Mushroom Gratin

Prep time: 10 minutes | Cook time: 40 minutes | Serves: 8

4 tablespoons butter
1 large onion, chopped
1-pound shiitake mushrooms, coarsely chopped
1 cup heavy cream
1 cup milk
2 tablespoons cornstarch
2 tablespoons cold water
¼ teaspoon grated nutmeg

⅛ teaspoon salt
⅛ teaspoon black pepper
1 (16-ounce) package frozen chopped spinach, thawed and squeezed dry
½ cup freshly grated parmesan cheese
½ cup grated gruyere cheese

1. At 400 degrees F, preheat your oven. 2. Melt the butter in a heavy-bottomed saucepan over medium heat; add the onion and cook for 5 minutes; add the mushrooms and cook for 10 minutes or until browned. 3. In a suitable bowl, beat the heavy cream and milk. 4. In another small bowl, mix the cornstarch and cold water until the cornstarch dissolves. Add this slurry to the milk mixture and stir to combine. 5. Pour the milk mixture over the mushrooms. Stir in the nutmeg, salt, and pepper. Cook for almost 5 minutes until the sauce thickens. 6. Add the spinach to the sauce. Stir in the parmesan cheese. 7. Spoon the spinach and mushroom mixture into a gratin baking dish. Sprinkle the gruyere cheese on top. 8. Bake for almost 20 minutes until hot and bubbly.
Per Serving: Calories 211; Total Fat 22g; Sodium 166mg; Total Carbs 1.1g; Fiber 0g; Sugars0.1g; Protein 2.9g

Eggplant Moussaka

Prep time: 30 minutes | Cook time: 90 minutes | Serves: 6

For the Eggplant
4 eggplants, cut into ½-inch-thick rounds

Olive oil, for brushing

For the Tomato Sauce
½ cup olive oil
2 large onions, sliced
2 large red bell peppers, seeded and cut into ½-inch-thick slices
1 (28-ounce) can of diced

tomatoes
2 tablespoons tomato paste
1 teaspoon dried oregano
⅛ teaspoon salt

For the Cheese Sauce
4 cups milk
¼ cup cornstarch
½ cup water

1 cup crumbled feta cheese
1 teaspoon dried oregano

To Make the Eggplant: 1. Preheat the broiler. 2. Place the eggplant slices on a suitable baking sheet. Brush lightly with olive oil. Broil for almost 5 minutes until golden. Remove and set aside.
To Make the Tomato Sauce: 1. In a suitable saucepan over medium heat, preheat the olive oil. 2. Add the onions and cook for almost 8 minutes, often stirring, until golden. 3. Add the red bell peppers and cook for 2 minutes. 4. Stir in the tomatoes, tomato paste, oregano, and salt. Increase the heat and bring the sauce to a boil. Reduce its heat to medium, cover this pan, and simmer for 10 minutes.
To Make the Cheese Sauce: 1. In a suitable saucepan over medium heat, preheat the milk for almost 5 minutes until warm. Set aside. 2. In a suitable bowl, Beat the cornstarch and water until the cornstarch dissolves. Add this slurry to the heated milk. Place this pan over medium heat and cook for almost 15 minutes, stirring continuously, until the sauce thickens. Stir in the feta cheese and oregano.
To Assemble: 1. At 375 degrees F, preheat your oven. 2. In a 9-by-13-inch baking dish, arrange half the eggplant slices in a single layer. 3. Spoon half the tomato sauce evenly over the eggplant. Repeat with the rest eggplant and tomato sauce. 4. Spread the cheese sauce over the top. 5. Bake for almost 40 minutes until golden. 6. Serve and enjoy.
Per Serving: Calories 267; Total Fat 28.5g; Sodium 207mg; Total Carbs 1.5g; Fiber 0.3g; Sugars0.2g; Protein 2.4g

Tomato Sourdough Gratin

Prep time: 20 minutes | Cook time: 45 minutes | Serves: 6

1 sourdough loaf, cut into 1-inch cubes
1 cup pitted cured black olives, halved lengthwise
1 (12-ounce) can of diced tomatoes
6 scallions, chopped
1 cup chopped fresh basil

⅛ teaspoon salt, plus more as needed
⅛ teaspoon black pepper, plus more as needed
1 cup shredded manchego cheese
4 cups cherry tomatoes, halved lengthwise

1. At 375 degrees F, preheat your oven. 2. Place the bread in a suitable bowl. Chop half the olives and add them to the bread, including the diced tomatoes, scallions, basil, salt, and pepper. Stir until good mix. Taste and season with more salt and pepper, as needed. 3. Spoon the prepared mixture into a 9-by-13-inch baking dish. Top the bread mixture with the manchego cheese. Arrange the cherry tomatoes and the rest olives on top of the cheese. Cover the dish with aluminum foil. 4. Bake for 20 minutes. Remove the foil and bake for 15 minutes more until the cheese is melted and the edges of the bread are golden. 5. Let the food rest for 10 minutes before serving.
Per Serving: Calories 225; Total Fat 6.3g; Sodium 7mg; Total Carbs 38.1g; Fiber 5.9g; Sugars27.7g; Protein 3.1g

Ratatouille

Prep time: 20 minutes | Cook time: 35 minutes | Serves: 4

¼ cup olive oil
1 onion, chopped
4 garlic cloves, crushed
1 large eggplant, cut into 1-inch cubes
1 zucchini, cut into 1-inch cubes
1 red bell pepper, seeded and

chopped
⅛ teaspoon salt, plus more as needed
3 tomatoes, chopped
1 tablespoon dried oregano
1 teaspoon dried thyme
¼ cup chopped fresh basil

1. In a heavy-bottomed skillet over medium heat, preheat the olive oil. 2. Add the onion and cook for 5 minutes or until soft. 3. Add garlic and continue to cook for 2 minutes. 4. Add the eggplant and cook for 10 minutes, stirring often. 5. Stir in the zucchini, red bell pepper, and salt—Cook for 5 minutes. 6. Stir in the tomatoes, oregano, thyme, and basil—Cook for 10 minutes. Taste and season with more salt, as needed.
Per Serving: Calories 141; Total Fat 0.4g; Sodium 4mg; Total Carbs 31.8g; Fiber 5.6g; Sugars23.4g; Protein 0.6g

French Bean Stew

Prep time: 10 minutes | Cook time: 40 minutes | Serves: 4

¼ cup olive oil
1 onion, chopped
1 pound French green beans, trimmed and cut into 2-inch pieces
4 ripe tomatoes, seeded and diced

4 garlic cloves, minced
⅛ teaspoon salt
⅛ teaspoon black pepper
2 tablespoons tomato paste
2 cups vegetable broth

1. In a soup pot over medium heat, preheat the olive oil. Add the onion and cook for 5 minutes, often stirring, until softened. 2. Add the green beans, cover the pot, and cook for 10 minutes, stirring often. If necessary, add 2 tablespoons of water to prevent the beans from sticking. 3. Stir in the tomatoes and their juices, garlic, salt, and pepper—Cook for 10 minutes. 4. Beat the tomato paste and vegetable broth in a suitable bowl until thoroughly mixed. Pour the broth into the pot. 5. Bring the stew to a boil. Cover the pot and simmer for 15 minutes. 6. Taste and season with more salt and pepper, as needed, before serving.
Per Serving: Calories 184; Total Fat 2.7g; Sodium 58mg; Total Carbs 33.4g; Fiber 0.2g; Sugars5.7g; Protein 6.3g

Roasted Cauliflower Tagine

Prep time: 15 minutes | Cook time: 35 minutes | Serves: 6

2 cauliflower heads, cut into florets
½ cup olive oil, divided
½ cup chopped fresh cilantro
1 onion, chopped
6 garlic cloves, peeled
1 teaspoon ground coriander

1 (32-ounce) can of diced tomatoes
1 tablespoon tomato paste
6 cups water
⅛ teaspoon salt, plus more as needed
⅛ teaspoon black pepper, plus

more as needed
2 large russet potatoes, peeled and cut into 1-inch cubes

1 (15-ounce) can of chickpeas, drained
¼ cup chopped lemons

1. Preheat the broiler. 2. Toss the cauliflower and 2 tablespoons of olive oil in a suitable bowl until well coated. 3. Transfer the florets to a suitable baking sheet and broil for almost 5 minutes until golden. Remove and set aside. 4. Heat 2 tablespoons of olive oil in the skillet over medium heat. Add the cilantro and sear for a few seconds. Set aside. 5. Preheat the rest 4 tablespoons of olive oil in a heavy-bottomed pot. Add the onion and sauté for 2 to 3 minutes until golden over medium heat. Stir in the garlic and coriander—Cook for 1 minute more. 6. Stir in the tomatoes, tomato paste, water, salt, and pepper until mixed. Taste and season with more salt and pepper, as needed. Increase the heat to medium-high and cook to a boil. Turn the heat to low and cook for 5 minutes. 7. Stir in the potatoes, increase the heat to high, and return the prepared mixture to a boil. Reduce its heat to medium and cook for almost 10 minutes until the potatoes are fork-tender but not overcooked. 8. Add the chickpeas, roasted cauliflower, and cilantro. Stir gently and cook over low heat for 10 minutes to warm through. Sprinkle with the preserved lemons and serve.
Per Serving: Calories 211; Total Fat 22g; Sodium 166mg; Total Carbs 1.1g; Fiber 0g; Sugars0.1g; Protein 2.9g

Eggplant Parmesan

Prep time: 30 minutes | Cook time: 80 minutes | Serves: 6

2 cups bread crumbs
1 teaspoon dried oregano
¼ teaspoon salt
1 cup skim milk
12 small or 6 medium eggplants, cut into ½-inch-thick slices

3 cups basic tomato basil sauce
4 cups diced fresh mozzarella cheese
1 cup freshly grated parmesan cheese

1. At 375 degrees F, preheat your oven. 2. Stir together the bread crumbs, oregano, and salt in a suitable bowl. Pour the milk into another large bowl. 3. Dip the eggplant slices in the milk and the bread crumb mixture. Place the coated eggplant slices on a suitable baking sheet. 4. Bake for 30 minutes. Remove and set aside. 5. Spread a few spoonsful of tomato sauce on the bottom of a 9-by-13-inch baking dish. Arrange half the eggplant over the sauce. 6. Cover the eggplant with mozzarella cheese. Top with the rest eggplant. 7. Spoon the rest tomato sauce over the eggplant. Cover the sauce with parmesan cheese. 8. Bake for 40 minutes. Let rest for 10 minutes before serving.
Per Serving: Calories 390; Total Fat 1.9g; Sodium 7mg; Total Carbs 100.3g; Fiber 17.8g; Sugars69.7g; Protein 3.2g

Mushroom Pastilla

Prep time: 30 minutes | Cook time: 35 minutes | Serves: 4

3 large eggs
¼ cup olive oil
1 onion, chopped
1 pound of mushrooms, chopped
1 teaspoon ground cinnamon
½ teaspoon ground allspice
½ teaspoon ground ginger
½ teaspoon ground coriander
½ cup chopped fresh parsley
1 tablespoon freshly squeezed

lemon juice
½ cup toasted slivered almonds
Salt
Black pepper
8 sheets of filo dough; follow the instructions on the package to prevent drying
4 tablespoons butter, melted
1 tablespoon powdered sugar

1. At 400 degrees F, preheat your oven. 2. In a small bowl, beat the eggs and then set them aside. 3. In a skillet over medium heat, preheat the olive oil; stir fry the onion for 5 minutes or until softened; add the mushrooms and sauté for 5 minutes. Stir in ½ teaspoon of cinnamon, the allspice, ginger, coriander, parsley, and lemon juice. 4. Add the eggs to this skillet. Cook for almost 3 minutes, stirring until the eggs are fully cooked. 5. Add the almonds. Season the prepared mixture with black pepper and salt and set aside. 6. One at a time, brush both sides of each filo sheet with melted butter and layer into an 8-inch round baking dish. 7. Spoon the prepared mushroom filling in the center of the ready dough and spread it evenly. Fold the extra dough over the filling, ensuring all the filling is covered. Brush the top with the rest melted butter. 8. Bake the food for 15 to 20 minutes until the filo is golden brown. 9. Dust with the powdered sugar and the remaining ½ teaspoon of cinnamon. 10. Serve hot.
Per Serving: Calories 385; Total Fat 41.2g; Sodium 11mg; Total Carbs 6.8g; Fiber 4g; Sugars2.4g; Protein 1.7g

Chapter 6 Soups and Salads Recipes

Classic Gazpacho

Prep time: 20 minutes | Chill time: 60 minutes | Serves: 6

4 small slices slightly stale bread
1 cup water
1 cup blanched almonds
2 garlic cloves, peeled
3 tablespoons apple cider vinegar
¼ cup olive oil

4 cups ice water
Salt
Freshly ground black pepper
24 green seedless grapes, for serving

1. To blanch the almonds, place raw almonds in boiling water and let sit for 1 minute. Drain and rinse under cold water. Gently squeeze the nuts from their skins. 2. Combine the bread and water in a shallow bowl, soak the bread for almost 10 minutes till tender, Drain off the water. Put the bread in a food processor. 3. Combine the almonds and garlic. Put the vinegar, olive oil, and ice water in the food processor to pulse. 4. Process till the mixture shows white liquid, Sprinkle salt and pepper to the top of the food. 5. Place the soup to a large bowl, cover and freeze for at least 1 hour. 6. Top with the grapes and serve it.
Variation tip:4 cups almond milk could substitute the almonds and ice water.
Per Serving: Calories 134; Fat 9.5g; Sodium 167mg; Carbs 11g; Fiber 0.7g; Sugar 3.8g; Protein 1.5g

Nutrition-Richness Tabboulief Salad

Prep time: 20 minutes | Cook time: 0 | Serves: 6

1 cup fine bulgur wheat
1 cup hot water
4 cups finely chopped fresh parsley
2 tomatoes, diced
1 sweet onion, chopped

½ cup olive oil
½ cup freshly squeezed lemon juice, plus more as needed
⅛ teaspoon salt, plus more as needed

1. Add and mix the bulgur and hot water in a medium bowl. Set aside for almost 5 minutes, till become tender. 2. Mix and stir the parsley, tomatoes, and onion in another medium bowl. Strain the water for the bulgur. Add it into the tomato mixture. 3. Add and mix the olive oil and lemon juice. Drizzle with the salt, and add more salt or lemon juice if needed. Serve it. 4. Cool to refrigerate leftovers in an airtight container for at most 1 week.
Variation tip: If someone is allergic to gluten, you could use cooked quinoa to substitute for bulgur.
Per Serving: Calories 244; Fat 18g; Sodium 83mg; Carbs 15g; Fiber 4g; Sugar 5g; Protein 3g

Fattoush with Roasted Pita Bread

Prep time: 20 minutes | Cook time: 5 minutes | Serves: 6

2 loaves slightly stale pita bread, cut into 2-inch squares
½ cup olive oil
¼ cup freshly squeezed lemon juice
2 tablespoons pomegranate molasses, or cranberry juice
1 tablespoon Sanaa's Za'atar, or store-bought
6 romaine lettuce leaves, chopped
2 tomatoes, diced

2 Persian cucumbers, diced
1 red bell pepper, seeded and diced
4 scallions, white and green parts, chopped
2 radishes, thinly sliced
1 cup chopped fresh parsley
½ cup chopped fresh mint
Salt
Freshly ground black pepper

1. Heat the oven to 350°F in advance. 2. Use a single layer of a baking sheet to plate the pia squares, bake for almost 5 minutes until brown. Set aside. 3. Stir the olive oil, lemon juice, molasses, and za'atar until blended in a medium bowl. Set aside. 4. Mix and combine the lettuce, tomatoes, cucumbers, red bell pepper, scallions, radishes, parsley, and mint in a large bowl. Sprinkle the dressing and stir to coat. 5. If needed, add salt and pepper. Top with the pita chips. Serve it.
Per Serving: Calories 299; Fat 20g; Sodium 120mg; Carbs 30g; Fiber 7g; Sugar 16g; Protein 4.4g

Healthy Tomato Cauliflower Salad

Prep time: 15 minutes | Cook time: 0 | Serves: 4

¼ cup extra-virgin olive oil
¼ cup lemon juice
Zest of 1 lemon
¾ teaspoon kosher salt
½ teaspoon ground turmeric
¼ teaspoon ground coriander

¼ teaspoon ground cumin
¼ teaspoon black pepper
⅛ teaspoon ground cinnamon
1 pound riced cauliflower
1 English cucumber, diced
12 cherry tomatoes, halved

1 cup fresh parsley, chopped   ½ cup fresh mint, chopped

1. In a large bowl, add the olive oil, lemon juice, lemon zest, salt, turmeric, coriander, cumin, black pepper, and cinnamon, mix them well. 2. Add the cauliflower rice, cucumber, tomatoes, parsley, and mint and gently mix them together. Enjoy.
Per Serving: Calories 188; Fats 14.58g; Sodium 483mg; Carbs 13.91g; Fiber 4.2g; Sugar 6.87g; Protein 3.58g

Quinoa Spinach Salad with Pomegranate Dressing

Prep time: 15 minutes | Cook time: 15 minutes | Serves: 6

For the Quinoa
1½ cups water
1 cup quinoa
For the Dressing
1 cup extra-virgin olive oil
½ cup pomegranate juice
½ cup freshly squeezed orange juice
1 small shallot, minced
1 teaspoon pure maple syrup
For the Salad
3 cups baby spinach
½ cup fresh parsley, coarsely chopped
½ cup fresh mint, coarsely chopped
Approximately ¾ cup

¼ teaspoon kosher salt

1 teaspoon za'atar
½ teaspoon ground sumac
½ teaspoon kosher salt
¼ teaspoon freshly ground black pepper

pomegranate seeds, or 2 pomegranates
¼ cup pistachios, shelled and toasted
¼ cup crumbled blue cheese

To Make the Quinoa: In the saucepan, add the water, quinoa, salt and then bring to a boil; lower the heat, cover the pan and then simmer for 10 to 12 minutes. Fluff the quinoa with a fork.
To Make the Dressing: 1. In a medium bowl, add the olive oil, pomegranate juice, orange juice, shallot, maple syrup, za'atar, sumac, salt, and black pepper, mix them well. 2. In a large bowl, add about ½ cup of dressing. 3. Transfer the remaining dressing to the airtight container and refrigerate the dressing for up to 2 weeks. Let the chilled dressing reach room temperature before using.
To Make the Salad: 1. In a bowl, gently toss the spinach, parsley, mint, quinoa and pomegranate seeds. 2. Or, if using whole pomegranates: Cut the pomegranates in half; fill a large bowl with water and hold the pomegranate half, cut side-down; hit the back of the pomegranate so the seeds fall into the water; immerse the pomegranate in the water and gently pull out any remaining seeds. Repeat with the remaining pomegranate. Skim the white pith off the top of the water. Drain the seeds and add them to the greens. 3. Add the pistachios and cheese and toss gently.
Per Serving: Calories 355; Fats 21.86g; Sodium 686mg; Carbs 33.62g; Fiber 4.6g; Sugar 10.5g; Protein 7.85g

Mediterranean-Flavor Stone Soup

Prep time: 20 minutes | Cook time: 30 minutes | Serves: 6

8 cups vegetable broth
2 potatoes, peeled and cut into 1-inch cubes
2 celery stalks, chopped
2 cups cut green beans
1 yellow summer squash, cut into 1-inch cubes
1 carrot, cut into ½-inch slices
1 onion, chopped
1 green bell pepper, seeded and diced

¼ cup quick cooking barley
1 (16-ounce) can diced tomatoes
2 tablespoons chopped fresh oregano
⅛ teaspoon salt
⅛ teaspoon freshly ground black pepper
½ cup freshly grated Parmesan cheese (optional)
2 cups bread croutons (optional)

1. Heat a large soup pot to medium heat to cook the vegetable broth, potatoes, celery, green beans, squash, carrot, onion, and green bell pepper. Mix to combine. 2. Boil the dish in the pot with a lid. Lower the heat to simmer for 10 minutes. Whisk and simmer the barley for over 10 minutes. 3. After adding the tomatoes, oregano, salt, and pepper, heat to medium-heat to boil the soup. And then lower the heat to keep a simmer for over 5 minutes. 4. Remove the soup from heat. Set the soup aside for 5 minutes. Garnish with the Parmesan cheese and croutons (if desired) on the top of the dish. 5. Serve and enjoy. Leftover need to be stored in the refrigerator for up to 1 month. To serve, thaw in the refrigerator overnight. Combine the soup and ½ cup water in a small pot over medium heat and cook until warmed completely.
Variation tip: Frozen cut green beans could substitute fresh beans.
Per Serving: Calories 354; Fat 4.5g; Sodium 1064mg; Carbs 67g; Fiber 12g; Sugar 10g; Protein 15g

Classic Salad

Prep time: 30 minutes | Cook time: 20 minutes | Serves: 4

1 pound small red potatoes, halved	¼ cup white wine vinegar
8 ounces green beans, trimmed	3 tablespoons Dijon mustard
1 head Boston lettuce, leaves separated	⅛ teaspoon salt
4 large hardboiled eggs, peeled and quartered (see tip)	⅛ teaspoon freshly ground black pepper
8 cherry tomatoes, halved	¼ cup olive oil
	1 cup cured black olives

1. Heat the saucepan to high heat to boil the potatoes, add water to cover it. Boil for 5 minutes till the potatoes are tender but not mushy. Drain the water and set aside. 2. Heat another saucepan to medium-high heat to boil the green beans. Cook for almost 2 minutes to blanch. 3. Prepare a shallow salad bowl, plate the lettuce leaves. Divide the potatoes, green beans, egg quarters, and cherry tomatoes among the bowls evenly. 4. Stir and combine the vinegar, mustard, salt, and pepper in a small bowl. At the same time, gently drizzle the olive oil till the dressing become well-emulsified. 5. Sprinkle the season and add the olive to the top of the salad. 6. Serve it.
Per Serving: Calories 326; Fat 22g; Sodium 488mg; Carbs 26g; Fiber 5.4g; Sugar 3.5g; Protein 7g

Homemade Mediterranean Salad with Potato

Prep time: 15 minutes | Cook time: 15 minutes | Serves: 6

4 russet potatoes	¼ cup olive oil
1 red bell pepper, seeded and finely diced	¼ cup freshly squeezed lemon juice
1 red onion, finely chopped	Grated zest of 1 lemon
2 cups chopped fresh parsley	1 teaspoon dried thyme
½ cup capers, drained	⅛ teaspoon salt

1. Heat a medium saucepan to high heat to boil the potatoes, add water to cover it. Boil for 15 minutes till the potatoes are tender but not mushy. Drain off the water and set aside. 2. Peel and cut the potatoes into ½-inch cubes, and then put it in a medium bowl. 3. Prepare another bowl, add the red bell pepper, red onion, parsley, and capers into it. Set aside. 4. Whisk the olive oil, lemon juice, lemon zest, thyme, and salt in a small bowl, Sprinkle the dressing over the potato salad and stir to coat. 5. Chill to room temperature and serve.
Per Serving: Calories 296; Fat 9.5g; Sodium 94mg; Carbs 49g; Fiber 4.4g; Sugar 3g; Protein 6g

Panzanella Salad with Olive Bread

Prep time: 20 minutes | Cook time: 5 minutes | Serves:6

1 small loaf French bread, cut into 1-inch cubes (about 6 cups)	1 small red onion, thinly sliced
¼ cup olive oil, divided	1 cup chopped fresh basil
3 large tomatoes	1 garlic clove, mashed to a paste
2 Persian cucumbers, cut into ½-inch-thick rounds	¼ cup red wine vinegar
	⅛ teaspoon salt

1. Heat the oven to 350°F in advance. 2. Add 2 tablespoons of olive oil into the bread cubes and mix to coat in a large bowl. Plate the cubes in a single layer on a baking sheet. Roast for 5 minutes till the bread shows lightly brown. Distribute the baked cubes evenly among bowls Dice the tomatoes, and use a colander to collect the juices. Set it aside. Plate the tomatoes to a medium bowl. 3. Add the cucumbers, red onion, basil, and garlic to the tomatoes. 4. Add and stir the remaining 2 tablespoons of olive oil, the vinegar, and salt to the bowl containing the tomato juice. Sprinkle the season into the vegetables and stir to combine well. 5. Distribute the vegetable and dressing among the bowls with the bread. Serve the dish.
Per Serving: Calories 318; Fat 11g; Sodium 514mg; Carbs 45g; Fiber 3.5g; Sugar 7g; Protein 10g

Fresh Salad with Lentil Feta

Prep time: 10 minutes | Cook time: 15 minutes | Serves:6

2 cups chopped fresh parsley	¼ cup olive oil
2 celery stalks, diced	½ cup freshly squeezed lemon juice
2 baby cucumbers, diced	1 teaspoon chopped fresh oregano
1 red onion, diced	1 pound dried brown lentils, rinsed and picked over for debris
1 yellow bell pepper, seeded and diced	
8 cups water	½ cup crumbled feta cheese

1. Add and mix the parsley, celery, cucumbers, red onion, and yellow bell pepper in a large bowl. 2. Stir and combine the olive oil, lemon juice, and oregano in a small bowl. Add the dressing to the vegetables and mix to coat. Set aside. 3. Combine and boil the lentils and water in a large pot over medium-high heat. Once boiled, lower the heat to simmer for 15 minutes till the lentils are done well. Drain off the water and add the lentils. 4. At the same time, continue to cook and add the vegetables. Mix them to combine well. Drizzle with the feta cheese. Serve it. Leftovers need to be stored in an airtight container for up to 1 week. Thaw in advance to room temperature before serving.
Per Serving: Calories 229; Fat 12g; Sodium 148mg; Carbs 25g; Fiber 3g; Sugar 3g; Protein 10g

Greek Salad with Olive and Cheesy Feta

Prep time: 20 minutes | Cook time: 0 | Serves: 6

10 romaine lettuce leaves, chopped	slices
1 red onion, thinly sliced	1 cup pitted Kalamata olives
1 green bell pepper, seeded and chopped	¼ cup chopped fresh oregano
2 large tomatoes, diced	6 tablespoons olive oil
2 Persian cucumbers, cut into	¼ cup freshly squeezed lemon juice
	1 cup crumbled feta cheese

1. Mix and combine the lettuce leaves, red onion, green bell pepper, tomatoes, cucumbers, olives, and oregano in a large bowl. Set aside. 2. Whisk and blend the olive oil and lemon juice in a small bowl. Sprinkle the dressing over the salad and stir to coat well. 3. Drizzle with the feta cheese. Taste to adjust season and serve.
Per Serving: Calories 238; Fat 21g; Sodium 402mg; Carbs 8g; Fiber 3g; Sugar 4g; Protein 5g

Shepherd's Salad with Fresh Vegetables

Prep time: 15minutes | Cook time: 0 | Serves: 6

4 large ripe tomatoes, diced	(optional)
4 Persian cucumbers, diced	½ cup chopped fresh parsley
6 scallions, white and green parts, chopped	¼ cup olive oil
1 green bell pepper, seeded and chopped	3 tablespoons red wine vinegar
1 cup crumbled feta cheese	⅛ teaspoon salt
	⅛ teaspoon freshly ground black pepper

1. Mix and combine the tomatoes, cucumbers, scallions, green bell pepper, feta cheese (if using), and parsley in a large bowl, 2. Stir the olive oil, vinegar, salt, and pepper in a small bowl. Sprinkle the dressing over the vegetables. Stir to coat well.
Per Serving: Calories 195; Fat 15g; Sodium 296mg; Carbs 11g; Fiber 3g; Sugar 7g; Protein 6g

Lemony Zucchini Salad with Quinoa

Prep time: 20-30 minutes | Cook time: 25 minutes | Serves: 4

For the Quinoa

1½ cups water	¼ teaspoon kosher salt
1 cup quinoa	

For the Salad

2 tablespoons extra-virgin olive oil	pepper
1 zucchini, thinly sliced into rounds	2 garlic cloves, sliced
6 small radishes, sliced	Zest of 1 lemon
1 shallot, julienned	2 tablespoons lemon juice
¾ teaspoon kosher salt	¼ cup fresh mint, chopped
¼ teaspoon freshly ground black	¼ cup fresh basil, chopped
	¼ cup pistachios, shelled and toasted

To Make the Quinoa: In the saucepan, add the water, quinoa, salt and bring to a boil; reduce the heat, cover the pan and simmer the quinoa for 10 to 12 minutes. Fluff the quinoa with a fork.
To Make the Salad: 1. In the skillet, heat the olive oil over medium-high heat; add the zucchini, radishes, shallot, salt, black pepper and sauté them for 7 to 8 minutes; add the garlic and sauté for 30 seconds to 1 minute longer. 2. In a large bowl, add the cooked quinoa, zucchini mixture, lemon zest and lemon juice, mint, basil, pistachios and gently mix them well.
Per Serving: Calories 244; Fats 9.35g; Sodium 647mg; Carbs 33.2g; Fiber 4.1g; Sugar 2.38g; Protein 7.99g

Homemade Panzanella

Prep time: 15 minutes | Cook time: 0 | Serves: 4

½ loaf baguette or Italian country loaf or similar, cut into 1-inch cubes
4 large ripe tomatoes, cored and cut into 1 inch cubes
2 garlic cloves, minced
1 bunch fresh basil, chopped
½ cup extra-virgin olive oil
¼ cup red wine vinegar
1½ teaspoons salt
½ teaspoon freshly ground black pepper

1. In a suitable bowl, add the bread, tomatoes, garlic, basil in a large bowl and then stir to moisten the bread with the juice from the tomatoes. 2. Mix in the olive oil, vinegar, salt and pepper. 3. Let the mixture sit for 5 to 15 minutes to allow the flavors develop before serving.
Per Serving: Calories 176; Fats 12.28g; Sodium 1187mg; Carbs 14.1g; Fiber 2.6g; Sugar 5.36g; Protein 3.16g

Tuna Veggie Salad

Prep time: 20 minutes | Cook time: 0 | Serves: 4-6

1 (5-ounce) package baby spinach
2 (5-ounce) cans tuna packed in water, drained
4 medium ripe tomatoes, cored and cut into 1-inch cubes
1 red bell pepper, seeded and thinly sliced
½ red onion, thinly sliced
1 garlic clove, minced
½ cup pitted Niçoise olives
2 hard-boiled eggs, peeled and cut into quarters
2 tablespoons capers
¼ cup extra-virgin olive oil
2 tablespoons red wine vinegar
1 teaspoon salt
¼ teaspoon freshly ground black pepper

1. In a large bowl, combine all the ingredients. 2. Let the mixture sit for 5 to 10 minutes to allow the flavors to develop. 3. Place in a serving bowl and serve immediately.
Per Serving: Calories 173; Fats 12.53g; Sodium 643mg; Carbs 8.07g; Fiber 2.4g; Sugar 4.24g; Protein 8.66g

Veggie Fruit Crab Salad with Lemon Dressing

Prep time: 15 minutes | Cook time: 0 | Serves: 4

1 head romaine lettuce, washed and chopped
1 fennel bulb, shaved or sliced very thin
1 large pink grapefruit, peeled and cut into ½-inch cubes
pound crabmeat
2 teaspoons salt, divided
¼ teaspoon freshly ground black
pepper
⅓ cup extra-virgin olive oil
1 shallot, minced
1 teaspoon Dijon mustard
Zest and juice of 1 lemon
2 tablespoons chopped fresh flatleaf parsley
¼ teaspoon red pepper flakes

1. Prepare a large platter, arrange the lettuce on it and then top the lettuce with the fennel, grapefruit, and crabmeat; sprinkle with the pepper and 1 teaspoon of the salt. 2. In a small bowl, mix together the remaining salt, olive oil, shallot, mustard, parsley, red pepper flakes, lemon zest and juice until well combined; pour the mixture over the salad. 3. The leftover dressing can be refrigerated for several days.
Per Serving: Calories 247; Fats 9.65g; Sodium 1707mg; Carbs 17.99g; Fiber 6.3g; Sugar 10.63g; Protein 24.01g

Tuna Potato Salad

Prep time: 15 minutes | Cook time: 20 minutes | Serves: 4

1 pound small red or fingerling potatoes, halved
1 pound green beans or haricots verts, trimmed
1 head romaine lettuce, chopped or torn into bite-size pieces
½ pint cherry tomatoes, halved
8 radishes, sliced thin
½ cup olives, pitted (any kind you like)
2 (5-ounce) cans no-salt-added tuna packed in olive oil, drained
8 anchovies (optional)

1. Fill a large pot fitted with a steamer basket with 2 to 3 inches of water. 2. Put the potatoes in the steamer basket and place the green beans over the potatoes. Bring the water to a boil over high heat; reduce the heat to low, cover the pot and then simmer the food for 7 minutes, or until the green beans are tender but crisp. 3. Remove the green beans and continue to steam the potatoes for an additional 10 minutes. 4. Place the romaine lettuce on a serving platter. Arrange the potatoes, green beans, tomatoes, radishes, olives, and tuna in different areas of the platter. If using the anchovies, place them around the platter.
Per Serving: Calories 259; Fats 6.24g; Sodium 484mg; Carbs 34.53g; Fiber 9.9g; Sugar 5.65g; Protein 17.68g

Roasted Golden Beet and Avocado Salad

Prep time: 15 minutes | Cook time: 60 minutes | Serves: 4

1 bunch (about 1½ pounds) golden beets
1 tablespoon extra-virgin olive oil
1 tablespoon white wine vinegar
½ teaspoon kosher salt
¼ teaspoon freshly ground black pepper
1 bunch (about 4 ounces)
watercress
1 avocado, peeled, pitted, and diced
¼ cup crumbled feta cheese
¼ cup walnuts, toasted
1 tablespoon fresh chives, chopped

1. Heat the oven to 425°F ahead of time. 2. Wash and trim the beets, then wrap each beet individually in foil. 3. Arrange the beets on the baking sheet and roast them for 45 to 60 minutes until fully cooked (if the beets can be easily pierced with a fork, they are cooked). 4. Remove the beets from the oven and allow them to cool. Under cold running water, slough off the skin. Cut the beets into bite-size cubes or wedges. 5. In a large bowl, whisk together the olive oil, vinegar, salt, and black pepper; add the watercress, beets, avocado, feta, walnuts and chives and mix gently.
Per Serving: Calories 245; Fats 16.33g; Sodium 525mg; Carbs 22.14g; Fiber 8.7g; Sugar 12.42g; Protein 6.53g

Wild Rice and Chickpeas Salad

Prep time: 20 minutes | Cook time: 45 minutes | Serves: 4-6

For the Rice
1 cup water
4 ounces (⅔ cup) wild rice
¼ teaspoon kosher salt
For the Pickled Radish
1 bunch radishes (6 to 8 small), sliced thin
½ cup white wine vinegar
½ teaspoon kosher salt
For the Dressing
2 tablespoons extra-virgin olive oil
2 tablespoons white wine vinegar
½ teaspoon pure maple syrup
½ teaspoon kosher salt
¼ teaspoon freshly ground black pepper
For the Salad
1 (15-ounce) can no-salt-added or low-sodium chickpeas, rinsed and drained
1 bulb fennel, diced
¼ cup walnuts, chopped and
toasted
¼ cup crumbled feta cheese
¼ cup currants
2 tablespoons fresh dill, chopped

To Make the Rice: In a saucepan, add the water, rice, salt and bring to a boil; lower the heat, cover the pan and simmer the rice for 45 minutes.
To Make the Pickled Radish: In a medium bowl, mix up the radishes, vinegar, and salt. Let the mixture rest for 15 to 30 minutes.
To Make the Dressing In a large bowl, mix up the olive oil, vinegar, maple syrup, salt and black pepper.
To Make the Salad: 1. Add the rice to the bowl with the dressing while still warm and mix well; mix in the chickpeas, fennel, walnuts, feta, currants and dill. 2. Garnish with the pickled radishes, enjoy.
Per Serving: Calories 327; Fats 11.37g; Sodium 1058mg; Carbs 45.51g; Fiber 11.37g; Sugar 7.58g; Protein 13.21g

Flavorful Gazpacho

Prep time: 15 minutes | Cook time: 0 | Serves: 4

2 pounds' tomatoes, cut into chunks
1 bell pepper, cut into chunks
1 cucumber, cut into chunks
1 small red onion, cut into chunks
1 garlic clove, smashed
2 teaspoons sherry vinegar
½ teaspoon kosher salt
¼ teaspoon freshly ground black pepper
⅓ cup extra-virgin olive oil
Lemon juice (optional)
¼ cup fresh chives, chopped, for garnish

1. In a high-speed blender, add the tomatoes, bell pepper, cucumber, onion, garlic, vinegar, salt, black pepper and then blend them until smooth. 2. While blending, add the olive oil and purée until smooth; add more vinegar or a spritz of lemon juice as needed. Garnish with the chives.
Per Serving: Calories 214; Fats 18.58g; Sodium 346mg; Carbs 11.88g; Fiber 2.6g; Sugar 2.33g; Protein 3.09g

White Bean Salad with Bell Peppers

Prep time: 15 minutes | Cook time: 0 | Serves: 4

2 tablespoons extra-virgin olive oil
2 tablespoons white wine vinegar
½ shallot, minced
½ teaspoon kosher salt
¼ teaspoon freshly ground black pepper
3 cups cooked cannellini beans,

or 2 (15-ounce) cans no-salt-added or low-sodium cannellini beans, drained and rinsed
2 celery stalks, diced
½ red bell pepper, diced
¼ cup fresh parsley, chopped
¼ cup fresh mint, chopped

In a large bowl, mix up all the ingredients and enjoy.
Per Serving: Calories 98; Fats 7.5g; Sodium 303mg; Carbs 7.17g; Fiber 2.5g; Sugar 2.42g; Protein 1.54g

Mint Lentil Salad

Prep time: 20 minutes | Cook time: 30 minutes | Serves: 4-6

For the Lentils
1 cup French lentils
1 garlic clove, smashed
1 dried bay leaf

For the Salad
2 tablespoons extra-virgin olive oil
2 tablespoons red wine vinegar
½ teaspoon ground cumin
½ teaspoon kosher salt
¼ teaspoon freshly ground black

pepper
2 celery stalks, diced small
1 bell pepper, diced small
½ red onion, diced small
¼ cup fresh parsley, chopped
¼ cup fresh mint, chopped

To Make the Lentils: 1. In a large saucepan, add the lentils, garlic, bay leaf and enough water to cover them by about 3 inches and bring to a boil; lower the heat, cover the pan and simmer them for 20 to 30 minutes, or until tender. 2. Drain the lentils to remove any remaining water after cooking. Discard the garlic and bay leaf.
To Make the Salad: In a large bowl, mix up the olive oil, vinegar, cumin, salt, black pepper, celery, bell pepper, onion, parsley, mint and cooked lentils.
Per Serving: Calories 240; Fats 8.05g; Sodium 310mg; Carbs 33.95g; Fiber 12.4g; Sugar 2.15g; Protein 9.32g

Dijon Fruit Chicken Salad

Prep time: 15 minutes | Cook time: 0 | Serves: 2

2 cups chopped cooked chicken breast
2 Granny Smith apples, peeled, cored, and diced
½ cup dried cranberries
¼ cup diced red onion
¼ cup diced celery

2 tablespoons honey Dijon mustard
1 tablespoon olive oil mayonnaise
½ teaspoon salt
¼ teaspoon freshly ground black pepper

1. In a medium bowl, mix up the chicken, apples, cranberries, onion and celery. 2. In another small bowl, mix the mustard, mayonnaise, salt and pepper until well blended. 3. Stir the dressing into the chicken mixture until thoroughly combined. Enjoy.
Per Serving: Calories 225; Fats 5.17g; Sodium 847mg; Carbs 34.26g; Fiber 5.8g; Sugar 24.45g; Protein 10.32g

Cherry Tomato Chicken Salad with Feta Cheese

Prep time: 15 minutes | Cook time: 0 | Serves: 2

¼ cup balsamic vinegar

1 teaspoon freshly squeezed lemon juice
¼ cup extra-virgin olive oil
¼ teaspoon salt
¼ teaspoon freshly ground black pepper
2 grilled boneless, skinless

chicken breasts, sliced (about 1 cup)

½ cup thinly sliced red onion
10 cherry tomatoes, halved
8 pitted Kalamata olives, halved
2 cups roughly chopped romaine lettuce
½ cup feta cheese

1. In a medium bowl, stir the vinegar and lemon juice well. Slowly whisk in the olive oil, salt, pepper and continue whisking vigorously until well blended 2. Add the onion, tomatoes, olives, chicken and stir well. Cover the bowl and refrigerate the mixture for at least 2 hours or overnight. 3. Divide the romaine between 2 salad plates and top each with half of the chicken-vegetable mixture. You can serve the salad

with feta cheese on the top.
Per Serving: Calories 513; Fats 26.25g; Sodium 1677mg; Carbs 22.73g; Fiber 2.9g; Sugar 17.26g; Protein 45.44g

Vegetable and Flank Steak Salad

Prep time: 20 minutes | Cook time: 10 minutes | Serves: 4

1-pound flank steak
1 teaspoon extra-virgin olive oil
1 tablespoon garlic powder
½ teaspoon salt
½ teaspoon freshly ground black pepper

4 cups baby spinach leaves
10 cherry tomatoes, halved
10 cremini or white mushrooms, sliced
1 small red onion, thinly sliced
½ red bell pepper, thinly sliced

1. Preheat your broiler. Line a baking sheet with aluminum foil. 2. Rub the top of the flank steak with the olive oil, garlic powder, salt, and pepper and let marinate for 10 minutes. 3. Transfer the flank steak to the prepared baking sheet and broil for 5 minutes on each side for medium rare. Allow the meat to rest on a cutting board for 10 minutes. 4. In a large bowl, toss the spinach, tomatoes, mushrooms, onion and bell pepper well. 5. Divide the salad among 4 dinner plates. Slice the steak on the diagonal and place 4 to 5 slices on top of each salad. 6. Serve with your favorite vinaigrette.
Per Serving: Calories 226; Fats 6.57g; Sodium 393mg; Carbs 14.7g; Fiber 2.9g; Sugar 7.97g; Protein 27.24g

Simple Feta Veggie Salad

Prep time: 10 minutes | Cook time: 0 | Serves: 4

For the Salad
1 head romaine lettuce, torn
½ cup black olives, pitted and chopped
1 red onion, thinly sliced
For the Dressing
2 tablespoons extra-virgin olive oil
2 tablespoons red wine vinegar
Juice of 1 lemon
1 tablespoon dried oregano (or
2 tablespoons chopped fresh

1 tomato, chopped
1 cucumber, chopped
½ cup crumbled feta cheese

oregano leaves)
3 garlic cloves, minced
½ teaspoon Dijon mustard
½ teaspoon sea salt
¼ teaspoon freshly ground black pepper

To Make the Salad: In a large bowl, mix up the lettuce, olives, red onion, tomato, cucumber and feta.
To Make the Dressing: 1. In a small bowl, whisk the olive oil, vinegar, lemon juice, oregano, garlic, mustard, sea salt, and pepper. 2. Pour the dressing over the salad and enjoy.
Per Serving: Calories 178; Fats 13.09g; Sodium 610mg; Carbs 12.1g; Fiber 5.3g; Sugar 4.61g; Protein 5.68g

Eggplant Soup

Prep time: 15 minutes | Cook time: 40 minutes | Serves: 6

Olive oil cooking spray
2 pounds (1 to 2 medium to large) eggplant, halved lengthwise
2 beefsteak tomatoes, halved
2 onions, halved
4 garlic cloves, smashed
4 rosemary sprigs
2 tablespoons extra-virgin olive oil

1 to 2 cups no-salt-added vegetable stock
1 teaspoon pure maple syrup
1 teaspoon ground cumin
1 teaspoon ground coriander
1 teaspoon kosher salt
¼ teaspoon freshly ground black pepper
Lemon juice (optional)

1. Preheat the oven to 400°F. 2. Line two baking sheets with parchment paper or foil. Lightly spray with olive oil cooking spray. 3. Spread the eggplant, tomatoes, onions, and garlic on the prepared baking sheets, cut-side down. Nestle the rosemary sprigs among the vegetables and drizzle with the olive oil; roast the vegetables for 40 minutes, checking halfway through and removing the garlic before it gets brown. 4. When cool enough to touch, remove the eggplant flesh and tomato flesh from the skin, then transfer them to a high-powered blender; add the rosemary leaves, onions, garlic, maple syrup, cumin, coriander, salt, black pepper, 1 cup of the vegetable stock and purée them until smooth. 5. The soup should be thick and creamy. If the soup is too thick, add another cup of stock slowly, until your desired consistency is reached. You can serve with lemon juice.
Per Serving: Calories 99; Fats 2.61g; Sodium 444mg; Carbs 18.36g; Fiber 6.7g; Sugar 9.6g; Protein 2.94g

Dijon Cucumber Salad

Prep time: 15 minutes | Cook time: 0 | Serves: 4

4 medium cucumbers, chopped or spiralized into spaghetti noodles
1 tomato, chopped
3 scallions, white and green parts, chopped
2 tablespoons extra-virgin olive oil

¼ cup red wine vinegar
2 tablespoons chopped fresh dill
2 garlic cloves, minced
1 teaspoon Dijon mustard
½ teaspoon sea salt
¼ teaspoon freshly ground black pepper

1. In a large bowl, add the cucumber, tomato, scallions and mix well. 2. In a small bowl, mix up the olive oil, vinegar, dill, garlic, mustard, sea salt and pepper. 3. Toss the dressing with the salad and enjoy.
Per Serving: Calories 109; Fats 7.69g; Sodium 314mg; Carbs 8.91g; Fiber 2.9g; Sugar 3.87g; Protein 2.36g

Homemade Caprese Salad

Prep time: 15 minutes | Cook time: 0 | Serves: 4

3 large tomatoes, sliced
4 ounces' part-skim mozzarella cheese, cut into ¼-inch-thick slices
¼ cup balsamic vinegar

2 tablespoons extra-virgin olive oil
½ teaspoon sea salt
¼ cup loosely packed basil leaves, torn

1. On the platter, arrange the tomatoes and cheese slices alternating in a row. 2. Drizzle with the olive oil and vinegar. 3. Sprinkle with sea salt and basil, enjoy.
Per Serving: Calories 115; Fats 7.54g; Sodium 530mg; Carbs 3.94g; Fiber 0.1g; Sugar 3g; Protein 7.08g

Lemon Chickpea Salad

Prep time: 10 minutes | Cook time: 0 | Serves: 6

2 (14-ounce) cans chickpeas (3 cups), drained
½ red onion, finely chopped
2 cucumbers, finely chopped
¼ cup extra-virgin olive oil
Juice of 2 lemons
Zest of 1 lemon

1 tablespoon tahini
3 garlic cloves, minced
2 teaspoons dried oregano
½ teaspoon sea salt
¼ teaspoon freshly ground black pepper

1. In a medium bowl, add the chickpeas, red onion and cucumbers. 2. In a small bowl, mix up the olive oil, lemon juice and zest, tahini, garlic, oregano, sea salt and pepper. 3. Toss the dressing with the salad and enjoy.
Per Serving: Calories 244; Fats 12.9g; Sodium 409mg; Carbs 27.71g; Fiber 6.7g; Sugar 7.09g; Protein 7.46g

Basil Lettuce Salad

Prep time: 15 minutes | Cook time: 0 | Serves: 6

2 heads romaine lettuce, chopped
3 cups chopped skinless cooked chicken breast
1 cup canned or jarred (in water) artichoke hearts, drained, rinsed, and chopped
2 tomatoes, chopped
2 zucchinis, chopped
½ red onion, finely chopped
3 ounces' mozzarella cheese, chopped
⅓ cup unsweetened nonfat plain Greek yogurt

1 tablespoon Dijon mustard
2 tablespoons extra-virgin olive oil
Zest of 1 lemon
3 garlic cloves, minced
2 tablespoons chopped fresh basil leaves
2 tablespoons chopped fresh chives
½ teaspoon sea salt
⅛ teaspoon freshly ground black pepper

1. In a large bowl, add the lettuce, chicken, artichoke hearts, tomatoes, zucchini, red onion and mozzarella. 2. In a small bowl, mix up the yogurt, mustard, olive oil, lemon zest, garlic, basil, chives, sea salt, and pepper. 3. Toss the vegetables with the dressing and enjoy.
Per Serving: Calories 257; Fats 8.02g; Sodium 423mg; Carbs 16.29g; Fiber 8g; Sugar 6.15g; Protein 31.96g

Chill Gazpacho

Prep time: 15 minutes | Cook time: 0 | Serves: 4

6 tomatoes, chopped
3 garlic cloves, minced

2 red bell peppers, finely chopped
1 red onion, finely chopped

3 cups tomato juice
¼ cup red wine vinegar
¼ cup extra-virgin olive oil
¼ cup basil leaves, torn

½ teaspoon sea salt
¼ teaspoon freshly ground black pepper

1. In a blender, combine the tomatoes, garlic, red bell peppers, red onion, tomato juice, vinegar, olive oil, basil, sea salt, and pepper, then pulse them for 20 to 30 (1-second) pulses until blended. 2. Chill for 1 hour and serve.
Per Serving: Calories 156; Fats 6.8g; Sodium 633mg; Carbs 22.55g; Fiber 6.8g; Sugar 14.81g; Protein 4.35g

Easy Panzanella

Prep time: 15 minutes | Cook time: 10 minutes | Serves: 4

6 tablespoons extra-virgin olive oil, divided
4 whole-grain bread slices, crusts removed, cut into pieces
1 cup yellow cherry tomatoes, halved
1 cup red cherry tomatoes, halved
1 plum tomato, cut into wedges
½ red onion, very thinly sliced

¼ cup chopped fresh basil leaves
1 tablespoon capers, drained and rinsed
¼ cup red wine vinegar
2 garlic cloves, minced
½ teaspoon Dijon mustard
½ teaspoon sea salt
¼ teaspoon freshly ground black pepper

1. In a large skillet, heat 2 tablespoons of olive oil over medium-high heat until it shimmers; add the bread slices and cook for 6 to 8 minutes, flipping occasionally, until crisp and browned. 2. Drain and cool the bread on paper towels. 3. In a large bowl, add the cooled bread, yellow, red, and plum tomatoes, red onion, basil, and capers, mix well. 4. In a small bowl, whisk the remaining 4 tablespoons of olive oil with the vinegar, garlic, mustard, sea salt, and pepper. 5. Toss cooked bread slices and vegetables with the dressing and serve.
Per Serving: Calories 234; Fats 11.04g; Sodium 705mg; Carbs 27.38g; Fiber 4.5g; Sugar 8.27g; Protein 6.97g

Roasted Cauliflower and Arugula Salad

Prep time: 20 minutes | Cook time: 20 minutes | Serves: 4

1 head cauliflower, trimmed and cut into 1-inch florets
2 tablespoons extra-virgin olive oil, plus more for drizzling (optional)
1 teaspoon ground cumin

½ teaspoon kosher salt
¼ teaspoon freshly ground black pepper
5 ounces' arugula
⅓ cup pomegranate seeds
¼ cup pine nuts, toasted

1. Preheat your oven to 425°F. Line a baking sheet with parchment paper. 2. In a large bowl, toss the cauliflower with olive oil, cumin, salt, and black pepper. Spread the coated cauliflower in a single layer on the prepared baking sheet and roast for 20 minutes, tossing halfway through. 3. Divide the arugula among 4 plates, then top them with the cauliflower, pomegranate seeds, and pine nuts. 4. Serve with a simple drizzle of olive oil.
Per Serving: Calories 164; Fats 13.34g; Sodium 322mg; Carbs 10.39g; Fiber 3.2g; Sugar 5.49g; Protein 3.84g

Lentil Soup with Lemon Juice

Prep time: 15 minutes | Cook time: 30 minutes | Serves: 6

1 tablespoon extra-virgin olive oil
1 teaspoon ground cumin
1 teaspoon ground coriander
1 teaspoon ground turmeric
1 teaspoon kosher salt
¼ teaspoon freshly ground black pepper
1 tablespoon no-salt-added tomato paste
1 onion, diced

1 carrot, diced
1 celery stalk, diced
3 garlic cloves, minced
4 cups no-salt-added vegetable stock
2 cups water
1 cup red lentils
3 tablespoons lemon juice
¼ cup fresh parsley, chopped

1. In the stockpot, heat the olive oil over medium-high heat; add the cumin, coriander, turmeric, salt, black pepper and sauté for 30 seconds; add the tomato paste and sauté for 30 seconds to 1 minute; add the onion, carrot, celery and sauté 5 to 6 minutes; add the garlic and sauté for 30 seconds. 2. Add the vegetable stock, water, lentils and then bring to a boil. Lower the heat and cover the pot partially, simmer the food for 20 minutes or until the lentils are tender. 3. Mix in the lemon juice and parsley, serve and enjoy.
Per Serving: Calories 189; Fats 2.13g; Sodium 456mg; Carbs 33.67g; Fiber 8.2g; Sugar 4.54g; Protein 10.01g

Lentil Veggie Soup

Prep time: 15 minutes | Cook time: 40 minutes | Serves: 6

1 tablespoon extra-virgin olive oil
1 onion, diced
1 carrot, diced
1 celery stalk, diced
1 sweet potato, unpeeled and diced
1 cup green or brown lentils
1 dried bay leaf
1 teaspoon ground turmeric
1 teaspoon ground cumin
1 teaspoon kosher salt
¼ teaspoon freshly ground black pepper
4 cups no-salt-added vegetable stock

1. In the stockpot, heat the olive oil over medium-high heat; add the onion, carrot, celery, sweet potato and sauté them for 5 to 6 minutes; add the lentils, bay leaf, turmeric, cumin, salt, black pepper and sauté for 30 seconds to 1 minute longer. 2. Add the stock and bring to a boil, then lower the heat to low, cover the pot and simmer for 20 to 30 minutes, or until the lentils and sweet potato are tender. If you find the soup becoming thick and stew-like, feel free to add additional stock or water as it cooks.
Per Serving: Calories 164; Fats 1.52g; Sodium 1059mg; Carbs 30.2g; Fiber 5g; Sugar 4.21g; Protein 8.69g

Kale and Bean Soup with Parmesan Cheese

Prep time: 20 minutes | Cook time: 25 minutes | Serves: 4

2 tablespoons extra-virgin olive oil
1 onion, diced
1 carrot, diced
1 celery stalk, diced
1 teaspoon kosher salt
4 cups no-salt-added vegetable stock
1 (15-ounce) can no-salt-added or low-sodium cannellini beans, drained and rinsed
1 tablespoon fresh thyme, chopped
1 tablespoon fresh sage, chopped
1 tablespoon fresh oregano, chopped
¼ teaspoon freshly ground black pepper
1 bunch kale, stemmed and chopped
¼ cup grated Parmesan cheese (optional)

1. In the pot, heat the olive oil over medium-high heat; add the onion, carrot, celery, salt and sauté for 5 to 6 minutes, or until translucent and slightly golden. 2. Add the vegetable stock, beans, thyme, sage, oregano, black pepper and bring to a boil; lower the heat and simmer for 10 minutes; stir in the kale and let it wilt about 5 minutes. 3. You can serve with 1 tablespoon of Parmesan cheese.
Per Serving: Calories 201; Fats 9.55g; Sodium 765mg; Carbs 24.39g; Fiber 9.5g; Sugar 7.34g; Protein 6.54g

Rosemary Vegetable Soup

Prep time: 15 minutes | Cook time: 35 minutes | Serves: 6

2 sweet potatoes, peeled and sliced
2 parsnips, peeled and sliced
2 carrots, peeled and sliced
2 tablespoons extra-virgin olive oil
1 teaspoon chopped fresh rosemary
1 teaspoon chopped fresh thyme
1 teaspoon salt
½ teaspoon freshly ground black pepper
4 cups vegetable or chicken broth
Grated Parmesan cheese for garnish (optional)

1. Preheat the oven to 400°F. Line a baking sheet with aluminum foil. 2. In a large bowl, coat the sweet potatoes, parsnips, carrots with the olive oil, rosemary, thyme, salt and pepper. 3. Transfer the coated vegetables on the baking sheet and roast them for 30 to 35 minutes until tender and brown at the edges. Remove the baking sheet from the oven and allow to cool until just warm. 4. Transfer the vegetables and broth to a blender and blend until smooth, working in batches. Pour each blended batch into a large saucepan. 5. When all of the vegetables have been puréed, heat the soup over low heat just until heated through. 6. Ladle into bowls and top with Parmesan cheese if desired.
Per Serving: Calories 184; Fats 6.78g; Sodium 786mg; Carbs 27.06g; Fiber 4.7g; Sugar 7.76g; Protein 5.05g

Hearty Chicken Veggie Soup

Prep time: 20 minutes | Cook time: 30 minutes | Serves: 2

1 teaspoon extra-virgin olive oil
1 medium yellow onion, diced
1 large carrot, peeled and diced
1 celery stalk, peeled and diced
2 (6-ounce) boneless, skinless chicken breasts, cut into 1-inch pieces
1 medium zucchini, diced
2 yellow squash, diced
½ cup chopped fresh parsley, plus extra for garnish
1 teaspoon chopped fresh oregano
1 teaspoon chopped fresh basil
½ teaspoon salt
¼ teaspoon freshly ground black pepper
2 cups chicken stock

1. In your skillet, heat the olive oil over medium-high heat; add the onion, carrot, celery and sauté for 5 minutes; add the chicken and sauté for 10 minutes longer. 2. Add the zucchini, squash, parsley, oregano, basil, salt, pepper and sauté for 5 minutes; reduce the heat to medium, and pour in the stock. Cover the skillet and cook for an additional 10 minutes. 3. Apportion the soup between bowls, garnish with additional parsley and enjoy.
Per Serving: Calories 366; Fats 11.5g; Sodium 2021mg; Carbs 33.84g; Fiber 7.9g; Sugar 16.92g; Protein 33.99g

Tomato Tofu Soup

Prep time: 20 minutes | Cook time: 30 minutes | Serves: 4

1 tablespoon extra-virgin olive oil
1 onion, diced
2 garlic cloves, sliced
1 tablespoon no-salt-added tomato paste
2 pounds' tomatoes, chopped
½ cup no-salt-added vegetable stock
¾ cup fresh basil, chopped and divided
1 teaspoon kosher salt
¼ teaspoon freshly ground black pepper
8 ounces' silken tofu, drained
1 cup cherry tomatoes, quartered

1. In the saucepan, heat the olive oil over medium-high heat; add the onion and sauté for 5 to 6 minutes until slightly golden; add the garlic and sauté for 30 seconds; add the tomato paste and sauté for 30 seconds; add the tomatoes and slightly cook for 5 to 10 minutes; add the stock, salt, black pepper and ½ cup of the basil. 2. Carefully transfer the mixture, in batches, to a high-powered blender. Add the tofu, and purée. Return the soup to the saucepan and simmer for 10 minutes. 3. Divide the cherry tomatoes among 4 bowls. Ladle the soup into the bowls and garnish with the remaining ¼ cup basil, enjoy.
Per Serving: Calories 160; Fats 7.05g; Sodium 752mg; Carbs 16.49g; Fiber 5.2g; Sugar 8.49g; Protein 11.87g

Butternut Squash, Carrot and Onion Soup

Prep time: 15 minutes | Cook time: 40 minutes | Serves: 4

2 tablespoons extra-virgin olive oil
1 onion, chopped
1 carrot, chopped
1 celery stalk, chopped
4 cups unsalted vegetable broth
3 cups chopped butternut squash
1 teaspoon dried thyme
½ teaspoon sea salt
¼ teaspoon freshly ground black pepper

1. In a large pot, heat the olive oil over medium-high heat until it shimmers; add the carrot, onion, celery and sauté them for 5 to 7 minutes, or until the onion and carrot begin to brown. 2. Add the broth, squash, thyme, sea salt, pepper and bring to a simmer; reduce the heat to medium and simmer for 20 to 30 minutes until the squash is soft. 3. In an immersion blender, purée the soup.
Per Serving: Calories 137; Fats 6.94g; Sodium 1250mg; Carbs 19.6g; Fiber 3.1g; Sugar 6.25g; Protein 1.55g

Spanish Potato Salad

Prep time: 10 minutes | Cook time: 10 minutes | Serves: 6-8

4 russet potatoes, peeled and chopped
3 large hard-boiled eggs, chopped
1 cup frozen mixed vegetables, thawed
½ cup plain full-fat Greek yogurt, unsweetened
5 tablespoons pitted Spanish olives
½ teaspoon freshly ground black pepper
½ teaspoon dried mustard seed
½ tablespoon freshly squeezed lemon juice
½ teaspoon dried dill
Salt

1. Boil potatoes for 5 to 7 minutes, until just fork-tender, checking periodically for doneness. You don't want to overcook them. 2. While the potatoes are cooking, in a suitable bowl, mix the eggs, vegetables, yogurt, olives, pepper, mustard, lemon juice, and dill. 3. Season with black pepper and salt. Add the potatoes to the large bowl, mix well and serve once the potatoes are cooled somewhat.
Per Serving: Calories 267; Total Fat 28.5g; Sodium 207mg; Total Carbs 1.5g; Fiber0.3g; Sugars0.2g; Protein 22.4g

White Bean and Sausage Soup

Prep time: 15 minutes | Cook time: 20 minutes | Serves: 6

2 tablespoons extra-virgin olive oil
8 ounces' Italian chicken sausage (uncooked), sliced
1 onion, chopped 1 carrot, chopped
1 red bell pepper, seeded and chopped
3 garlic cloves, minced

6 cups unsalted vegetable broth
1 (14-ounce) can white beans, drained
4 cups chopped kale
1 teaspoon dried thyme
½ teaspoon sea salt
¼ teaspoon freshly ground black pepper
Pinch red pepper flakes

1. In a large pot, heat the olive oil over medium-high heat until it shimmers. 2. Add the sausage and cook for about 5 minutes, stirring occasionally, until browned. Leave the oil in the pot and set the sausage aside for later use. 3. Still in the pot, add the onion, carrot, red bell pepper and sauté them for about 5 minutes, until the vegetables are soft; add the garlic and sauté for 30 seconds. 4. Stir in the broth, beans, kale, thyme, sea salt, pepper, and red pepper flakes. Bring to a simmer, then reduce the heat to low and simmer for about 5 minutes more until the kale is soft. 5. Return the sausage to the pot and cook for 1 minute more until the sausage heats through. Serve immediately.
Per Serving: Calories 241; Fats 6.2g; Sodium 297mg; Carbs 32.82g; Fiber 10g; Sugar 9.83g; Protein 14.69g

Pepper Lentil Soup

Prep time: 10 minutes | Cook time: 20 minutes | Serves: 4

2 tablespoons extra-virgin olive oil
2 onions, chopped
2 celery stalks, chopped
2 carrots, chopped
4 garlic cloves, minced
1 (14-ounce) can lentils, drained

2 bay leaves
6 cups unsalted vegetable broth
1 teaspoon sea salt
¼ teaspoon freshly ground black pepper
Pinch red pepper flakes
¼ cup red wine vinegar

1. In a large pot, heat the olive oil over medium-high heat until it shimmers; add the onions, carrots, celery and sauté for 5 to 10 minutes until the vegetables are soft; add the garlic and sauté for 30 seconds. 2. Stir in the lentils, bay leaves, red pepper flakes, sea salt, pepper, and broth; bring to a simmer and reduce the heat to medium-low; simmer for 10 minutes longer, stirring occasionally. 3. Discard the bay leaves. Stir in the vinegar and serve.
Per Serving: Calories 289; Fats 3.81g; Sodium 773mg; Carbs 53.94g; Fiber 14.8g; Sugar 13.01g; Protein 12.27g

Zucchini Chicken Soup

Prep time: 10 minutes | Cook time: 20 minutes | Serves: 8

2 tablespoons extra-virgin olive oil
12 ounces boneless, skinless chicken breast, sliced
2 carrots, chopped
1 onion, chopped
1 red bell pepper, seeded and chopped
1 fennel bulb, chopped
5 garlic cloves, minced

6 cups unsalted chicken broth
1 (14-ounce) can crushed tomatoes, undrained
2 zucchinis, chopped
1 tablespoon dried Italian seasoning
½ teaspoon sea salt
¼ teaspoon freshly ground black pepper

1. In a large pot, heat the olive oil over medium-high heat until it shimmers; add the chicken breast slices and sauté for 5 minutes until browned. Leave the oil in the pot and set the cooked chicken breast slices aside for later use. 2. Add the carrots, onion, red bell pepper, and fennel to the pot, sauté them for about 5 minutes until the vegetables are soft; add the garlic and sauté for 30 seconds. 3. Add the broth, tomatoes, zucchini, Italian seasoning, sea salt, and pepper, bring to a boil and reduce the heat; simmer them for about 5 minutes more until the vegetables are soft. 4. Put the cooked chicken breast slices back to the pot and wait for 1 minute longer until the chicken heats through. 5. Serve immediately.
Per Serving: Calories 127; Fats 4.6g; Sodium 1147mg; Carbs 18.29g; Fiber 3.5g; Sugar 7.31g; Protein 6.58g

Turkey-Meatball Soup

Prep time: 20 minutes | Cook time: 25 minutes | Serves: 6

12 ounces ground turkey

1 yellow onion, grated and

squeezed of excess water (see tip)
1 tablespoon dried Italian seasoning
1 teaspoon garlic powder
1 teaspoon sea salt, divided
½ teaspoon freshly ground black pepper, divided
2 tablespoons extra-virgin olive oil

1 red onion, chopped
5 garlic cloves, minced
6 cups unsalted chicken broth
1 (14-ounce) can chopped tomatoes, drained
3 medium zucchini, chopped or spiralized
¼ cup chopped fresh basil leaves

1. In a medium bowl, mix together the turkey, yellow onion, Italian seasoning, garlic powder, ½ teaspoon of sea salt and ¼ teaspoon of pepper. 2. Form the mixture into ¾-inch balls and place them on a plate, set aside for later use. 3. In a large pot, heat the olive oil over medium-high heat until it shimmers; add the red onion and sauté for 5 minutes until soft; add the garlic and sauté for 30 seconds. 4. Stir in the broth, tomatoes, the remaining salt and the remaining pepper. Bring to a boil, then add the meatballs and return to a boil. 5. Reduce the heat to medium-low and simmer for about 15 minutes, stirring occasionally, until the meatballs are cooked through; add the zucchini and wait for 3 minutes longer or until soft. 6. Stir in the basil, serve and enjoy.
Per Serving: Calories 155; Fats 7.12g; Sodium 1570mg; Carbs 9.31g; Fiber 2.4g; Sugar 4.6g; Protein 14.2g

Orzo Chicken Soup

Prep time: 10 minutes | Cook time: 20 minutes | Serves: 8

1 tablespoon extra-virgin olive oil
1 cup chopped onion
½ cup chopped carrots
½ cup chopped celery
3 garlic cloves, minced
9 cups low-sodium chicken broth

2 cups shredded cooked chicken breast
½ cup lemon juice
Zest of 1 lemon, grated
1 to 2 teaspoons dried oregano
8 ounces cooked orzo pasta

1. Preheat the oil over medium heat in a suitable pot, add the onion, carrots, celery, and garlic, and cook for almost 5 minutes until the onions are translucent. 2. Add the broth, cook to a boil, and then cook on a simmer and cook for 10 more minutes until the flavors melt. 3. Add the lemon juice, shredded chicken, zest, and oregano. 4. Plate the orzo in serving bowls first, then add the chicken soup.
Per Serving: Calories 211; Total Fat 22g; Sodium 166mg; Total Carbs 1.1g; Fiber 0g; Sugars 0.1g; Protein 22.9g

Curry Zucchini Soup

Prep time: 10 minutes | Cook time: 20 minutes | Serves: 4-6

¼ cup extra-virgin olive oil
1 medium onion, chopped
1 carrot, shredded
1 small garlic clove, minced
4 cups low-sodium chicken broth

2 medium zucchinis, sliced
2 apples, peeled and chopped
2½ teaspoons curry powder
¼ teaspoon salt

1. In a suitable pot, preheat the oil over medium heat. Sauté the onion, carrot, and garlic and cook until tender. 2. Add the chicken broth, zucchini, apples, and curry powder. 3. Boil the food for 2 minutes, reduce its heat, and simmer for 20 minutes until the vegetables are tender. 4. Season with the salt and serve.
Per Serving: Calories 234; Total Fat 10.8g; Sodium 124mg; Total Carbs 2.3g; Fiber 0.4g; Sugars 2.1g; Protein 6.3g

Rustic Winter Salad

Prep time: 10 minutes | Cook time: 0 | Serves: 4

1 small green apple, sliced
6 stalks of kale, chopped
½ cup crumbled feta cheese
½ cup dried currants
½ cup chopped pitted kalamata olives
½ cup sliced radicchio

2 scallions, sliced
¼ cup peeled, julienned carrots
2 celery stalks, sliced
¼ cup sweet red wine vinaigrette
Salt and freshly ground black pepper (optional)

1. In a suitable bowl, mix the apple, kale, feta, currants, olives, radicchio, scallions, carrots, and celery and mix well. 2. Drizzle with the vinaigrette. Season with black pepper and salt (optional), then serve.
Per Serving: Calories 390; Total Fat 1.9g; Sodium 7mg; Total Carbs 100.3g; Fiber 17.8g; Sugars 69.7g; Protein 3.2g

Chapter 7 Snack and Appetizers Recipes

Easy Sweet Potato Sticks

Prep time: 10 minutes | Cook time: 40 minutes | Serves: 4

4 large sweet potatoes, peeled and cut into finger-like strips
2 tablespoons extra-virgin olive oil
½ teaspoon salt
½ teaspoon freshly ground black pepper

1. Heat the oven over to 350°F in advance. Lay the baking sheet with aluminum foil. Prepare a large bowl to put the sweet potatoes and olive oil, salt, and pepper. Toss them well. 2. Set a single layer on the baking sheet, and then put sweet potatoes to it. Bake it for almost 40 minutes until the edges of the food become brown. 3. Set piping hot.
Per Serving: Calories 190; Fat 3g; Sodium 416mg; Carbs 37g; Fiber 6g; Sugar 12g; Protein 4g

Pesto Cucumber Boats with Walnuts

Prep time: 15 minutes | Cook time: 15 minutes | Serves: 4-6

3 medium cucumbers
¼ teaspoon salt
1 packed cup fresh basil leaves
1 garlic clove, minced
¼ cup walnut pieces
¼ cup grated Parmesan cheese
¼ cup extra-virgin olive oil
½ teaspoon paprika

1. Make each cucumber into 4 stocky pieces by cutting them in half lengthwise and crosswise. 2. Scoop out the seeds and leave a shallow for each cucumber. Slightly sprinkle salt and put them aside on a platter. 3. Mix and blend the basil, garlic, walnuts, Parmesan cheese, and olive oil in a blender or food processor. 4. Spread pesto into each cucumber "boat" by using a spoon. Add a bit of paprika for each cucumber "boat".
Per Serving: Calories 88; Fat 7g; Sodium 252mg; Carbs 3g; Fiber 1g; Sugar 1.5g; Protein 2g

Refreshing Citrus-Kissed Melon

Prep time: 15 minutes | Cook time: 0 | Serves: 4

2 cups cubed melon, such as Crenshaw, Sharlyn, or honeydew
2 cups cubed cantaloupe
½ cup freshly squeezed orange juice
¼ cup freshly squeezed lime juice
1 tablespoon orange zest

1. Mix up the melon cubes in a container. 2. In a bowl, mix together the orange juice, lime juice, and orange zest and pour over the fruit. 3. Cover and put into the refrigerator and store for at least 4 hours, stirring now and then. 4. Serve chilled.
Per Serving: Calories 81; Fat 0.39g; Sodium 29mg; Carbs 19.76g; Fiber 1.8g; Sugar 17.08g; Protein 1.79g

Tasty Spicy-Sweet Roasted Walnuts

Prep time: 15 minutes | Cook time: 15 minutes | Serves: 8 to 10

4 cups walnut halves
2 tablespoons extra-virgin olive oil
1 tablespoon mild curry powder
1 teaspoon salt
¼ cup lightly packed light brown sugar

1. Turn on the oven and heat it to 250°F. Line a baking sheet with aluminum foil. 2. Toss the walnuts with the olive oil to coat with your clean hands in a large bowl. Put in some curry powder and salt and mix well. 3. Spread out the walnuts on the baking sheet and bake them for 15 minutes. 4. Take out carefully for the oven and let it sit to cool just until warm to the touch, about 10 minutes. 5. Sprinkle the warm walnuts with the brown sugar and let it sit to cool to room temperature before storing in an airtight container.
Per Serving: Calories 225; Fat 22.28g; Sodium 259mg; Carbs 5.1g; Fiber 2.5g; Sugar 0.96g; Protein 5.04g

Refreshing Café Cooler

Prep time: 15 minutes | Cook time: 0 | Serves: 4

Ice cubes
2 cups low-fat milk
½ teaspoon ground cinnamon
½ teaspoon pure vanilla extract
1 cup espresso, cooled to room temperature
4 teaspoons sugar (optional)

1. Put in some ice cube to fill four tall glassess. 2. In a blender, add the milk, cinnamon, and vanilla and blend until the mixture is frothy. 3.

Pour the milk over the ice cubes and top each drink with one-quarter of the espresso. If using sugar, stir it into the espresso until it has dissolved. 4. Serve immediately, with chilled teaspoons for stirring.
Per Serving: Calories 78; Fat 2.53g; Sodium 66mg; Carbs 9.68g; Fiber 0.2g; Sugar 8.69g; Protein 4.11g

Diary-free and Easy Hummus

Prep time: 10 minutes | Cook time: 0 | Serves: 16

1 (14-ounce) can chickpeas, drained
3 garlic cloves, minced
2 tablespoons tahini
2 tablespoons extra-virgin olive oil
Juice of 1 lemon
Zest of 1 lemon
½ teaspoon sea salt
Pinch cayenne pepper
2 tablespoons chopped fresh Italian parsley leaves

1. In a blender, add the chickpeas, garlic, tahini, olive oil, lemon juice and zest, sea salt and cayenne; then blend them for about 60 seconds until the mixture is smooth. 2. Garnish with parsley, enjoy.
Per Serving: Calories 63; Fat 3.45g; Sodium 136mg; Carbs 6.66g; Fiber 1.9g; Sugar 1.14g; Protein 2.17g

Diary-Free Baba Ganoush

Prep time: 10 minutes | Cook time: 15 minutes | Serves: 6

1 eggplant, peeled and sliced
¼ cup tahini
½ teaspoon sea salt
Juice of 1 lemon
¼ teaspoon ground cumin
⅛ teaspoon freshly ground black pepper
2 tablespoons extra-virgin olive oil
2 tablespoons sunflower seeds (optional)
2 tablespoons fresh Italian parsley leaves (optional)

1. Turn on the oven and heat it to 350°F. 2. Spread the eggplant slices in an even layer on a baking sheet, Bake them for about 15 minutes until it is soft. Cool for a moment and roughly chop the eggplant. 3. Blend the eggplant with the tahini, sea salt, lemon juice, cumin, and pepper for about 30 seconds in a blender. 4. Put the food to a plate. Drizzle with the olive oil and put in some the sunflower seeds and parsley.
Per Serving: Calories 120; Fat 9.09g; Sodium 248mg; Carbs 8.78g; Fiber 4g; Sugar 3.56g; Protein 3.31g

Terrific Spiced Almonds

Prep time: 10 minutes | Cook time: 7 minutes | Serves: 8

2 cups raw unsalted almonds
1 tablespoon extra-virgin olive oil
1 teaspoon ground cumin
½ teaspoon garlic powder
½ teaspoon sea salt
⅛ teaspoon cayenne pepper

1. Cook the almonds for about 3 minutes in a large nonstick skillet over medium-high heat, shaking the pan constantly, until the almonds become fragrant. Replace to a bowl and put aside. 2. Heat the olive oil until it shimmers in the same skillet over medium-high heat. 3. Put in the cumin, garlic powder, sea salt, and cayenne. Cook them for 30 to 60 seconds, until the spices become fragrant. 4. Add the almonds to the skillet and sauté them for 3 minutes more, or until the spices coat the almonds. 5. Let the food sit to cool naturally and then serve.
Per Serving: Calories 215; Fat 18.66g; Sodium 161mg; Carbs 7.98g; Fiber 4.5g; Sugar 1.57g; Protein 7.65g

Thyme Manoushe Flatbread

Prep time: 10 minutes | Cook time: 10 minutes | Serves: 6

Nonstick cooking spray
1 (16-ounce) bag whole-wheat pizza dough
3 tablespoons dried thyme
3 tablespoons sesame seeds
3 tablespoons extra-virgin olive oil
¼ teaspoon kosher or sea salt

1. At 450 degrees F, preheat your oven. 2. Grease a suitable, rimmed baking sheet with nonstick cooking spray. 3. Divide the prepared dough into three equal balls. 4. Spread some flour on the work surface, then roll each dough ball on it with a rolling pin into a 6-inch circle. 5. Place all three dough circles on the baking sheet. 6. Beat together the thyme, sesame seeds, oil, and salt in a suitable bowl. 7. Brush the oil onto the three dough circles with a spoon until it's all used up. 8. Bake the prepared dough circles for 10 minutes, or until the edges just start to brown and crisp and the oil is cooked into the dough. 9. Remove the flatbreads from the oven, cut each circle in half, and serve.
Per Serving: Calories 288; Total Fat 30.8g; Sodium 12mg; Total

Carbs 5.2g; Fiber 3.5g; Sugars 1.6g; Protein 1.5g

Easy Sweet-and-Savory Popcorn

Prep time: 5 minutes | Cook time: 15 minutes | Serves: 8

8 cups air-popped popcorn
2 tablespoons extra-virgin olive oil
2 tablespoons packed brown sugar

2 tablespoons Chinese five-spice powder
¼ teaspoon sea salt

1. Turn on the oven and heat it to 350°F. 2. Put the popcorn in a large bowl. Put aside. 3. In a bowl, mix the olive oil, brown sugar, five-spice powder, and sea salt. Coat the popcorn with the mixture. Transfer the coated popcorn to the 9-by-13-inch baking dish. 4. Bake the popcorn for 15 minutes and at the same timr stir every 5 minutes. 5. Serve hot, or cool and store in resealable bags in single-serve (1-cup) batches.
Per Serving: Calories 75; Fat 3.76g; Sodium 75mg; Carbs 9.83g; Fiber 1.2g; Sugar 3.44g; Protein 1.14g

Quick and Easy White Bean Dip

Prep time: 5 minutes | Cook time: 0 | Serves: 8

1 (14-ounce) can white beans, drained
¼ cup extra-virgin olive oil
2 garlic cloves, minced
2 tablespoons chopped fresh

thyme leaves
1 teaspoon Dijon mustard
Zest of 1 orange
Juice of 1 orange
½ teaspoon sea salt

In a blender, add all of the ingredients and then blend them until the mixture is smooth.
Per Serving: Calories 75; Fat 6.96g; Sodium 153mg; Carbs 3.15g; Fiber 0.8g; Sugar 1.17g; Protein 0.56g

Terrific Marinated Olives

Prep time: 10 minutes | Cook time: 0 | Serves: 8

¼ cup extra-virgin olive oil
¼ cup red wine vinegar
3 garlic cloves, minced
2 tablespoons chopped fresh rosemary leaves
1 tablespoon chopped fresh thyme

leaves
Zest of 1 lemon
½ teaspoon sea salt
2 cups black or green olives, drained and rinsed

1. In a bowl, mix the olive oil, vinegar, garlic, rosemary, thyme, lemon zest, and sea salt. 2. Put in the olives to your container and pour the marinade over the top. Seal and put into the refrigerator and store for at least 2 hours. The olives can be stored in the refrigerator for up to 2 weeks.
Per Serving: Calories 129; Fat 13.68g; Sodium 847mg; Carbs 2.4g; Fiber 1.7g; Sugar 0.29g; Protein 0.58g

Mediterranean Tzatziki Sauce

Prep time: 10 minutes | Cook time: 0 minute | Serves: 8

1 cup unsweetened nonfat plain Greek yogurt
1 cucumber, peeled and grated
1 tablespoon chopped fresh dill

1 garlic clove, minced
¼ teaspoon sea salt
⅛ teaspoon freshly ground black pepper

1. In a bowl, mix the yogurt, cucumber, dill, garlic, sea salt, and pepper. 2. Cover and put into the refrigerator and store for 1 hour or more and then serve.
Per Serving: Calories 29; Fat 0.3g; Sodium 86mg; Carbs 3.24g; Fiber 0.4g; Sugar 1.77g; Protein 3.97g

Garlicky White Bean Dip

Prep time: 10 minutes | Cook time: 15 minutes | Serves: 6

1 (16-ounce) can white cannellini beans, drained and rinsed
Juice of 1 lemon

2 garlic cloves
1 teaspoon dried thyme
¼ cup extra-virgin olive oil

1. In a blender, mix well the beans, lemon juice, garlic, thyme, and olive oil and blend. 2. Stop and scrape down the sides of the food processor a few times, then continue blending until the mixture is smooth. put into the refrigerator and store for up to 5 days in an airtight container.

Per Serving: Calories 167; Fat 9.27g; Sodium 4mg; Carbs 16.14g; Fiber 4g; Sugar 0.42g; Protein 5.94g

Quick Olive Tapenade

Prep time: 10 minutes | Cook time: 0 | Serves: ½ cup

½ cup kalamata olives
1 tablespoon capers
2 tablespoons coarsely chopped fresh parsley

1 tablespoon extra-virgin olive oil
1 tablespoon freshly squeezed lemon juice
Sea salt

1. In a blender, add the olives, capers, parsley, olive oil, and lemon juice and pulse until the mixture is thick and chunky. 2. Add some salt as you like. Adjust the flavor using more salt and lemon juiceto taste. Leftovers can keep for 5 days in the refrigerator.
Per Serving: Calories 51; Fat 5.21g; Sodium 757mg; Carbs 1.54g; Fiber 0.7g; Sugar 0.12g; Protein 0.26g

Quick and Easy Trail Mix

Prep time: 10 minutes | Cook time: 0 minute | Serves: 8

½ cup unsalted roasted cashews
¼ cup dried cranberries
¼ cup dried apricots

½ cup walnut halves
½ cup toasted hazelnuts

1. Mix all ingredients in a container. 2. Store the mixture in ¼ cup servings in resealable bags for up to six weeks.
Per Serving: Calories 149; Fat 12.38g; Sodium 2mg; Carbs 8.51g; Fiber 1.7g; Sugar 4.04g; Protein 3.47g

Healthy Sauerkraut Avocado Mash

Prep time: 5 minutes | Cook time: 0 | Serves: ⅔ cup

¼ cup sauerkraut, chopped
1 medium avocado

Sea salt
Freshly ground black pepper

1. Mash together the sauerkraut and avocado in a bowl. 2. Add some salt and pepper to taste and then serve.
Per Serving: Calories 166; Fat 14.78g; Sodium 1287mg; Carbs 9.72g; Fiber 7.4g; Sugar 0.98g; Protein 2.23g

Homemade Red Pepper and Lentil Dip

Prep time: 10 minutes | Cook time: 0 | Serves: 2 cups

1 (16-ounce) can red lentils, drained and rinsed
4 ounces roasted red peppers, from a jar
Juice of 1 lemon

2 tablespoons extra-virgin olive oil
1 tablespoon tahini
1 garlic clove
Sea salt

1. Blend the lentils, roasted red peppers, lemon juice, olive oil, tahini, and garlic in a food processor, until the mixture is smooth, stopping to scrape down the sides of the bowl as necessary. 2. Add some salt as you like. 3. Put into the refrigerator and store for up to 5 days in an airtight container.
Per Serving (⅓ cup): Calories 123; Fat 6.14g; Sodium 1323mg; Carbs 13.28g; Fiber 4g; Sugar 1.2g; Protein 4.8g

Terrific Eggplant Caviar

Prep time: 10 minutes | Cook time: 10 minutes | Serves: 4

2 (1-pound) eggplants
2 garlic cloves, mashed
½ cup finely chopped fresh parsley
½ cup finely diced red bell pepper

¼ cup freshly squeezed lemon juice, plus more as needed
2 tablespoons tahini
⅛ teaspoon salt, plus more as needed

1. Preheat the broiler. 2. Pierce the eggplants with a fork in several places and place them on a rimmed baking sheet. 3. Broil the eggplants for about 3 minutes until the skin is charred on one side; flip them and broil the other side for 3 minutes more until charred. Remove and let the food sit to cool naturally. 4. Remove the skin from the eggplants and scoop the pulp into a bowl carefully. Mash the pulp into a smooth purée with a fork. 5. Put in the garlic, parsley, red bell pepper, lemon juice, tahini, and salt (you can add more salt to your likimg), stir them well. 6. Put into the refrigerator and store for at least 1 hour and then serve. Leftover "caviar" can be kept refrigerated in an airtight container for up to 5 days, or frozen for up to 1 month.

Per Serving: Calories 124; Fat 4.64g; Sodium 97mg; Carbs 20.26g; Fiber 9.3g; Sugar 10.46g; Protein 4.44g

Delicious Roasted Grape, Olive, and Tahini

Prep time: 15 minutes | Cook time: 25 minutes | Serves: 4

2½ cups seedless red grapes	1 teaspoon sea salt
1 tablespoon extra-virgin olive oil	1 cup cherry tomatoes
2 tablespoons dried rosemary	1 cucumber, cut into ½-inch-thick
½ cup tahini	slices
½ cup water	1 cup black olives, pitted

1. Turn on the oven and heat it to 425°F. 2. Toss the grapes in the olive oil and rosemary. 3. Arrange the grapes on a small rimmed baking sheet in a single layer and then roast them for 25 minutes, stirring now and then through cooking. 4. In a bowl, mix together the tahini, water, and salt while the grapes are roasting. 5. Serve the roasted grapes, tomatoes, cucumber slices, and olives with the tahini dip.
Per Serving: Calories 335; Fat 23.36g; Sodium 870mg; Carbs 31.21g; Fiber 5.5g; Sugar 19.42g; Protein 6.57g

Tasty Avocado Pudding

Prep time: 10 minutes | Cook time: 0 | Serves: 4

1 ripe banana	½ cup unsweetened nondairy milk
2 avocados	⅓ cup unsweetened cocoa powder
2 tablespoons pure maple syrup	

1. In a blender, add the banana, avocados, maple syrup, and milk and blend until the mixture is smooth, scraping down the sides when necessary. 2. Slowly put in the cocoa powder and blend to mix well. 3. Serve it chilled.
Per Serving: Calories 235; Fat 15.78g; Sodium 23mg; Carbs 26.7g; Fiber 9.5g; Sugar 11.48g; Protein 4.61g

Rosemary Olives

Prep time: 10 minutes | Cook time: 0 | Serves: 4

¼ cup olive oil	1 teaspoon chopped fresh
¼ cup red wine vinegar	rosemary
Grated zest of 1 lemon	2 cups jarred olives, drained

1. In a medium bowl, mix the olive oil, vinegar, lemon zest, and rosemary until blended. 2. Put in the olives and gently stir to coat. Toss properly and let marinate for at least 3 hours and then serve.
Per Serving: Calories 202; Fat 20.72g; Sodium 496mg; Carbs 5.11g; Fiber 2.2g; Sugar 0.3g; Protein 0.62g

Savory Walnut and Red Pepper Spread

Prep time: 20 minutes | Cook time: 10 minutes | Serves: 6

3 slices whole-wheat bread	bought
1 red bell pepper, seeded and	2 tablespoons pomegranate
coarsely chopped	molasses, or cranberry juice
½ onion, chopped	½ teaspoon ground coriander
1 cup walnuts	½ teaspoon ground cumin
3 tablespoons Harissa, or store-	¼ cup olive oil

1. In a blender, mix well the bread, red bell pepper, onion and walnuts. 2. Process for a few seconds until combined but coarse. Do not overprocess. You want to retain some texture of the walnuts in this spread. 3. Put in the harissa, molasses, coriander, cumin and olive oil, process them for a few seconds until smooth. 4. The leftovers can be stored in an airtight container in the regrigeraror for up to 1 week.
Per Serving: Calories 298; Fat 19.27g; Sodium 181mg; Carbs 30.39g; Fiber 6.5g; Sugar 15g; Protein 5.46g

Lemony Green Olive Tapenade

Prep time: 20 minutes | Cook time: 10 minutes | Serves: 6

2 cups pitted green olives	¼ cup freshly squeezed lemon
1 cup coarsely chopped walnuts	juice
1 onion, chopped	¼ cup olive oil
½ cup chopped fresh parsley	1 teaspoon dried oregano

1. In a blender, mix well the olives, walnuts, onion, and parsley. Pulse about 5 times until coarsely chopped. 2. Put in the lemon juice, olive oil, and oregano. Process for a few seconds more. The spread should be finely chopped but not puréed.
Per Serving: Calories 180; Fat 17.92g; Sodium 18mg; Carbs 4.71g; Fiber 1.5g; Sugar 1.44g; Protein 2.44g

Easy Stuffed Grape Leaves

Prep time: 40 minutes | Cook time: 65 minutes | Serves: 60 Grape Leaves

½ cup plus 1 tablespoon olive oil, divided	1 teaspoon ground allspice
1 onion, finely chopped	Salt
1½ cups short-grain rice	Freshly ground black pepper
6 cups cold water, divided	1 (16-ounce) can grape leaves,
1 cup finely chopped fresh parsley	drained, rinsed, stems cut off
10 garlic cloves, peeled	4 potatoes, peeled and cut into
2 tomatoes, finely chopped	½-inch-thick rounds
	½ cup freshly squeezed lemon juice

1. In the skillet, heat ¼ cup of olive oil over medium-low heat; put in the onion and sauté for 5 minutes. 2. Stir in the rice and cook for 1 minute. Stir in 2 cups of cold water and cook for 5 minutes, or until the water evaporates. Remove from the heat and stir in the parsley, 3 cloves of the garlic (minced), tomatoes, and allspice and add some salt and pepper. Transfer the rice mixture to a bowl and put aside. 3. Put the grape leaves, shiny-side down, on a work surface. Add 1 tablespoon of the stuffing into the center of each leaf. 4. Fold the stem side horizontally over the stuffing, then fold the 2 vertical sides over the first fold; roll until reaching the leaf point until it form a cylinder 2 inches long by 1 inch thick. 5. Cover the bottom of a heavy round pot with the potato slices and drizzle with 1 tablespoon of olive oil. 6. Layer the stuffed grape leaves, tightly side by side, on top of the potato slices. Each layer will have about 30 stuffed leaves. Place the remaining 7 garlic cloves between the stuffed leaves. Drizzle with the remaining ¼ cup of olive oil. 7. Put a round flat glass plate on top of the rolls and press down. The plate should be smaller than the pot, leaving ¼ inch between the plate and the edge of the pan. Put in the remaining 4 cups of cold water. The water should cover the plate and the grape leaves, and decrease as the grape leaves cook. 8. Over medium heat, place the plate and cook for 15 minutes. Turn the heat to low and cook for 40 minutes. 9. Turn off the heat, carefully remove the plate, and drizzle the grape leaves with the lemon juice. Cover and let the food Place a round flat glass plate on top of the rolls and press down lightly. The plate should be slightly smaller than the pot, leaving about ¼ inch between the plate and the pot's edge. 10. Sit to cool naturally and then serve.
Per Serving (5 leaves): Calories 258; Fat 4.31g; Sodium 489mg; Carbs 50.83g; Fiber 4.5g; Sugar 6.57g; Protein 5.17g

Filo-Wrapped Brie

Prep time: 30 minutes | Cook time: 20 minutes | Serves: 12

4 tablespoons butter, melted	1 (14-ounce) wheel Brie cheese,
6 (18-by-14-inch) sheets frozen	unwrapped, rind left on
filo dough, thawed; follow the	½ cup orange marmalade
instruction on the package to	Crackers, for serving
prevent drying	

1. Turn on the oven and heat it to 400°F. 2. Brush a baking sheet with melted butter. Place 1 sheet of filo dough on the baking sheet; brush it lightly with melted butter. Place another filo sheet on top; brush it lightly with melted butter. Repeat the same process. 3. Place the cheese wheel in the center of the filo dough stack. Spread the orange marmalade over the cheese with a spoon. 4. Fold the filo dough over the cheese gently and marmalade until the cheese is covered. Press slightly to seal. Brush the filo bundle with the remaining melted butter. 5. Bake the food for 20 minutes until golden brown. Let the food sit to cool naturally for 10 minutes and serve with crackers.
Per Serving: Calories 207; Fat 13.63g; Sodium 294mg; Carbs 14.15g; Fiber 0.3g; Sugar 8.19g; Protein 7.64g

Mediterranean Trail Mix

Prep time: 10 minutes | Cook time: 0 | Serves: 6

1 cup roughly chopped unsalted walnuts	½ cup shelled salted pistachios
½ cup roughly chopped salted almonds	½ cup roughly chopped apricots
	½ cup roughly chopped dates
	⅓ cup dried figs, sliced in half

In a suitable zip-top bag, mix the walnuts, almonds, pistachios, apricots, dates, and figs and mix well.
Per Serving: Calories 214; Total Fat 11.8g; Sodium 80mg; Total Carbs 24.6g; Fiber 2.5g; Sugar 2.2g; Protein 24.6g

Garlicky Tomato Bruschetta

Prep time: 15 minutes | Cook time: 5 minutes | Serves: 4

2 tablespoons olive oil
2 garlic cloves, mashed
½ baguette, cut into 12 slices
3 small ripe tomatoes, seeded and

chopped
1 cup chopped fresh basil
Salt
Pepper

1. Preheat the broiler. 2. In a bowl, stir together the olive oil and garlic. Brush the bread slices with this mixture and place them on a baking sheet. Put aside. 3. Mix together the tomatoes and basil in another container and add some salt and pepper. Taste, and adjust seasoning as you like. 4. Put the bread under the broiler for 1 minute until crisp. Take out carefully for the oven, add 1 tablespoon of the tomato mixture on top of each piece slice.
Per Serving: Calories 113; Fat 7.25g; Sodium 658mg; Carbs 10.6g; Fiber 1.4g; Sugar 2.96g; Protein 2.4g

Spinach-Walnut Fatayers

Prep time: 30 minutes | Cook time: 15 minutes | Serves: 12

2 (10-ounce) packages fresh spinach, chopped
¼ teaspoon salt, plus more for sprinkling
1 small onion, finely chopped
¼ cup coarsely chopped walnuts

¼ cup olive oil
½ teaspoon ground sumac
½ yield Pizza Dough, or 1 pound store-bought, thawed, at room temperature
All-purpose flour, for dusting

1. Turn on the oven and heat it to 375°F. 2. Put the spinach in a medium bowl and sprinkle it with add some salt. Gently massage the spinach and set aside for 5 minutes. Squeeze out the excess moisture and return the spinach to the bowl. 3. Put in the onion, walnuts, olive oil, sumac, and salt. Stir to combine and put aside. 4. Cut the dough into 12 balls. Flour a work surface and roll out the dough balls on it into ⅛-inch-thick circles. 5. Place 1 heaping tablespoon of the spinach stuffing in the center of each circle. Fold up the sides to the center, squeezing them to seal and form a triangle. Place the fatayers on a baking sheet. 6. Bake for 15 minutes and then serve.
Per Serving: Calories 113; Fat 8.52g; Sodium 171mg; Carbs 6.92g; Fiber 0.8g; Sugar 1.07g; Protein 2.69g

Beet-Grapefruit Salad

Prep time: 20 minutes | Cook time: 20 minutes | Serves: 4

For the Dressing
¼ cup olive oil
2 tablespoons orange juice
1 tablespoon apple cider vinegar
Juice and zest of 1 lime
For the Salad
6 beets, peeled and cut in half
1 teaspoon olive oil
6 cups chopped mixed greens
2 large ruby red grapefruits, peeled, pith removed, segmented,

1 tablespoon chopped fresh basil
Sea salt
Black pepper

and cut into chunks
One scallion, sliced
½ cup chopped pecans
½ cup crumbled goat cheese

To Make the Dressing: Beat together the olive oil, orange juice, vinegar, lime juice, lime zest, and basil in a suitable bowl. Season with black pepper and salt and set aside.
To Make the Salad: 1. At 400 degrees F, preheat your oven. 2. In an 8-by-8-inch baking dish, toss the beets with olive oil. Roast until the beets are tender, about 20 minutes. 3. Remove the beets from the oven and chill them in the refrigerator for about 2 hours. Cut the beets into wedges. 4. In a suitable bowl, toss the greens together with half the dressing until well coated. 5. Evenly divide the greens between serving plates. Top each salad with beet wedges, grapefruits, scallion, pecans, and goat cheese. 6. Evenly drizzle the rest dressing over the salads and serve.
Per Serving: Calories 355; Total Fat 24g; Sodium 116mg; Total Carbs 32g; Sugar 25g; Fiber 6g; Protein 9g

Honey Crostini with Goat Cheese

Prep time: 10 minutes | Cook time: 10 minutes | Serves: 4

½ baguette, cut into 12 thin slices
4 tablespoons olive oil, divided
¼ teaspoon salt
4 ounces' goat cheese, at room

temperature
½ teaspoon dried thyme
4 tablespoons honey

1. Turn on the oven and heat it to 375°F. 2. Arrange the bread slices on a baking sheet. Brush with 2 tablespoons of olive oil. Put in some the salt and bake for 10 minutes or until lightly toasted. Remove and put aside. 3. Wisk well the goat cheese, the remaining 2 tablespoons of olive oil, and the thyme in a medium bowl. 4. Put the toast on a platter and spread with the goat cheese. Drizzle with the honey and enjoy the delicious food.
Per Serving: Calories 344; Fat 23.88g; Sodium 339mg; Carbs 24.17g; Fiber 0.3g; Sugar 18.41g; Protein 10.01g

Savory Popcorn

Prep time: 10 minutes | Cook time: 5 minutes | Serves: 6

3 tablespoons extra-virgin olive oil
¼ teaspoon garlic powder
¼ teaspoon freshly ground black pepper

¼ teaspoon sea salt
⅛ teaspoon dried thyme
⅛ teaspoon dried oregano
12 cups plain popped popcorn

1. In a suitable sauté pan, preheat the oil over medium heat until shimmering, and then add the garlic powder, pepper, salt, thyme, and oregano until fragrant. 2. Drizzle the oil over the popcorn, toss, and serve in a bowl.
Per Serving: Calories 327; Total Fat 29g; Sodium 888mg; Total Carbs 6g; Fiber 1g; Sugar 1g; Protein 11g

Mediterranean Crostini

Prep time: 15 minutes | Cook time: 15 minutes | Serves: 6

One baguette, sliced ¼ inch thick
5 tablespoons extra-virgin olive oil
¼ teaspoon salt
⅛ teaspoon black pepper
½ cup hummus
1 cup quartered grape tomatoes

1 cup diced cucumber
Four chopped pitted kalamata olives
½ cup crumbled feta cheese
½ cup chopped flat-leaf parsley, for garnish
⅓ cup pickled turnips (optional)

1. At 350 degrees F, preheat your oven. 2. On baking sheet, arrange the baguette slices and carefully brush the tops and sides with the oil. Sprinkle with black pepper and salt. 3. Bake the baguette slices for 10 minutes or until the toasts become slightly crispy. Remove them from the oven and set them aside. 4. Arrange the hummus in a thin layer on the toast when the slices are cool enough to handle. 5. Individually, spoon tomatoes, cucumber, olives, and feta cheese onto the toast. 6. Garnish with fresh parsley and pickled turnips.
Per Serving: Calories 115; Total Fat 11.6g; Sodium 17mg; Total Carbs 1.7g; Fiber 0.2g; Sugars 0.1g; Protein 1.7g

Honey-Rosemary Almonds

Prep time: 10 minutes | Cook time: 10 minutes | Serves: 6

1 cup raw, whole, shelled almonds
1 tablespoon minced fresh rosemary

¼ teaspoon kosher or sea salt
1 tablespoon honey
Nonstick cooking spray

1. Mix the almonds, rosemary, and salt in a suitable skillet over medium heat. Stir frequently for 1 minute. 2. Add honey and cook for another 3 to 4 minutes, frequently stirring, until the almonds are coated and darken around the edges. 3. Now remove it from the heat. Using a spatula, spread the almonds onto a pan coated with nonstick cooking spray. Cool for 10 minutes. 4. Break up the almonds before serving.
Per Serving: Calories 355; Total Fat 40.3g; Sodium 14mg; Total Carbs 1.3g; Fiber 0.6g; Sugars 0.6g; Protein 0.7g

Marinated Strawberries

Prep time: 10 minutes | Cook time: 0 | Serves: 4

⅓ cup balsamic vinegar
1 tablespoon honey
2 teaspoons pure vanilla extract

8 cups hulled and halved strawberries

1. In a suitable bowl, beat together the balsamic vinegar, honey, and vanilla until blended. 2. Stir in the strawberries and let the berries marinate in the refrigerator for 15 minutes. 3. Drain the vinegar mixture out of the strawberries and serve immediately.
Per Serving: Calories 223; Total Fat 25g; Sodium 389mg; Total Carbs 0.3g; Fiber 0g; Sugars 0g; Protein 0.3g

Fig- Energy Bites

Prep time: 20 minutes | Cook time: 0 | Serves: 6

¾ cup diced dried figs (six to eight)	2 tablespoons ground flaxseed
½ cup chopped pecans	2 tablespoons regular peanut butter
¼ cup rolled oats (old fashioned or quick oats)	2 tablespoons honey

1. Mix the figs, pecans, oats, flaxseed, and peanut butter in a suitable bowl. 2. Drizzle with the honey, and mix everything. 3. Press the figs and nuts into the honey and powdery ingredients. 4. Divide the prepared dough evenly into four sections in the bowl. 5. Dampen your hands with water-but do not get them too wet. Using your hands, roll three bites out of each of the four sections of dough. 6. Enjoy directly or chill this dish in the freezer for 5 minutes. 7. The bites can be stored in a sealed container in the refrigerator for up to 7 days.
Per Serving: Calories 185; Total Fat 16.5g; Sodium 9mg; Total Carbs 7.3g; Fiber 1.1g; Sugars 0.5g; Protein 4.2g

Fruit Cheese Board

Prep time: 10 minutes | Cook time: 0 | Serves: 4

2 cups sliced fruits, such as apples, pears, plums, or peaches	sticks
2 cups finger-food fruits, such as berries, cherries, grapes, or figs	1 cup roasted peppers or artichoke hearts
2 cups raw vegetables cut into	1 cup cubed cheese

1. Wash all the fresh produce and cut into slices or bite-size pieces. 2. Put all of the ingredients on a wooden board or serving tray. 3. Include small spoons for items like the berries and olives and a fork or knife for the cheeses. 4. Serve with small plates and napkins.
Per Serving: Calories 165; Total Fat 18.4g; Sodium 1mg; Total Carbs 1g; Fiber 0.5g; Sugars 0g; Protein 0.3g

Fruit-Topped Meringues

Prep time: 10 minutes | Cook time: 50 minutes | Serves: 24 Cookies

Four large egg whites, at room temperature	Pinch sea salt
¼ teaspoon cream of tartar	½ cup honey
	1 cup raspberries

1. At 200 degrees F, preheat your oven. 2. Layer two baking sheets with parchment paper and set aside. 3. In a suitable stainless steel bowl, beat the egg whites until they are frothy. 4. Add the cream of tartar and salt, and beat them for 4 to 5 minutes until soft peaks form. 5. Beat in the honey, 1 tablespoon at a time, until stiff glossy peaks form. 6. Spoon meringue batter onto the baking sheets, and create an appropriate well in the center of each batter. 7. Bake until firm, 45 to 50 minutes. Put off the heat in the oven and open the door to cool the meringues for at least 1 hour. 8. Serve.
Per Serving: Calories 46; Total Fat 4.3g; Sodium 21mg; Total Carbs 1.4g; Fiber 0.6g; Sugars 0.2g; Protein 1.1g

Yogurt Chocolate Pudding

Prep time: 10 minutes | Cook time: 5 minutes | Serves: 4

½ cup unsweetened almond milk	1 teaspoon pure vanilla extract
4 ounces' dark chocolate, at least 60 percent cacao, chopped	Whipped coconut cream for garnish
2 cups low-fat plain Greek yogurt	

1. In a saucepan, bring about 1-inch water to a simmer over low heat. 2. Place a suitable heat-resistant bowl over the saucepan. 3. Add the almond milk and chocolate to the bowl, and stir them for 5 minutes until the chocolate is completely melted, and the prepared mixture is smooth. 4. Remove the bowl from the heat, and beat in the yogurt and vanilla until well blended. 5. Cover the blended mixture with plastic wrap, and place the bowl in the refrigerator to refrigerate the food for

at least 3 hours. 6. Serve topped with whipped coconut cream.
Per Serving: Calories 255; Total Fat 18.4g; Sodium 1mg; Total Carbs 1g; Fiber 0.5g; Sugars 0g; Protein 0.3g

Pomegranate Granita

Prep time: 10 minutes | Cook time: 0 | Serves: 4

4 cups pomegranate juice, no sugar added	¼ teaspoon ground cinnamon
¼ cup honey	Pinch sea salt

1. In a suitable bowl, beat together the pomegranate juice, honey, cinnamon, and salt until well blended. Pour the pomegranate mixture into a 9-by-13-by-3-inch metal baking dish. 2. Freeze the prepared mixture for at least 4 hours, scraping the surface with a fork every 30 minutes until the ready mix looks like colored snow. 3. Store the granita in the freezer in a sealed container for 2 weeks, scraping with a fork before serving.
Per Serving: Calories 205; Total Fat 0g; Sodium 221mg; Total Carbs 56g; Sugar 54g; Fiber 0g; Protein 0g

Creamy Panna Cotta

Prep time: 10 minutes | Cook time: 2 minutes | Serves: 4

½ cup unsweetened almond milk	¼ cup honey
1 (¼-ounce) packet of unflavored gelatin	1 teaspoon cornstarch
	½ teaspoon almond extract
1½ cups low-fat milk	1 cup fresh berries

1. Add the almond milk into a suitable saucepan and sprinkle the gelatin over it; let stand for 5 minutes. 2. Heat them for 2 minutes over medium-low heat until the gelatin is dissolved. Beat in the milk, honey, cornstarch, and almond extract. 3. Pour this panna cotta mixture into 4 (6-ounce) ramekins and wrap them in plastic wrap. Refrigerate until set, about 3 hours. 4. Loosen this panna cotta by running a knife around the inside edges of the ramekins and invert them onto serving plates. Top with berries and serve.
Per Serving: Calories 129; Total Fat 1g; Sodium 122g; Total Carbs 26g; Sugar 24g; Fiber 1g; Protein 5g

Spiced Oranges with Dates

Prep time: 10 minutes | Cook time: 0 | Serves: 4

4 large oranges	⅛ teaspoon ground cloves
2 large blood oranges	2 tablespoons chopped hazelnuts
¼ cup chopped Medjool dates	

1. Peel off and pith off the oranges, so you just have the flesh. 2. Follow the membranes to cut the sections of the oranges out, and place them in a suitable bowl. Squeeze any remaining juice from the membranes into the bowl with the fruit. 3. Add the dates, cloves, and hazelnuts to the bowl and toss to mix. 4. Store this dish in a sealed container in the refrigerator. Serve spooned into individual bowls.
Per Serving: Calories 184; Total Fat 2g; Sodium 220g; Total Carbs 43g; Sugar 35g; Fiber 8g; Protein 3g

Roasted Cauliflower with Dipping Sauce

Prep time: 10 minutes | Cook time: 15 minutes | Serves: 4

For the Cauliflower

¼ cup olive oil	One head cauliflower, stem trimmed, cut into florets
2 teaspoons salt	½ lemon
1 teaspoon smoked hot paprika (or chipotle powder)	

For the Saffron Sauce

¼ teaspoon saffron threads	½ teaspoon ground turmeric
1 tablespoon water	1 scallion, finely chopped
1 cup Greek yogurt	1 tablespoon chopped fresh cilantro
1 teaspoon salt	

To Make the Cauliflower: 1. At 400 degrees F, preheat your oven. 2. Mix the olive oil, salt, and paprika or chipotle powder in a suitable bowl. Add the cauliflower 3. In a single layer, place the cauliflower on a rimmed baking sheet. 4. Roast until the cauliflower is brown around the edges, about 15 minutes, with occasional stirring. 5. Squeeze the lemon juice over the cauliflower.
To Make the Saffron Sauce: 1. Mix the saffron threads with the water in a suitable bowl or saucer. This step releases the color and flavor. 2. Mix the yogurt, saffron-water mixture, salt, turmeric, scallion, and

cilantro in another bowl. Mix well. 3. Arrange the cauliflower on a serving dish along with a suitable bowl of saffron dip, and serve. 4. The cooked cauliflower will keep five days in the refrigerator, and the sauce will keep four days in the fridge.
Per Serving: Calories 399; Total Fat 27.5g; Sodium 32mg; Total Carbs 45g; Fiber 3.8g; Sugars 38.8g; Protein 3.1g

Fruit Crumble Muesli

Prep time: 20 minutes | Cook time: 0 | Serves: 4

1 cup gluten-free rolled oats	1 cup sliced fresh strawberries
¼ cup chopped pecans	1 nectarine, pitted and chopped
¼ cup almonds	2 kiwis, peeled and chopped
4 pitted Medjool dates	½ cup blueberries
1 teaspoon vanilla extract	1 cup low-fat plain Greek yogurt
¼ teaspoon ground cinnamon	

1. In a food processor, mix the oats, pecans, almonds, dates, vanilla, and cinnamon, and pulse until the prepared mixture resembles coarse crumbs. 2. Stir together the strawberries, nectarine, kiwis, and blueberries in a suitable bowl until well mixed. Divide the fruit and yogurt between bowls and top each bowl with the oat mixture. 3. Enjoy.
Per Serving: Calories 258; Total Fat 6g; Sodium 130g; Total Carbs 45g; Sugar 28g; Fiber 7g; Protein 11g

Toasted Pita Wedges

Prep time: 10 minutes | Cook time: 15 minutes | Serves: 6-8

1 (12-ounce) package of whole-wheat pita bread	¼ cup extra-virgin olive oil
	1 teaspoon sea salt

1. At 375 degrees F, preheat your oven. 2. Cut each pita bread into 12 wedges. 3. Place the pita wedges in a suitable bowl and drizzle with olive oil and sea salt. 4. Place the pita in a single layer on the baking sheet and place the baking sheet in the oven. 5. Toast the pita until crisp and lightly browned, about 10 to 15 minutes. 6. You can store the pita wedges in an airtight container at room temperature for almost ten days.
Per Serving: Calories 353; Total Fat 37.9g; Sodium 221mg; Total Carbs 1.2g; Fiber 0.1g; Sugars 0.2g; Protein 3g

Feta with Olive Oil and Herbs

Prep time: 10 minutes | Cook time: 0 | Serves: 4

8 ounces' feta cheese	1 tablespoon red wine vinegar
¼ cup extra-virgin olive oil	2 teaspoons lemon zest
1 tablespoon chopped fresh oregano	¼ teaspoon red pepper flakes

1. Place the feta in a shallow bowl. 2. Pour the olive oil over the feta and sprinkle with the oregano, vinegar, lemon zest, and pepper flakes. 3. Cover the shallow bowl with a lid or plastic wrap, marinate at room temperature for 1 hour, or refrigerate for several days. 4. To serve, cut the feta into bite-size pieces. 5. The cheese can be kept for 7 days in the refrigerator.
Per Serving: Calories 168; Total Fat 3.1g; Sodium 412mg; Total Carbs 28.5g; Fiber 6.9g; Sugars 5g; Protein 7.5g

Sautéed Olives with Basil

Prep time: 10 minutes | Cook time: 5 minutes | Serves: 6-8

2 tablespoons extra-virgin olive oil	One garlic clove, minced
	One scallion, sliced
2 cups pitted olives (kalamata and Sicilian or a pitted Greek blend)	½ teaspoon dried rosemary
⅛ teaspoon red pepper flakes (optional)	1 tablespoon slivered preserved lemons (optional)

1. Place a suitable frying pan over high heat. 2. Add the olive oil, olives, red pepper flakes (optional), and garlic. 3. Sauté for 5 minutes or until the olives start to wilt. 4. Add the scallions, rosemary, and preserved lemon (optional). 5. Serve warm.
Per Serving: Calories 196; Total Fat 13.2g; Sodium 67mg; Total Carbs 16.9g; Fiber 3.1g; Sugars 8.4g; Protein 4.8g

Moroccan Zucchini Spread

Prep time: 10 minutes | Cook time: 20 minutes | Serves: 4

¼ cup plus 1 tablespoon extra-	virgin olive oil

4 large zucchinis, cut in half lengthwise	¼ cup lemon juice
	½ teaspoon dried oregano
2 teaspoons salt, divided	¼ teaspoon cayenne pepper
¼ cup tahini	Two scallions, sliced
One garlic clove, minced	1 tablespoon chopped fresh mint

1. At 375 degrees F, preheat your oven. 2. Brush a suitable baking sheet with olive oil. 3. Brush the zucchini with ¼ cup of olive oil and sprinkle with one teaspoon of salt. 4. Arrange the zucchini on the oiled baking sheet, skin side down. 5. Roast the zucchini for 15 to 20 minutes or until it is soft. 6. Place the zucchini in a suitable bowl and mash with a fork or potato masher. 7. Mix in the tahini, garlic, lemon juice, oregano, cayenne, 1 tablespoon of olive oil, and 1 teaspoon of salt. 8. Add the scallions and mint, and mix well. 9. Spoon the prepared mixture into a serving bowl, drizzle with olive oil, and serve warm or at room temperature. 10. The spread will keep for five days in the refrigerator or the freezer for several months.
Per Serving: Calories 187; Total Fat 8.9g; Sodium 517mg; Total Carbs 18g; Fiber 2.8g; Sugars 0.6g; Protein 7.5g

Almonds with Apricots

Prep time: 10 minutes | Cook time: 5 minutes | Serves: 4

2 tablespoons extra-virgin olive oil	⅛ teaspoon red pepper flakes (optional)
1 cup blanched (skinless) unsalted almonds	⅛ teaspoon ground cinnamon
	½ cup dried apricots, chopped
½ teaspoon sea salt	

1. Place a suitable frying pan over high heat. 2. Add the olive oil, almonds, and sea salt and sauté until the almonds are a light golden brown, 5 to 10 minutes. 3. Spoon the hot almonds into a serving dish and add the red pepper flakes (optional), cinnamon, and apricot pieces. 4. Let this dish cool for a while before serving. 5. These nuts can be stored in a sealed container at room temperature for up to 5 days.
Per Serving: Calories 256; Total Fat 24.2g; Sodium 13mg; Total Carbs 10g; Fiber 0.5g; Sugars 9g; Protein 2g

Crispy Chickpeas

Prep time: 10 minutes | Cook time: 15 minutes | Serves: 4

1 (15-ounce) can of cooked chickpeas, drained	⅛ teaspoon chili powder
	⅛ teaspoon garlic powder
1 tablespoon olive oil	⅛ teaspoon paprika
¼ teaspoon salt	

1. At 380 degrees F, preheat your oven. 2. In a suitable bowl, toss all ingredients together until the chickpeas are well coated. 3. Pour the chickpeas into the air fryer and spread them out in a single layer. 4. Roast the chickpeas for 15 minutes, stirring once halfway through the cooking time. 5. Serve and enjoy.
Per Serving: Calories 172; Total Fat 1.8g; Sodium 135mg; Total Carbs 41.1g; Fiber 6.2g; Sugars 28.7g; Protein 6.2g

Crunchy White Beans

Prep time: 5 minutes | Cook time: 20 minutes | Serves: 2

1 (15 ounces) can of cooked white beans	¼ teaspoon garlic powder
	¼ teaspoon salt
2 tablespoons olive oil	1 teaspoon chopped fresh basil
1 teaspoon fresh sage, chopped	

1. At 380 degrees F, preheat your oven. 2. Mix the beans, olive oil, sage, garlic, ⅛ teaspoon of salt, and basil in a suitable bowl. 3. Pour the white beans into the air fryer and spread them out in a single layer. 4. Bake the white beans for 10 minutes. Stir and continue cooking for 5 to 9 minutes. 5. Toss the beans with the rest salt before serving.
Per Serving: Calories 364; Total Fat 29.6g; Sodium 489mg; Total Carbs 27g; Fiber 10.6g; Sugars 9.3g; Protein 5.5g

Beet Chips

Prep time: 10 minutes | Cook time: 30 minutes | Serves: 6

4 medium beets, rinse and slice thin	2 tablespoons olive oil
	Hummus, for serving
1 teaspoon sea salt	

1. At 380 degrees F, preheat your oven. 2. Toss the beets with sea salt and olive oil in a suitable bowl until well coated. 3. Put the beet slices

into the air fryer and spread them out in a single layer. 4. Fry the food in the oven for 10 minutes. Stir, then fry for an additional 10 minutes. Stir again, then fry for 5 to 10 minutes, or until the chips reach the desired crispiness. 5. Serve with a favorite hummus.

Per Serving: Calories 134; Total Fat 10.8g; Sodium 124mg; Total Carbs 2.3g; Fiber 0.4g; Sugars 2.1g; Protein 6.3g

Yogurt Deviled Eggs

Prep time: 15 minutes | Cook time: 15 minutes | Serves: 4

¼ cup nonfat plain Greek yogurt
Four eggs
1 teaspoon chopped fresh dill
⅛ teaspoon paprika

⅛ teaspoon garlic powder
⅛ teaspoon salt
Chopped fresh parsley for garnish

1. At 260 degrees F, preheat your air fryer. 2. Place the eggs in a single layer in the air fryer basket and cook for 15 minutes. 3. Quickly remove the eggs from the air fryer and place them into a cold water bath. Let the eggs cool in the water for 10 minutes before removing and peeling them. 4. After peeling the eggs, cut them in half. 5. Spoon the yolk into a suitable bowl. Add the dill, yogurt, paprika, salt, and garlic powder, and mix until smooth. 6. Spoon or pipe the yolk mixture into the halved egg whites. 7. Serve with a sprinkle of fresh parsley on top.

Per Serving: Calories 211; Total Fat 22g; Sodium 166mg; Total Carbs 1.1g; Fiber 0g; Sugars 0.1g; Protein 2.9g

Popcorn with Garlic Salt

Prep time: 5 minutes | Cook time: 10 minutes | Serves: 2

2 tablespoons olive oil
¼ cup popcorn kernels

1 teaspoon garlic salt

1. At 380 degrees F, preheat your oven. 2. Tear a square of aluminum foil the size of the bottom of the air fryer and place it into the air fryer. 3. Drizzle olive oil on the top of the foil, and then stir in the popcorn kernels. 4. Roast the food for 8 to 10 minutes, or until the popcorn stops popping. 5. Transfer the popcorn to a suitable bowl and sprinkle with garlic salt before serving.

Per Serving: Calories 225; Total Fat 6.3g; Sodium 7mg; Total Carbs 38.1g; Fiber 5.9g; Sugars 27.7g; Protein 3.1g

Roasted Spiced Cashews

Prep time: 5 minutes | Cook time: 10 minutes | Serves: 4

2 cups raw cashews
2 tablespoons olive oil
¼ teaspoon salt

¼ teaspoon chili powder
⅛ teaspoon garlic powder
⅛ teaspoon smoked paprika

1. At 360 degrees F, preheat your air fryer. 2. In a suitable bowl, toss all of the ingredients together. 3. Pour the cashews into the air fryer basket and roast them for 5 minutes. 4. Shake the basket, then cook for 5 minutes more. 5. Serve immediately.

Per Serving: Calories 223; Total Fat 6.3g; Sodium 7mg; Total Carbs 38.1g; Fiber 5.9g; Sugars 27.7g; Protein 3.1g

Chapter 8 Starchy Mains Recipes

Jeweled Rice with Peas and Carrots

Prep time: 15 minutes | Cook time: 30 minutes | Serves: 6

½ cup olive oil, divided
1 onion, finely chopped
1 garlic clove, minced
½ teaspoon chopped peeled fresh ginger
4½ cups water
1 teaspoon salt, divided, plus more as needed
1 teaspoon ground turmeric

2 cups basmati rice
1 cup fresh sweet peas
2 carrots, peeled and cut into ½-inch dice
½ cup dried cranberries
Grated zest of 1 orange
⅛ teaspoon cayenne pepper
¼ cup slivered almonds, toasted

1. Heat ¼ cup of olive oil in a large heavy-bottomed pot over medium heat. 2. Cook the onion about 4 minutes. Add the garlic and ginger and then cook for 1 minute. 3. Add ¾ teaspoon of salt, water, and turmeric and stir. Bring the mixture to a boil. Add the rice and stir. Bring together to a boil. Taste and adjust seasoning as needed. 4. Then decrease the heat to low. Cover and cook for 15 minutes. Then remove from the heat. Let the rice rest about 10 minutes with the lid closed. 5. At the same time, heat the remaining olive oil in a medium skillet over the medium-low heat. Stir in carrots and peas and cook for 5 minutes. 6. Add the cranberries and orange zest. Add the remaining salt and the cayenne to season and cook for 1 to 2 minutes. 7. Serve the rice onto a serving plate and add the peas and carrots on the top. Sprinkle the toasted almonds over and serve.
Variation tip: Use thawed frozen peas and frozen diced carrots instead of fresh. Cook for 2 minutes instead of 5.
Per Serving: Calories 330; Fat 26g; Sodium 408mg; Carbs 30g; Fiber 10g; Sugar 6g; Protein 6g

Asparagus Risotto

Prep time: 15 minutes | Cook time: 30 minutes | Serves: 4

5 cups vegetable broth, divided
3 tablespoons unsalted butter, divided
1 tablespoon olive oil
1 small onion, chopped
1½ cups Arborio rice

1-pound fresh asparagus, ends trimmed, cut into 1-inch pieces, tips separated
¼ cup grated Parmesan cheese, additional cheese for serving

1. In a saucepan, bring the vegetable broth to a boil over medium heat. Turn the heat to low and keep the broth at a steady simmer. 2. In a 4-quart heavy-bottomed saucepan over medium heat, melt 2 tablespoons of butter with the olive oil. Add the onion and cook for 2 to 3 minutes. 3. Add the rice and stir with a wooden spoon while cooking for 1 minute until the grains are well coated in the butter and oil. 4. Stir in ½ cup of warm broth. Cook, and stirring occasionally, for about 5 minutes until the broth is completely absorbed. 5. Add the asparagus stalks and another ½ cup of broth. Cook, stirring occasionally, until the liquid is absorbed. Continue adding the broth, ½ cup at a time, and cooking until it is completely absorbed before adding the next ½ cup. Stir frequently to prevent sticking. After 20 minutes, the rice should be cooked but still firm. 6. Add the asparagus tips, the remaining 1 tablespoon of butter, and the Parmesan cheese. Stir vigorously to combine. 7. Remove from the heat, top with additional Parmesan cheese, if desired, and serve immediately.
Variation tip: Use other vegetables in place of asparagus. Try butternut squash, zucchini, or mushrooms. Sauté until cooked through and tender, and add to the risotto when you would add the asparagus tips.
Per Serving: Calories 285; Fat 19g; Sodium 1242mg; Carbs 34g; Fiber 12g; Sugar 6g; Protein 11g

Enticing Vegetable Paella

Prep time: 25 minutes | Cook time: 45 minutes | Serves: 6

¼ cup olive oil
1 large sweet onion, chopped
1 large red bell pepper, seeded and minced
1 large green bell pepper, seeded and minced
3 garlic cloves, finely minced

1 teaspoon smoked paprika
5 saffron threads (see tip)
1 zucchini, cut into ½-inch cubes
4 large ripe tomatoes, peeled, seeded, and chopped
1½ cups short-grain Spanish rice
3 cups vegetable broth, warmed

1. Preheat the oven to 350 degrees F before cooking. 2. Heat olive oil in a large oven-safe skillet over medium heat. 3. Cook the red and green bell peppers and onion in the skillet. 4. Add the saffron threads, zucchini, tomatoes, garlic, and paprika and cook over medium-low

heat about 10 minutes. 5. Add the rice and pour the vegetable broth. Bring the boil by increasing the heat. Then cook for 15 minutes over medium-low heat. Use aluminum foil to cover and place inside the oven. 6. Bake until the broth is absorbed about 10 minutes.
Variation tip: Skip the saffron and use ¼ teaspoon ground turmeric instead to get the lovely yellow hue of traditional paella.
Per Serving: Calories 319; Fat 10g; Sodium 770mg; Carbs 53g; Fiber 4g; Sugar 8g; Protein 5g

Mouthwatering Eggplant and Rice Casserole

Prep time: 30 minutes | Cook time: 35 minutes | Serves: 4

For the Sauce
½ cup olive oil
1 small onion, chopped
4 garlic cloves, mashed
6 ripe tomatoes, peeled and chopped

2 tablespoons tomato paste
1 teaspoon dried oregano
¼ teaspoon ground nutmeg
¼ teaspoon ground cumin

For the Casserole
4 (6-inch) Japanese eggplants, halved lengthwise
2 tablespoons olive oil

1 cup cooked rice
2 tablespoons pine nuts, toasted
1 cup water

To Make the Sauce: 1. Heat the olive oil in a heavy-bottomed saucepan over medium heat. Cook the onion about 5 minutes. 2. Add tomatoes, tomato paste, nutmeg, oregano, cumin, and garlic and stir. Bring to a boil. Cover. Simmer for 10 minutes over low heat. Remove and set aside.
To Make the Casserole: 1. Heat the broiler before cooking. 2. Meanwhile simmering the sauce, brush olive oil over the eggplant and transfer onto a baking sheet. Broil the eggplant until golden, about 5 minutes. Remove and set it aside to cool. 3. Heat the oven to 375 degrees F and then arrange the cooled eggplant in a 9-by-13-inch baking dish with cut-side up. Spoon out its flesh from the peel. 4. Combine ½ the tomato sauce, the cooked rice, and pine nuts in a bowl. Then fill each spooned eggplant with the mixture. 5. Combine the rest tomato sauce and water in the same bowl. Drizzle over the stuffed eggplant. 6. Bake the eggplant until tender about 20 minutes.
Per Serving: Calories 582; Fat 42g; Sodium 30mg; Carbs 58g; Fiber 25g; Sugar 26g; Protein 12g

Vegetable Medley Couscous

Prep time: 15 minutes | Cook time: 45 minutes | Serves: 8

¼ cup olive oil
1 onion, chopped
4 garlic cloves, minced
2 jalapeño peppers, pierced with a fork in several places
½ teaspoon ground cumin
½ teaspoon ground coriander
1 (28-ounce) can crushed tomatoes
2 tablespoons tomato paste
⅛ teaspoon salt
2 bay leaves

11 cups water, divided
4 carrots, peeled and cut into 2-inch cubes
2 zucchinis, cut into 2-inch pieces
1 acorn squash, halved, seeded, and cut into 1-inch-thick slices
1 (15-ounce) can chickpeas, drained and rinsed
¼ cup chopped preserved lemons (optional)
3 cups couscous

1. Heat olive oil in a large heavy-bottomed pot over medium heat. Cook the onion for 4 minutes and then stir in jalapenos, cumin, coriander, and garlic. Cook together for 1 minute. 2. Then add tomato paste, tomato, salt, bay leaves, and pour 8 cups of water. Bring together to a boil. 3. Add zucchini, acorn squash, and carrots and bring to a boil. Slightly decrease the heat and cook until the vegetables are tender but not mushy, for about 20 minutes. Spoon out 2 cups of the cooking liquid and set it aside. Season as needed. 4. Then add the chickpeas and preserved lemons and cook for 2 to 3 minutes. Turn off the heat. 5. Boil the rest 3 cups of water in a medium pan over high heat. Stir in the couscous. Cover the pan. Turn off the heat and then let the couscous rest for 10 minutes. Drizzle half the reserved cooking liquid and fluff the couscous with a fork. 6. Transfer onto a large platter and drizzle with the remaining cooking liquid. Arrange the vegetables on the top. Transfer the remaining stew into a serving bowl.
Per Serving: Calories 242; Fat 8g; Sodium 260mg; Carbs 37.8g; Fiber 7.5g; Sugar 7.8g; Protein 7g

Chickpea Pilaf with Raisin

Prep time: 15 minutes | Cook time: 30 minutes | Serves: 4

¼ cup olive oil
½ teaspoon ground turmeric
½ teaspoon ground cardamom
4½ cups water
2 cups basmati rice

1 cup raisins
½ cup chopped dried apricots
1 cup cooked chickpeas
⅛ teaspoon salt, plus more as needed

1. Heat the olive oil in a heavy-bottomed pot over medium heat. 2. Cook the turmeric and cardamom and stir for 15 to 20 seconds. Pour water and bring to a boil. 3. Add rice, raisins, chickpeas, salt, and apricots and stir well. Taste and adjust seasoning as needed. 4. Bring the mixture to a boil again. Cover and simmer over low heat for about 15 minutes. 5. Remove from heat and let the pilaf rest for 10 minutes with the lid covered. Use a fork to fluff. 6. Serve and enjoy!
Variation tip: Use any dried fruits you have in your pantry—dried dates and cranberries work especially well.
Per Serving: Calories 415; Fat 27g; Sodium 91mg; Carbs 51g; Fiber 17g; Sugar 11g; Protein 12g

Herbed Lentil Ragout

Prep time: 15 minutes | Cook time: 50 minutes | Serves: 6

¼ cup olive oil
1 onion, finely chopped
4 carrots, peeled and cut into ¼-inch dice
2 celery stalks, cut into ¼-inch-thick slices
4 garlic cloves, mashed
1 pound dried French green lentils, rinsed and picked over for debris

4 thyme sprigs
2 bay leaves
½ teaspoon dried oregano
½ teaspoon cayenne pepper
⅛ teaspoon salt
⅛ teaspoon freshly ground black pepper
4 cups vegetable broth
2 tablespoons red wine vinegar

1. Heat the olive oil in a heavy-bottomed pot over medium heat. 2. Cook the onion in the pot for 5 minutes. 3. Stir in carrots, garlic, and celery and cook for 10 minutes or more. 4. Add thyme, bay leaves, oregano, cayenne, salt, black pepper, vegetable broth, and the lentils and bring to a boil by increasing the heat. Then cook over medium-low heat until the lentils are tender, about 30 minutes. 5. Discard the thyme and bay leaves. Stir in the vinegar. Serve and enjoy!
Variation tip: Use 1 cup pearl onions, 4 baby zucchini, halved, and 8 ounces baby carrots instead of the large vegetables.
Per Serving: Calories 202; Fat 10g; Sodium 454mg; Carbs 27g; Fiber 3g; Sugar 5g; Protein 7g

Egyptian Beans, Rice, and Pasta Mix

Prep time: 25 minutes | Cook time: 1 hour 20 minutes | Serves: 8

For the Sauce
2 tablespoons olive oil
2 garlic cloves, minced
1 (16-ounce) can tomato sauce
For the Rice
1 cup olive oil
2 onions, thinly sliced
2 cups dried brown lentils, rinsed and picked over for debris
4 quarts plus ½ cup water, divided
2 cups short-grain rice

¼ cup white vinegar
¼ cup Harissa, or store-bought
⅛ teaspoon salt

1 teaspoon salt, plus more for cooking the pasta
1-pound short elbow pasta
1 (15-ounce) can chickpeas, drained and rinsed

To Make the Sauce: 1. Heat olive oil in a pan over medium heat. 2. Add the garlic and cook for 1 minute. 3. Stir in tomato sauce, harissa, vinegar, and salt. Bring the sauce to a boil by increasing the heat. Cook the sauce until thickened over low heat about 20 minutes. Remove and set aside.
To Make the Rice: 1. Prepare a paper towel-lined plate and set aside for later use. 2. Heat olive oil in a pan over medium heat. 3. Cook the onion in the pan until crisp and golden about 7 to 10 minutes, stirring often. 4. Drain and transfer to a separate bowl. Reserve 2 tablespoons of the cooking oil. Set aside. Reserve the pot. 5. Combine together 4 cups of water and the lentils in a large pot over high heat. Bring to a boil and cook for 20 minutes. Drain and transfer to a bowl. Toss the lentil with the reserved cooking oil. Set aside. 6. Heat the onion pan over medium-high heat and add rice, salt, and 4½ cups of water into the pan. Bring to a boil and decrease the heat to low. Cover and cook for 20 minutes. Remove from the heat and let rice rest for 10 minutes. 7. Pour the remaining 8 cups of water, salt, and the cooked lentils in

the same pot and then bring to a boil over high heat. Add the pasta in the liquid and cook for 6 minutes according to the package directions. Drain and set aside. 8. Transfer the rice onto a serving plate. Add the lentils, chickpeas, and pasta on the top. Drizzle the hot tomato sauce over and sprinkle the crispy fried onion.
Per Serving: Calories 597; Fat 32g; Sodium 472mg; Carbs 70g; Fiber 7.6g; Sugar 3g; Protein 9g

Simple Chickpeas and Bulgur

Prep time: 10 minutes | Cook time: 35 minutes | Serves: 6

½ cup olive oil
1 onion, chopped
6 tomatoes, diced, or 1 (16-ounce) can diced tomatoes
2 tablespoons tomato paste
2 cups water

1 tablespoon Harissa, or store-bought
⅛ teaspoon salt
2 cups coarse bulgur
1 (15-ounce) can chickpeas, drained and rinsed

1. Heat the olive oil in a heavy-bottomed pot over medium heat. 2. Sauté the onion in the pot for 5 minutes. 3. Then add the tomatoes and their juice. Cook for 5 minutes. 4. Add the tomato paste, harissa, water, and salt in the pot and stir well. Bring to a boil. 5. Stir in the chickpeas and bulgur. Bring to a boil again. Cover and then cook over low heat for 15 minutes. Let it rest for 15 minutes. 6. Serve and enjoy!
Variation tip: To make this dish gluten free, replace the bulgur with quinoa.
Per Serving: Calories 311; Fat 19g; Sodium 390mg; Carbs 30g; Fiber 10g; Sugar 8g; Protein 7g

Tasty Bulgur and Lentils

Prep time: 5 minutes | Cook time: 1 Hour| Serves: 6

½ cup olive oil
2 yellow onions, thinly sliced
1 teaspoon salt, divided
1 pound dried brown lentils,

rinsed and picked over for debris
8 cups water
1½ cups coarse bulgur

1. Prepare a plate lined with paper towels and set it aside. 2. Heat the olive oil in a medium saucepan over medium heat. 3. Toss the onions with ¼ teaspoon of salt and add into the hot oil. Cook until crispy and golden brown, about 7 to 10 minutes, stirring from time to time. Transfer the onions to the prepared plate and set aside. Remove from the heat and let it cool. 4. In the pot, add the lentils, water, and ¾ teaspoon of salt. Bring the mixture to a boil over high heat. Cook the mixture over the medium heat until the lentils are just cooked, about 15 minutes. Remain 3 cups of cooking liquid. 5. Stir in the bulgur and then bring to a boil. Taste and adjust seasoning as needed. Cover and cook for 20 minutes over low heat. Remove from heat and sit for 10 minutes. 6. Transfer the lentils and bulgur onto a serving plate. Add the crispy onions on the top. 7. Serve and enjoy.
Serving Tip: Serve this dish with tzatziki sauce but note that it will no longer be vegan.
Per Serving: Calories 292; Fat 18g; Sodium 406mg; Carbs 28g; Fiber 4g; Sugar 2g; Protein 8g

Egyptian Fava Beans

Prep time: 15 minutes | Cook time: 15 minutes | Serves: 6

1 (15-ounce) can fava beans, undrained
4 garlic cloves, minced
1 tablespoon ground cumin
⅛ teaspoon salt
⅛ teaspoon freshly ground black pepper

½ cup freshly squeezed lemon juice
¼ cup olive oil
1 sweet onion, chopped, divided
2 ripe tomatoes, diced, divided
2 cups finely chopped fresh parsley, divided

1. Combine the fava beans with their liquid, cumin, garlic, salt, and pepper in a medium saucepan over medium heat. Bring to a boil. 2. Mash the fava beans partially with a potato masher or fork. Then continue to cook over medium heat for 10 minutes more. 3. Add the olive oil, lemon juice, and half of each of the onion, tomatoes, and parsley. Taste and adjust seasoning as needed. Turn off the heat. 4. Transfer the bean mixture into a serving plate and add the remaining onion, tomatoes, and parsley.
Per Serving: Calories 134; Fat 10g; Sodium 73mg; Carbs 12g; Fiber 3g; Sugar 5g; Protein 2g

Black-Eyed Pea Pilaf with Swiss Chard

Prep time: 20 minutes | Cook time: 50 minutes | Serves: 4

10 cups water, divided
1 pound Swiss chard, or kale, chopped
¼ cup olive oil
1 onion, chopped

1 cup canned black-eyed peas, drained and rinsed (see tip)
1 garlic clove, mashed
½ teaspoon ground coriander
1 cup coarse bulgur

1. Bring 8 cups of water to a boil in a large soup pot over medium heat. Add the Swiss chard and return it to a boil. Cook for 5 minutes. Turn off the heat. Drain and set aside to cool. 2. Heat the soup pot to medium heat and warm the olive oil. Then add the onion and cook for 5 minutes. Then cook the black-eyed peas for 10 minutes. 3. Add the garlic, coriander, and Swiss chard in the pot and cook for 1 minute, stirring from time to time. 4. Add the bulgur and bring all together to a boil. Cover and then cook over medium-low heat for 10 minutes. Remove from heat and then let the pilaf rest for 10 minutes. 5. Serve and enjoy!
Variation tip: You can use frozen black-eyed peas, but thaw them before cooking.
Per Serving: Calories 191; Fat 14g; Sodium 257mg; Carbs 16g; Fiber 4g; Sugar 2.5g; Protein 4g

Spiced Lentils with Dumplings

Prep time: 20 minutes | Cook time: 40 minutes | Serves: 8

1 cup olive oil
2 large onions, thinly sliced
2 cups chopped fresh cilantro
6 garlic cloves, minced
1 tablespoon ground coriander
1 tablespoon ground cumin
1 pound dried brown lentils, rinsed and picked over for debris
10 cups water
⅛ teaspoon salt

⅛ teaspoon freshly ground black pepper
1 cup pomegranate molasses, or aged balsamic vinegar
½ cup freshly squeezed lemon juice
½ yield Pita Bread dough, or 3 (4-inch) balls store-bought pizza dough
½ cup all-purpose flour

1. Prepare a paper towel-lined plate and set aside. 2. Heat the olive oil in a soup pot or Dutch oven over medium heat. 3. Fry the onions until golden and crispy about 10 minutes. Transfer the onions to the prepared plate to drain with a slotted spoon. 4. Add the garlic, coriander, cumin, and cilantro to the oil. Cook and stir for 1 minute. Plate half the herb mixture and set aside. 5. In the pot, add the water, salt, lentils, and pepper to the remaining herb mixture. Bring to a boil and then cook until the lentils are tender, for about 20 minutes. 6. Add the molasses and lemon juice and stir well. 7. Divide the dough into ½-inch balls. Flour the dough and add in the cooking lentils. Cook for 5 minutes. 8. Serve the lentils and dumplings in a shallow plate. Add the reserved herb mixture and then arrange on the top with the crispy onions. Serve and enjoy!
Per Serving: Calories 387; Fat 28g; Sodium 67mg; Carbs 32g; Fiber 3g; Sugar 7g; Protein 7g

Enticing Lentil and Mushroom Lasagna

Prep time: 20 minutes | Cook time: 40 minutes | Serves: 4

2 cups dried brown lentils, rinsed and picked over for debris
6 cups water
¼ cup olive oil
1 onion, finely chopped
4 garlic cloves, minced
1 pound white mushrooms, cut into slices
½ cup chopped fresh cilantro
4 cups basic tomato basil sauce,

or store-bought, divided
⅛ teaspoon salt, plus more as needed
⅛ teaspoon black pepper, plus more as needed
1 (9-ounce) package no-boil lasagna sheets
1 cup shredded fresh mozzarella cheese

1. Heat the oven to 400 degrees F before cooking. 2. Combine the lentils and water in a large saucepan over high heat. Bring to a boil. Cook over medium-low heat until the lentils are just tender. Drain and set aside. 3. Heat the olive oil in a sauté pan over medium heat. 4. Cook the onion in the pan for 5 minutes. Add the garlic, cilantro, and mushrooms and cook for 5 minutes, stirring occasionally. 5. Add 2 cups of tomato sauce, salt, pepper, and lentils and stir well. Taste and adjust seasoning as needed. Turn off the heat. 6. Transfer 1 cup of tomato sauce at the bottom of a 9-by-13-inch baking dish and spread over. Layer the lasagna sheets on the top. 7. Spread the lentil mixture evenly over the lasagna. Use a layer of lasagna sheets to cover. Drizzle over with 1 cup of tomato sauce. 8. Bake for 15 minutes and top with the mozzarella cheese. Bake until the cheese is browned and bubbling about 5 minutes or more.

Per Serving: Calories 625; Fat 17g; Sodium 400mg; Carbs 87g; Fiber 21g; Sugar 36g; Protein 28g

Mushroom Farro with Scallions

Prep time: 20 minutes | Cook time: 1 Hour 10 minutes | Serves: 6

1½ cups dried farro
Hot water, for soaking the farro
½ cup olive oil
1 onion, finely chopped
1 pound mixed shiitake and cremini mushrooms, cleaned and cut into slices
1 garlic clove, minced
⅛ teaspoon salt, plus more as needed

½ cup dry white wine, or vegetable broth
3 cups vegetable broth
¼ cup chopped fresh oregano
½ cup chopped scallions, white and green parts
2 tablespoons pine nuts, toasted
Shaved Parmesan cheese, for serving (optional)

1. In a bowl, add the farro and soak the farro with hot water. Let it rest for 1 hour. 2. Heat olive oil in a skillet over medium-low heat. Cook the onion until golden about 5 minutes. 3. Then cook the mushrooms, salt, and garlic until tender, about 5 minutes. 4. Drain the farro and add to the onion and mushrooms. Cook for 2 minutes. 5. Pour wine and stir well. Cook until the liquid has been absorbed about 15 minutes. 6. Add the oregano and pour in the vegetable broth. Taste and adjust seasoning as needed. Cover and cook over low heat for 30 minutes. Turn off the heat and let it rest for 10 minutes or more. 7. Transfer the farro onto a serving plate and sprinkle the scallions and pine nuts over and add the Parmesan cheese on the top.
Per Serving: Calories 309; Fat 20g; Sodium 501mg; Carbs 32g; Fiber 5g; Sugar 19g; Protein 4g

Butternut Squash and Bulgur Pilaf

Prep time: 25 minutes | Cook time: 50 minutes | Serves: 4

3 pounds butternut squash, peeled, seeded, and cut into ½-inch-thick half-moons
¼ cup olive oil, divided
1 small onion, finely chopped
4 scallions, white and green parts, chopped
1 zucchini, diced

1 jalapeño pepper, seeded and finely chopped
½ red bell pepper, chopped
2 tomatoes, diced
¼ cup chopped fresh cilantro
½ cup coarse bulgur #3
¼ cup coarsely chopped walnuts

1. Heat the oven to 400 degrees F before cooking. 2. Coat the butternut squash with 1 tablespoon of olive oil in a baking sheet. Spread into a single layer and bake for 10 minutes. Remove and set aside. 3. Heat the remaining 3 tablespoons of olive oil in a large skillet over medium heat. 4. Cook the onion for 5 minutes and then add the scallions, zucchini, jalapenos, red bell pepper, cilantro, and tomatoes. Cook over medium-low heat for 15 minutes and toss to coat. 5. Add the bulgur in the pot and bring to a boil. Cover and cook over low heat for 15 minutes. 6. Turn off the heat. Add the butternut squash and walnuts and stir well. Cover and let it rest for 10 minutes. 7. Serve and enjoy.
Per Serving: Calories 337; Fat 17g; Sodium 20mg; Carbs 47g; Fiber 8g; Sugar 4g; Protein 6g

Homemade Mushroom Tortellini

Prep time: 40 minutes | Cook time: 20 minutes | Serves: 6

¼ cup olive oil
1 onion, chopped
1 pound white mushrooms, chopped
1 garlic clove, mashed

½ teaspoon salt
½ teaspoon freshly ground black pepper
All-purpose flour, for dusting
Pita Bread dough

1. In a medium skillet, heat the olive oil over medium heat; add the onion and cook for 5 minutes until golden; add the mushrooms and cook them for 10 minutes until their natural water evaporates, stirring often; add the garlic, salt and pepper, stir and then remove the skillet from the heat. 2. Preheat the oven to 350°F. 3. Dust a work surface with flour and roll out the pita dough on it to ⅛ inch thick. Using a 2-inch round glass or cookie cutter, cut rounds from the dough. Place ½ teaspoon of mushroom stuffing in the center of each dough circle. Fold the circle in half and pinch the edges together to form a hat-like shape. 4. Arrange the tortellini on the baking sheet. Bake the tortellini for 5 minutes. 5. Let the tortellini cool. Once cooled, use them in the Tortellini in Yogurt Sauce or freeze in a freezer bag for up to 3 months.
Per Serving: Calories 371; Fats 10.52g; Sodium 697mg; Carbs 59.02g; Fiber 4.1g; Sugar 3.77g; Protein 10.53g

Easy Fig Couscous

Prep time: 10 minutes | Cook time: 10 minutes | Serves: 5

1½ tablespoons olive oil
¼ cup chopped onion
1 garlic clove, minced
1 teaspoon sea salt
2¾ cups chicken broth
1½ cups dried couscous

1½ cups dried figs, thinly sliced
¼ cup baby spinach
1 teaspoon ground cinnamon
¼ teaspoon ground allspice
¼ cup crumbled feta cheese (optional)

1. Heat the olive oil in a saucepan over medium heat; add the onion, garlic, salt and sauté them for 5 minutes until softened; add the broth and bring to a boil. 2. Remove saucepan from the heat and stir in the couscous, figs, spinach, cinnamon, and allspice. 3. Cover the saucepan and let stand for 10 minutes until the water has been absorbed. 4. Serve topped with the feta cheese (optional).
Per Serving: Calories 233; Fats 6.46g; Sodium 1051mg; Carbs 41.68g; Fiber 5.5g; Sugar 22.63g; Protein 5.37g

Vegetable Tagine with Olive

Prep time: 25 minutes | Cook time: 50 minutes | Serves: 6

½ cup olive oil
1 onion, chopped
2 celery stalks, chopped
1 (32-ounce) can diced tomatoes
4 cups water
4 garlic cloves, slivered
2 bay leaves
Grated zest of 1 lemon
1 teaspoon chopped fresh thyme
⅛ teaspoon salt, plus more as needed
8 ounces baby potatoes, halved
2 carrots, peeled and cut into

1-inch matchsticks
1 fennel bulb, quartered, white parts only
2 tablespoons Ghee, or butter
½ teaspoon ground cumin
½ teaspoon ground coriander
½ teaspoon freshly ground black pepper
¼ cup freshly squeezed lemon juice
1 (15-ounce) can chickpeas, drained and rinsed
½ cup pitted green olives

1. Heat the olive oil in a Dutch oven or tagine over medium heat. 2. Cook the onion and celery in the tagine for 5 minutes. 3. Add tomatoes, garlic, water, bay leaves, lemon zest, thyme, and salt and stir well. Taste and adjust seasoning as needed. Bring to a boil and simmer over low heat for 5 minutes. 4. Cook the potatoes, fennel, and carrots by bringing to a boil. Cover and cook over medium-low heat for 20 minutes. 5. When the vegetables are almost cooked, in a small skillet, melt the ghee over medium heat. Stir in coriander, pepper, and cumin. Cook for 30 seconds. Add lemon juice and stir. 6. Add the spice mixture, chickpea, and olives into the stew and stir. Cover and cook over medium heat for 5 minutes or more. 7. Remove from the heat. Cover and let it rest for 10 minutes. 8. Serve and enjoy!
Ingredient tip: Fennel is a bulb vegetable very popular around the Mediterranean region. When buying fennel, look for a large, tight, white bulb free of bruises. Check the fronds or feathers to ensure there are no signs of a flower head, which signals the fennel has passed its prime.
Variation tip: Skip the ghee or butter for a vegan dish.
Per Serving: Calories 344; Fat 24g; Sodium 370mg; Carbs 30g; Fiber 9g; Sugar 9g; Protein 6g

Fresh Sauce Penne Pasta

Prep time: 15 minutes | Cook time: 15 minutes | Serves: 4

⅛ teaspoon salt, plus more for cooking the pasta
1 pound penne pasta
¼ cup olive oil
1 garlic clove, crushed
3 cups chopped scallions, white and green parts

3 tomatoes, diced
2 tablespoons chopped fresh basil
⅛ teaspoon freshly ground black pepper
Freshly grated Parmesan cheese, for serving

1. Bring a large pot of salted water to a boil, then add the pasta, stir, and return the water to a boil. Boil the pasta for about 6 minutes or until al dente. 2. A couple minutes before the pasta is completely cooked. 3. In a medium saucepan, heat the olive oil and then add the garlic, cook for 30 seconds; add the tomatoes and scallion, cover the pan and cook for 2 to 3 minutes. 4. Drain the pasta and then add it to the vegetables, then stir in the basil and season with the salt and pepper. 5. Top with the Parmesan cheese, serve and enjoy.
Per Serving: Calories 418; Fats 16.69g; Sodium 745mg; Carbs 56.66g; Fiber 9.6g; Sugar 6.94g; Protein 10.79g

Tortellini in Yogurt Sauce

Prep time: 15 minutes | Cook time: 25 minutes | Serves: 6

¼ cup cornstarch
1 cup cold water
6 cups plain yogurt, or store-bought
¼ teaspoon ground nutmeg
½ teaspoon salt, plus more as needed
2 tablespoons ghee, butter, or

olive oil
3 garlic cloves, minced
1 tablespoon dried mint
1 pound store-bought mushroom-filled tortellini, cooked according to the package directions

1. In a large bowl, mix up the cornstarch and cold water until the cornstarch dissolves; whisk in the yogurt. Place a fine-mesh sieve over a medium saucepan and pour the yogurt mixture through the sieve to remove any lumps. 2. Stir in the nutmeg and salt. Place the pan over medium heat and cook them for 20 minutes, stirring continuously, or until the sauce thickens and begins to coat the back of a spoon. 3. In a small saucepan, melt the ghee over medium heat; add the garlic to the ghee and then cook for 1 minute; stir in the mint and then remove the pan from the heat; stir the mixture into the yogurt sauce. 4. Add the cooked tortellini to the yogurt sauce, stirring so they are coated; cook them for 5 minutes over low heat or until heated through.
Per Serving: Calories 234; Fats 9.87g; Sodium 352mg; Carbs 27.85g; Fiber 1.8g; Sugar 14.34g; Protein 9.87g

Lentils and Rice in Broth

Prep time: 15 minutes | Cook time: 25 minutes | Serves: 4

2¼ cups low-sodium or no-salt-added vegetable broth
½ cup uncooked instant brown rice
½ cup uncooked brown or green lentils
½ cup diced celery (about 1 stalk)
½ cup diced carrots (about 1 carrot)
¼ cup chopped fresh curly-leaf parsley
1 (2.25-ounce) can sliced olives, drained

¼ teaspoon freshly ground black pepper
1 tablespoon freshly squeezed lemon juice
¼ cup diced red onion (about ⅛ onion)
1 garlic clove, minced (about ½ teaspoon)
1½ tablespoons extra-virgin olive oil
¼ teaspoon kosher or sea salt
¼ teaspoon freshly ground black pepper

1. In a medium saucepan, bring vegetable broth and lentils to a boil over high heat; cover and adjust heat to medium-low; cook food for 8 minutes. 2. Increase heat to medium and stir in rice. Cover the pot again and then cook the mixture for about 15 minutes, or till the liquid is absorbed. Then remove pot from the heat and let it sit for 1 minute, then uncover and stir. 3. In a bowl, while the lentils and rice are cooking, combine the carrots, celery, olives, onion and parsley. 4. In a small bowl, whisk oil, garlic, lemon juice, salt and pepper together. Set aside. 5. Add the cooked lentils and rice to the carrot bowl. Pour the dressing over the top and mix everything together.6. Serve hot or cold, or store in a sealed container in the refrigerator for up to 7 days.
Per Serving: Calories 208; Fats 6.27g; Sodium 527mg; Carbs 33.78g; Fiber 3g; Sugar 2.43g; Protein 5.23g

Parmesan Spaghetti Pesto

Prep time: 10 minutes | Cook time: 40 minutes | Serves: 6

12 ounces' ricotta
1 cup Garlic Basil Pesto, or store-bought
2 tablespoons olive oil

¼ cup freshly grated Parmesan cheese
Salt
1 pound spaghetti

1. Preheat the oven to 400°F. 2. In a food processor, mix up the ricotta and basil pesto; purée into a smooth cream and transfer to a large bowl. Set aside. 3. Coat a 10-cup Bundt pan with the olive oil and sprinkle with Parmesan cheese. Set aside. 4. Boil a large pot of salted water over high heat. Once the water is boiling, add the pasta to pot and then cook for about 6 minutes until al dente. 5. Drain the pasta well and add it to the pesto cream. Mix well. 6. Spoon the pasta into the prepared cooking pan, pressing to ensure it is tightly packed. Bake the food for 30 minutes. 7. Place a flat serving platter on top of the cake pan. Quickly and carefully invert the pasta cake. Gently remove the pan. 8. Cut into slices and serve topped with your favorite sauce.
Per Serving: Calories 245; Fats 12.46g; Sodium 476mg; Carbs 23.23g; Fiber 3.5g; Sugar 0.82g; Protein 11.87g

Cheese Pizza

Prep time: 10 minutes | Cook time: 10 minutes | Serves: 4

1 tablespoon olive oil
½ yield Homemade Pizza Dough, or 1 pound store-bought
8 ounces' fresh mozzarella cheese, cut into 1-inch cubes
All-purpose flour, for dusting
1 teaspoon cornmeal

1 cup Homemade Tomato Basil Sauce, or store-bought
½ cup chopped fresh basil, divided
1 tablespoon freshly grated Parmesan cheese

1. Coat a medium bowl with the olive oil and then place the dough in the bowl; cover the bowl with a clean kitchen towel and let the dough rise for 1 hour or until the dough doubles in size. 2. Preheat the oven to 500°F. 3. Use the paper towels to pat the mozzarella cheese dry with paper towels. 4. Dust a work surface with flour and place the dough on it. Flatten the dough into a 10-inch circle. Sprinkle the cornmeal on a baking sheet. Place the dough circle on the baking sheet. 5. Spread the tomato sauce on the dough, leaving a ½-inch border all around. Scatter the mozzarella and half the basil over the sauce. 6. Bake the dough for about 10 minutes until the crust is golden and the cheese is bubbling. 7. Sprinkle with the remaining basil and the Parmesan cheese. Serve hot!
Per Serving: Calories 383; Fats 9.64g; Sodium 1697mg; Carbs 46.65g; Fiber 5.9g; Sugar 10.18g; Protein 25.34g

Penne Pasta in Tomato-Caper Sauce

Prep time: 10 minutes | Cook time: 15 minutes | Serves: 4

2 tablespoons olive oil
2 garlic cloves, minced
1 cup sliced cherry tomatoes
2 cups Homemade Tomato Basil

Sauce, or store-bought
1 cup capers, drained and rinsed
Salt
4 cups penne pasta

1. In a medium saucepan, heat olive oil over medium heat; then add the garlic and cook for 30 seconds; add the cherry tomatoes and cook them for 2 to 3 minutes. 2. Pour in the tomato sauce and bring the mixture to a boil; stir in the capers and then turn off the heat. 3. Boil a large pot of salted water over high heat. 4. Once boiling, add the pasta to the pot of water and cook for about 7 minutes until al dente. 5. Drain the pasta and stir it into the sauce. Toss gently and cook over medium heat for 1 minute or until warmed through.
Per Serving: Calories 382; Fats 8.22g; Sodium 2459mg; Carbs 66.85g; Fiber 14.9g; Sugar 14.52g; Protein 7.28g

Beans in Tomato-Honey Sauce

Prep time: 5 minutes | Cook time: 20 minutes | Serves: 6

2 teaspoons extra-virgin olive oil
2 (15-ounce) cans cannellini or great northern beans, undrained
2 tablespoons honey
1 (12-ounce) can low-sodium tomato paste

½ cup water
½ cup minced onion (about ¼ onion)
¼ cup red wine vinegar
¼ teaspoon ground cinnamon

1. In a medium saucepan, heat the oil over medium heat; cook the onion for 5 minutes, stirring frequently; add the vinegar, honey, cinnamon, tomato paste, water and mix well. Lower the heat. 2. Drain and rinse one can of the beans in a colander and then add to the saucepan. Then pour the entire second can of beans (including the liquid) into saucepan. Cook the food for 10 minutes, stirring occasionally. 3. Serve and enjoy.
Per Serving: Calories 287; Fats 1.53g; Sodium 67mg; Carbs 53.77g; Fiber 15g; Sugar 10.05g; Protein 16g

Cannellini Lettuce Wraps

Prep time: 10 minutes | Cook time: 10 minutes | Serves: 4

1 tablespoon extra-virgin olive oil
¼ teaspoon freshly ground black pepper
¾ cup chopped fresh tomatoes
½ cup diced red onion (about ¼ onion)
¼ cup finely chopped fresh curly

parsley
1 (15-ounce) can cannellini or great northern beans, drained and rinsed
8 romaine lettuce leaves
½ cup prepared hummus

1. In a large saucepan, heat oil over the medium heat; add onion and cook 3 minutes, stirring occasionally; add tomatoes and peppers and cook 3 minutes, stirring occasionally; add beans and cook 3 minutes more, stirring occasionally. Remove pan from heat; toss in parsley. 2.

Spread 1 tablespoon hummus on each lettuce leaf. Spread hot bean mixture evenly in center of each leaf. 3. Fold one side of lettuce leaf lengthwise over filling, then fold other side to form a wrap and serve.
Per Serving: Calories 188; Fats 9.64g; Sodium 115mg; Carbs 28.31g; Fiber 9g; Sugar 2.13g; Protein 9.64g

Broiled Eggplant Slabs

Prep time: 5 minutes | Cook time: 15 minutes | Serves: 6

Nonstick cooking spray
1 tablespoon extra-virgin olive oil
1 medium globe eggplant, stem removed
2 tablespoons balsamic vinegar
2 tablespoons freshly squeezed lemon juice
¼ teaspoon kosher or sea salt
¼ cup chopped or torn mint leaves

1 teaspoon ground cumin
1 cup sliced sweet onion
1 (15-ounce) can chickpeas, drained and rinsed
1 tablespoon sesame seeds, toasted if desired
1 (15-ounce) can chickpeas, drained and rinsed
1 garlic clove, finely minced (about ½ teaspoon)

1. Place one oven rack about 4 inches below the broiler element and then preheat the broiler to high. Brush a large, rimmed baking sheet with nonstick cooking spray. 2. Cut the eggplant lengthwise into four slabs and then arrange the eggplant slabs on the prepared baking sheet. Set aside. 3. In a small bowl, add the oil, lemon juice, vinegar, cumin, salt and mix them well. 4. Brush or drizzle both sides of the eggplant slab with 2 tablespoons of the lemon sauce. Reserve remaining dressing. 5. Broil the eggplant slabs in the preheated broiler for 4 minutes; flip them, then broil for another 4 minutes, until golden brown. 6. While broiling the eggplant slabs, in a bowl, add the chickpeas, onion, mint, sesame seeds, garlic and the reserved dressing, then gently mix to incorporate all the ingredients. 7. When the time is up, transfer the eggplant slabs to a cooling rack and cool for 3 minutes. After cooling slightly, place eggplant on a cutting board and slice each slice horizontally into ½-inch strips. 8. Place eggplant slices in the bowl with the onion mixture. Gently put everything together and serve warm or at room temperature.
Per Serving: Calories 124; Fats 3.04g; Sodium 223mg; Carbs 21.23g; Fiber 6.2g; Sugar 8.63g; Protein 4.77g

Brown Rice Pilaf

Prep time: 15 minutes | Cook time: 15 minutes | Serves: 6

1 tablespoon extra-virgin olive oil
1 cup chopped onion (about ½ medium onion)
½ cup shredded carrot (about 1 medium carrot)
1 teaspoon ground cumin
½ teaspoon ground cinnamon

2 cups instant brown rice
1¾ cups 100% orange juice
¼ cup water
1 cup golden raisins
½ cup shelled pistachios
Chopped fresh chives (optional)

1. In a medium saucepan, heat the oil over medium-high heat; sauté the onion for 5 minutes; add the carrot, cumin, and cinnamon, and sauté them for 1 minute. 2. Stir in the rice, orange juice, and water. Cover it and bring to a boil, reduce the heat to medium-low. Cook for about 7 minutes, or till the rice is cooked through and liquid is absorbed. 3. Stir in the raisins, pistachios and chives (optional) and serve.
Per Serving: Calories 271; Fats 6.57g; Sodium 36mg; Carbs 51g; Fiber 4.3g; Sugar 24.59g; Protein 5.56g

Green Lentil Rice Balls

Prep time: 5 minutes | Cook time: 15 minutes | Serves: 6

¼ white onion, minced
2 garlic cloves, minced
5 basil leaves
1 tablespoon lemon juice
¼ cup parsley leaves

1 cup cooked brown rice
½ teaspoon salt
1 tablespoon olive oil
½ cup cooked green lentils

1. Preheat the air fryer to 380°F. 2. In a food processor, add the cooked lentils, garlic, onion, parsley, basil and pulse them until mostly smooth. 3. Prepare a large bowl, pour the lentil mixture, and stir in brown rice, lemon juice, olive oil and salt. 4. Form 1-inch balls from the rice mixture and then arrange the rice balls in a single layer in air fryer basket without touching each other. 5. Fry the rice balls in the preheated air fryer for 6 minutes; when the time is up, flip the rice balls and fry for another 4 to 5 minutes, or until all sides are browned. 6. Serve and enjoy.
Per Serving: Calories 83; Fats 2.65g; Sodium 199mg; Carbs 12.5g; Fiber 2.1g; Sugar 1.2g; Protein 2.6g

Brown Rice and Pasta in Vegetable Broth

Prep time: 10 minutes | Cook time: 20 minutes | Serves: 6

1 tablespoon extra-virgin olive oil
1 cup (about 3 ounces) uncooked vermicelli or thin spaghetti, broken into 1- to 1½-inch pieces
3 cups shredded cabbage (about half a 14-ounce package of coleslaw mix or half a small head of cabbage)
3 cups low-sodium or no-salt-added vegetable broth
½ cup water
1 cup instant brown rice
2 garlic cloves
¼ teaspoon kosher or sea salt
⅛ to ¼ teaspoon crushed red pepper
½ cup loosely packed, coarsely chopped cilantro
Fresh lemon slices, for serving (optional)

1. In a large saucepan, heat the oil over medium-high heat; add the pasta and cook for 3 minutes to toast, stirring often; add the cabbage and sauté for 4 minutes; add the broth, water, rice, garlic, salt, and crushed red pepper, and bring to a boil over high heat. Stir, cover, and reduce the heat to medium-low; simmer them for 10 minutes. 2. Remove the pan from the heat, with the lid still on. Let sit for 5 minutes. Fish out the garlic cloves, mash them with a fork, then stir the garlic back into the rice. Stir in the cilantro. Serve with the lemon slices (optional).
Per Serving: Calories 136; Fats 4.28g; Sodium 405mg; Carbs 21.59g; Fiber 3.5g; Sugar 5.71g; Protein 4.17g

Lemon Avocado Farro Bowl

Prep time: 5 minutes | Cook time: 30 minutes | Serves: 6

1 tablespoon add 2 teaspoons extra-virgin olive oil, divided
1 cup chopped onion (about ½ medium onion)
2 garlic cloves, minced (about 1 teaspoon)
1 carrot, shredded (about 1 cup)
2 cups low-sodium or no-salt-added vegetable broth
1 cup (6 ounces) uncooked pearled or 10-minute farro
2 avocados, peeled, pitted, and sliced
1 small lemon
¼ teaspoon kosher or sea salt

1. In a medium saucepan, heat 1 tablespoon of oil over medium-high heat; add the onion and sauté for 5 minutes; add the garlic and carrot, sauté them for 1 minute; add the broth and farro, and bring to a boil over high heat. 2. Lower the heat to medium-low, cover, and simmer for about 20 minutes or until the farro is plump and slightly chewy (al dente). 3. Pour the farro into a serving bowl, and add the avocado slices. Using a citrus zester, zest the peel of the lemon directly into the bowl of farro. Halve the lemon, and squeeze the juice out of both halves using a citrus juicer or your hands. 4. Drizzle the remaining 2 teaspoons of oil over the bowl, and sprinkle with salt. Gently mix all the ingredients and serve.
Per Serving: Calories 209; Fats 10.74g; Sodium 153mg; Carbs 28.72g; Fiber 7g; Sugar 14.03g; Protein 3.43g

Parmesan Barley Risotto

Prep time: 5 minutes | Cook time: 25 minutes | Serves: 6

4 cups low-sodium or no-salt-added vegetable broth
1 tablespoon extra-virgin olive oil
1 cup chopped yellow onion (about ½ medium onion)
2 cups uncooked pearl barley
¼ teaspoon kosher or sea salt
½ cup dry white wine
1 cup freshly grated Parmesan cheese (about 4 ounces), divided
¼ teaspoon freshly ground black pepper
Fresh minced chives and lemon wedges, for serving (optional)

1. In the skillet, pour in the broth and bring to a simmer. 2. In a large stockpot, heat oil over the medium-high heat; sauté the onion for 8 minutes, stirring occasionally; add the barley and sauté for 2 minutes until the barley is toasted. 3. Pour in wine and then cook for about 1 minute, or till most of the liquid evaporates; add 1 cup of warm broth to the pot and then cook for 2 minutes, stirring often, or till most of the liquid is absorbed; then add the remaining broth, 1 cup at a time, and cook until each cup has been absorbed (about 2 minutes each time), then add the next cup. The last broth added will take longer to absorb, about 4 minutes. 4. Remove pot from the heat and then stir in the salt, pepper and ½ cup of cheese. Serve with the remaining cheese on the side, along with the chives and lemon wedges (optional).
Per Serving: Calories 367; Fats 9.95g; Sodium 1198mg; Carbs 57.52g; Fiber 10.7g; Sugar 2.56g; Protein 13.49g

Garlicky Asparagus Couscous

Prep time: 5 minutes | Cook time: 25 minutes | Serves: 6

1 cup garlic-and-herb goat cheese (about 4 ounces)
1½ pounds asparagus spears, ends trimmed and stalks chopped into 1-inch pieces (about 2¾ to 3 cups chopped)
1 tablespoon extra-virgin olive oil
1 garlic clove, minced (about ½ teaspoon)
¼ teaspoon freshly ground black pepper
1¾ cups water
1 (8-ounce) box uncooked whole-wheat or regular Israeli couscous (about 1⅓ cups)
¼ teaspoon kosher or sea salt

1. Preheat the oven to 425°F. 2. Put the goat cheese on the counter to bring to room temperature. 3. In a large bowl, add the asparagus, oil, garlic, pepper and mix them well. Spread the asparagus on a large baking sheet and roast in the preheated oven for 10 minutes, stirring a few times. Then remove the baking sheet from oven and transfer the asparagus with a spoon to a large bowl. 4. While roasting the asparagus, in a medium saucepan, boil the water; add the couscous and salt. Reduce the heat to medium-low, cover and then cook for 12 minutes, or till the water is absorbed. 5. Pour the hot couscous into the bowl with asparagus. Then add goat cheese, mix thoroughly until completely melted. Enjoy.
Per Serving: Calories 104; Fats 2.13g; Sodium 343mg; Carbs 18.84g; Fiber 4.4g; Sugar 2.44g; Protein 5.43g

Sweet Potato and Black Bean Burgers

Prep time: 10 minutes | Cook time: 10 minutes | Serves: 4

1 (15-ounce) can black beans, drained and rinsed
1 cup mashed sweet potato
½ teaspoon dried oregano
¼ teaspoon dried thyme
¼ teaspoon dried marjoram
1 garlic clove, minced
For Serving:
Whole wheat buns or whole wheat pitas
Plain Greek yogurt
Avocado
¼ teaspoon salt
¼ teaspoon black pepper
1 tablespoon lemon juice
1 cup cooked brown rice
¼ to ½ cup whole wheat bread crumbs
1 tablespoon olive oil

Lettuce
Tomato
Red onion

1. Preheat the air fryer to 380°F. 2. In a large bowl, add the black beans and mash them until there are no large pieces left; add the oregano, thyme, marjoram, garlic, salt, pepper, mashed sweet potato and lemon juice, mix them well. 3. Stir in the cooked rice; Add ¼ cup whole wheat bread crumbs and stir. If it seems too wet and fluffy, add another ¼ cup of bread crumbs and stir. 4. Form 4 patties from the dough and arrange them in the basket of the air fryer without touching each other. 5. Brush half of the olive oil onto the patties and bake them in the preheated oven for 5 minutes; Turn the meatloaf over, and brush the other side with the remaining oil and bake for 4 to 5 minutes. 6. Serve on toasted whole wheat bread or whole wheat pita with a dollop of yogurt, avocado, lettuce, tomato, and red onion as desired.
Per Serving: Calories 247; Fats 12.05g; Sodium 187mg; Carbs 28.41g; Fiber 7.7g; Sugar 5.29g; Protein 9.89g

Roasted White Beans with Peppers and Onion

Prep time: 5 minutes | Cook time: 15 minutes | Serves: 4

1 rosemary sprig
2 (15-ounce) cans white beans, or cannellini beans, drained and washed
¼ to ½ teaspoon salt
3 garlic cloves, minced
1 red bell pepper, diced
½ red onion, diced
1 tablespoon olive oil
½ teaspoon black pepper
1 bay leaf
Olive oil cooking spray

1. Preheat the air fryer to 360°F. Then lightly coat the inside of a 5-cup capacity casserole dish with cooking spray. 2. In a large bowl, add the garlic, bell pepper, onion, beans, olive oil, salt, and pepper, combine them well. 3. Place the bean mixture into the prepared casserole dish, top the mixture with the rosemary and bay leaf, and then place the casserole dish into the air fryer. 4. Roast the food for 15 minutes. 5. Remove the rosemary and bay leaves, and then stir well before serving.
Per Serving: Calories 79; Fats 4.46g; Sodium 152mg; Carbs 9.67g; Fiber 3.7g; Sugar 2.03g; Protein 2g

Spicy Lentil Carrot Patties

Prep time: 15 minutes | Cook time: 10 minutes | Serves: 4

1 cup cooked brown lentils
¼ cup fresh parsley leaves
½ cup shredded carrots
¼ red onion, minced
¼ red bell pepper, minced
1 jalapeño, seeded and minced
2 garlic cloves, minced
1 egg
For Serving:
Whole wheat buns or whole wheat pitas
Plain Greek yogurt

2 tablespoons lemon juice
2 tablespoons olive oil, divided
½ teaspoon onion powder
½ teaspoon smoked paprika
½ teaspoon dried oregano
¼ teaspoon salt
¼ teaspoon black pepper
½ cup whole wheat bread crumbs

Tomato
Lettuce
Red Onion

Preheat the air fryer to 380°F. 2. In a food processor, add the lentils, parsley and pulse them mostly smooth, then pour the lentils into a large bowl. 3. Mix the lentils with the onion, egg, bell pepper, carrot, jalapeño, lemon juice, garlic and 1 tablespoon of olive oil. 4. Add the onion powder, bread crumbs, oregano, salt, pepper and paprika. Mix everything together until the seasonings and bread crumbs are well combined. 5. Form the mixture into 4 patties and arrange them in the air fryer basket, making sure they don't touch each other. Brush the patties with the remaining olive oil. 6. Bake the patties for 10 minutes, flipping halfway through. 7. Serve on toasted whole wheat bread or whole wheat pita with a dollop of yogurt and lettuce, tomatoes, and red onions, as desired.
Per Serving: Calories 279; Fats 10.63g; Sodium 307mg; Carbs 32.3g; Fiber 7.1g; Sugar 7.84g; Protein 15.64g

Red Lentil-Cheese Stuffed Tomatoes

Prep time: 10 minutes | Cook time: 15 minutes | Serves: 4

4 tomatoes
½ cup cooked red lentils
1 garlic clove, minced
1 tablespoon minced red onion
4 basil leaves, minced

¼ teaspoon salt
¼ teaspoon black pepper
4 ounces' goat cheese
2 tablespoons shredded Parmesan cheese

1. Preheat the air fryer to 380°F. 2. Slice the top off of each tomato; cut and scoop out half of the flesh inside of the tomato. Place it into a medium bowl. 3. To the bowl with tomato, add the cooked lentils, pepper, onion, basil, garlic, salt, goat cheese and stir them until well combined. 4. Spoon the filling into the scooped-out cavity of each of the tomatoes, top each one with ½ tablespoon of shredded Parmesan cheese. 5. Arrange the tomatoes to the air fryer basket in a single layer and bake them for 15 minutes. 6. Serve and enjoy.
Per Serving: Calories 192; Fats 11.14g; Sodium 317mg; Carbs 11.34g; Fiber 3.5g; Sugar 4.41g; Protein 12.79g

Baked Beans with Feta Cheese

Prep time: 5 minutes | Cook time: 30 minutes | Serves: 4

Olive oil cooking spray
1 (15-ounce) can cannellini beans, drained and rinsed
1 (15-ounce) can great northern beans, drained and rinsed
½ yellow onion, diced
1 (8-ounce) can tomato sauce
1½ tablespoons raw honey
¼ cup olive oil

2 garlic cloves, minced
2 tablespoons chopped fresh dill
½ teaspoon salt
½ teaspoon black pepper
1 bay leaf
1 tablespoon balsamic vinegar
1 ounce of feta cheese, finely chopped, for serving

1. Preheat your air fryer to 360°F, then lightly coat the inside of a 5-cup capacity casserole dish with olive oil cooking spray. 2. In a large bowl, add all of ingredients except the feta cheese and stir them until well combined. 3. Then pour the bean mixture into the prepared casserole dish. 4. Bake the bean mixture in the preheated air fryer for 30 minutes. 5. When cooked, discard the bay leaf. Top with the crumbled feta and serve.
Per Serving: Calories 336; Fats 18g; Sodium 499mg; Carbs 36.47g; Fiber 9.3g; Sugar 11.83g; Protein 11.28g

Baked Mushroom Pilaf

Prep time: 5 minutes | Cook time: 40 minutes | Serves: 4

Olive oil cooking spray

2 cups vegetable broth

2 tablespoons olive oil
½ yellow onion, diced
1 cup pearl barley
2 garlic cloves, minced
1 tablespoon fresh thyme, chopped

½ teaspoon salt
8 ounces' button mushrooms, diced
¼ teaspoon smoked paprika
Fresh parsley, for garnish

1. Preheat your air fryer to 380°F, then lightly coat the inside of a 5-cup capacity casserole dish with olive oil cooking spray. 2. Add the rice, stock, cumin, chickpeas, turmeric, black pepper, peas, salt, ginger, garlic powder, carrot, cinnamon and onion powder to the casserole dish. Stir them well to combine. 3. Cover the casserole dish loosely with aluminum foil. 4. Bake the mixture for 20 minutes. When time is up, remove from air fryer and stir well. 5. Return casserole to air fryer and bake, uncovered, for an additional 25 minutes. 6. Fluff with a spoon, sprinkle with fresh chopped parsley, plate and enjoy.
Per Serving: Calories 271; Fats 7.65g; Sodium 577mg; Carbs 46.09g; Fiber 8.9g; Sugar 4.63g; Protein 7.2g

Rice-Chickpea Bake

Prep time: 10 minutes | Cook time: 45 minutes | Serves: 6

Olive oil cooking spray
1 cup long-grain brown rice
2 ¼ cups chicken stock
1 (15.5-ounce) can chickpeas, drained and rinsed
½ cup diced carrot
½ cup green peas
1 teaspoon ground cumin

½ teaspoon ground turmeric
½ teaspoon ground ginger
½ teaspoon onion powder
½ teaspoon salt
¼ teaspoon ground cinnamon
¼ teaspoon garlic powder
¼ teaspoon black pepper
Fresh parsley, for garnish

1. Preheat your air fryer to 380°F, then lightly coat the inside of a 5-cup capacity casserole dish with olive oil cooking spray. 2. Add the rice, stock, chickpeas, carrot, peas, cumin, turmeric, ginger, onion powder, salt, cinnamon, garlic powder, and black pepper to the casserole dish. Stir them well to combine. 3. Cover the casserole dish loosely with aluminum foil. 4. Bake the mixture for 20 minutes. When the time is up, remove from the air fryer and stir well. 5. Place the casserole back into the air fryer, uncovered, and bake for 25 minutes more. 6. Fluff with a spoon and sprinkle with fresh chopped parsley, serve and enjoy.
Per Serving: Calories 224; Fats 3.31g; Sodium 462mg; Carbs 40.11g; Fiber 5g; Sugar 4.29g; Protein 8.61g

Flavorful Flatbread with Olive Tapenade

Prep time: 30 minutes | Cook time: 5 minutes | Serves: 6

For the Flatbread
¾ cup warm water (120°F to 125°F)
1 tablespoon honey
1 package quick-rising yeast
¾ cup whole-wheat flour, plus
For the Tapenade
1 cup black olives, pitted and chopped
1 cup green olives, pitted and chopped
2 roasted red pepper slices, chopped
1 tablespoon capers, drained and

more for dusting the work surface
¼ cup all-purpose flour
½ teaspoon sea salt
1 tablespoon extra-virgin olive oil

rinsed
1 garlic clove, minced
1 tablespoon chopped fresh basil leaves
1 tablespoon chopped fresh oregano leaves
¼ cup extra-virgin olive oil

To Make the Flatbread: 1. Mix the water, honey, and yeast in a large bowl. Let sit for 5 minutes, covered with a clean kitchen towel, until the yeast foams. 2. Mix the whole-wheat and all-purpose flours and sea salt in a large bowl. Put in the yeast mixture and stir until a ball forms. 3. Turn the dough out onto a floured surface and knead for about 5 minutes until the mixture is smooth. 4. Brush a bowl with olive oil. Put in the dough and turn to coat with the oil. Cover and place in a warm spot to rise for about 1 hour until doubled. 5. Turn on the oven and heat it to 450°F. 6. Place it in the oven as it preheats if you have a pizza stone. 7. Split the dough into 6 portions. Roll each into a thin oblong shape, ¼ to ½-inch thick. Bake the flatbreads on the pizza stone (or directly on the rack) for about 5 minutes until browned.
To Make the Tapenade: Mix the black and green olives, roasted pepper, capers, garlic, basil, oregano, and olive oil in a food processor. Process them for 10 to 20 (1-second) pulses until coarsely chopped.
Per Serving: Calories 168; Fat 7.92g; Sodium 564mg; Carbs 22.71g; Fiber 3.2g; Sugar 5.24g; Protein 3.63g

Chapter 9 Sweet, Dessert, and Staple Recipes

Classic Baklava

Prep time: 40 minutes | Cook time: 50 minutes | Serves: 12

4 cups crushed walnuts
½ cup sugar
2 tablespoons ground cinnamon
1 cup melted Ghee or butter, divided

24 sheets filo dough; follow the instructions on the package to prevent drying
4 cups Orange Blossom Syrup

1. Add the walnuts, sugar, and cinnamon in a small bowl and set aside for later use. 2. Brush some ghee inside the bottom and sides of a 9-by-13-inch baking dish and arrange 2 sheets of filo. Brush some ghee over the filo thoroughly. 3. Then top with 2 more and brush with ghee as well. Repeat with the rest 8 sheets of filo. 4. Arrange evenly over the top filo dough with the walnut mixture. Drizzle with 1 tablespoon of ghee. 5. Brush the top 2 sheets of filo with ghee and repeat with the rest filo. Brush the top layer with the remaining ghee. Cool in the refrigerator for 10 minutes. 6. At 300 degrees F, heat your oven in advance. 7. Cut the baklava into diamond shape with a sharp knife. 8. Bake in your oven until golden about 50 minutes. 9. Serve with the orange blossom syrup completely on the top. Let rest overnight before serving.
Per Serving: Calories 393; Fat 33g; Sodium 123mg; Carbs 25g; Fiber 4g; Sugar 19g; Protein 5g

Cinnamon Fruit Biscotti

Prep time: 20 minutes | Cook time: 55 minutes | Serves: 15

2 cups all-purpose flour
3 teaspoons ground cinnamon, divided
1 teaspoon baking powder
¼ teaspoon salt
1 cup sugar, divided

6 tablespoons unsalted butter, at room temperature
3 large eggs
¼ cup freshly squeezed orange juice
1 teaspoon vanilla extract

1. At 325 degrees F, heat your oven in advance. Line parchment paper over a baking sheet. 2. Whisk the flour, 2 teaspoons of cinnamon, the baking powder, and salt in a medium bowl and set aside for later use. 3. Combine 2 tablespoons of sugar and butter in a large bowl. Beat with a handheld electric mixer until fluffy. 4. Beat in 2 eggs and combine well. Pour the orange juice and vanilla and mix well. 5. Then mix together the butter mixture with the flour mixture to form a dough. Divide the dough in half and shape the halves into a 9-inch- long log. Arrange evenly on the preheated baking sheet. 6. Whisk the rest egg in a small bowl. Brush the logs with the egg wash. 7. Bake in your oven for 40 minutes. When cooked, remove and let cool for 20 minutes. 8. Stir together the remaining 2 tablespoons of sugar and 1 teaspoon of cinnamon. 9. Cut the cogs at a 45-degree angle with serrated knife into ½-inch-thick slices. Place the biscotti, cut-side down, on a baking sheet. Dust with the cinnamon-sugar and bake for 15 minutes. Let cool for a couple hours before serving.
Per Serving: Calories 134; Fat 4g; Sodium 56mg; Carbs 21g; Fiber 1g; Sugar 7g; Protein 3g

Almond Orange Cake

Prep time: 15 minutes | Cook time: 45 minutes | Serves: 8

½ cup olive oil, plus more for preparing the cake pan
1 cup ground almonds
1½ cups sugar, divided
2 teaspoons baking powder
4 large eggs

Grated zest of 2 oranges
1 cup freshly squeezed orange juice
5 whole cloves
Grated zest of 1 lemon
¼ teaspoon ground cardamom

1. At 350 degrees F, heat your oven in advance. 2. Prepare an 8-inch cake pan and coat with olive oil. Set aside for later use. 3. Stir together the almonds, 1 cup of sugar, and the baking powder in a medium bowl. 4. Add the olive oil and orange zest and whisk the eggs in another medium bowl. Then whisk together the egg mixture with the almond mixture until well combined. Spoon into the prepared cake pan. 5. Cook in your oven about 45 minutes until the top is golden. 6. Stir together the remaining sugar, orange juice, cloves, cardamom, and lemon zest in a medium saucepan over medium heat. Bring to a boil and stir from time to time. Cook for 5 to 8 minutes until syrupy and set aside for serving. 7. Remove the baked cake and drizzle the syrup over the top to soak the cake. Allow the cake to rest for 30 minutes before serving.
Per Serving: Calories 249; Fat 16g; Sodium 6mg; Carbs 26g; Fiber 1g; Sugar 21g; Protein 2g

Flavorful Semolina Syrup Cake

Prep time: 15 minutes | Cook time: 40 minutes | Serves: 12

1 tablespoon tahini
3 cups semolina flour, or uncooked Cream of Wheat cereal
¾ cup Ghee, or store-bought, at room temperature
½ cup sugar

1 cup Plain Yogurt plus 1 tablespoon, or store-bought
1½ teaspoons baking soda
12 almonds
2 cups Orange Blossom Syrup

1. At 400 degrees F, heat your oven in advance. 2. Prepare a 9-by-13-inch baking dish and coat with tahini. 3. Add semolina, ghee, and sugar in a medium bowl and set aside. 4. Whisk the baking soda with 1 cup of yogurt in a small bowl. Allow it to sit for 5 minutes. 5. Mix together the semolina mixture with yogurt mixture until well combined. Then transfer the batter to the prepared baking dish. 6. Moisten your palms with 1 tablespoon of yogurt to smooth the top of the cake. Shake the pan lightly and settle the batter. 7. Press lightly a knife blade into the batter to mark 2-inch squares or diamond-shaped pieces and make sure not to cut all the wat through. 8. Place 1 almond in the center of each piece. 9. Bake in the preheated oven for 40 minutes or until golden. 10. Pour the syrup over the warm cake and let it soak into the cake. 11. Put in the refrigerator for at least 2 hours before serving.
Per Serving: Calories 334; Fat 16g; Sodium 170mg; Carbs 41g; Fiber 2g; Sugar 9g; Protein 7g

Classic French Clafoutis

Prep time: 10 minutes | Cook time: 30 minutes | Serves: 4 to 6

3 tablespoons melted butter, at room temperature, plus more for preparing the pan
½ cup all-purpose flour
½ cup sugar
¼ teaspoon salt

3 large eggs
Grated zest of 2 lemons
⅓ cup whole milk
3 cups cherries, pitted
1 tablespoon powdered sugar, for serving

1. At 350 degrees F, heat your oven in advance. Prepare a 9-inch round baking pan and coat with butter. 2. Whisk sugar, flour, and salt in a medium bowl and set aside. 3. Whisk in eggs in another medium bowl. Then add the lemon zest, milk, and melted butter. Combine together. Mix together the egg mixture with the flour mixture until very smooth, for 3 minutes. 4. Arrange the batter onto the prepared pan, and add cherries on the top. 5. Bake in your oven until the clafoutis is set and golden about 30 minutes. 6. Before serving, let it cool for 10 minutes and drizzle on the top with the powdered sugar.
Per Serving: Calories 256; Fat 10g; Sodium 194mg; Carbs 38g; Fiber 2g; Sugar 25g; Protein 5g

Classic Tahini Sauce

Prep time: 15 minutes | Cook time: 0 | Serves: 32

3 garlic cloves, minced or mashed into a paste
½ cup tahini
½ cup freshly squeezed lemon

juice
1 cup water
¼ teaspoon ground cumin
⅛ teaspoon salt

1. Whisk the tahini, garlic, lemon juice, cumin, water, and salt in a small bowl until smooth. 2. Serve or store in an airtight container in the refrigerator for up to 1 month.
Per Serving: Calories 24; Fat 2g; Sodium 14mg; Carbs 1g; Fiber 1g; Sugar 0.1g; Protein 1g

Garlic Basil Pesto

Prep time: 15 minutes | Cook time: 0 | Serves: 16

2 cups packed chopped fresh basil
3 garlic cloves, peeled
¼ cup pine nuts
½ cup olive oil

½ teaspoon salt
½ cup freshly grated Parmesan cheese

1. Combine the garlic, basil, and pine nuts in a food processor or blender and pulse well until coarsely chopped. 2. Add salt, olive oil, and parmesan cheese and process for 5 minutes until smooth. 3. Serve or store in an airtight container in the refrigerator for up to 1 month.
Per Serving: Calories 85; Fat 8g; Sodium 102mg; Carbs 1.5g; Fiber 0.1g; Sugar 0.1g; Protein 1g

Simple Garlic Aioli

Prep time: 15 minutes | Cook time: 0 | Serves: 16

3 garlic cloves, minced
½ teaspoon salt
1 large egg yolk, at room

temperature
1 cup olive oil

1. Combine the salt, egg yolk, and the garlic together in a food processor and process for 1 minute. 2. Meanwhile processing, add the olive oil drop by drop until the olive oil is incorporated and smooth. 3. Serve or store in an airtight container in the refrigerator for up to 1 week.
Prep Tip: Make this aioli by hand: In a medium bowl, mash the garlic and salt into a smooth paste. Add the egg yolk and, using a fork or small whisk, whisk while slowly adding the oil drop by drop until incorporated.
Per Serving: Calories 85; Fat 8g; Sodium 102mg; Carbs 1.5g; Fiber 0.1g; Sugar 0.1g; Protein 1.4g

Greek Tzatziki Sauce

Prep time: 15 minutes | Cook time: 0 | Serves: 8

2 garlic cloves, minced
1 teaspoon dried mint flakes (see tip)
½ teaspoon salt
2 cups Plain Yogurt, or store-

bought
½ cup cold water
2 Persian cucumbers, chopped (optional)

1. Stir together the mint, salt, and garlic in a medium bowl. 2. Then pour in cold water and yogurt until smooth. 3. Add the chopped cucumber in the paste. Chill before serving. 4. Serve or store in an airtight container in the refrigerator for up to 1 week.
Per Serving: Calories 45; Fat 3g; Sodium 175mg; Carbs 4g; Fiber 0.4g; Sugar 4g; Protein 2.5g

Homemade Tomato Basil Sauce

Prep time: 10 minutes | Cook time: 20 minutes | Serves: 8

¼ cup olive oil
4 garlic cloves, crushed
1 (28-ounce) can crushed tomatoes
1 cup water

⅛ teaspoon salt
⅛ teaspoon freshly ground black pepper
1 cup chopped fresh basil

1. Heat the olive oil in a medium saucepan over medium heat. 2. Sear the garlic in the saucepan about 30 seconds. 3. Add tomatoes, water, salt, and pepper in the pan and stir well. Then bring to a boil, cover the pan and simmer for 15 minutes, stirring from time to time to avoid sticking. 4. Then add the basil and cook for 2 to 3 minutes or more. 5. Serve cooled or store in an airtight container for up to 1 week or freeze for up to 6 weeks.
Per Serving: Calories 79; Fat 7g; Sodium 161mg; Carbs 4g; Fiber 2g; Sugar 3g; Protein 1g

Awesome Béchamel Sauce

Prep time: 10 minutes | Cook time: 15 minutes | Serves: 8

2 cups whole milk
1 tablespoon butter
2 tablespoons all-purpose flour

¼ cup freshly grated Parmesan cheese
⅛ teaspoon freshly grated nutmeg

1. Heat the milk in a medium saucepan over low heat for 2 to 3 minutes. Turn off the heat and cover to keep the milk warm. 2. Melt the butter in a medium saucepan over medium heat. Add flour and cook until smooth, for about 2 minutes, whisking continuously. 3. Pour ¼ cup of warm milk in the flour paste and whisk well. Then resume cooking for 10 minutes, slowly whisking in the warm milk until the mixture thickens. 4. Turn off heat and combine together the mixture, Parmesan cheese, the grated nutmeg together. 5. Serve and enjoy.
Per Serving: Calories 84; Fat 3.5g; Sodium 67mg; Carbs 10g; Fiber 0.1g; Sugar 8g; Protein 3g

Simple Preserved Lemons

Prep time: 10 minutes | Cook time: 5 minutes | Serves: 5

5 lemons
2 tablespoons salt, divided

Freshly squeezed lemon juice, as needed

1. In a large saucepan, pour water into three-fourth full and bring to a boil over high heat. 2. Add the lemons and reduce heat to medium, and then boil for 2 minutes. Turn off the heat and set aside to cool. 3. In a large(1-pint) Mason jar, add 1 tablespoon salt. 4. Cut off ½ inch from the top of each lemon and cut evenly into four servings for each lemon from the top to within ½ inch of the bottom. 5. Drizzle over the lemon flesh with ½ teaspoon of salt for each serving. Then close the lemon and push into the jar. Repeat with the rest lemons. 6. Press the lemons to release the juices with a wooden spoon. To submerge the lemons, add freshly squeezed lemon juice to cover if needed. 7. Tightly seal the jar and set aside to sit for 3 days, shaking the jar a few times each day. 8. After 3 days, put the jar in the refrigerator and let sit for 1 month before using. It can be stored in the sealed jar for up to 1 year.
Per Serving: Calories 13; Fat 0.1g; Sodium 2791mg; Carbs 4g; Fiber 0.2g; Sugar 1.5g; Protein 0.2g

Authentic Ghee

Prep time: 5 minutes | Cook time: 20 minutes | Serves: 32

1 pound (4 sticks) unsalted butter, cut into 3-inch cubes

1 tablespoon salt

1. In a large heavy-bottomed saucepan, place the butter to evenly melt the butter and prevent it from burning. 2. Simmer the butter over medium-low heat until the milk solids float to the top, for about 5 minutes. Then skim off and discard the solids to remove all the floaters. 3. Cook for 10 more minutes or until the milk solids sink to the bottom and the butter turns clear. 4. Cook again until the milk solids on the bottom of the pan turn light brown and the clarified butter becomes fragrant, about 5 minutes. Check from to time to get the ghee. 5. Allow it to cool for 3 to 5 minutes. Then pour into a clean jar with tight-fitting lid. 6. Ghee can be preserved in an air-tight jar on a pantry shelf for up to 1 year without refrigeration.
Per Serving: Calories 71; Fat 8g; Sodium 223mg; Carbs 0g; Fiber 0g; Sugar 0g; Protein 0.5g

Herbed Butter

Prep time: 15 minutes | Cook time: 0 | Serves: 16

½ cup finely chopped fresh basil, thyme, or cilantro
1 garlic clove, mashed
1 tablespoon freshly squeezed lemon juice

8 tablespoons (1 stick) unsalted butter, at room temperature
½ teaspoon white pepper
¼ teaspoon salt
Grated zest of 1 lemon

1. Combine the garlic, lemon juice, and basil in a food processor and process until smooth. 2. Then add white pepper, salt, lemon zest, and butter in the processor and mix well. 3. Transfer the butter into an airtight container and put in the refrigerator until firm. Store the butter in an airtight container in the refrigerator for up to 2 months or frozen up to 6 months. To freeze, wrap the butter tightly in wax paper. 4. Remove from the freezer and thaw in the refrigerator for 24 hours before using. 5. **Variation Tip:** Flavor the butter with fruit for a sweeter spread option. Stir together ½ cup butter, at room temperature, with ¼ cup of your favorite jam.
Per Serving: Calories 38; Fat 4g; Sodium 39mg; Carbs 0.7g; Fiber 0.2g; Sugar 0.1g; Protein 0.3g

Easy Harissa

Prep time: 15 minutes | Cook time: 15 minutes | Serves: 16

½ cup olive oil, plus more as needed
1 red bell pepper, seeded and chopped
5 habanero peppers, seeded and chopped
2 tablespoons freshly squeezed

lemon juice
1 tablespoon tomato paste
1 tablespoon ground cumin
1 teaspoon ground coriander
1 teaspoon paprika
½ teaspoon salt

1. Add olive oil in a skillet and heat over medium heat. 2. Add the habaneros and red bell pepper and cook for 10 minutes. 3. Add tomato paste, cumin, coriander, paprika, salt, and lemon juice in the skillet and combine well. Cook for 2 to 3 minutes or more. 4. In a food processor or blender, add the ingredients and blend until smooth. If the paste seems dry, add olive oil, 1 tablespoon at a time, until it reaches your desired consistency. 5. Serve or store in an airtight container in the refrigerator for up to 2 months.
Per Serving: Calories 69; Fat 7g; Sodium 75mg; Carbs 2g; Fiber 0.4g; Sugar 1g; Protein 0.5g

Greek Plain Yogurt

Prep time: 15 minutes | Cook time: 30 minutes | Serves: 10

6 cups 2% milk, or whole milk   ¼ cup plain yogurt

1. Pour the milk in a heavy-bottomed pot and heat over medium heat until it begins to bubble at the edge and reaches 180 degrees F, stirring occasionally. 2. Then transfer the hot milk into a large glass or stainless steel bowl. Allow it to cool to 120 degrees F, about 10 minutes. 3. Add yogurt in a small bowl and whisk well. Spoon to the warm milk and stir to combine well. 4. Then allow the mixture to sit warm for at least 8 hours or up to 12 hours to get it thicker and tangier. 5. Remove the bowl and refrigerate the yogurt for 8 hours, or until cold.
Per Serving: Calories 93; Fat 5g; Sodium 66mg; Carbs 7g; Fiber 0g; Sugar 8g; Protein 5g

Tasty Orange Blossom Syrup

Prep time: 5 minutes | Cook time: 15 minutes | Serves: 32

2 cups sugar   lemon juice
1½ cups water   1 tablespoon orange blossom
1 tablespoon freshly squeezed   water

1. Stir in sugar, lemon juice, and water in a small saucepan and bring to a boil over medium heat. Cook for 15 minutes or until the syrup shapes. 2. Turn off the heat and add the orange blossom water. Allow it to cool before serving and store in an airtight container in the refrigerator for up to 1 month.
Per Serving: Calories 25; Fat 0g; Sodium 0mg; Carbs 6g; Fiber 0g; Sugar 6g; Protein 0g

Aromatic Pita Bread

Prep time: 20 minutes | Cook time: 20 minutes | Serves: 8

1 tablespoon active dry yeast   more for dusting, divided
1 tablespoon sugar   1 teaspoon salt
1½ cups water, divided   1 tablespoon olive oil
2½ cups all-purpose flour, plus

1. Add sugar, yeast, and ½ cup of warm water in a cup and stir well. Allow it to sit for about 5 minutes to let the yeast activate. 2. Whisk 2 cups of flour and salt in a medium bowl and combine well. Mix in the yeast mixture, 1 tablespoon at a time, and then add the remaining warm water to form a dough. 3. Dust flour over your hands and a clean work surface. Transfer the dough out on to the flour and knead it until smooth, for about 5 minutes. You can dust more flour in your palms to prevent the dough from sticking. 4. Prepare another medium bowl and brush inside with olive oil. Transfer the dough in the prepared bowl. Cover the dough and let it sit for 1 hour. 5. At 500 degrees F, heat your oven in advance. 6. Divide the dough into 8 3-inch ball. Cover them with a clean kitchen towel and let it sit for 10 minutes. 7. Dust flour over a clean work surface. Then roll each ball into a ⅛-inch-thick round and let it rest for 5 minutes. 8. Arrange 2 rounds on a baking pan and bake until the bread puffs up, for 3 to 5 minutes. 9. When cooked, remove from the oven and repeat with the remaining dough rounds.
Per Serving: Calories 166; Fat 2g; Sodium 293mg; Carbs 31g; Fiber 1g; Sugar 1g; Protein 5g

Homemade Pizza Dough

Prep time: 30 minutes | Cook time: 0 | Serves: 8

3 cups bread flour, plus more as   yeast
needed   1½ cups warm water, plus more
1 teaspoon sugar   as needed
2 teaspoons salt   ¼ cup olive oil, divided
1 (0.25-ounce) packet instant dry

1. Combine sugar, salt, yeast, and flour in a bowl of a stand mixer fitted with dough hook attachment. 2. At low speed, mixing while slowly adding the warm water and 2 tablespoons of olive oil and then at medium-low speed to form a ball of dough. To make a smooth dough, add 2 tablespoons water or more or a couple tablespoons of flour as needed. 3. Prepare a medium bowl and brush inside with the remaining 2 tablespoons of olive oil. 4. Then transfer the dough in the prepared bowl and knead until smooth but firm. 5. Use directly or store covered in the refrigerator for up to 2 days. Punch it down when take it out of the refrigerator and allow it to warm to room temperature

about 30 minutes before using.
Per Serving: Calories 99; Fat 7g; Sodium 692mg; Carbs 7g; Fiber 0.4g; Sugar 1g; Protein 1g

Simple Falafel Mix

Prep time: 15 minutes | Cook time: 15 minutes | Serves: 10

1 pound dried chickpeas   teaspoon garlic powder
1 large onion, chopped   1 tablespoon ground coriander
2 cups chopped fresh parsley   1 tablespoon ground cumin
½ cup chopped fresh cilantro   1 teaspoon salt
2 garlic cloves, mashed, or ¼   1 tablespoon baking powder

1. Soak the chickpeas in cold water in a large bowl for 24 hours. Then drain and transfer to a medium bowl. 2. Mix in parsley, onion, and cilantro. Then transfer to a food processor and blender until thick. 3. Pour the paste into a colander and let it sit to drain the liquid. Transfer the chickpea to a large bowl. 4. Add garlic, cumin, coriander, salt, and baking powder and stir well. 5. Use directly, or store in an airtight container in the refrigerator for up to 5 days.
Per Serving: Calories 190; Fat 3g; Sodium 252mg; Carbs 31g; Fiber 6g; Sugar 6g; Protein 10g

Fragrant Herbed Oil

Prep time: 5 minutes | Cook time: 0 | Serves: 2

½ cup extra-virgin olive oil   1 teaspoon fresh rosemary leaves
1 teaspoon dried basil   2 teaspoons dried oregano
1 teaspoon dried parsley   ⅛ teaspoon salt

1. In a small bowl, pour oil and add basil, rosemary, parsley, oregano, and salt. Stir well and add oil to mix with a fork. 2. Make the herbed oil up to 2 days in advance and store in the refrigerator.
Per Serving: Calories 213; Fat 23g; Sodium 620mg; Carbs 1g; Fiber 0.6g; Sugar 0g; Protein 0g

Easy Red Wine Vinaigrette

Prep time: 5 minutes | Cook time: 0 | Serves: 2

¼ cup plus 2 tablespoons extra-   2 teaspoons Dijon mustard
virgin olive oil   ½ teaspoon minced garlic
2 tablespoons red wine vinegar   ⅛ teaspoon kosher salt
1 tablespoon apple cider vinegar   ⅛ teaspoon freshly ground black
2 teaspoons honey   pepper

1. Combine vinegars, honey, garlic, mustard, pepper, olive oil, and salt in a jar. Shake well. 2. Store in an airtight container for 1 to 2 days.
Per Serving: Calories 135; Fat 12g; Sodium 444mg; Carbs 6g; Fiber 0.3g; Sugar 6g; Protein 0.4g

Gluten-Free Cider Dressing

Prep time: 5 minutes | Cook time: 0 | Serves: 2

2 tablespoons apple cider vinegar   Salt
⅓ lemon, juiced   Freshly ground black pepper
⅓ lemon, zested

1. Combine together the lemon juice, lemon zest, vinegar, salt, and pepper in a jar. Shake well. 2. Store in an airtight container for 1 to 2 days.
Per Serving: Calories 7; Fat 0.04g; Sodium 1mg; Carbs 1g; Fiber 0g; Sugar 0.5g; Protein 0g

Crunchy Pickled Turnips

Prep time: 5 minutes | Cook time: 0 | Serves: 1 quart

1 pound turnips, washed well,   1 teaspoon dried Turkish oregano
peeled, and cut into 1-inch batons   3 cups warm water
1 small beet, roasted, peeled, and   ½ cup red wine vinegar
cut into 1-inch batons   ½ cup white vinegar
2 garlic cloves, smashed

1. Combine together beet, oregano, garlic, and turnips in a jar. 2. Pour vinegars and water to soak the vegetables. Cover and shake well. 3. Put in the refrigerator for an hour and the turnip will be pickled well. 4. Store in an airtight container in the refrigerator for up to 2 weeks.
Per Serving (1 to 2 tablespoons): Calories 6; Fat 0g; Sodium 4mg; Carbs 0.8g; Fiber 0.4g; Sugar 0.3g; Protein 0.4g

Homemade Pickled Onions

Prep time: 5 minutes | Cook time: 15 minutes | Serves: 8 to 10

3 red onions, finely chopped
½ cup warm water
¼ cup granulated sugar
¼ cup red wine vinegar
1 teaspoon dried oregano

1. Combine water, sugar, vinegar, oregano, and onions in a jar and shake well. Then put in the refrigerator for an hour and the onions will be pickled. 2. Store in an airtight container in the refrigerator for up to 2 weeks.
Per Serving: Calories 6; Fat 0g; Sodium 4mg; Carbs 0.8g; Fiber 0.4g; Sugar 0.3g; Protein 0.4g

Citrusy Berry and Honey Compote

Prep time: 5 minutes | Cook time: 15 minutes | Serves: 2 to 3

½ cup honey
¼ cup fresh berries
2 tablespoons grated orange zest

1. Add all the ingredients in a small saucepan and heat over medium-low heat until that sauce thickens, for about 2 to 5 minutes. For microwave, 15 seconds will be enough. 2. You can add this to pancakes, muffins, or French toast. Store in an airtight container in the refrigerator.
Per Serving: Calories 328; Fat 1g; Sodium 58mg; Carbs 83g; Fiber 1g; Sugar 77g; Protein 1g

Refreshing Yogurt Dip

Prep time: 5 minutes | Cook time: 15 minutes | Serves: 2 to 3

1 cup plain, unsweetened, full-fat Greek yogurt
½ cup cucumber, peeled, seeded, and diced
1 tablespoon freshly squeezed
lemon juice
1 tablespoon chopped fresh mint
1 small garlic clove, minced
Salt
Freshly ground black pepper

1. Combine cucumber, lemon juice, garlic, mint, and yogurt in a food processor and pulse several times with noticeable cucumber chunks. 2. Taste and add salt and pepper as you like. Store in an airtight container for 1 to 2 days.
Per Serving: Calories 213; Fat 23g; Sodium 620mg; Carbs 1g; Fiber 0.6g; Sugar 5mg; Protein 0.4g

Lemony Cucumber Dressing

Prep time: 5 minutes | Cook time: 0 | Serves: 2

1½ cups plain, unsweetened, full-fat Greek yogurt
1 cucumber, seeded and peeled
½ lemon, juiced and zested
1 tablespoon dried, minced garlic
½ tablespoon dried dill
2 teaspoons dried oregano
Salt

1. Combine together cucumber, yogurt, lemon juice, dill, oregano, a pinch of salt, and garlic together in a food processor. 2. Taste and adjust the seasoning as you like. Transfer to a serving bowl and enjoy! 3. Store in an airtight container for 1 to 2 days.
Per Serving: Calories 151; Fat 6g; Sodium 89mg; Carbs 18g; Fiber 2g; Sugar 11g; Protein 8g

Easy Tzatziki Sauce

Prep time: 5 minutes | Cook time: 0 | Serves: 2

1 medium cucumber, peeled, seeded and diced
½ teaspoon salt, divided, plus more½ cup plain, unsweetened, full-fat Greek yogurt
½ lemon, juiced
1 tablespoon chopped fresh parsley
½ teaspoon dried minced garlic
½ teaspoon dried dill
Freshly ground black pepper

1. In a colander, put the cucumber and then sprinkle with ¼ teaspoon of salt. Toss well. 2. Allow it to sit at room temperature in the colander for 30 minutes. 3. Under cool water, rinse the cucumber and then arrange in a single layer on several layers of paper towels to remove the excess liquid. 4. Then pulse the cucumber to finely chop and drain off extra liquid. 5. In a mixing bowl, add the cucumber, yogurt, parsley, dill, garlic, the remaining ¼ teaspoon of salt, and lemon juice and mix well. 6. Add salt and pepper to season and whisk well. Then put in an airtight container in the refrigerator. It can be stored for 1 to 2 days.
Per Serving: Calories 55; Fat 2g; Sodium 613mg; Carbs 6g; Fiber 1g; Sugar 5g; Protein 3g

Dijon Garlic Dressing

Prep time: 5 minutes | Cook time: 0 | Serves: 2

¼ cup extra-virgin olive oil
2 tablespoons freshly squeezed orange juice
1 orange, zested
1 teaspoon garlic powder
¾ teaspoon za'atar seasoning
½ teaspoon salt
¼ teaspoon Dijon mustard
Freshly ground black pepper

1. Combine together the orange juice, orange zest, garlic powder, za'atar, mustard, and salt in a jar. 2. Add pepper to season and shake well. 3. Store in a manson jar or an old tomato sauce jar for up to 4 days.
Per Serving: Calories 269; Fat 27g; Sodium 666mg; Carbs 7g; Fiber 2g; Sugar 1g; Protein 1g

Herbed Cider Yogurt Dressing

Prep time: 5 minutes | Cook time: 0 | Serves: 3

1 cup plain, unsweetened, full-fat Greek yogurt
½ cup extra-virgin olive oil
1 tablespoon apple cider vinegar
½ lemon, juiced
1 tablespoon chopped fresh
oregano
½ teaspoon dried parsley
½ teaspoon kosher salt
¼ teaspoon garlic powder
¼ teaspoon freshly ground black pepper

1. Combine olive oil, lemon juice, oregano, parsley, salt, garlic powder, pepper, and yogurt in a large bowl. Whisk well. 2. Use directly or store in the refrigerator for up to 1 week, shaking to emulsify again before use.
Per Serving: Calories 373; Fat 39g; Sodium 427mg; Carbs 5g; Fiber 0.3g; Sugar 4g; Protein 3g

Meringues with Strawberries

Prep time: 25 minutes | Cook time: 90 minutes | Serves: 6

4 large egg whites
1 teaspoon vanilla extract
½ teaspoon cream of tartar
¾ cup sugar
8 ounces' strawberries, diced
¼ cup fresh mint, chopped
¼ cup unsweetened shredded coconut, toasted

1. Preheat the oven to 225°F. Line 2 baking sheets with parchment paper. 2. Place the egg whites, vanilla, and cream of tartar in the stand mixer bowl (or use a suitable bowl with an electric hand mixer); beat at medium speed until soft peaks form, about 2 to 3 minutes. 3. Increase the speed to high, and gradually add the sugar, beating until stiff peaks form and the prepared mixture looks shiny and smooth for about 2 to 3 minutes. 4. Using a spatula or spoon, drop ⅓ cup of meringue onto a prepared baking sheet; smooth out and make shapelier as desired. Make 12 dollops, 6 per sheet, leaving at least 1 inch between dollops. 5. Bake them for 1½ hours, rotating baking sheets between top and bottom, front and back, halfway through. After 1½ hours, turn off the oven, but keep the door closed. Leave the meringues in the oven for an additional 30 minutes. 6. You can leave the meringues in the oven even longer (or overnight), or you may let them finish cooling to room temperature. 7. Mix the strawberries, mint, and coconut in a suitable bowl. Serve 2 meringues per person topped with the fruit mixture.
Per Serving: Calories 270; Total Fat 7.3g; Sodium 250mg; Total Carbs 44.8g; Fiber4.1g; Sugars9.2g; Protein 8.1g

Creamy Citrus Dressing

Prep time: 5 minutes | Cook time: 0 | Serves: 2

1 cup plain, unsweetened, full-fat Greek yogurt
1 large lemon, zested and juiced
½ teaspoon dried oregano
½ teaspoon dried parsley
1½ teaspoons garlic salt
Freshly ground black pepper

1. Whisk together lemon juice, lemon zest, yogurt, oregano, garlic salt, and parsley in a medium bowl. 2. Add pepper to season. Serve with salad as you like or store in an airtight container for no longer than 2 days.
Per Serving: Calories 88; Fat 2g; Sodium 669mg; Carbs 12g; Fiber 0g; Sugar 9g; Protein 7g

Spain-inspired Romesco Dip

Prep time: 10 minutes | Cook time: 10 minutes | Serves: 10

1 (12-ounce) jar roasted red peppers, drained
1 (14.5-ounce) can diced tomatoes, undrained
½ cup dry-roasted almonds
2 garlic cloves
2 teaspoons red wine vinegar
1 teaspoon smoked paprika or ½ teaspoon cayenne pepper
¼ teaspoon kosher or sea salt

¼ teaspoon freshly ground black pepper
¼ cup extra-virgin olive oil
⅔ cup torn, day-old bread or toast (about 2 slices)
Assortment of sliced raw vegetables such as carrots, celery, cucumber, green beans, and bell peppers, for serving

1. Combine tomatoes and their juices, almonds, garlic, salt, pepper, vinegar, smoked paprika, and roasted peppers in a high-powered blender or food processor. 2. At medium speed, puréeing the mixture and slowly drizzle in the oil until well incorporated. 3. Add bread and purée. 4. Serve with raw vegetables or store in an airtight container in the refrigerator for up to one week.
Per Serving: Calories 113; Fat 9g; Sodium 223mg; Carbs 6g; Fiber 2g; Sugar 3g; Protein 2g

Fragrant Roasted Garlic

Prep time: 2 minutes | Cook time: 25 minutes | Serves: 16

2 cups peeled garlic cloves
½ cup low-fat milk

1 tablespoon olive oil

1. At 350 degrees F, heat our oven in advance. 2. Combine milk and garlic in a medium ovenproof skillet and bring to a boil over medium-high heat. 3. Then reduce the heat to low and simmer for 5 minutes, stirring from time to time. 4. Turn off the heat and drain the milk. Stir in olive oil. Cover and roast garlic in the oven about 20 minutes, or until tender and golden. 5. Serve or store in an airtight container in the refrigerator for up to 1 week.
Per Serving: Calories 46; Fat 2g; Sodium 35mg; Carbs 6g; Fiber 0.4g; Sugar 0.2g; Protein 2g

Chocolate Mousse with Berries

Prep time: 10 minutes | Cook time: 0 | Serves: 4

2 cups plain Greek yogurt
¼ cup heavy cream
¼ cup pure maple syrup
3 tablespoons unsweetened cocoa powder

2 teaspoons vanilla extract
¼ teaspoon kosher salt
1 cup fresh mixed berries
¼ cup chocolate chips

1. Place the yogurt, cream, maple syrup, cocoa powder, vanilla, and salt in the bowl of a stand mixer or use a suitable bowl with an electric hand mixer. 2. Mix at medium-high speed until fluffy, about 5 minutes. 3. Spoon evenly among 4 bowls and put in the refrigerator to set for at least 15 minutes. 4. Serve each bowl with ¼ cup mixed berries and 1 tablespoon mixed chocolate chips.
Per Serving: Calories 216; Total Fat 5.2g; Sodium 37mg; Total Carbs 37.8g; Fiber4.3g; Sugars0.4g; Protein 8.1g

Pistachio-Stuffed Dates

Prep time: 10 minutes | Cook time: 0 | Serves: 4

½ cup unsalted pistachios shelled
¼ teaspoon kosher salt

8 Medjool dates, pitted

1. Add the pistachios and salt to a food processor-process them for 3 to 5 minutes until mixed with chunky nut butter. 2. Split open the dates and spoon the pistachio nut butter into each half.
Per Serving: Calories 271; Total Fat 22.9g; Sodium 30mg; Total carbs 17.1g; Fiber 2.6g; Sugars 9.6g; Protein 3g

Summer Fruit Granita

Prep time: 10 minutes | Cook time: 0 | Serves: 4

¼ cup sugar
1 cup fresh strawberries
1 cup fresh raspberries

1 cup fresh blackberries
1 teaspoon freshly squeezed lemon juice

1. In a suitable saucepan, bring 1 cup of water to a boil over high heat. Add the sugar and stir well until dissolved. 2. Remove this

pan from the heat, add the berries and lemon juice, and cool to room temperature. Once cooled, place the fruit in a blender or food processor and blend on high until smooth. 3. Pour the puree into a shallow glass baking dish and place in the freezer for 1 hour. Stir with a fork and freeze for 30 minutes, then repeat. 4. Use an ice cream scoop to portion the granita into dessert dishes to serve.
Per Serving: Calories 170; Total Fat 0.3g; Sodium 1mg; Total carbs 18g; Fiber 2.1g; Sugars 9.6g; Protein 0.9g

Hot Chocolate

Prep time: 10 minutes | Cook time: 10 minutes | Serves: 4

4 cups of low-fat milk
2 teaspoons sugar
4 (1-ounce) squares of dark chocolate

½ teaspoon salt
½ teaspoon ground cinnamon
¼ teaspoon chili powder

1. In a suitable, heavy saucepan, preheat the milk and sugar over low heat until it reaches a simmer. 2. Place the dark chocolate, salt, cinnamon, and chili powder in a suitable bowl and pour just enough hot milk over the chocolate to cover. 3. Return this pan to the heat and Reduce its heat to low. 4. Beat the hot milk and chocolate together until the chocolate has melted, then pour the prepared mixture into the rest milk in the saucepan, whisking constantly. 5. To serve, divide among 4 mugs.
Per Serving: Calories 245; Total Fat 24.3g; Sodium 36mg; Total carbs 34.9g; Fiber 6.8g; Sugars 23.8g; Protein 3.7g

Baked Biscotti

Prep time: 10 minutes | Cook time: 20 minutes | Serves: 8

2 cups whole-wheat flour
¾ cup sugar
1 teaspoon baking powder
¼ teaspoon salt
¾ cup slivered almonds

3 large eggs
2 tablespoons pure almond extract
1 teaspoon pure vanilla extract
1 teaspoon olive oil

1. Place your oven rack in the middle position and preheat the oven to 275°F. 2. Mix the flour, sugar, baking powder, salt, and almonds in a suitable bowl and stir with a wooden spoon until well mixed. 3. Beat the eggs, almond extract, and vanilla in a suitable bowl. 4. Pour the prepared egg mixture into the dry ingredients and use a wooden spoon to mix well, stirring for almost 2 minutes to ensure that the ingredients are well mixed. 5. Use your hands to grease a suitable baking sheet with the olive oil, and then use your greased hands to spread the prepared dough onto the baking sheet in a rectangle of about 11 x 4 inches. 6. Bake for almost 45 minutes, remove from the oven and use a sharp, greased knife to cut the rectangle crosswise into ½-inch slices. Lay the pieces cut side up to about ½ inch apart and return the baking sheet to the oven. 7. Bake until the cut sides are pretty dry, about 20 minutes. 8. Cool on the baking sheet to room temperature, then store in an airtight container.
Per Serving: Calories 166; Total Fat 16.2g; Sodium 15mg; Total carbs 5.6g; Fiber 1.9g; Sugars 3.1g; Protein 2.5g

Chocolate-Dipped Fruit Bites

Prep time: 10 minutes | Cook time: 5 minutes | Serves: 4-6

½ cup semisweet chocolate chips
¼ cup low-fat milk
½ teaspoon pure vanilla extract
½ teaspoon ground nutmeg
¼ teaspoon salt

2 kiwis, peeled and sliced
1 cup honeydew melon chunks (about 2-inch chunks)
1 pound of whole strawberries

1. Place the chocolate chips in a suitable bowl. 2. Microwave the milk until hot in another small bowl for about 30 seconds. Pour the milk over the chocolate chips, sit for 1 minute, and then Beat until the chocolate is melted and smooth. Stir in the vanilla, nutmeg, and salt and allow to cool for 5 minutes. 3. Line a suitable baking sheet with wax paper. Dip each piece of fruit halfway into the chocolate, tap gently to remove excess chocolate, and place the fruit on the baking sheet. 4. When all the fruit has been dipped, allow it to sit until dry, about 30 minutes. Arrange on a platter and serve.
Per Serving: Calories 122; Total Fat 10.7g; Sodium 40mg; Total carbs 8.8g; Fiber 1.2g; Sugars 6.6g; Protein 0.8g

Baked Pears in Wine Sauce

Prep time: 10 minutes | Cook time: 1 hr. 15 minutes | Serves: 4

4 just-ripe firm pears, cored and peeled
1 cup sweet red wine
1 cinnamon stick

2 teaspoons light brown sugar
½ teaspoon pure almond extract
4 mint sprigs for garnish

1. At 325 degrees F, preheat your oven. 2. Cut a slice from the bottom of each to allow them to stand easily. 3. Place the pears in a suitable baking dish. 4. In a suitable saucepan, mix the red wine, cinnamon stick, and brown sugar and heat over low heat until it just reaches a simmer. Stir in the almond extract, remove the cinnamon stick, and pour the liquid into the baking dish. Slide the plate into the oven, careful not to tip the pears. 5. Bake until the pears are golden and fork-tender, about 1 hour. The bottom one-third to one-half will be a deep red. 6. Gently transfer the pears to a platter and pour the red wine mixture back into the saucepan. Heat over medium heat and simmer until reduced by half, about 15 minutes. Remove this pan from the heat and allow the sauce to cool for 10 minutes. 7. To serve, place each pear in a shallow dessert bowl and pour a little red wine sauce around it. Garnish with fresh mint.
Per Serving: Calories 113; Total Fat 2.8g; Sodium 139mg; Total carbs 24.3g; Fiber 2.7g; Sugars 19.2g; Protein 1.5g

Classic Hummus

Prep time: 10 minutes | Cook time: 0 | Serves: 12

2 (15-ounce) cans low-sodium chickpeas, drained and rinsed
3 garlic cloves, peeled
¼ cup tahini

½ cup olive oil
Juice of 1 lemon
¼ teaspoon sea salt

1. Combine together the garlic, tahini, olive oil, lemon juice, and chickpeas in a food processor. Add salt to season and puree to smooth. 2. Serve with pita bread or crudités. Store in an airtight container in the refrigerator for up to 1 week.
Per Serving: Calories 177; Fat 13g; Sodium 154mg; Carbs 12g; Fiber 4g; Sugar 2g; Protein 5g

Roasted Honey-Cinnamon Apples

Prep time: 10 minutes | Cook time: 20 minutes | Serves: 2

1 teaspoon olive oil
4 firm apples, peeled, cored, and sliced
½ teaspoon salt

1 ½ teaspoon ground cinnamon
2 tablespoons low-fat milk
2 tablespoons honey

1. At 375 degrees F, preheat your oven. Grease a suitable casserole dish with olive oil. 2. Toss the apple slices with the salt and ½ teaspoon of cinnamon in a suitable bowl. 3. Spread the apples in the baking dish and bake for 20 minutes. 4. Meanwhile, in a suitable saucepan, preheat the milk, honey, and remaining 1 teaspoon cinnamon over medium heat, stirring frequently. When it reaches a simmer, remove this pan from the heat and cover to keep warm. 5. Divide the apple slices between 2 dessert plates and pour the prepared sauce over the apples. Serve warm.
Per Serving: Calories 170; Total Fat 9.8g; Sodium 49mg; Total carbs 17.4g; Fiber 1.5g; Sugars 15.5g; Protein 3.2g

Pineapple and Melon

Prep time: 10 minutes | Cook time: 10 minutes | Serves: 4

8 fresh pineapple rings, rind removed
8 watermelon triangles with rind

1 tablespoon honey
½ teaspoon black pepper

1. Preheat an outdoor grill over high heat. 2. Drizzle the fruit slices with honey and sprinkle one side of each piece with pepper. Grill for 5 minutes, turn, and grill for another 2 minutes. 3. Serve.
Per Serving: Calories 226; Total Fat 1g; Sodium 4g; cholesterol: 31mg; Total Carbs 20g; Fiber 3g; Protein 6g

Red Grapefruit Granita

Prep time: 10 minutes | Cook time: 0 | Serves: 4-6

3 cups red grapefruit sections
1 cup red grapefruit juice
¼ cup honey

1 tablespoon lime juice
Fresh basil leaves for garnish

1. Remove as much pith (white part) and membrane from the grapefruit segments. 2. Add all ingredients except the basil to your blender, and pulse just until smooth. 3. Pour the prepared mixture into a shallow glass baking dish and place in the freezer for 1 hour. Stir with a fork and freeze for another 30 minutes, then repeat. 4. Scoop into small dessert glasses and garnish with fresh basil leaves to serve.
Per Serving: Calories 271; Total Fat 11g; Sodium 8mg; Total Carbs 46.7g; Fiber 3.2g; Sugars 32.8g; Protein 4.2g

Lemon and Watermelon Granita

Prep time: 10 minutes | Cook time: 0 | Serves: 4

4 cups watermelon cubes
¼ cup honey

¼ cup lemon juice

1. Blend the watermelon, honey, and lemon juice in a suitable blender. Purée all the ingredients, then pour into a 9-by-9-by-2-inch baking pan and place in the freezer. 2. Every 30 to 60 minutes, run a fork across the frozen surface to fluff and create ice flakes. Freeze for almost 3 hours total and serve.
Per Serving: Calories 120; Total Fat 1.1g; Sodium 1mg; Total Carbs 29.1g; Fiber 2g; Sugars 22.2g; Protein 3.2g

Wine Poached Pears

Prep time: 10 minutes | Cook time: 45 minutes | Serves: 4

2 cups dry red wine
¼ cup honey
Zest of ½ orange
2 cinnamon sticks

1 (1-inch) piece of fresh ginger
Four pears, bottom inch sliced off, so the pear is flat

1. Add the wine, honey, orange zest, cinnamon, and ginger to the pot over medium-high heat, stir well. 2. Cook to a boil with occasional stirring. Reduce its heat to medium-low and cook for 5 minutes to let the flavors blend. 3. Add the pears to the pot and cover the pot; bring them to simmer and simmer for 20 minutes until the pears are tender, turning every 3 to 4 minutes to ensure even color and contact with the liquid. 4. Refrigerate the pears in the liquid for 3 hours to allow for more flavor absorption. 5. Bring the pears and liquid to room temperature. Place the pears on individual dishes and return the poaching liquid to the stovetop over medium-high heat. 6. Simmer the pears for 15 minutes until the liquid is syrupy. 7. Serve the pears with the juice drizzled over the top.
Per Serving: Calories 224; Total Fat 6.8g; Sodium 7mg; Total Carbs 15.4g; Fiber 0.6g; Sugars 11.3g; Protein 1.1g

Vanilla Pudding with Strawberries

Prep time: 10 minutes | Cook time: 10 minutes | Serves: 4

2¼ cups skim milk, divided
1 egg, beaten
½ cup sugar
1 teaspoon vanilla extract

Pinch sea salt
3 tablespoons cornstarch
2 cups sliced strawberries

1. Beat 2 cups of milk with the egg, sugar, vanilla, and sea salt in a suitable bowl. 2. Transfer the prepared mixture to a suitable pot, place it over medium heat, and slowly cook to a boil, whisking constantly. 3. In a suitable bowl, Beat the cornstarch with the rest ¼ cup of milk. In a thin stream, Beat this slurry into the boiling mixture in the pot. Cook until it thickens, stirring constantly. Boil for 1 minute more, stirring constantly. 4. Spoon the pudding into 4 dishes and refrigerate to chill. Serve topped with sliced strawberries.
Per Serving: Calories 207; Total Fat 3.5g; Sodium 54mg; Total Carbs 20.6g; Fiber 1g; Sugars 19.7g; Protein 3.9g

Mixed Berry Frozen Yogurt Bar

Prep time: 10 minutes | Cook time: 0 | Serves: 8

8 cups vanilla frozen yogurt
1 cup sliced fresh strawberries
1 cup fresh blueberries

1 cup fresh blackberries
1 cup fresh raspberries
½ cup chopped walnuts

1. Apportion the yogurt among eight dessert bowls. 2. Serve the toppings family-style, and let your guests choose their toppings and spoon them over the yogurt.
Per Serving: Calories 150; Total Fat 3.2g; Sodium 9mg; Total Carbs 31.1g; Fiber 3g; Sugars 24.4g; Protein 1.6g

Fruit Salad with Yogurt

Prep time: 10 minutes | Cook time: 0 | Serves: 4

1½ cups grapes, halved
1 cup chopped cantaloupe
2 plums, chopped
1 peach, chopped
½ cup fresh blueberries

1 cup unsweetened plain nonfat Greek yogurt
2 tablespoons honey
½ teaspoon ground cinnamon

1. Mix the grapes, cantaloupe, plums, peach, and blueberries in a suitable bowl. Toss to mix. Divide among four dessert dishes. 2. In a suitable bowl, Beat the yogurt, honey, and cinnamon. Spoon over the fruit.
Per Serving: Calories 177; Total Fat 9.5g; Sodium 20mg; Total Carbs 21.4g; Fiber 0.1g; Sugars 16.8g; Protein 5.9g

Date Energy Balls

Prep time: 10 minutes | Cook time: 0 | Serves: 24

1 cup walnuts
1 cup almonds
2 cups Medjool dates, pitted
2 tablespoons olive oil
¼ cup unsweetened cocoa powder

¼ cup shredded unsweetened coconut, plus additional for coating
Pinch sea salt

1. In a blender, blend the walnuts, almonds, dates, olive oil, cocoa powder, coconut, and sea salt for 1-second until everything is well chopped. 2. Form the prepared mixture into 24 balls. 3. Spread the additional coconut on a plate and roll the balls in the coconut to coat. 4. Serve, refrigerate, or freeze.
Per Serving: Calories 179; Total Fat 11.9g; Sodium 30mg; Total Carbs 41.9g; Fiber 4.3g; Sugars 23.5g; Protein 7.9g

Pasta flora

Prep time: 15 minutes | Cook time: 35 minutes | Serves: 24

Nonstick cooking spray
2 cups all-purpose flour
½ cup sugar
1 teaspoon vanilla extract
½ cup (1 stick) unsalted butter

2 teaspoons baking powder
2 eggs
2 tablespoons orange zest
¼ cup apricot jam

1. At 400 degrees F, preheat your oven. 2. Grease a suitable 9-by-13-inch baking dish with cooking spray. 3. Mix the sugar, flour, vanilla, butter, baking powder, eggs, and orange zest in a food processor. Pulse until a stiff dough forms—Press three-fourths of the prepared dough into the prepared dish. 4. Spread the jam over the prepared dough. 5. Roll out the rested dough to the ¼-inch thickness and cut it into ½-inch-wide strips. 6. Make a lattice over the top of the jam with the strips. Bake for almost 35 minutes until golden. Cool on a wire rack. 7. Cut into 24 cookies and serve.
Per Serving: Calories 213; Total Fat 12.1g; Sodium 60mg; Total Carbs 26.5g; Fiber 4.4g; Sugars 18g; Protein 2.4g

Toasted Almonds with Honey

Prep time: 15 minutes | Cook time: 5 minutes | Serves: 4

½ cup raw almonds

3 tablespoons good-quality honey

1. Fill suitable saucepan three-quarters full with water and cook to a boil over high heat. 2. Stir in the almonds and cook for 1 minute. 3. Drain the cooked almonds in a fine-mesh sieve and rinse. 4. Remove the skins from the almonds by rubbing them in a clean kitchen towel. Place the almonds on a paper towel to dry. 5. In the same saucepan, mix the almonds and honey and cook over medium heat until the almonds get golden for 4 to 5 minutes. 6. Let them cool for 15 minutes before serving.
Per Serving: Calories 178; Total Fat 1.4g; Sodium 20mg; Total carbs 12.3g; Fiber 4.2g; Sugars 6.9g; Protein 1.9g

Cretan Cheese Pancakes

Prep time: 10 minutes | Cook time: 25 minutes | Serves: 4

2 cups all-purpose flour, plus extra for kneading
½ cup water
2 tablespoons olive oil, plus extra for frying

1 tablespoon lemon juice
1 tablespoon brandy
1 teaspoon sea salt
5 tablespoons crumbled feta cheese

2 tablespoons olive oil
½ cup chopped nuts of your choice

⅛ to ¼ teaspoon ground cinnamon for topping
1 tablespoon honey for drizzling

1. In a suitable bowl, stir together the flour, water, olive oil, lemon juice, brandy, and salt until a ball of dough forms. 2. Turn the prepared dough onto a lightly floured surface and knead for 10 minutes. 3. Divide the prepared dough into 5 equal pieces and roll each piece into a ball. 4. Place each dough ball on a floured surface and roll it out into a 6-inch-wide circle about ¼ inch thick. 5. Place 1 tablespoon of the feta in the center, fold the prepared dough over, and knead the ready dough and cheese together. 6. Once the cheese is well incorporated, roll the prepared dough out flat to the same size. Repeat with the rest balls of dough. 7. In a suitable skillet, preheat the oil over medium-high heat. Place one round of dough in this skillet and cook for 5 to 6 minutes on each side, until golden brown. 8. Transfer the cooked pancake to a paper towel-lined plate to drain. 9. Repeat to cook the rest dough pancakes. 10. Sprinkle these pancakes evenly with the nuts and cinnamon, drizzle with the honey, and serve.
Per Serving: Calories 480; Total Fat 24g; Sodium 396mg; total Carbs 57g; Sugar 6g; Fiber 3g; Protein 11g

Fruit with Crème Fraiche

Prep time: 10 minutes | Cook time: 0 | Serves: 4

4 cups chopped fresh fruit
1 cup crème Fraiche

1 teaspoon sugar
¼ cup chopped fresh mint leaves

1. Evenly divide the fruit among four bowls. 2. In a suitable bowl, mix the crème Fraiche and sugar, if desired. 3. Top the fruit with a generous spoonful or two of the crème Fraiche. 4. Sprinkle the mint over each bowl, garnish with 1 to 2 whole sprigs of mint, and serve.
Per Serving: Calories 113; Total Fat 1.9g; Sodium 68mg; Total carbs 24.6g; Fiber 3.5; Sugars 16.3g; Protein 2.4g

Honey-Cinnamon Doughnuts

Prep time: 80 minutes | Cook time: 5 minutes | Serves: 5-6

3½ cups all-purpose flour
1 cup of warm water
1 (¼-ounce) packet of instant yeast
1 cup milk
2 large eggs
¼ cup sugar
1 teaspoon sea salt
1 cup water

¾ cup honey
4 cups safflower oil for frying (enough for the prepared dough balls to float)
¼ teaspoon ground cinnamon for topping
¼ cup chopped nuts of your choice for topping (optional)

1. Stir together the flour, warm water, and yeast in a suitable bowl and mix well. Add the milk, eggs, sugar, and salt and mix until a thick batter is formed. Cover the batter, and let it rest for 45 to 60 minutes. 2. When the batter has about 20 minutes of resting time left, stir together the water and honey in a suitable saucepan and cook to a simmer over medium heat. Simmer the food for 5 minutes, then pour into an eligible bowl. 3. Rinse and dry the saucepan. Stir in the safflower oil and heat over medium-high heat. 4. When the oil is hot, scoop 1 tablespoon of batter, form it into a ball, and gently drop it into the hot oil. Fry the batter for 3 to 4 minutes on each side until golden brown. Transfer the prepared doughnut to a paper towel-lined plate to drain and repeat fry the rest batter. 5. Add the fried doughnuts to the honey mixture, coating them evenly, then transfer them to a plate. Dust with the cinnamon, top with chopped nuts, if desired, and serve immediately.
Per Serving: Calories 374; Total Fat 27.9g; Sodium 3mg; Total carbs 35.1g; Fiber 3.8g; Sugars 26.1g; Protein 1.3g

Yogurt with Honey and Pomegranates

Prep time: 10 minutes | Cook time: 0 | Serves: 4

4 cups plain full-fat Greek yogurt
½ cup pomegranate seeds

¼ cup honey
Sugar, for topping

1. Evenly divide the yogurt among four bowls. Evenly divide the pomegranate seeds among the bowls and drizzle each with the honey. 2. Sprinkle each bowl with a pinch of sugar, if desired, and serve.
Per Serving: Calories 232; Total Fat 27.9g; Sodium 3mg; Total carbs 35.1g; Fiber 3.8g; Sugars 26.1g; Protein 1.3g

Pistachio Cookies

Prep time: 20 minutes | Cook time: 15 minutes | Serves: 6

1 cup all-purpose flour, plus extra for dusting
¼ cup cornstarch
1 teaspoon baking powder
Pinch sea salt
1 large egg

½ cup confectioners' sugar
½ cup (1 stick) unsalted butter
½ teaspoon lemon zest
½ teaspoon pure vanilla extract
½ cup finely ground pistachios

1. At 400 degrees F, preheat your oven. Line a suitable baking sheet with parchment paper. 2. Stir the flour, cornstarch, baking powder, and salt until well blended in a suitable bowl. 3. Add the egg, confectioners' sugar, butter, lemon zest, and vanilla and stir until the prepared dough is uniform. 4. Turn the prepared dough onto a lightly floured surface and flatten it out with your hands. Place the ground pistachios in the center of the ready dough and knead the prepared dough to incorporate the nuts evenly. 5. Roll the prepared dough into 2-inch balls and place them on the prepared baking sheet, then use your palm to flatten them slightly. 6. Bake the cookies for 10 to 12 minutes, until golden brown. 7. Let the cookies cool for a while before serving.
Per Serving: Calories 336; Total Fat 31.2g; Sodium 75mg; Total carbs 40.4g; Fiber 6g; Sugars 31.7g; Protein 4.4g

Grilled Peaches with Yogurt

Prep time: 10 minutes | Cook time: 30 minutes | Serves: 4

4 ripe peaches, halved and pitted
2 tablespoons olive oil
1 teaspoon ground cinnamon, plus

extra for toppingh
2 cups plain full-fat Greek yogurt
¼ cup honey, for drizzling

1. At 350 degrees F, preheat your oven. 2. Place the peaches in a baking dish, cut-side up. 3. Stir together the olive oil and cinnamon in a suitable bowl, then brush the prepared mixture over the peach halves. 4. Bake the peaches for almost 30 minutes until they are soft. 5. Top the peaches with the yogurt, drizzle them with honey, and then serve.
Per Serving: Calories 207; Total Fat 6g; Sodium 32mg; Total carbs 39.5g; Fiber 3.9g; Sugars 31.1g; Protein 2.2g

Strawberry Parfaits

Prep time: 10 minutes | Cook time: 0 | Serves: 4

2 cups ricotta cheese
¼ cup honey
2 cups sliced strawberries
1 teaspoon sugar

Topping such as sliced almonds, fresh mint, and lemon zest (optional)

1. Toppings such as sliced almonds, fresh mint, and lemon zest 2. In a suitable bowl, beat together the ricotta and honey until well blended. 3. Place this bowl in the refrigerator for a few minutes to firm up the prepared mixture. 4. In a suitable bowl, toss together the strawberries and sugar. 5. In each of four small glasses, layer 1 tablespoon of the ricotta mixture, then top with a layer of the strawberries and another layer of the ricotta. 6. Finish with your preferred toppings, if desired, then serve.
Per Serving: Calories 279; Total Fat 14.3g; Sodium 493mg; Total carbs 12.3g; Fiber 2.4g; Sugars 8.7g; Protein 0.9g

Greek Yogurt with Chocolate

Prep time: 10 minutes | Cook time: 0 | Serves: 4

4 cups plain full-fat Greek yogurt
½ cup heavy (whipping) cream

2 ounces' dark chocolate (at least 70% cacao), grated, for topping

1. In the bowl of a mixer fitted with the mixing paddle using a handheld mixer, whip the yogurt and cream for almost 5 minutes, or until peaks form. 2. Evenly divide the whipped yogurt mixture among bowls and top with the grated chocolate. 3. Serve.
Per Serving: Calories 337; Total Fat 17g; Sodium 17mg; Total carbs 18.8g; Fiber 2.9g; Sugars 14g; Protein 5.4g

Churro Bites with Chocolate Sauce

Prep time: 10 minutes | Cook time: 35 minutes | Serves: 6

1 cup water
1 teaspoon pure vanilla extract

2 tablespoons unsalted butter
½ teaspoon sea salt

½ cup sugar
1 teaspoon ground cinnamon
1 cup all-purpose flour
2 cups safflower oil for frying

2 large eggs
1 cup dark chocolate chips
¼ cup heavy (whipping) cream

1. Mix the water, vanilla, butter, salt, sugar, and cinnamon in a suitable saucepan—Cook to a boil over high heat. 2. Reduce its heat to low and add the flour, then stir quickly until a ball of dough forms. Let stand for 5 minutes. 3. Add the eggs to the prepared dough one at a time, stirring after each addition until mixed. 4. Transfer the prepared dough to a piping bag fitted with the tip of your choice. 5. Clean and dry the saucepan you used for the prepared dough, then stir in the safflower oil and heat over high heat to 350°F. 6. To make bite-size pieces, pipe 2-inch-long strips of dough, then use a knife or fork to slice off the prepared dough at the tip of the piping bag. 7. Fry until golden on all sides, being careful not to overcrowd this pan, then transfer to a paper towel-lined plate to drain. Repeat to fry the rested dough. 8. Mix some sugar and cinnamon in a shallow bowl and dredge the churros in the prepared mixture. 9. In a suitable microwave-safe bowl, mix the chocolate chips and cream and microwave in 30-second intervals, stirring until melted and well mixed. 10. Serve the churros immediately, with the chocolate sauce alongside.
Per Serving: Calories 429; Total Fat 2.5g; Sodium 35mg; Total carbs 46.4g; Fiber 1g; Sugars 37.3g; Protein 1g

Baked Apples with Walnuts

Prep time: 10 minutes | Cook time: 45 minutes | Serves: 4

4 apples
¼ cup chopped walnuts
2 tablespoons honey
1 teaspoon ground cinnamon

¼ teaspoon ground nutmeg
¼ teaspoon ground ginger
Pinch sea salt

1. At 375 degrees F, preheat your oven. 2. Chop the tops off the apples; use a metal spoon or paring knife to remove the cores, leaving the bottoms of the apples intact. Place the apple cut-side up in a 9-by-9-inch baking pan. 3. Stir together the walnuts, honey, cinnamon, nutmeg, ginger, and sea salt in a suitable bowl. Spoon the prepared mixture into the centers of the apples. Bake the apples for almost 45 minutes until browned, soft, and fragrant. Serve warm.
Per Serving: Calories 284; Total Fat 23g; Sodium 14mg; Total Carbs 17.5g; Fiber 11.1g; Sugars 4g; Protein 6.1g

Conclusion

The Mediterranean diet is one of the healthier and simplest diets. It is simple to follow and easy to adopt. You can enjoy your favorite while following this diet. Some foods are restricted in the diet. Doctors and health care professionals recommend this diet because it is good for heart health. It reduces the risk of many diseases such as heart diseases, cancer, type-2 diabetes, asthma, and many more. There are a lot of health benefits of this diet. It keeps you active, strong, and fit. It manages weight loss. It increases your life longevity. This diet focuses on fresh vegetables such as broccoli, Brussels sprouts, tomatoes, and many more, fresh fruits such as apples, strawberries, bananas, and many more, legumes, whole grains, seafood, quality dairy products, and limiting poultry. Drink plenty of water while following this diet. In this cookbook, you will get healthy, delicious, and satisfying Mediterranean diet recipes – breakfast, main dishes, dinner, desserts, snacks, etc. If you want to stay healthy and active, exercise, eat a healthy diet and drink plenty of water. This diet consists of healthy nutrients such as healthy fats, vitamins, minerals, and proteins. Olive oil is the main ingredient in this diet. You should cook all foods using olive oil.

Appendix 1 Measurement Conversion Chart

VOLUME EQUIVALENTS (LIQUID)

US STANDARD	US STANDARD (OUNCES)	METRIC (APPROXIMATE)
2 tablespoons	1 fl.oz	30 mL
¼ cup	2 fl.oz	60 mL
½ cup	4 fl.oz	120 mL
1 cup	8 fl.oz	240 mL
1½ cup	12 fl.oz	355 mL
2 cups or 1 pint	16 fl.oz	475 mL
4 cups or 1 quart	32 fl.oz	1 L
1 gallon	128 fl.oz	4 L

VOLUME EQUIVALENTS (DRY)

US STANDARD	METRIC (APPROXIMATE)
⅛ teaspoon	0.5 mL
¼ teaspoon	1 mL
½ teaspoon	2 mL
¾ teaspoon	4 mL
1 teaspoon	5 mL
1 tablespoon	15 mL
¼ cup	59 mL
½ cup	118 mL
¾ cup	177 mL
1 cup	235 mL
2 cups	475 mL
3 cups	700 mL
4 cups	1 L

TEMPERATURES EQUIVALENTS

FAHRENHEIT (F)	CELSIUS (C) (APPROXIMATE)
225°F	107°C
250°F	120°C
275°F	135°C
300°F	150°C
325°F	160°C
350°F	180°C
375°F	190°C
400°F	205°C
425°F	220°C
450°F	235°C
475°F	245°C
500°F	260°C

WEIGHT EQUIVALENTS

US STANDARD	METRIC (APPROXINATE)
1 ounce	28 g
2 ounces	57 g
5 ounces	142 g
10 ounces	284 g
15 ounces	425g
16 ounces (1 pound)	455 g
1.5pounds	680 g
2pounds	907g

Appendix 2 Recipes Index

Made in United States
Troutdale, OR
11/29/2023

15123752R00067